AA

999 PLACES TO EAT OUT FOR AROUND £5

Contents and Key to Regions

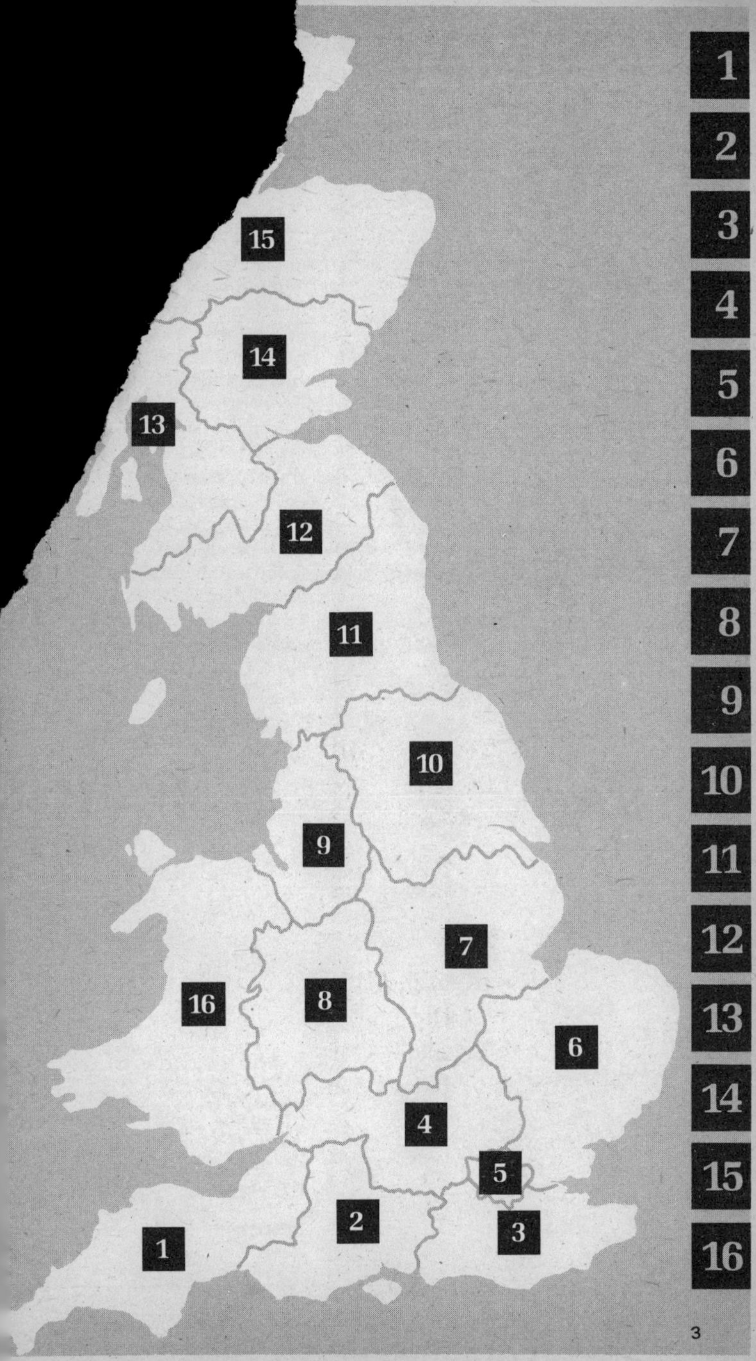
15
14
13
12
11
10
9
7
16
8
6
4
5
1
2
3
1
2
3
4
5
6
7
8
9
10
11
12
13
14
15
16

Eating Out

There is no doubt that a good meal with a glass of wine is one of the simplest yet most profound pleasures life can offer, but 'paying through the nose' for it at an uncaring restaurant can sometimes take the edge off that pleasure.
That's why the AA Hotel and Restaurant Inspectors have again taken to the road to bring you an even more comprehensive and far-reaching guide to low-price, yet high-standard eating places.
In these days of rising costs, when many people worry about high mortgages and growing families, it seems almost immoral to have to blow the week's wages – or the housekeeping budget – on a meal out for two people.
Fortunately, as this book demonstrates, there are at least 999 restaurants in Britain where excellence and economy are combined to prov
for good eating out
congenial surround
serve traditional Briti
to satisfy the growing i
Continental and ethnic
guide covers French, Itali
Greek, Indian and Chinese
What is more, the 999 eating
described in these pages rang
from fashionable grill-rooms in
renowned hotels to small inns, bistros, trattorias, exotic restaurants, and wine bars.
However different, they all have several things in common: an appealing atmosphere, pleasant service, well-prepared food. Most important – they give value for money. Choices may be better in some cases than in others, but in each case the quality of cuisine has been carefully considered.
At most of the establishments

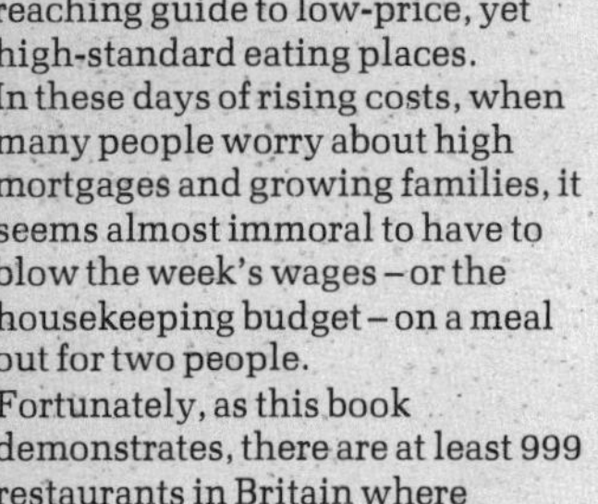

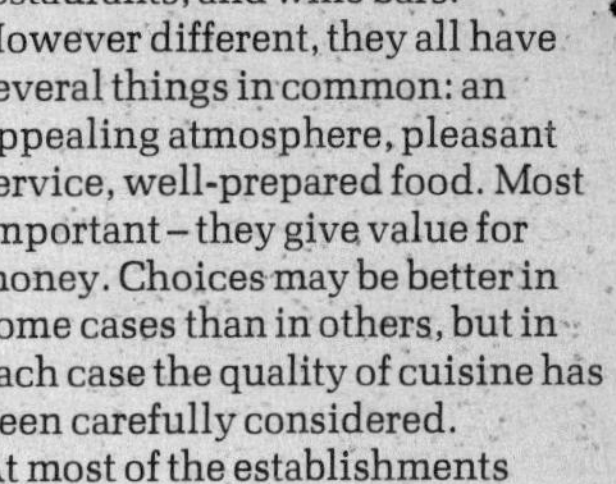

joy a three-course
s of wine for
asionally a pub or
been mentioned for
bar snacks or lunches.
there is somewhere for
here – roadside inns and
r tourists and business-
smart restaurants for
rsary or birthday
rations, intimate bistros or
ntry pubs to impress the
irlfriend without giving the bank
manager apoplexy and friendly
family restaurants to treat the wife
and children to Sunday lunch.

The AA Hotel and Restaurant inspectors have visited and recommended all these places – a seal of approval from a group of established eaters-out!

My inspectors are not peak-capped grading machines with slide rules, but thirty professional men and women with a profound appreciation of what is best and worst in hotels and restaurants.

The guide is divided into England, Scotland and Wales. Each region is introduced by a map which indicates the location of the towns listed. In certain cases it may be advisable to use a road atlas where an inn is out of town.

All prices quoted are the latest available before going to press, but care has been taken to exclude places where prices are likely substantially to exceed £5 during 1981. As far as possible VAT and service charges have been included in the calculation.

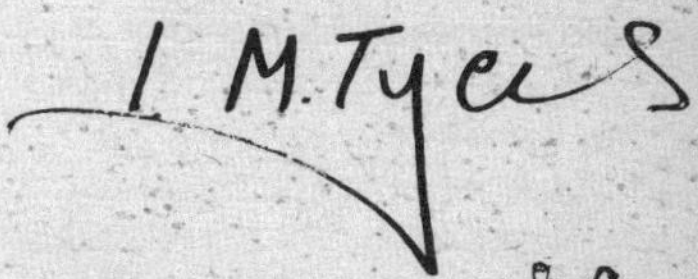

999 plus ONE

THE PILGRIM'S HALT
98 High Street (Maidstone 57281)
Open: Tue-Sat 12noon-2.30pm, 7-10.30pm, Sun 12.30-2.30pm

At first sight a dry-cleaning business has very little in common with a restaurant offering an intimate, relaxing atmosphere and a traditionally-English menu, but Dennis and Ruth Treadaway run both businesses very successfully and they only need to climb a flight of stairs to go from one to the other.
So successful are they that the Treadaways are the proud owners of the restaurant which readers chose as the place they would have liked to have seen in last year's '999' Guide.
The Pilgrim's Halt at Maidstone, Kent, was one of numerous restaurants looked at by AA inspectors up and down the country to find the 1000th entry.
Chief Hotel Inspector Geoffrey Lerway had the task of inspecting the four shortlisted nominations and as he says; 'The Pilgrim's Halt was without question my top choice because it reflected the warmth of the owners' personality'.
The Treadaways, married forty-two years, have been mixing haute cuisine with hot vapours for fifteen years. Before that, they opened a dry-cleaning business in Horsham, Surrey but hankered after running a restaurant. For several years they had run a hotel and country club in Bishop's Stortford, where they learned the basics of the restaurant trade, then when premises above the dry-cleaners in Horsham fell vacant, they opened their own restaurant there.
With an imaginative Czech chef called Louis at the kitchen range, the restaurant became so successful that ten years later they were able to open a similar restaurant in Maidstone, again above a dry-cleaners, combining two contrasting but surprisingly complementary trades.
The Pilgrim's Halt is a medieval building in the centre of Maidstone – one of the very few to have survived from an early date. Low-

...but
...rant
...gh-
...,
...nd
...effect.
...e in

...ent,
...home-made and
...(with a bias
...d English) and a
...erican influence. This
...ly from Ruth
...y, originally from
...SA, whose home-made
...colate fudge or
...scotch sauces transform ice
... into a transatlantic delight.
...harge of the kitchen is Gary
...imstead, only twenty-two, and
...escribed by Dennis Treadaway as
'a brilliant young English chef'. Particularly recommended is the Aberdeen Scotch steak, charcoal-grilled and served with a hunting knife, or the old English casserole made with breast of chicken, mushrooms, carrots, onions and served with a fresh cream sauce laced with cider. Fresh salads and juicy vegetables, picked from the Treadaway's garden, complete a memorable meal from the à la carte menu, but always watch the blackboard for details of Gary's low-priced and imaginative special dishes, changing daily. Meals are well-presented with colourful garnish, on crockery made by Ruth herself.

Ruth and Dennis employ a very young staff at the Pilgrim's Halt; the emphasis in their words, is on 'efficient youth'. All decisions are made jointly and manageress Sue Turner makes sure that everyone feels involved in the day-to-day running of the restaurant. To keep prices low and customers happy they employ a limited mark-up on popular dishes and resist the temptation to make over-large profits.

The restaurant is a family concern, (Ruth and Dennis have two children and ten grandchildren, all interested in the trade) and was designed to be a long-lasting and valuable part of Maidstone, not just a money-making business venture. Plans for the future include turning the old barn at the back of the restaurant into a room for conferences and private parties, and the conversion of the medieval cellar, which with its gigantic brick arches and sewer pipes resembles a Paris nightclub, into a wine bar. We wish them continued success!

Standards in the competition to find the 1000th entry were high, and details of the several close runners-up can be found within the text. They are:

Applejacks, Ledbury p 168
Badger's Holt, Dartmeet p 24
Le Bol à Toute Faire, Malvern p 169

A–Z of Towns

GLAND

The Punch + Judy, Petersfield

Lion Hotel, Shrewsbury

Tea House, Sandwich

The Red House Hotel, Exeter

The Ashburnian, Derby

South West Peninsula

Rolling hills, rugged coastlines, bleak moorlands, balmy beaches – the South West has it all, with a dramatic history to match. Intrepid seafarers when not fending off the Spanish, sailed from Plymouth and Bristol in search of treasures and returned laden with foods we now take for granted – not to mention the illicit liquor landed by moonlight in countless Cornish smugglers' caves. The sweet potato introduced by Drake in 1563 never quite caught on, but the ordinary potato, brought back from the New World by Raleigh has never looked back – a fitting complement to the variety of fish caught around West Country shores. Our debt to these gentlemen exceeds this – our palates would be the poorer were it not for the herbs and spices they discovered in foreign lands. Imagine baked Cornish pilchards without cloves and allspice or Somerset jugged hare in cider vinegar without juniper berries and rosemary!

Land and sea are equally fertile around these parts – thanks to the warm Gulf Stream and a variety of rich soils. The apple orchards of Somerset and Devon have long yielded that unique fermented juice of the apple – scrumpy. Not only is cider a heady drink, but also

it is
iti
Som
with
delici
many
cider is v
Devon, ha
sauce is a s
which manage
press may end t
Somerset apple
Vale of Pewsey in S
succulent walnuts w
als use to stuff prune
braising steak.

Fish and seafood are
in Devon and Cornwal
giant lobsters, prawns an
grace many a fisherman's pla
the local hostelries, with dev
crab a Brixham special. Macker

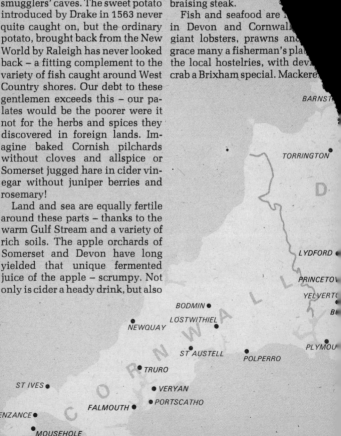

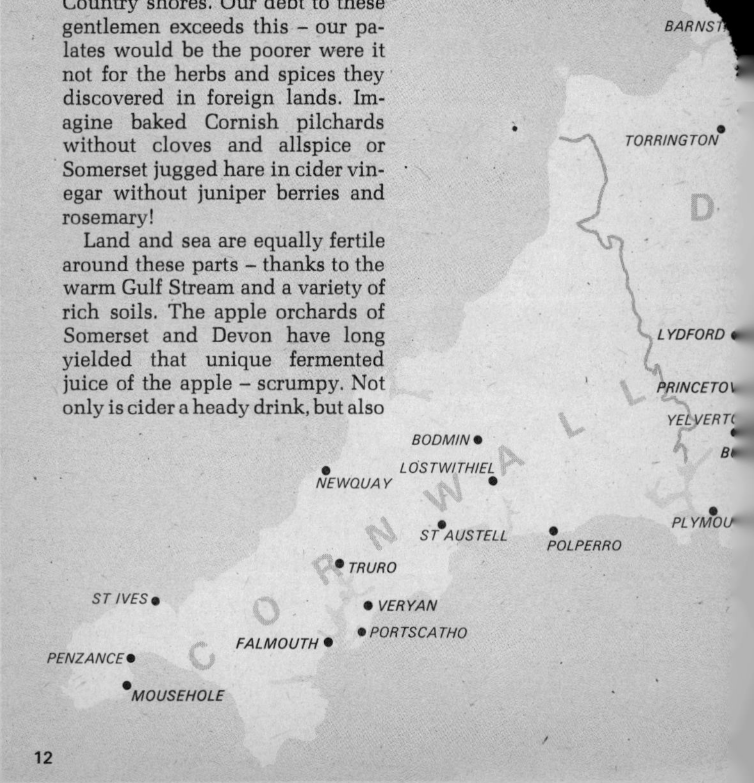

only
gh's
. The
ulent
ermen
le with

tion here if
Even the fam-
ream have been
e interest of such
hts such as fillet
erry and cream or
syllabub.

And what of Chudleighs, Dartmouth Pie, Widecombe gingerbread, lardy cakes, saffron cakes, Cornish pasties and clotted cream? The list of traditional West Country fare is endless and you can be sure to find at least some examples to tempt you in the places found in the following pages.

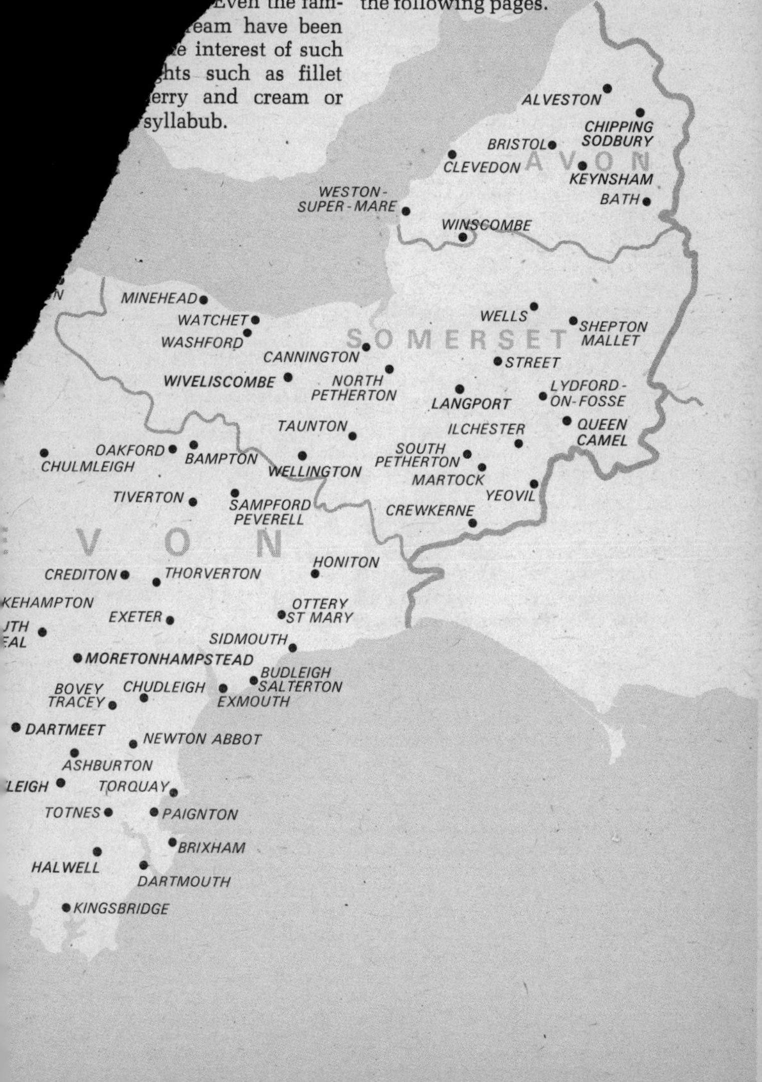

Alveston

THE SHIP RESTAURANT, Post House Hotel, Thornbury Road
(Thornbury 412521)
Open: Mon-Sun 12.30-2.30pm

[icon]

'The Wealth of Avon' is the name coined by staff at this modern Trusthouse Forte establishment for their special carvery lunch at £4.65. For that price you can choose a starter such as home-made pâté, egg mayonnaise or grapefruit and orange segments and follow it with roast prime ribs of beef, the chef's daily selected joint or special entrée with traditional accompaniments, roast potatoes and a choice of vegetables, or a cold buffet of interesting meats and salads with various dressings. A sweet such as Black Forest gâteau or chocolate profiteroles is extra at 80p, but coffee is included in the overall price.

Ashburton

THE DARTMOOR MOTEL ☆☆
(Ashburton 52232)
Open: Mon-Sun 12noon-2pm, 7-9.30pm

[C] [P] [icon]

The
pleas
offers
around
extreme
on fish a
scampi, p
cooked in s
delight, but y
lower priced st
within your budg
Children are offered
lunch at around £2.

RISING SUN INN, Woo
(Ashburton 52544)
1½m off southbound A38 E
Plymouth
Open: Mon-Sun 11.30am-2p
7-10.30pm

[C] [♫] [P]

Once used by sheep drovers as a
overnight stop on the road to Dart
this rustic old inn houses an interes
collection of prints dating from the e
1920s. Many of the people depicted st
form a faithful band of locals who meet
and drink here. A sumptuous cold buffet, which includes home-cooked cold meats, fresh salmon, salads and pies, is very reasonably priced, and there are grills and basket meals for those who like it hot. You can buy a

ook

m, 5.30pm

Exmoor at this
iped awning and
y-run and offering
snacks throughout the
day may be followed by
and kidney pie, Cornish
ham – all served with chips
as an alternative main
, cheese or ham salad. Fruit
it pie with Devon cream,
ke or gâteaux are some of the
sserts provided. Three courses
st somewhere between £1.70-£3
large glass of house wine will set
back about another 60p.

Barnstaple

BARNSTAPLE MOTEL ☆☆☆ Braunton Road (Barnstaple 5016)
Open: Mon-Sun 12.30-2pm, 7-10pm

[C] [P]

The restaurant and bar of this pleasant motel are ideal places to break a journey and enjoy good food. Hot and cold bar snacks include cottage pie, chips and peas. A three-course lunch in the restaurant is around £4. Choices include grapefruit and mandarin cocktail, roast lamb or gammon and pineapple and sweets from the trolley. A similar three-course dinner is £5.50, with a slightly larger selection of main courses, including beef chasseur.

Bath

BARCELONA SPANISH RESTAURANT, 31 Barton Street (Bath 63924)
Open: Tue-Sun 12noon-2.15pm, 6.30-11.30pm

[C] [P] [S]

Suddenly it's Spain when you sample the intriguing cuisine at this bright and cheerful restaurant with its new, Spanish-style cocktail bar. Paella at around £3.60, kalamares marinera (squids with tomato and wine sauce) at about £3.20 or gambas parrilla (king prawns) for less than £4 are some choice examples. Tasty English dishes are also on offer, as are daily specialities shown on a board, including rape vizcanna (monkfish) and stuffed peppers. Choice of appetisers is wide, and an interesting sweet is pijama, a dish of assorted nuts and raisins served with a miniature flask of moscato.

CLARETS WINE AND SHERRY LOUNGE, 6-7 Kingsmead Square (Bath 66688)
Open: Mon-Fri 10am-2.30pm, 6.30-11pm (Sat 11.30pm), Sun 7-10.30pm

[C] [♫] [P] [S] [🍷]

Clarets is a beautifully converted white-walled cellar, with pine-wood furniture. In fine summer weather, chairs and tables are set out under the large plane tree in the cobbled square outside. The owners, David and Lisa Tearle are thoroughly experienced restaurateurs and serve tasty dishes prepared from good fresh food. Choose from starters, casseroles (including a vegetarian vegetable and cheese version) with bread and butter and green salad (about £2.25-£4.00) and home-made sweets, with filter coffee to complete a very pleasant meal.

DANISH FOOD AND WINE BAR Pierrepont Place (Bath 61603)
Open: Mon-Sat 11am-2.30pm

[♫] [P] [S] [🍷]

The Fernley's Danish Food and Wine Bar (behind the hotel), although small and simple, is both stylish and comfortable, and well worth a visit for the variety of its delicious open sandwiches of meat, fish and cheese (around 75p). To these you can add salads (for a small extra charge), and finish with pastries and cream and good filter coffee. As an alternative try the cold table where, for from about £2, you can help yourself to as much cold meat and salad as you can heap on your plate.

THE EDWARDIAN, 36 Westgate Street (Bath 61642)
Open: Dining Room: Mon-Sat 12noon-3pm, 6pm-11pm, Sun 12noon-2pm, 7-10.30pm, Cellar Bar: Mon-Sun 12noon-2.30pm, 6-9.30pm, 9.30-1am

[C] [♫] [S] [🍷]

You'll have no trouble in finding and enjoying variety at this Edwardian hotel, close to the Abbey. The first floor Edwardian Dining Room is tastefully furnished in the period and a good grill section is available, with ice cream, fruit pie and cream or cheeseboard included in the price. Starters are extra and, without care, some will take you over the £5 limit. Sunday lunch can be had here for around £5, with half-price meals for children. In the cellar you can select hot roasts from the carvery in a sophisticated yet informal atmosphere, every day including Sundays. For the night-birds, there are candlelight suppers of beefburgers or steaks and salads, accompanied by live music until 1am. Expect to pay £1-£2.

SPORTSMAN STEAK HOUSE, Rode Hill, Rode (Frome 830249)
11m south of Bath on B3109 Rode-Bradford-on-Avon road
Open: Mon-Fri 12noon-2.30pm

[C] [P]

This converted stone barn has a copper-topped bar on the first floor, in an open-plan area where you can enjoy an aperitif while Philip, the resident chef, prepares your meal. Starters include fruit juices, prawn cocktail, and Strasbourg pâté with fingers of hot toast. Main dishes are unfussy but good, with two lamb chops, a pork chop or gammon steak at about £2.30, or a luscious, tender T-bone steak at twice the price. Not only do those prices include freshly-cooked chips, peas and mushrooms, but also ice cream or cheese to follow. Even with wine, you can just keep within the £5.

TRATTORIA DA PIETRO
39 Gay Street (Bath 27919)
Open: Mon-Sat 12noon-2.30pm, 6.30-11pm

[P] [S]

This busy, informal little Italian restaurant is extremely popular with locals and businessmen who enjoy robust Italian food and wine. The splendid list of antipasti includes mozzarella in carozza – delicious soft cheese fried in breadcrumbs, which costs around 90p. Pasta dishes are about £2, meat dishes such as steak bordelaise in the £3.10-£4.50 range. Daily specialities are displayed on the bar blackboard. All the main meals are served with vegetables of the day. Salads are about £2.50, sweets around 85p. There is a good list of Italian wine. A glass of it will cost you about 50p.

Bodmin

CASTLE HILL HOUSE HOTEL ★★
(Bodmin 3009)
Open: Mon-Sat 7-8.30pm,
Sun 12.30-2pm

[P]

Ken and Sylvia Flint's Castle Hill House Hotel is an elegant Georgian mansion set in two acres of lawns and gardens. Delicious home-produced food such as soup, pâté and steak and kidney pie proves popular with guests and locals alike, and it's as well to book in advance for dinner. The table d'hôte menu offers a three-course meal and coffee for about £4, and most items on the small à la carte menu are within our price range. A good selection of freshly-made sweets, including gâteaux and home-made fruit pies is served with thick clotted Cornish cream.

THE CORNISH ARMS★★ Pendoggett, St Kew (Port Isaac 263)
Open: Mon-Sat 12.30-2pm, 7-9.30pm,
Sun 12.30-2pm

[C] [P]

This quaint Cornish inn, smothered in creepers, lies about four miles inland from Port Isaac. The low-beamed, flagstoned bar and lounges are aglow with log fires, polished oak, mahogany and brass. An excellent buffet lunch, comprising a choice of home-made hot dishes such as steak and kidney pie, well-prepared salads and tender beef, ham or pork carved at the table costs around £2.25. Home-made sweets are about 70p. Traditional Sunday lunch offers a wide choice for all three courses, and at around £4.50 is good value for money. The à la carte dinner, with careful choice, can be just within our budget. Tempting dishes include guinea fowl in sherry and red wine. A glass of French wine is about 50p.

Bovey Tracey

RIVERSIDE INN, Fore Street
(Bovey Tracey 832293)
Open: Mon-Sun 12noon-2pm, 7-10pm

[♫] [P]

This large inn by a stream enjoys a picturesque situation in the centre of Bovey Tracey, a popular touring area within a stone's throw of Hay Tor. On display is the sword, broken in two, which is said to have been used by the knight, De Tracey in the murder of Thomas à Becket. There are two eating places to choose from; the Cavalier Restaurant offers a substantial à la carte menu of grills, while the King Charles Buttery has a more budget-priced selection, such as basket meals, pizzas, sandwiches or salads. A choice from the à la carte of chef's own pâté, the Moorland grill (which includes kidney, egg, sausage, chop, gammon) with vegetables of the day and lemon sorbet, accompanied by wine and coffee would come just within our limit. On Sundays a set three-course lunch with coffee can be had for around £3 or thereabouts.

Bristol

ARNOLFINI, Narrow Quay
(Bristol 299191)
Open: Tue-Sat 11am-8pm

Popular with students who drift around the attractive Arnolfini public arts complex, this airy and spacious bistro-style restaurant predictably has taped background music and a blackboard menu, with salads, cold meats and cakes on display on long counters. There is always an exhibition of works of art on the walls. Once a docks warehouse, the restaurant overlooks St Augustine's Reach. Soups, pâtés and a hot dish of the day are all reasonably priced, and a three-course light meal can be enjoyed for around £2. Salads are particularly interesting, and a mixed salad of celery, apple, nuts, orange and mayonnaise costs about 40p. Wine by the glass is around 50p.

BISTRO TWENTY-ONE, 21 Cotham Road, South Kingsdown
(Bristol 421744)
Open: Mon-Sat 7-11.30pm

For food of the quality served by experienced gourmet cook Stephen Markwick, low prices cannot be
exp
tem
But t
cuisi
reaso
evident
Canaille
available)
green pepp
sweets are ge
good choice of
salads is included
price. Booking in ad

LE CHÂTEAU WINE B
32 Park Street (Bristol 2
Open: Mon-Sat 9.30pm-2
5.30-9pm

[♫] [P] [S]

This informal, busy city cent
brims over with business peop
lunchtime – a tribute to good fo
unpretentious but relaxing
surroundings, with wooden furnit
and lighting from candles in wax-
encrusted bottles. Behind the Victori
bar a blackboard proclaims the range o
hot lunchtime dishes – pork fillet kebabs in lemon garlic sauce, moussaka, chili con carne, kidneys Java at prices around £1.60-£2.20. Also at lunchtime and in the evening a selection of cold meats, pâté, cheeses, mackerel and attractively-prepared salads is on offer at about £1.75. Interesting desserts include peaches in brandy, and blueberry pie – both around 60p, as well as cheesecake, ices and sorbets. The better quality wines may prove too pricey, but a glass of French vin ordinaire costs about 50p.

THE CHEQUERS INN, Hanham Mills, Hanham (Bristol 674242)
Open: Mon-Sat 12noon-2.30pm, 6.30-11pm, Sun 12noon-2.30pm, 7-11pm

[C] [P] [?]

It pays to arrive early for dinner at this riverside haven, close to the City, for if you pay your bill before 8pm you get 30% discount. And at around £4 (after discount) for a three-course meal, that bargain can buy even an expensive dish like T-bone steak. No wonder The Chequers is a popular haunt, attracting not only local business people but family parties, particularly for Sunday lunch, and even yachtsmen taking a spot of shore-leave. Apart from the restaurant offering a comprehensive choice of grills or 'Fisherman's Choices', the self-service bar has a carvery specialising in 'Roasters' – succulent rare beef or roast pork with vegetables for around £3.30 or cold ham off the bone plus help-yourself salads

25. Lasagne, steak and r turkey and ham in white lso available for around £1.50 vegetables. Pastries and re on offer at give-away prices.

LES RESTAURANT, Dingles, ens Road, Clifton (Bristol 291471)
en: Mon-Fri 9am-5.30pm,
at 9am-6pm

[C] [♫] [S]

This comfortable, modern, self-service restaurant situated next to the Ladies Fashion Department, displays cold meats, salads, pâtés and a variety of sandwiches, all at very reasonable prices. Staff are on hand to help you to the various permutations of interesting salads which range in price from around £1-£1.60. Hot quiches and meat loaf are around 75p and soup costs about 30p. With cream gâteaux on offer at around 45p to complete the menu, this is a much sought-after filling station for shoppers. A bar dispenses glasses of house wine (about 50p), lager and aperitifs.

DRAGONARA HOTEL☆☆☆☆
Redcliffe Way (Bristol 20044)
Open: Captain's Cabin Bar: Mon-Fri 12.30-2pm, Garden Room: Mon-Fri 6.30-10.30pm, Sat-Sun 12.30-2pm, 6.30-10.30pm

[C] [♫] [P] [S] [♧]

The Garden Room is a bright and pleasant restaurant within Ladbroke's Dragonara Hotel. A typical meal here might consist of pâté in the pot, followed by chicken breast provençale, with ice-cream to finish, at a cost of around £5. However, take care, as several of the main dishes will take you over the budget. At the recently introduced Cabin Bar though, you can choose from a variety of hot and cold dishes (eg, moussaka or salad of the day) after a bowl of soup, for as little as £1.50. House wine is around 75p per goblet.

EDWARDS, 203 Whiteladies Road, Clifton (Bristol 311533)
Open: Mon-Sat 8am-6pm, 7-11pm

The former Victorian shop has been recently modernised by owner/chef James Orchard. Breakfast, lunch, afternoon tea and supper all offer an imaginative range of good food at sensible prices. Lunch can be chosen from an impressive selection of home-made soups (cream of watercress with almonds at about 50p), quiches, savoury pancakes (under £2) or main-meat dishes (£1.70-£4). Sweets and vegetables are under £1. The dinner is more ambitious from both culinary and price aspects, but home-made beef, Guinness and oyster pie with accompaniments should be about £5.

GIOVANNI PIZZERIA, 15 Union Street (Bristol 22731)
Open: Mon-Thu 11.30am-12mdnt, Fri-Sat 11.30am-2am, Sun 5.30-12mdnt

[C] [♫] [S] [♧]

Home-made pizzas are the speciality here. You can buy a simply-dressed tomato, oregano and garlic version, or go for a more elaborate one like pizza Giovanni – an extravagance of mozzarella cheese, tomato, oregano, salami and black olives, costing about £2.50. The skilful preparation of these and other dishes is on view to diners, providing interesting 'while-you-wait' entertainment. A more conventional form of entertainment is the nightly disco dancing and, occasionally, there is a live band at weekends.

THE GUILD RESTAURANT, Bristol Guild, 68-70 Park Street (Bristol 291874)
Open: Mon-Fri 9.30am-5pm, Sat 9.30am-1pm

[S]

The small Guild Restaurant, with its attractive extension on to a terrace, covered in winter, but opened in summer to allow patrons to eat in the sun, is a part of the smart Bristol Guild store in the city centre. Under the capable direction of Alison Moore, inexpensive lunchtime meals of good quality include a selection of home-made soup, quiches or pâtés chalked on a blackboard menu. Soup is around 60-75p, quiches are around 95p and pâtés with salad about £1.90. A hot main dish of the day could be spaghetti bolognese, moussaka, a roast or a casserole, all served with vegetables at around £2.50. Creamy desserts are delicious and modestly priced at around 85p. A glass of French house wine is about 50p.

LLANDOGER TROW, 5 King Street (Bristol 20783)
Open: Mon-Fri 12noon-2.30pm, 6-11pm (Sat 11.30), Sun 12noon-2pm, 7-10.30pm

[C] [♫] [P] [S]

King Street boasts a number of impressive 17th- and 18th-century buildings, including the long-running Theatre Royal, first opened to the public in 1766. But none is more interesting, or has attracted more legends, than Llandoger Trow, built in 1664, one of the oldest inns in the city and now run by Berni. Duckling and T-bone steaks are specialities of the house here and the steak and duck restaurant does an extremely good local trade. In the smaller steak and sole restaurant, prices range from about £3 for fillets of plaice and salad to just under £6 for fillet steak and salad. Half a duckling and salad costs around £5. Wine by the glass is about 70p.

MAXWELL PLUM ✕ 1-3 Frogmore Street (Bristol 291413)
Open: Tue-Fri 12noon-2pm, Mon-Fri 7-11pm (Sat 7-11.30pm)

[♫]

Maxwell Plum is an intimate and
char
listed
entert
like to
menu is
choose f
starters, m
inclusive p
is around 35
(French) costs
atmosphere are
posters from silent
interest to the attract

PARKS, 51 Park Street (
Open: Mon-Sat 11am-11
Sun 12noon-11pm

[♫] [P] [🍷]

Parks, situated in Bristol's bu
Street and close to the city's lo
university and museum buildi
one of the newest restaurants in t
though housed in a Georgian listed
building. It is fresh and bright,
bedecked with attractive plants, gran
mirrors and fans from the once-far-flu
Empire. Specialities here are savoury pancakes made with buckwheat and filled with such things as chicken in mushroom and white wine sauce, blue cheese with apple and walnuts, or cheese with spinach and nutmeg, all at about £2, and teas such as Earl Grey and jasmine served with milk or lemon, at around 30p per person. Main-course dishes, served with vegetables or salad, and jacket potato with butter or sour cream, include 8oz sirloin steak and country chicken casserole. In addition there is a Chef's Special. Desserts include gooseberry and elderflower ice cream at around £1. House wine is about 50p a glass, and for the discerning palate, there is a dry white wine-and-blackcurrant liqueur called 'Kir'.

LA ROMANINA, 25 The Mall, Clifton (Bristol 34499)
Open: Mon-Sat 12noon-2.30pm, 7-11.30pm

ours and cheerful f Bruno Sica's restaurant h of the Mediterranean to Clifton old town. Fresh e on every table, and service is s and prompt. The pizza and ishes are very good and cost £2. Add on a further £2 to cover ter and sweet. The à la carte meat hes, often accompanied by robust lian sauces, are more expensive, but otatoes and fresh vegetables in season are included in the main price. Fresh salmon and lobster are also available in season.

TRATTORIA SORRENTO
239 Cheltenham Road (Bristol 45879)
Open: Mon-Thu, Sun 6pm-2am, Fri-Sat 6pm-3am

[P]

This spacious, modern trattoria, bedecked with Chianti flasks, is noted for its home-made pastas and pizzas. Freshly made for each customer, the pizzas are rated by gourmets as 'the finest this side of Mount Vesuvius', and the Chef's Special is a particularly praiseworthy specimen – brimming over with Italian cheeses, tomatoes, bacon, salami, corn, peppers, mushrooms and anchovies! Pizzas and pasta dishes cost around £2 but the steak and chicken dishes, English or Italian style, are from £3. So generous are the main courses that the luscious sweets, Italian cheeses and speciality coffees prove to be quite a challenge. Whatever your choice, dishes will be served to you in true Italian style by cheerful (and sometimes singing) Italian waiters.

Brixham

THE ELIZABETHAN, 8 Middle Street (Brixham 3722)
Open: summer: Mon-Sun 12.15-2pm, Tue-Sat 7-9.30pm, winter: Mon-Sun 12.15-2pm

[C] [P] [S] [ ]

Small-paned windows, stuccoed walls, ceiling beams and dark, polished furniture lend an air of cosy antiquity to this small restaurant in the town centre. Fresh flowers are a complement to the fresh, home-made fare. The lunch menu offers a choice of main courses and desserts for around £2.20. Roast chicken, pork or fillet of plaice could be followed with apricot crumble or Devonshire junket with clotted cream. An appetiser such as home-made soup of the day, pâté or scampi, will set you back from 45p-£1.60. A large glass of house wine costs 55p. Dinners, served during the season, are 'Taste of England' dishes at their best. It would be easy to exceed the limit here, but soup, followed by honeyed chicken cooked with lemon and rosemary and a slice of fresh cream gâteau can be savoured – and a glass of wine too.

Buckfastleigh

DART BRIDGE INN, Totnes Road (Buckfastleigh 2214)
Open: Mon-Sun 12noon-2pm, 7-10pm

[P]

Just across the road from the River Dart, this mock Tudor inn has pleasant gardens and a sun terrace. It is less than 100 yards away from the A38 Exeter-Plymouth road. The interior is furnished in pub lounge-bar style. Hot and cold meals are served, the former consisting mainly of grills with chips and peas from £1.70 to £4. A seafood platter with shrimps, smoked mackerel, cockles and mussels is good value at £2.50. Fresh white or granary rolls are included.

Budleigh Salterton

THE LOBSTER POT (Budleigh Salterton 2731)
Open: Mar-Sep: Tue-Sat 12noon-2pm and 7-10pm, Sun 12noon-2pm

Jul-Aug: 7-10pm

♫ S

Near the sea front you will find this bright, white-painted restaurant with its small-paned windows and gay red canopy. Renowned for its fresh seafood specialities, you can enjoy an array of other dishes too in the comfortable, Georgian-style interior. A three-course set lunch is available for around £3.15, and the à la carte menu gives a good choice for under £5. Particularly recommended are the pâté with salad garni and mixed seafood and salad. Dinner offers specialities such as scallops à la crème (scallops cooked in white wine sauce), and vegetables are included in the price of the
A three-course dinner round
a French, Calypso or Jamaica
cost around £5.

Cannington

BLUE ANCHOR INN, Brook Street, Cannington (Combwich 652215)
Open: Mon-Sun 12noon-2pm, 7-10pm

P

This long, low, wisteria-clad inn was built in the 1600s. Rebuilt and greatly modernised in 1948, the Blue Anchor has enjoyed constant popularity for as long as anyone cares to remember.

...acks
...t
...ll the
...s a

...rch Road, Yate
...14367)
...Mon-Sat 12noon-
...pm, Sun 12noon-2pm,
...aurant: Mon-Sun 12.30-
...n

...Lawns is *genuine* Tudor – ...25. It is a popular eating place ... surroundings. The restaurant ...uthentic period plasterwork ... complements the comfortable ...ern furniture. A bright little buttery ...rs a wide range of hot or cold snacks. ...e former, in the 70p-90p price-range, ...clude curry, cottage pie, lasagne and ...hili con carne. A three-course meal in the restaurant costs from £4-£8. Accent is on grills. A glass of house wine is around 50p.

Chudleigh

THE WHEEL CRAFT CENTRE
Chudleigh Mill (Chudleigh 853255)
Open: Mon-Sun 10am-6pm

[P] [craft]

Created on the site of the original Town Mills which were used to grind corn, the Wheel Craft Centre has a restored watermill complete with working wheel. Individual hand crafts – pottery, woodwork and metalwork are displayed in the fascinating gift shop. The 'Tea Shoppe' provides much more than cream teas. Home-made soup with a hot roll costs 40p, and you may follow this with one of the Special Hot Lunches – farmhouse stew at £1 and chicken in red wine at £1.40 are examples. Home-made desserts served with clotted cream cost from 50p. Lighter snacks include 'Things on toast' for 60p, omelettes with salad at 90p and quiche or pizza salads from £1.50. As yet The Wheel is unlicensed, though one has been applied for. A steaming cup of Rombout coffee at 30p is an excellent substitute!

Chulmleigh

FOX AND HOUNDS HOTEL ★★
Eggesford (Chulmleigh 345)
Open: Bar: Mon-Thu 11.30am-1.45pm, 6-9.30pm, Fri-Sat 11.30am-1.45pm, 6-10pm, Sun 7-9.30pm; Restaurant: Mar-Oct, 7.30-9.30pm

[P]

The Fox and Hounds Hotel, close to the River Taw, halfway between Exeter and Barnstaple, is a rambling country hotel, the mecca of fishermen from Victorian days. It has a large bar, the Eggesford Bar, which offers a wide range of bar snacks at a reasonable price. A salad bar in summer offers an impressive choice from £1.80. A Fox's lunch, consisting of French bread, ham and cheese, garnished with tomato and pickle, costs £1. A glass of house wine is about 45p. In the tourist season, a four-course dinner may be had for around £5.50 in the hotel dining room. The menu is interesting and offers a good choice. You may even eat fish caught that very day as an entrée or a main course! A speciality is Chicken Fox and Hounds – chicken served in a white wine sauce with mushrooms and asparagus.

Clevedon

MON PLAISIR RESTAURANT
32-34 Hill Road (Clevedon 872307)
Open: Mon-Sat 12noon-2pm, 7-10pm

[P]

For Mr Luis Moran and his staff 'Mon Plaisir' is certainly the operative phrase, for here nothing is too much trouble and with their warm, friendly welcome they hope to make eating here 'your pleasure' too. You will dine in comfort at this Victorian house, set just off the sea front, where well-prepared food is served in generous portions. The three-course set lunch (with a choice of five main courses) is excellent value at around £2.25. In the evening you must be more selective when choosing from the à la carte menu, but most main dishes comply with our limit.

Crediton

DARTMOOR RAILWAY INN ✕
Station Road (Crediton 2489)
Open: Mon-Sun 11am-2.30pm, 6-10pm

[C] [♫] [P]

Off the Exeter Road and close to Crediton Station is the appropriately named Dartmoor Railway Restaurant and Bar. They are, in their own words, 'famous for fine foods' so one can only hope that the house soup 'grotti nosh' turns out to be a misnomer! Specialities such as the Dartmoor Kings (individual casseroles filled with savoury cottage pie), steak and kidney pie, coq au vin provençale or curry and rice, or seafood risotto and Andalusian Picadillo (chicken, ham and savoury rice in a spicy Spanish sauce) certainly sound more tempting. And for the lighter meal how about a 'Dartmoor commoner' – a type of cottage pie? There's a curried chicken commoner, steak and grotti commoner or a Dartmoor kedgeree commoner – all tasty fillers for around £1.25. Bar grills are extensive and reasonably priced from around £2.25. Indeed, a substantial three-course meal here, with a glass of wine, need not total more than £4.50.

Crewkerne

THE OLD PARSONAGE ★★
Barn Street (Crewkerne 73516)
Open: Mon-Sat 12noon-2pm, 7-8.30pm, Sun 12noon-2pm

[C] [P]

On the corner of a quiet lane you will find this charming old rectory, personally run by Kenneth Mullins. Home cooking is the big attraction here. Interesting dishes such as cockles in cheese sauce and grilled rainbow trout with almonds and Pernod, are scattered liberally throughout the à la carte menu (most of which are unfortunately outside our price limit). The table d'hôte menus for lunch and dinner are reasonably priced at around £4.80. A traditional Sunday lunch for four courses plus coffee and cream costs approximately the same, with a special children's version at £1 less.

Dartmeet

BADGER'S HOLT (Poundsgate 213)
Open: Mon-Sat 9.30am-6pm, Sun 10.30am-6pm. Closed: Nov-Apr

[C]

The
strew
paint
the sha
conflu
Rare bir
eared ph
view in th
exotic, but
d'hôte lunch
good value. A c
home-made chick
served with fresh h
roll-mop herring or m
main course dishes such
loin of pork with pineapp
scallops with tartare sauce
with ample portions of well
vegetables. Home-cooked ga
roast lamb with a mixed salad
the cold alternatives. Desserts,
with lashings of Devonshire cre
include a delicious almond-flavo
trifle, apple pie or junket. A glass o
wine costs 50p. Light or satisfying
snacks are served throughout the day

Dartmouth

FOSSEY'S, Foss Street
(Dartmouth 3895)
Open: summer: Mon-Sat 10.30am-2.30pm, 6-10.30pm, Sun 12noon-2.30pm, 7-10.30pm; winter: Wed-Sat 10.30am-2.30pm, 7-10.30pm, Sun 12noon-2.30pm, 7-10.30pm

[P] [S]

Whether you choose a snack such as a toasted sandwich (around 60p) or a main course grill such as fillet steak with chips, peas, tomato and mushrooms (about £4.25), you can be sure that it will be carefully prepared and nicely served. The same attention is given to diners, who are made to feel really welcome. Which all explains why Fossey's is proving a successful venture. Situated in one of Dartmouth's interesting narrow streets just behind the ancient Buttery Walk, the restaurant d

lace
se

Street
,

ape in this neat
wine bar situated just
iver front, and as one
om such a nautical
is a speciality. As seating
eighteen people you may
for a place or book in
either way you'll be well
n paying the Steam Packet a
ung owner David Hawke has a
ound of hotels and catering in
ountry where he did his training,
in the West Indies, Brazil and
itzerland where he worked. So you
n be sure that when you taste his
ome-made quiche, pizzas or steak and
kidney pie you're tasting some of the best around – and the price is right too!

Exeter

CLARE'S, 13 Princesshay
(Exeter 55155)
Open: Mon-Sat 9.30am-5.30pm

[P] [S]

There are some classy shops in Princesshay, a pedestrian area just off the High Street and not far from the Cathedral, and Clare Shattock's brightly modern counter-service restaurant is just the place for a snack or lunch when you tire of looking in the gift shops and boutiques. It's justly popular with office workers, too, who have to find the quickest and cheapest good food around. 'Country style' hot dishes such as lasagne with rice and salad garnish, steak and kidney pie and gammon and courgettes in a cheese sauce cost around £1.50. A salad with quiche, pizza or meat costs about £1.75, and a baked potato with butter is only 20p. Clare's is licensed to sell wines, beer and cider. A glass of house wine costs around 35p.

COOLINGS WINE BAR
11 Gandy Street (Exeter 34183)
Open: Mon-Sat 12noon-2.15pm, 5.30-11.30pm

[P] [S]

Tucked away in one of the older, interesting streets behind the main shopping area is this stylish, family-run wine and food bar where all the food is freshly-prepared on the premises. Beams and checked tablecloths create a welcoming interior and you can also dine in the converted cellars. An excellent range of meats, pies and salads is displayed on the long self-service bar, including such delights as chicken Waldorf and salad, tuna and rice salad and sugar-baked ham and salad, all around £1.45-£1.75. Hot dishes such as lasagne (about £1.55) and cottage pie (about £1.45) are chalked up on the blackboard. There is a choice of about six sweets for around 45p-65p. A glass of French house wine costs about 50p.

HOLE IN THE WALL, Little Castle Street (Exeter 73341)
Open: Restaurant: Mon-Thu 12noon-2.30pm, Fri-Sat 12noon-2.30pm, 7-11pm. Steak Bar: Mon-Thu 6-11pm, Fri-Sat 6-11.30pm

[C] [S]

One of the nationwide Berni Inn chain of restaurants, the Hole in the Wall is an old building of character. It provides a choice of two attractive, well-appointed restaurants, offering steak, fish and chicken dishes. Those familiar with Berni Inns will know that included in the price of each main dish are potatoes, vegetables, roll and butter, and to follow, ice cream or cheese and biscuits. The perfect finishing touch is the coffee, served in a glass with a generous topping of cream for about 30p.

NEW TAJ MAHAL, 50 Queen Street
(Exeter 58129)
Open: Mon-Sun 12noon-2.30pm, 5.30-11.30pm

[S]

A compact Indian restaurant with somewhat grand interior décor equal to its name, the New Taj Mahal has walls of pleated multi-coloured silk and a silk-draped ceiling. A wide choice of Indian dishes is available but do take care when ordering curry – it can be very hot! The Tandoori Specials won't burn a hole in your pocket, though – they are well-priced at around £2.25-£3.50.

THE NOBODY INN ✕ Doddiscombleigh
(Christow 52394)
South of Exeter, 2m east of Christow
Open: Restaurant: Tue-Sat 7.30-9.30pm. Bar snacks: normal licensing hours

[P]

At one time weary travellers would stop at this inn in vain. An unknown purchaser had refused hospitality by locking the door, causing them to continue on their journeys in the belief there was 'nobody in'. Now, in the heavily-beamed bar with its imposing stone fireplace, a varied range of bar snacks awaits you, and more substantial fare in the charming 'character' restaurant. The menu here includes some comparative rarities – gazpacho soup, squid and gammon in raisin sauce, but they will prepare your favourite dish on request. Wine is the owner's 'hobby' and there are about 200 to choose from. A large glass of house wine costs only about 40p.

POPPYS, 12 South Street (Exeter 73779)
Open: Tue-Thu 11.30am-2pm, 6.30-11.30pm, Fri 6.30pm-12mdnt, Sat 11.30am-2.30pm, 6.30pm-12mdnt, Sun 6.30-11.30pm

[C] [♫] [S] [🍷]

There are not many places in Exeter where you can get a not-too-expensive evening meal, and Poppys is understandably popular with theatre- and cinema-goers and students. Shoppers and staff from nearby offices find it handy for a good satisfying lunch too. Here they serve really beefy beefburgers with various toppings for £1.25-£1.50 inclusive of potato and salad: that's for the ¼lb size – the ½lb variety costs 30p more. There are slimburgers and vegetarian nutburgers too. Kebabs and quiches are in the same price range, and home-made cheesecake or chocolate gâteau costs about 75p.

THE RED HOUSE HOTEL★ 2 Whipton Village Road, Whipton (Exeter 56104)
Open: Mon-Thu 12noon-2.30pm, 7-10pm, Fri-Sat 12noon-2.30pm, 7-10.30pm, Sun 12noon-1.30pm, 7-9.30pm

[C] [P] [🍷]

This imposing red brick building about a mile from the city centre has a warm comfortable décor with oak refectory tables and settles. There is an excellent bar menu from which one may select a snack or a satisfying three-course meal. A crock of delicious home-made soup served with French bread is about 40p and this may be followed by a cold platter (a variety of cold meats, pâtés, pies and fish with self-service salad) from around £1.50-£2, or a bar grill such as minute steak, chicken or scampi for about the same price. There is always a good selection of sweets including gâteaux from around 60p-70p. Nicholas house wine is 55p a glass.

ROYAL OAK INN, Dunsford (Christow 52256)
6m s
B321
Open:
10.30p
2.30pm

[♫] [P] [🍷]

A charmir
setting, the
either in the c
dining room. A
includes home-ma
cocktail, chicken-li
weekends, avocado ar
'beginners' from aroun
selection of grills such as
peaches or English steaks
price from about £2-£3.50.
or steak and kidney pie are ar
and a selection of salads about
£2.25 (prawn salad). Desserts i
gâteaux with cream, or black che
with meringue and cream and var
price from around 65p-80p. A large
glass of house wine costs about 50p.

THE SHIP INN, Martin's Lane (Exeter 72040)
Open: Mon-Sat 12noon-2pm, 6.30-10.30pm

[C] [♫] [S] [🍷]

Sir Francis Drake wrote in a letter dated 1587 'Next to mine own shippe I do most love that old 'Shippe' in Exon'. Today, good wine and victuals are still there to be enjoyed, and at quite reasonable prices. The upstairs restaurant is perhaps a little dark and cramped, with deep red wallpaper and upholstery, high-backed settles, and windows within a few feet of the building across the lane, but the atmosphere is right and service is very quick and cheerful. All food is à la carte – the same menu for lunch and dinner. Starters include Scott's pâté at 75p and – a speciality of the house – whitebait, about 80p. Fresh Torbay sole is the most popular fish dish – around £3.95. Roasts and grills are equally reasonable, the most expensive being fillet steak garni which costs over £4.50. All dishes include peas or tossed salad, fried or croquette potatoes, roll and butter. Sweets include vanilla ice with cream and meringue Chantilly. House wine is around 50p a glass.

THE SWAN'S NEST, Exminster (Kennford 832371)
4m south of Exeter on the A379 to Dawlish
Open: Mon-Sat 12noon-2pm, 6-10pm, Sun 12noon-1.30pm, 7-10pm

[P]

Mervyn and Joan Ash have run the

a
ch,
ry
The
e –
ds, cold
esh
ion of
t flans.
ound £3.95
e.

DGE, Lympstone
79)
xmouth on the A376
Thu, Sat 12noon-2pm, 6.15-
12noon-2pm, 6.15-10.30pm,
0-2pm, 6.15-10pm

ast lounge of this rambling
rgian hotel with its massive, dark
oden bar, glowing pink-shaded
mps, antiques, oil-paintings and
intimate sunken area with soft upholstered settees serves a selection of snacks to tempt anyone's palate. Pork and red wine pâté with salad, chutney and toast is a meal in itself at about £1.50, and there is always a hot dish of the day, served in an earthenware pot and accompanied by a side-salad, chutney, hot roll and butter, for around £1.85. Platters of cold meats, crab, prawn, duck pie or game pie with salad are around £2.30, complete with hot roll and butter. Sweets such as apfel strüdel with cream, gâteaux and cheesecake vary from about 55p-75p.

PHANTASY, 19 The Strand
(Exmouth 5147)
Open: summer: Tue-Sun 12noon-2.30pm, 7-10pm; winter: Tue-Sun 12noon-2.30pm, Fri-Sat 7-10pm

[C] [♫] [S] [♧]

This town-centre 'emporium' sells gifts, groceries, confectionery – and good food. The candle-lit restaurant, above the shop, is ably run by Michael and Shirley Wilkes. Day-time eaters should secure a window-seat for the view over the flower-filled town gardens. Among the dishes they prepare is cuddled chicken (a charmingly-named concoction of chicken breast, ham and asparagus topped with a mushroom and cheese sauce – a favourite at about £3.75).

YE OLDE SADDLER'S ARMS
Lympstone (Exmouth 72798)
2m north of Exmouth on the A376
Open: Mon-Sat 12noon-2pm, 7-10pm, Sun 12noon-2pm

[C] [P] [♧]

Nestling in the picturesque village of Lympstone is this charming cream-painted inn, with tables and gay umbrellas in the pleasant garden when the sun shines. Bar meals are well worthwhile sampling, but so is lunch or dinner in the Manger Restaurant. An extensive à la carte menu offers some eight starters, including home-made soup at around 40p and prawn cocktail at about 95p. Grilled fish, poultry, veal and steaks feature as main courses, varying in price from around £2.25 for veal to £4.95 for T-bone steak. A selection of sweets at about 80p includes meringue glacé and home-made cheesecake.

Falmouth

COCKLESHELL RESTAURANT
Mawnan Smith (Falmouth 250714)
Open: summer: Mon-Sun 12noon-2.30pm, 7-10pm, winter: Tue-Sat 12noon-2.30pm, 7-10pm

[P] [♧]

Take the Maenporth road south west of Falmouth and you will come upon the small village of Mawnan Smith. Amongst the tiny cluster of shops, Mike and Sue's small restaurant offers a welcome in relaxed surroundings. Food is wholesome and fresh and lunches are good value for money. Typical dishes are seafood pancake at around £2, mushroom provençale at £1.50 or curry at £1.25. An interesting range of home-made sweets is available for 50p. Traditional Sunday lunch – three courses – is a bargain at £2.80.

GREENBANK HOTEL★★★
Harbourside (Falmouth 312440)
Open: Mon-Sun 12.30-2pm, 7-9pm

[P]

Officers and passengers would leave their full-rigged packet ships and tea clippers at anchorage just off the pier of this attractive harbourside hotel before unwinding with a good meal. The names of ships and their captains and other nautical memorabilia adorn the walls of the Greenbank. Today this traditional hotel offers good honest food to a different clientele. The lunch is especially good value at about £3, offering a fair choice. And how could one better complement a main course of fresh grilled fillet of mackerel meunière than to sit before spectacular views of the mouth of the River Fal?

Halwell

THE OLD INN (Blackawton 329)
On A381 6m from Totnes
Open: Mon-Sat 12noon-1.35pm, 7-10pm, Sun 12noon-1.30pm, 7-9.45pm

[C] [P]

There's an emphasis on home-cooked meats, soups and sweets at this old country inn. Choose from a wide range of grills and salads (the cold meat platter is particularly good at about £2.35) and eat from a refectory table in the wood-panelled bar or, weather p
the well-kept beer garden.
steak with chips, peas etc, c
but you'll be well within the
with the popular honey-roast
steak, fish, or basket meals. Swe
clotted cream are all well under £

Honiton

KNIGHTS, Black Lion Court, High Street (Honiton 3777)
Open: Mon-Sat 12noon-2.30pm, Wed-Sat 7.30-11pm
Closed: Mon during winter

[C] [P] [S]

Good, wholesome, home-made dishes are the order of the day at Knights. Try the cauliflower soup with cream and a slice or two of fresh granary bread for starters, followed by cider-baked ham, salad and foil-wrapped jacket potato and yoghurt with a dressing of your choice – and, if you feel there's room under your belt for more, you can top the meal off with home-made sherry trifle or cheesecake with cream for a mouth-watering finale. Like the food, the décor here is natural and unfussy, with pine-clad ceiling covered with menus, wine labels and wine bottles, stone walls and pine refectory tables. Food is served on attractive Honiton pottery dishes.

MONKTON COURT INN, Monkton (Honiton 2309)
On A30 2m north of Honiton
Open: Mon-Fri 10.30am-2.15pm, 5.30-10.15pm, Sat 10.30am-2.15pm, 5.30-10.45pm, Sun 12noon-2pm, 7-10.30pm

[C] [P] [☘]

This imposing stone-built 17th-century inn with distinctive mullioned windows has a comfortable, welcoming interior – all dark polished wood and soft seating. Appetisers include smoked mackerel, pâté and toast and trimmings

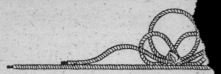

t
gh
Try
an
0p.
ould
n, beef
n fries,
nd
ad. 'Afters'
h as Dutch
ved with
t 60p. French
glass.

R HOTEL ✕ The Square
0)
-Sun 12noon-2pm, 7-9.15pm

n the centre of this sleepy
rset town, which is a through-
e to the West Country, you'll find
s unpretentious hotel-restaurant
here orders are taken at the bar for the excellent table d'hôte meals both at lunchtime and in the evening. A three-course lunch can cost as little as £3.50. Appetisers include home-made soup or fruit juice and there is a choice of five main courses, including roast duckling and apple sauce. A home-made sweet or ice cream completes the meal. For around £4.20, a three-course dinner offers four choices of starter, including rollmop herring, five main courses and a wide selection of sweets.

Keynsham

THE GRANGE HOTEL ★★, 42 Bath Road (Keynsham 2130)
Open: Bar snacks: Mon-Sun 11.30am-2.30pm; Restaurant: Mon-Fri 6.30-9pm, Sat-Sun 7-10pm

[P]

Once the main farmhouse in the area, this Georgian building in the centre of Keynsham has a comfortable air. A collection of Cries of London prints and medallioned cartoon prints adorn the restaurant walls. Lunchtime bar snacks range from 45p-£1.35, and include pâté, chicken drumsticks and traditional pastries. Dinner in the restaurant may be selected from an à la carte menu, where you will have to restrict your choice, or you may sample the four-course table d'hôte menu which costs £5.60. A typical meal could be country-style pâté, escalope of pork, apple pie and cream and coffee. A glass of wine adds another 55p.

Kingsbridge

GLOBE INN, Frogmore
(Frogmore 351)
Open: Mon-Sat 11am-2.30pm, 6-11pm, Sun 11am-2.30pm, 7-10.30pm

[C] [P]

Brian and Janet Edmond have given this 17th-century free house a complete face-lift since they took over in 1979. Emphasis is on local produce and home cooking, with starters, including a pâté of the day, ranging from 40p-£1. Devonshire lamb, baked in cider, tops the list of about ten main dishes, which are all under £2 (except rump steak – £3.80), and none of the delicious desserts is over 70p. Simple arithmetic will reveal that there's no need to forego the coffee and wine to stay under a fiver.

WOOSTERS, The Quay
(Kingsbridge 3434)
Open: Mon-Sun 12noon-2pm, 7-10.30pm (winter: closed Mon-Tue)

[C] [S]

Woosters – housed in a two-storey cottage – specialises in fish, which is not surprising since it is situated right on the quay. If you choose one of the superb dishes prepared from locally-caught fish you're likely not to be able to run to three courses within our £5 limit. Nevertheless, the lemon sole, at about £3.80, would allow for a starter – asparagus with hot butter for instance – and a choice of sweet; with coffee and a glass of good house wine you're just on the £5 mark – in fact you could replace the 'trolley' sweet by chocolate fudge cake with Devonshire cream at around 75p without breaking the bank. There is a good range of starters including smoked salmon pâté and a choice of two home-made soups. Salads range from £1.50 or so.

Langport

BROOKSIDE GUEST HOUSE AND RESTAURANT, Huish Episcopi
(Langport 250259)
Open: Mon-Sun: 8.30-9.30am, 12noon-2pm, 7.30-10pm

[P]

If you like the personal touch, then this intimate guesthouse-restaurant is the place for you. Hungry early morning travellers can snatch a typical English breakfast for £1.50, whilst at lunchtime a variety of bar snacks and salads are available costing from £1.50-£2 (including a soup with roll). In the evening, after the residents have been fed, a quality three-course meal is on offer – but most meat dishes take the price a little beyond our range. A glass of Spanish house wine is about 55p.

Lostwithiel

ROYAL OAK INN★★
(Lostwithiel 872552)
Open: Mon-Sun 12.30-2pm, 7-10pm

[P]

Charles I is said to have hidden in this 13th-century inn during the Civil War. Later it became the haunt of smugglers. Now, a less dramatic clientele is attracted by real ale and a wide range of bar meals. The ubiquitous fried chicken/scampi/steak/salad choice is supplemented by the chef's home-made soup of the day, or complete meal-in-a-pot for around £1.70, such as chicken commoner or steak and kidney. Sweets are home-made too; starters include escargots, and three filling courses can be well within the budget. Eat in a flagstoned or more formal lounge bar, or on the delightful sun terrace with views of the gentle valley.

THE TAWNY OWL RESTAURANT
19 North Street (Bodmin 872045)
Open: summer: Mon-Sun 9am-7pm, winter: Mon-Sat 9am-5.30pm

[P] [S] [🍷]

This informal restaurant in the centre of historic Lostwithiel has softly coloured walls adorned with the work of local artists. Bench seating and pleasant, friendly service enhance the warm teashop image and there are several outside tables for summer use. Emphasis is on home cooking which predominates the whole range of delicious dishes, savouries, gâteaux and pastries. Home-made soups are about 55p and unusual open sandwiches include cottage cheese, sultanas and apple as one costing around £1.30. Quic omelettes and salads are avai there is a hot dish of the day at lunchtime served with plain or s filled jacket potatoes for around £ A choice of wines by the glass is available from about 50p to 75p.

Lydford

THE CASTLE INN, Lydford
(Lydford 242)
Open: Mon-Sun 12noon-2pm, 7-8.30pm

[C] [P]

Close to the beautiful Lydford Gorge and next to the castle ruins is this superb example of a 16th-century English pub. The Foresters' Bar, where meals are served, has low lamp-lit beams and a great Norman fireplace ablaze with vast logs in winter or with a profusion of flowers in summer. At lunchtime, apart from a selection of soups, pâtés and basket meals, a sumptuous help-yourself buffet luncheon table is available which includes soups, roast chicken, duck, beef, home-cooked ham, crab, mackerel, smoked salmon, smoked trout, cold meat pies, salads, cheeses, sweets and coffee. The extensive à la carte evening menu could exceed our budget, but careful selection could give you a feast for around £5.

THE MANOR INN HOTEL★
Lydford Gorge (Lydford 208)
Open: Bar snacks: Mon-Sat 11am-2.15pm, 6-9.30pm, Sun 12noon-1.45pm, 7-9.30pm, Restaurant: Mon-Sun 12noon-2pm, 7.30-9.30pm

[C] [P]

French-style cuisine is the hallmark of this pleasant old inn, where Richard Squire prepares an enormous variety of fare. Satisfying bar snacks include curry

for
0p,
e
lt to
dinner
or
seafood
om the
and coffee –
menu
rs and main
lities such as vol-
(filled with
eads, bacon and
a white cream sauce) at
pe of chicken Devonshire
icken with apples,
n Felldownhead cider and
, finished with cream – a
or under £3. With starters under
sserts at 50p or less and a glass of
costing 40p, you can stay within
budget and still enjoy a wide choice.

Lydford-on-Fosse

THE LYDFORD
(Wheathill 217)
Open: Mon-Sat 10am-2.30pm, 6-10.30pm, Sun 10am-2pm, 7-10pm

[C] [♫] [P] [♧]

Situated at the A37/B3153 crossroads, this extended old inn could spoil you for choice; meals are available in the bar or in either of the restaurants. Basket or plate meals include steak, scampi, chicken and cod fries, and run from about £1.20 upwards. A three-course Sunday lunch consisting of a choice of starter and sweet with a set traditional roast, costs around £2.80. Snacks include a good display of cold meats, pies and pastries, plus a ploughman's, fisherman's or Fosseman's lunch (all under £1). A special fun meal for kiddies costs £1.35. A glass of wine costs from 50p.

Lynton

THE BLUE BALL INN, Countisbury Hill, Countisbury (Brendon 263)
A mile east of Lynton on the A39
Open: Mon-Sun 11am-2.30pm, 6-11pm

[♫] [P] [♧]

The Blue Ball Inn stands amid some of North Devon's most beautiful countryside, just over a mile from the picturesque villages of Lynton and Lynmouth. The Inn still retains the charm and character of its 17th-century hostelry days with beams, real ale and a welcoming open log fire. In the evening familiar bar snacks such as ploughman's, ham sandwiches and salads are served, along with a selection of more substantial meals like rump steak, breaded plaice or rainbow trout, all at reasonable cost.

Martock

THE GEORGE INN (Martock 2574)
2m off the A303
Open: Mon-Sat 12noon-2pm, 7.15-10pm, Sun 7.15-10pm

[P] [S]

The George first appeared in church records way back in 1512 and there's a list of licensees dating from 1677 on display. However, most people will be more concerned with the food, of which there is a wide selection at reasonable prices. At the bar, try the 'George Special' of tender steak with onions and mushrooms in a buttered bap for about £1.50, or alternatively you might prefer a modest cheese and pickle sandwich or the venerable ploughman's. The small restaurant, adjacent to the bar, was once the local bakery. It has been converted into a cosy eating place where you can enjoy a three-course meal during the day and choose from the extensive à la carte menu available in the evening.

Minehead

THE DRAGON HOUSE, Bilbrook (Washford 215)
Open: Mon-Sun 12noon-2pm, 7-9.20pm

[C] [P]

This delightful, stone-built 17th-century house is surrounded by over two acres of beautiful garden where fresh vegetables are grown for use in the restful restaurant and bar. The passing motorist will do well to stop and sample the excellent three-course table d'hôte lunch which offers a choice of three starters, four main courses and a selection of sweets from the trolley for around £5. Bar snacks include home-made soup or ploughman's lunch for well under £1, hot dish of the day at around £2.75, a selection of omelettes and chips for about £1.50 and a choice of salads, including prawn salad at around £3. The extensive à la carte menu and the dinner menu are beyond our budget.

THE GOOD FOOD INN, 34 The Avenue (Minehead 4660)
Open: summer: Mon-Sun 10am-10pm, winter: closed Mon

[C] [S] [&]

Ver
serv
stagg
la car
hours a
value f
price fr
speciality
seafood an
guises, fron
be served in a
for another 50p
pizzas, omelettes,
on offer. Sweets inc
fancy pancakes, som
liqueurs, priced aroun
Special two- and three-co
grills are available for chi
around £1, including a soft
special bonus, if you order ar
complete a three-course meal
2.30-4pm, soup and sweet are o
free.

NORTHFIELD HOUSE HOTEL ★★★
Northfield Road (Minehead 5155)
Open: Mon-Sun 12.45-1.30pm, 7-8.30pm

[P]

Built at the turn of the century as a tea planter's mansion, this splendid hotel has spectacular views of the sea and the Brendon Hills to the south. The

e acres of garden were
r Edwin Lutyens and
e Jekyll – the ideal setting
o remember. At £4.70 the
se lunch is exceptional value,
ices for each course. After a
cream of vegetable soup, roast
en and salad, lemon layer pudding
resh fruit or cheese, what better
a stroll around the tranquil
rdens? The five-course dinner is a
ittle out of our league at £7. A bonus to non-resident guests is the 9-hole clock golf course.

Moretonhampstead

WHITE HART HOTEL ★★ The Square (Moretonhampstead 406)
Open: Mon-Sun 12noon-2pm (Sun 1.30pm), 7-8.30pm

[P]

During the Napoleonic Wars, French officers on parole from Dartmoor Prison met at the White Hart. By then, this 300-year-old building was already established as a coaching inn. Its simple, elegant exterior is distinguished by the figure of a hind above the portico. The interior is unpretentious and comfortable. Lunchtime bar snacks are excellent and reasonably priced (chef's chicken curry at £1.35). As part of the 'Taste of England' scheme, the restaurant menu offers some good basic English dishes (including Devon apple cake) and an excellent value, three-course tourist menu at £3.75. An effort is made to use fresh local produce wherever possible. Afternoon teas are served in the hotel's charming lounge.

Mousehole

CAIRN DHU ★★ Raginnis Hill (Mousehole 233)
Open: Mon-Sun 12noon-2pm, 7-9.45pm
Closed: Oct-May

[P] [♧]

A crow's nest view of Mount's Bay, from Penzance, past St Michael's Mount to the Lizard, can be enjoyed from Cairn Dhu. Donald and Angela Sibley's hotel and restaurant, perched about two hundred feet above the bustling village of Mousehole, exudes warmth and friendliness. Cuisine in this small character hotel is well-prepared and suitable for any occasion. Based on recipes from the 16th-century to the present day, emphasis is on home-made British fare. Excellent value table d'hôte lunch or dinner offers four courses for less than £6. Typical dishes are farmhouse pâté or smoked mackerel fillets, followed by either skate with black butter, lamb Louise or home-made steak and kidney pie. Delicious desserts include strawberry shortcake, orange sorbet or peach and brandy ice cream. A wide range of international cheeses and a glass of French house wine round off an enjoyable meal. Bar food is available in the bar and on the sun terrace.

Newquay

THE BISTRO, 34 East Street (Newquay 5444)
Open: summer: Mon-Tue 10am-10pm, Wed 10am-7pm, Thu-Sun 10am-12mdnt

[S]

A family operation which caters for families is a fair description of The Bistro. In the courtyard sun-trap behind the shop and on the forecourt, white-painted ironwork tables and chairs and flowers in pots and hanging baskets lend a gay informality. Inside, wooden tables have red place mats, and red-flocked wallpaper and predominantly red carpet make this a cheerful environment in which to enjoy a meal. Miraculously, the family who run it can still serve a Sunday set lunch at around £1.50. A typical menu is soup, roast turkey with stuffing, three vegetables and ice cream. Apart from the à la carte menu, which includes such things as home-made steak and kidney pie with chips and peas at around £1.25, a good mixed grill and a 12oz steak with all the trimmings at under £5, there is a light supper menu at around £1.25 which includes pizza and side salad. Snacks are available all day. Flans and gâteaux are made on the premises and Cornish cream teas are served. A glass of the house wine costs about 50p.

CROSS MOUNT HOTEL ★★ Church Street, St Columb Minor (Newquay 2669)
Open: Mon-Sun: normal licensing hours. Restaurant: 12.30-1.30pm, 6.30-8.30pm. Bar: 12noon-2pm

[C] [P] [S]

The Cross Mount Hotel is just on the outskirts of Newquay but enjoys a village environment. The building is basically 17th-century and combines a small residential hotel with restaurant and bar. Burnt orange, toning with the mellow natural stone walls, is the basic colour in the dining room, giving a warm and cheerful setting for a nicely-presented meal. Table d'hôte lunch at around £3.50 and dinner (available 6.30-7.30pm) at about £4 are good value,

a
ar
la c
wic
8.30
mea
sandv
omele
and bu
salads a
glass.

THE SMUGG
Cubert (Crantoc
A mile off the A30
Open: Restaurant: M
11pm, Sun 12noon-2p
Oct-Apr weekends onl
during normal licensing

[C] [♫] [P] [♣]

The Smugglers Den really was
of smugglers, in the days when
of the Cornish coast was notoriou
freebooting. In spite of its modern
comfortable appearance, with carpe
and upholstered chairs – some of the
converted from barrels – it is not difficult to imagine this 16th-century thatched, stone-built hostelry in its former guise of farmhouse and centre of sinister activities. Sunday lunch is a speciality here, a starter, a cut off the joint with fresh vegetables and

, sweet and coffee
3.50. Apart from the
t dinner menu, there is
enu offering starters such
broth, corn-on-the-cob,
out or salmon, and as main
steaks and grills at £2.50
s, and omelettes, salads, fish
cken dishes. A good range of bar
s is available or there's a choice of
ulent meats, sweets and starters
ilable in the separate carvery.

Newton Abbot

THE DARTMOOR HALFWAY
Bickington (Bickington 270)
Open: Mon-Sat 11am-2.30pm, 6-10.30pm, Sun 12noon-2pm, 7-10.30pm

[C] [P]

A 'change' house in coaching days, this 17th-century cob and stone inn, three miles west of Newton Abbot, has a garden and patio where one may enjoy a meal on hot days. The large, open-area bar is furnished in oak, with wood panelling and hessian-covered walls. Here you may sample one of nine starters, a particular favourite being 'grotti nosh', a meal in itself for around 60p. Follow this with seafood risotto or steak and kidney pie at around £3, and complete the treat with fruit pie and cream washed down with fresh coffee and cream with a Turkish delight or mint. You will still have just enough change from your £5 for a glass of excellent French wine.

ROMA PIZZERIA, 50 Queen Street
(Newton Abbot 69580)
Open: Mon-Sat 12noon-2.30pm, 7-11pm

[S]

A little chunk of Italy exists in the heart of Devon. This ground floor restaurant with its blue painted chairs, polished tables and fishing net hangings is alive with Latin charm and colour. From the eight or so starters, a good choice would be seafood cocktail, followed by a speciality pizza or pasta dish costing from around £1.50-£2.50. Why not follow this by a sweet from the trolley at around 50p, or ask for 'today's special'? An Italian house wine is always available.

North Petherton

WALNUT TREE INN
(North Petherton 662255)
Open: Mon-Sat, 11am-2.30pm, 7-11pm (winter 10.30pm), Sun 12noon-2pm, 7-9pm

[C] [P]

A 19th-century coaching inn, this hotel has recently been renovated by its owners, Richard and Hilary Goulden, to make it a welcome overnight stop for the modern traveller. Meals in the small restaurant consist of a number of 'platters' (steak, fish, chicken or an omelette) served with vegetables or a mixed salad and jacket potatoes or chips. Prices are surprisingly low – from around £1.50 for an omelette to £4 for a steak. Snacks and light meals are available in the bar and there's a very accommodating children's menu, featuring all the old favourites.

Oakford

HIGHER WESTERN RESTAURANT
Oakford (Anstey Mills 210)
On the A361, 1½ miles west of Oakford
Open: Mon-Sun 12noon-2pm, 3-5.30pm, 7-10pm

[P]

This small, attractive restaurant is recommended mainly for its good lunchtime bar snacks, from a range of open sandwiches (such as chicken, prawns, salami from around 75p) to pâté and salad, lasagne, home-made steak and kidney pie or sirloin steak and chips. You can have a three-course meal, including soup and roll and a sweet, for anything from £3.50-£5 depending on your choice. There is a set Sunday lunch for around £3.50. Dinner is rather more expensive. Many a motorist will be relieved to find a good pull-in at such a remote spot.

Okehampton

THE COUNTRYMAN, Beacon Cross, Sampford Courtney (North Tawton 206) 5 miles north of Okehampton on the B3215
Open: Mon-Fri 12noon-2.30pm, 7-10.30pm, Sat 12noon-2.30pm, 7-11pm, Sun 12noon-2pm, 7-10.30pm

[P]

This sophisticated, unusual inn in the heart of Devon is frequented as much for its excellent bar food as for its draught beers. Out of season, a businessman's lunch can be had for around £2.25. A three-course meal from the à la carte menu will just about come within the £5 limit if carefully selected. A choice of ten starters, including pâté à la volaille (chicken pâté with Cognac) may be followed by one of six main fish courses, a grill, poultry, curry or home-made steak and kidney pie. Most of the home-made desserts, served with cream, will price the meal above £5, but an ice cream is an alternative. The cold buffet table includes a host of salads, ploughman's lunches and sandwiches.

Ottery St Mary

KING'S ARMS HOTEL★ Gold Street (Ottery St Mary 2486)
Open: Mon-Sun 12noon-2pm, 7-9pm

[C] [P] [S] [symbol]

Built in 1756, the King's Arms Hotel was originally an old coaching inn. Now the white-painted building commands a central p picturesque little town. decorated Tar Barrel Bar excellent range of food – eit a full three-course meal. Foll soup of the day, steak pie, plai chicken or beef curry, cider-bak Devon ham, and ham or cheese s are some of the choices for a main course, ranging in price from about £1.95-£2.50. Vegetables are included good choice of sweets is available for around 60p and a glass of house wine is about 40p. The à la carte dining room menu is more pricey, but still good value and children are catered for.

Paignton

LAI KIN, 33 Hyde Road (Paignton 551005)
Open: Mon-Sun 12noon-2pm, 5.30-11.30pm

♫ [P] [S]

The unusual marble-look frontage and smoked glass, 'porthole'-style door is an incongruous entrance to this Chinese restaurant in the main shopping area. Inside, the décor is more appropriate, with Chinese lanterns illuminating black chairs, white cloths and sparkling cutlery. Chicken with cashew nuts followed by apple fritters and syrup cost around £3.95 from the à la carte menu, and a table d'hôte lunch is always available at just about £3.50 – terrific value. Chinese or Russian tea is served, as well as coffee and a glass of French house wine – another incongruity in such oriental surroundings – costs about 55p.

LA TAVERNA, 53 Torbay Road (Paignton 551190)
Open: summer: Mon-Sat 10.30am-2.30pm, 5.30-11pm, Sun 12noon-2pm, 7-10.30pm, winter: Mon-Thu 10.30am-2.30pm, 5.30-10.30pm, Fri-Sat 10.30am-2.30pm, 5.30-11pm,

le

lent
nt is
o
placed
t
alls with
nate tiled floor
lete the illusion
nes outside. The
, Ernest Pelosi, has
since 1903, so it may
f nostalgia that the
n scene has been so
ated. Small portions of
s are served as starters, or
hoose spaghetti bolognese,
r cannelloni at about £1.80 as
ain course. Pizza specialities cost
nough the same. Other bar snacks
ut 75p-£1.10) include egg and
ps, sausages, egg, beans and chips,
d ploughman's lunch. There is a short
ist of other main dishes, including
steaks, chicken, fish and salads. A glass of Italian wine is about 60p.

Penzance

ADMIRAL BENBOW, Chapel Street (Penzance 3448)
Open: Mon-Sun 12noon-2pm, 6-10pm

[C]

In the early 18th-century, bands of smugglers known as the 'Benbow Brandy Men' made the Admiral Benbow

Inn their headquarters. Here it was that the surplus tea, 'baccy, perfume, silk and brandy were hidden. Today, it boasts an equally desirable list of goodies to be chosen from the 'Vittals Chart', such as Cornish lobster, shark's fin and bird's nest soup, roasts, grills and various curries. Ice creams are the speciality – try the 'gooseberry lagoon' (coffee ice, gooseberries and iced fruit syrup) or the Southern Star (banana, paw-paw, peach and iced fruits), and wash it all down with a shot of finest rum. Buffet lunches are available in the bar upstairs at around £2.60. There is usually a set 'dish of the week' at around £3.

PATCHES, 36a Market Jew Street (Penzanze 5003)
Open: summer: Mon-Sun 12noon-3pm, 7-10pm, winter: Mon-Thu 12noon-3pm, Fri-Sat 12noon-3pm, 7-10pm, Sun 7-10pm

[P] [S]

An informal, relaxed bistro in the heart of the shopping complex of Penzance, Patches' alcoved interior, complete with original gas lamps and character prints is a haven for both shoppers and tourists. Interesting daily menus offer wholesome, well-prepared food such as quiche Lorraine served with new potatoes, vegetables or salad at £2, Chesham Pie (pork and chicken) at £1.75 and sherry trifle or Black Forest gâteau at 65p. A wide range of good wines is available to complement the food – at 50p a glass.

ROSIE'S RESTAURANT, 12-13 Chapel Street (Penzance 3540)
Open: Mon-Sat 12noon-2pm, 5.30-10pm

[S]

Rosie's Restaurant, situated within the heart of Penzance town centre, and under the personal supervision of attractive, auburn-haired Rosie, offers informality in cuisine, service and surroundings. A congenial bistro-style atmosphere is attained by the use of dark-stained wood walls and furniture, cheery red-checked tablecloths and half curtains, low-hanging white lamps and lush green potted plants and palms – the perfect surroundings in which to enjoy the well-prepared plat du jour. Typical dishes are home-made pâté, beef soup and pizzas, with chili con carne, moussaka and cheese and potato pie as main courses. Good-choice mixed salads and interesting vegetarian dishes are also on offer. A limited but attractive range of sweets is available and an adequately stocked wine cellar offers a good French house wine at about 60p per glass.

Plymouth

BEETONS RESTAURANT
14 Athenaeum Street, The Hoe (Plymouth 61895)
Open: Mon-Fri 12noon-2.30pm, Mon-Sat 7.30-11.15pm

[C] [S]

Beetons has a good reputation with local business people and residents. It has an old English atmosphere and is bright with copperware, but the tables are inclined to be close together – a result, no doubt, of the restaurant's popularity. Service is good, so do book for lunch or Saturday dinner, or you may be disappointed. The three-course table d'hôte lunch, with a starter of soup or fruit juice, main course of plaice, roast lamb, or steak and mushroom pie (plus a couple of additional dishes each day), together with a sweet or cheese and biscuits, is excellent value at about £2. The à la carte lunch or dinner menu is around the £5 mark. The French house wine is about £4 a litre carafe or around 50p a glass.

DARTMOOR UNION, Holbeton
(Holbeton 288)
6m south east of Plymouth off the A379
Open: Mon-Sat 12noon-2.30pm,
6-11pm (10.30 in winter)
Sun 12noon-2pm, 7-10.30pm

[C] [P] [&]

Good wholesome food here in solid oak surroundings. An old English cider press and barrels are housed here. This old-established inn is in the Devon tradition – it's the centre of village life but caters for holidaymakers too. Tasty vegetable soup served with hot crisp bread and butter at around 60p is just the thing to stay your hunger on a cold day. Basket meals cost from about £1.50, and there's a generous selection of main dishes including home-made steak and kidney pie and vegetab
£2.20. Sweets are about 6
could be nicer than a freshl
crumble with Devonshire cre
wine comes at around 55p a gla
Dinner in the restaurant is likely
in the region of £6.

THE KHYBER RESTAURANT ✕✕
44 Mayflower Street
(Plymouth 266036)
Open: Mon-Sun 12noon-2.30pm,
6-12pm

[C] [P]

Pass the Khyber and you will miss the chance of enjoying a friendly, well-established Indian restaurant run with family pride since 1960. Décor and furnishings are very Indian, cuisine is authentic and of a high standard. Table d'hôte lunch includes a starter such as shami kebab (delicious round pats of finely chopped meat with spices and onions), a selection of curries and English dishes, and a sweet – try guavas and clotted cream – to follow. Several dinner menus are also around £5, and the reasonable prices also allow you the pick of the à la carte menus. Wine at about 50p a glass is Spanish or German.

MERLIN'S RESTAURANT ★ 2 Windsor Villas, Cockyer Street (Plymouth 28133)
Open: Mon-Sat 12.30-2.30pm,
6.30-9.30pm

[C] [♫]

There's often something extra going on in this small hotel close to the city centre. Barbecues, Hallowe'en night parties, French or Greek evenings and beggar's banquets are Anne and Bill Proudman's specialities, but a no-nonsense lunch or dinner is always readily available. You'll be pleasantly surprised at the low prices of the well prepared dishes, served in an atmosphere of intimate friendliness. Table d'hôte menus offer, for example, delicious home-made soup, chicken chasseur with fresh and tender vegetables, and a sweet from the trolley for under £3; and even much of the more exclusive à la carte menu is also within our budget (bar the lobster!). House wine is French, around 50p a glass.

ZORBA GREEK TAVERNA
1 Moneycentre Precinct, Drake Circus (Plymouth 28032)
Open: Mon-Sat 11.30am-2.30pm, 7pm-2am

[C] [♫] [P] [S] [🍷]

Comfortable wickerwork chairs, bouzuki music in the background and shining cleanliness create a pleasant atmosphere in which to enjoy a relaxed meal. Prices are a little on the high side but it is not difficult to choose an interesting meal within the £5 limit. Meze à la Zorba is, in fact, a meal in itself as it consists of a selection of fifteen starters and main dishes. It costs around £12 for two people. Main courses include grills and fish, as well as dishes with exciting Greek names such as dolmadakia and at prices between about £3.60 and £6. Vegetables are extra. A starter could add quite a bit to the bill, but only if you treat yourself to a real luxury such as smoked salmon or avocado with prawns, will it be likely to take you far 'over the top'. Trolley sweets or cheese are available. A three-course business lunch comes well within the limit and always includes a Greek main dish. Wines are mostly Greek or Cypriot but house wine is either Greek or French and comes at about 60p a glass. This is a place for an evening out rather than just a place to eat as there is a small dance floor, and entertainments such as displays by Greek dancers take place from time to time.

Polperro

CRUMP'S (Polperro 72312)
Open: Mon-Sun 10.30am-5.45pm, 7.30-10pm

[P]

Mike and Wendy Costello's tea room and bistro, in this most picturesque of Cornish fishing villages, is a low-beamed 250-year-old farmhouse, furnished in the late Victorian/Edwardian style and offering a range of cuisine to suit all tourist tastes. Daytime meals are pâtisserie-style; snacks and light lunches. Freshly prepared salads with fish or home-made quiche Lorraine cost around £2.50, including soup, fruit juice or melon as appetisers. The bistro atmosphere is enhanced in the evening with white tablecloths and candles, when a plat du jour blackboard lists the dinner selections and the wine list. All dishes listed include a starter, sweet and coffee, but some are beyond the limit of our budget. A glass of French wine costs around 50p.

Portscatho

SMUGGLERS COTTAGE OF TOLVERNE, King Harry Ferry, Roseland Peninsula (Portscatho 309)
Open: May-Oct: Mon-Sun 10am-2.30pm, 3.30-5pm, 7-9pm

[P] [🍷]

Sailing and boating enthusiasts can drop anchor and pop in to sample the delicious home-made cuisine offered by Elizabeth and Peter Newman at this picturesque thatched cottage nestling close to King Harry's Ferry. Part of the cottage and the beach were used by the Americans in the preparation and planning of D-Day in the last war. At lunchtime there's an attractive cold buffet of home-produced quiches, fish mousses and meats, accompanied by original fresh salads. Alternatively, the Boathouse Bar-B-Q offers simple grills and hamburgers – ideal for the children. Informal suppers are superb value. Starters include stockpot soup at around 50p or smoked mackerel fillet for about £1. For your main course there could be locally-caught lemon sole, veal escalope or chicken marengo (all around £3.50) or savoury pancakes or omelettes for something over £2.50. Gooseberry fool or strawberry Pavlova are a couple of the tempting desserts.

Princetown

FOX TOR, Two Bridges Road (Princetown 238)
Open: Apr-Oct: Mon-Fri, Sun 9.30am-5.30pm, later times by arrangement

[P]

Just a little more than a stone's throw from the famous Dartmoor prison, this licensed restaurant specialises in fresh, home-made fare ranging from scones and Devon cream to full three-course meals. Appetisers at 50p and under, include egg mayonnaise or soup of the day with home-made bread. For your main course you can enjoy entrecôte steak with mushrooms, tomatoes, peas and buttered new potatoes for as little as £2.20. Sweets such as fruit tart or Devonshire junket are served with cream for 60p or less. With a glass of wine at 50p, you will still have more than £1 change from your fiver.

Queen Camel

MILDMAY ARMS
(Marston Magna 850456)
On the A359 Yeovil to Sparkford road
Open: Bar: Mon-Sat 12noon-2.30pm, 7-10.30pm, Sun 12noon-2pm, 7-10pm
Restaurant: Tue-Sat 7-10.30pm

P

Mildmay Arms is a local stone-built 17th-century inn situated on the edge of this attractive village with a considerable history. Personally run by Maggie and Ken Evans, this is a friendly place to eat where home-made specialities such as poacher's game pie, or Somerset casserole of beef, cooked in cider are served complete with Maggie's secret additives. For a cheaper alternative to the restaurant the bar menu offers a comprehensive range of goodies from the Wiltshire ploughman's to the daily special and quiche Lorraine all at around £1. A meal with any of these main courses plus appetiser, coffee and a glass of wine will cost around £2.50.

St Austell

HICKS WINE BAR, Church Street
(St Austell 4833)
Open: summer: Mon-Sat 11am-2.30pm, Tue-Sat 7-11pm (10.30pm in winter)

The Tudor frontage of Hicks gives way to a small, intimate wine bar of simple design with wooden tables and stools, and wine racks against the walls. Food is attractively displayed at one end of the bar and dishes can be chosen from a blackboard menu. Main meals are served with a selection of three salads such as curried rice or tomato, cucumber and onion, and an apple and celery mixture. These accompany various salamis, home-made quiche, gala pie or chef's home-made pâté – all around £1.20. There is a range of tasty hot dishes such as cottage pie, chicken casserole or sausage provençale for around £1.30. For dessert choose from Stilton, apple and biscuits, gâteau or cheesecake all at around 50p.

PIER HOUSE HOTEL ★★ Harbour Front, Charlestown (St Austell 5272)
Open: summer: Mon-Sun 12noon-2.30pm, 8-10pm

P

The Pier House Hotel, magnificently located right at the harbour's edge at the picturesque Georgian village of Charlestown, is well worth a visit though you must choose your dishes with care to keep within budget. The small harbour still exports china clay, and from the split-level restaurant of the charming, period hotel, adorned with masts, riggings and other nautical relics, one can view the complex manoeuvring of ships, laden with china clay, in the outer basin of the tiny docks. A la carte dinner offers good choices of French and English cuisine, such as Charlestown smoked mackerel pâté (about £1.15), followed by fresh local sole or râgout of seafood (both around £3.80), rounded off with lemon meringue or crème caramel (both about 90p), or a good choice of cheeses. Fresh seafood salads are also always available. A glass of French house wine costs around 60p.

St Ives

GLENCOE HOUSE HOTEL AND RESTAURANT ★★ Gwithian
(Hayle 752216)

Open: Mar-Oct: Mon-Sun 6.30-9pm

C P ♧

You can be sure of a homely welcome and personal attention from owners Trevor Greenaway and his wife in this country hotel in an idyllic village setting. The high standard of cuisine and the comfortable surroundings make this a popular eating place, so it is advisable to book for dinner. The table d'hôte menu is good value at around £5.50 and offers four courses such as melon cocktail, pork fillet with mushroom and Marsala sauce, a choice from the sweet trolley, cheese and biscuits plus coffee. At lunchtimes the lighter bar snack menu includes a cold buffet and will cost around £3. You can even enjoy a relaxing swim in the indoor, heated hotel pool before lunch. A glass of French wine is around 65p.

MASTER ROBERT'S HOTEL ★★★
Street-on-Pol (St Ives 6042)
Open: Mon-Sun 12noon-2.30pm, 7.30-10pm

C ♫

Ideal for an informal 'quickie' lunch or the most well organised dinner party, this tastefully-decorated hotel with its character bar is located in the heart of the interesting and historic town of St Ives. An extensive buffet lunch of cold meats and fresh salad can be had to the accompaniment of live music and entertainment in season, or a more formal meal may be taken in the steak bar and carvery with it's small central dance area – try the locally-caught sole. There's a well-laden trolley of home-made sweets to follow, and wine at about 50p a glass.

Sampford Peverell

THE FARM HOUSE INN, Leonard's Moor (Sampford Peverell 820824)
Open: Mon-Sat 7am-12mdnt, Sun 12noon-10.30pm

C ♫ P ♧

This restaurant is a conversion of two cottages and set back off the road in its own grounds. Cooking is predominantly of the wholesome English variety and all meals from breakfast through morning coffee, lunch, afternoon tea, dinner and supper are served here. At lunchtime, as well as the à la carte choice, there is a special 'dish of the day' which costs from £1.50 to £2, and the three-course Sunday lunch, featuring traditional roast beef, carved in the restaurant, is around £4. The wine list is extensive and a glass of wine costs about 50p. If you prefer a lighter meal, a cold buffet is set out in the attractive bar.

Shepton Mallet

THE CENTRE, 7 Market Place (Shepton Mallet 3544)
Open: Colonel Kirk's Kitchen: Tue-Sat 10am-3pm, Restaurant: Tue-Sat 12noon-2.30pm, 7-10pm

P

There are no less than three ghost stories connected with this very old building, which once provided stabling for over a hundred horses during the days of the Monmouth Rebellion in 1685. Today, the well-documented narratives of spooky happenings can be read before partaking of a set lunch, which might consist of soup, and roast beef with Yorkshire pudding (one of four main courses), followed by gooseberry pie, plus coffee. At £3, you certainly shouldn't be frightened of the price! Add 60p if you'd like a glass of house wine. On the ground floor, a variety of cakes, snacks and salads are available at competitive prices. The evening meal in the restaurant is likely to be beyond our limit.

Sidmouth

APPLEGARTH HOTEL ★ Sidford (Sidmouth 3174)
Open: Mon, Wed-Sun, 12.30-1.30pm, Mon-Sat 7-9.30pm

C P S ♧

One-time tea planters Jimmy and Barbara Lyness have earned themselves an enviable reputation for first-class cuisine and excellent service since 1969, when they made their drastic change of career and took over the Applegarth Hotel. But it's not only the owners who can boast an interesting background, for Applegarth itself dates back to the 16th century when it was used as a staging post for monks who transported salt from the mines of Salcome Regis to Exeter. The 'olde-worlde' character pervades the building to this day, not least in the restaurant with its beamed ceiling. The cuisine is always new and exciting – Barbara being a Cordon Bleu cook. For lunch, her array of dishes such as pâté Strasbourg, veau a la crème flambée and trout Applegarth will tempt the most discerning palate. More conventional dishes such as braised steak and chicken with honey and lemon sauce (both including starter and vegetables)

cost around £3.50. Desserts are the responsibility of young chef Tracey, who produces tasty concoctions with the aid of fresh cream, sherry, brandy or liqueurs. Liqueurs makes a second appearance in the speciality coffee which, as a relaxing plus to a good meal, is served in the sun lounge or the garden, where you are welcome to linger as long as you wish.

BOWD INN, Bowd Cross
(Sidmouth 3328)
On A3052 2m from Sidmouth seafront
Open: Mon-Thu 11am-2.30pm, 6-10.30pm, Fri-Sat 11am-2.30pm, 6-11pm, Sun 12noon-2pm, 7-10.30pm

[P]

Strategically placed at Bowd Cross en route to Sidmouth is this attractive 12th-century inn, set in a welcoming shrub and flower garden. Low ceilinged, beamed bars are cosy and inviting and the choice of food is excellent. Starters such as whitebait at 70p, melon frappé at 60p or kidney turbigo at £1 are on offer. Main courses include home-made quiche Lorraine at £1.30, tongue, beef or crab platter at £1.60, beef braised in wine or sauté of chicken Parisienne at £2.40 and roast duckling with apple or orange sauce at £3.40. All dishes include potatoes or French fries and salad or vegetables of the day. Steak, fish, curries and Chef's dish of the day are also available. A selection of home-made sweets are from 50p. French, Italian or Spanish wines may be savoured for 48p a glass.

SHERIDAN'S WINE BAR, Fore Street
(Sidmouth 6724)
Open: Mon-Sat 10.30am-2.30pm, 7-10pm (10.30pm Fri and Sat)

[S]

Sheridan's is a smart double-fronted building near the seafront, serving inexpensive home-cooked 'rustic' fare. The well-presented range of savouries includes lasagne, sardine and tomato or ham, cheese and tomato flan with salad, rough pâté with French bread, smoked salmon with brown bread, and a variety of cheeses served with bread or biscuits. A large portion of fresh strawberry flan or chocolate gâteau with cream costs around 70p, and there's plenty of good, strong coffee. A generous glass of French house wine will set you back about 50p. With good quality cutlery and china, and tables decorated with fresh flowers, this is a place for people who enjoy being pampered.

South Petherton

THE PUMP ROOM, Oaklands
Palmer Street (South Petherton 40272)
Open: Mon-Sun: 12noon-2pm, 7-9.15pm

[C] [P]

This attractive little food and wine bar lies at the back of Oaklands Restaurant (a good evening à la carte AA-appointed rosette and two knife and fork restaurant with menus a little above our limit). A tasty home-cooked meal of a high standard can be enjoyed here, with dishes such as smoked mackerel pâté as a starter, followed by scampi and French fries or two savoury pancakes with salad, plus sherry trifle, coffee and wine costing around £3.50. There is a staggering choice of wines.

South Zeal

OXENHAM ARMS★★
(Sticklepath 244)
Open: Bar snacks: Mon-Sat 12noon-2pm, 7-9pm, Sun 12noon-1.30pm, 7-9pm, Restaurant: Mon-Sun 12noon-1.30pm, 7.30-9pm

[C] [P]

'The stateliest and most ancient abode in the hamlet' is how Eden Phillpotts described this beautiful, beamed inn, which was first licensed in 1477. The hamlet quoted is South Zeal, a cluster of houses found by taking a slight detour off the A30 east of Okehampton. Bar snacks offer an array of fish and seafood – from rainbow trout with potatoes and vegetables for around £2 to plaice and French fries for £1. Home-made fruit pie and cream is about 55p. On Sundays cold meals only are served in the bar – salads include roast beef or chicken for £1.65 and cheese for just over £1. Three-course meals served in the cottagey restaurant are excellent in both choice and value for money. Lunches are priced by the main course and vary from £3 for home-made steak, kidney and mushroom pie to £4.50 for rump steak. Dinner is £5.50 and could include lamb cutlets garni with vegetables.

Street

GREYLAKE, Greinton
(Ashcott 210383)
Open: Tue-Fri, Sun 9am-11pm,
Sat 7am-11pm

[C] [P] [♤]

Greylake is all things to all men, women and children, but it is not one of your brash modern complexes, for the restaurant is housed in a 17th-century, whitewashed stone cottage, full of charm and character. There is a wide choice of food at painless prices. At midday, eleven different main courses are on offer (including deep-fried scampi and a mixed grill), and with starter, dessert and coffee, only the dearest steak dishes will take you over the £5 mark. A 'Sunday special', with roast pork as the main course, is around £3 (half-portions are available for children). Various salads and light meals can be had throughout the day.

KNIGHT'S TAVERN☆☆☆
Wessex Hotel
(Street 43383)
Open: Mon-Sat 10.30am-2.30pm, 7.30-10pm, Sun 12noon-2pm, 7.30-10pm

[C] [♬] [P] [♤]

With direct access from the car park, there's no need to go through the hotel to reach the Knight's Tavern, so it is a good place to know about, especially for families with children. Pleasant cheerful service and comfortable modern surroundings make it a worthwhile stopping place. Rest awhile in the King Arthur Bar – aptly named in this Camelot Country, where at lunchtime you can choose from a wide variety of bar snacks, and there are charcoal grills, omelettes, pizzas or pasta dishes, curries, fish and many other favourites at budget-prices. You could choose a good dinner in the grill room/restaurant under the £5 limit too, though you could bust the budget if you ignored the menu prices. Fruit juice, followed by fillet of plaice and a sweet from the trolley would come within our limit, leaving plenty over for a glass of wine at 50p and a tip – and there are a number of other permutations under our price limit.

Taunton

HEATHERTON GRANGE HOTEL ★
Bradford-on-Tone
(Taunton 46777/8)
On A38 1m from M5, junction 26
Open: Mon-Sat 12noon-2pm, 7-10.30pm,
Sun 12noon-2pm, 7-9pm

[C] [P]

This former coaching inn, dating from 1826 or earlier is easily accessible from Taunton or the M5. A wide variety of bar meals cost around the £1.50 mark and include Madras curry, steakburgers, home-made pies and salads (including fresh lobster and crab in season). Most of the à la carte menu presented in the small dining room is within our three-course budget. Basic favourites are supplemented by sweetbreads in sherry sauce or Swiss pork chop (stuffed with oregano, cheese, onions and mushrooms).

Thorverton

DOLPHIN INN (Exeter 860205)
Open: during licensing hours. Meals: Mon-Sun 12noon-1.45pm, 7-10pm

[P] [garden]

This two-storey inn enjoys a central position amid a picturesque village setting. Décor and furnishing in the Victoria Lounge bar would have pleased even the most discerning Victorian, and the deep-seated armchairs offer a place to relax with an after-dinner coffee. An archway leads through the bar to the attractive Gueridon Restaurant, romantically illuminated with oil lamps to produce a complementary atmosphere in which to enjoy some of the homely fare offered on the extensive menu. House specials include lemon sole with prawns and mushrooms, and home-made steak and kidney pie with Mackeson. Try the soup (also home-made) to start with, and for dessert there is a choice of cold sweets or ice cream –

all reasonably-priced. Traditional bar snacks are available every day – the locally-produced pasty with gravy sounds like a tempting and cheap filler at about 40p. On warmer days, lunch can be taken in the wisteria-clad beer garden.

Tiverton

POACHERS POCKET, Burlescombe (Greenham 672286)
10m west of Tiverton on the A373
Open: Restaurant: Mon-Sat 12noon-2.30pm, 6-10pm, Sun 12noon-2.30pm, Bar: Mon-Sat 11am-2.30pm, 6-10pm Sun 12noon-2.30pm, 7-10pm

[P] [♧]

This 17th-century inn gives you the choice of a pleasant bar or a peaceful restaurant. The bar offers a wide range of snacks, including seafood platter, scampi, chicken or sausage in the basket, gammon and pineapple, rump steak and turkey pie as well as ploughman's lunches and sandwiches. In the restaurant, the à la carte menu gives excellent value and you can feast on terrine provençale (a rough, spicy pâté), pheasant cooked in Madeira wine, and apfel strudel with Devon cream for around £5. All main courses include vegetables. Children are welcome and can eat food from the bar menu in the restaurant if their parents wish to eat à la carte.

Torquay

THE COPPER KETTLE, Ilsham Road, Wellswood (Torquay 23025)
Open: summer: Mon-Sun 9.30am-10.30pm, winter: Tue-Sat 10am-5pm

[♬] [P] [S] [♧]

This 'copper kettle' brews up not only for guests enjoying a refreshing cuppa after a meal but also for the picnicker on his way to the beach some yards away. Later in the day, day trippers about to make the long drive home are catered for. This is a special service offered by Leslie Bentham at his neat little Georgian restaurant in the heart of this holiday town. Many a thirsty tourist has had his flask filled to the brim with piping hot tea or freshly-percolated coffee by the enterprising Mr B. His wife, Elaine, specialises in high-standard home cooking – and the well-cooked roast lunch (with a starter) at around £1.50 and a Devonshire cream tea (with home-made scones) about 95p is very popular. Salads are the house speciality; egg mayonnaise, chicken, fresh crab, salmon and many more – all from around £1.40 with special reduced prices for children.

THE EPICURE, 34 Torwood Road (Torquay 23340)
Open: summer: Mon-Sun 10am-9.30pm, winter: Mon-Tue, Thu-Sun 10am-5pm

[♬] [P] [S] [♧]

With some thirty years' experience in hotels and catering behind him, proprietor Gary Dowland runs his attractive little restaurant with the emphasis on personal service and quality grill-style fare. Situated some 600yds from the harbour, in a row of shops, The Epicure is one of Torquay's oldest restaurants and instantly recognisable by its green stucco exterior with green woodwork and sun canopy. The deceptively small frontage leads into a long, brightly-decorated dining room. The cool exterior colouring is echoed inside with lush green plants. Best china and cutlery is used here and the walls bear framed prints of old sheet music. An extensive menu of fish dishes and grills is available, with home-made soups a starter speciality. Parents please note the special children's menu with main dishes less than half the standard price.

GRAEL WHOLE FOODS
59 Abbey Road (Torquay 211141)
Open: Mon-Sat 11am-6pm

[C] [P] [S]

Close to the main shopping centre is this pleasant whole-food shop and restaurant, easily recognised by the brown canopy over the door. The restaurant,at the rear of the shop, boasts a suitably natural décor with cane-shaded table lamps on pine refectory tables and brown semi-glazed crockery. A wall-board menu offers a small but interesting range of substantial dishes such as soup of the day, nut rissoles and salad, fresh fruit with cream plus coffee for about £2.30.

THE PANTRY, Strand (Torquay 25123)
Open: Mon-Fri 10.15am-5pm, Sat 10.15am-12.15pm

[C] [S] [♧]

The Pantry is part of the Williams and Cox department shore – a family business founded in 1837, which still upholds its reputation for quality and personal service. Overlooking the harbour, the restaurant has a modern décor with bentwood chairs and polished tables; service is provided by uniformed waitresses. Bill of fare is traditional, with omelettes, quiche Lorraine and a chef's daily special (roast leg of lamb or Caribbean chicken, perhaps) on the hot table, and a selection of cold meats, salmon or cheese with salad on the cold table.

You may, however, take a break from shopping any time as sandwiches, tea and pastries are served all day.

PIZZA-KING, 2 The Terrace, Fleet Street (Torquay 24365)
Open: summer: Mon-Sun 12noon-12mdnt, winter: Mon-Sat, 12 noon-2pm, 6-11pm

[S]

A cheerful, bright red canopy invites you into this rustic-style restaurant with wood-panelled walls and oak refectory tables. Red-painted chairs add warmth and colour to the simple yet attractive décor. There are twenty tantalising man-sized pizzas to choose from; and you can see them being prepared in the open cooking areas. You can make a feast out of the Pizza-King Special which is topped with cheese, tomato, salami, onion, mushroom, ham, pimentoes, to name but a phew! It costs about £2.40 and if your appetite can take it, 20p or so will add a baked potato and, at around 55p, a green salad. And for a mouth-watering finale, try cassata Seville – layers of chocolate and orange ice cream with raisins, walnuts and Grand Marnier – all for less than 60p. Wine is sold by the glass at about 60p. Between 12noon and 2pm, and after 7pm, there is a minimum charge of £1, though a special lunch for children costs around 75p.

Torrington

CASTLE HILL HOTEL ★★ South Street (Torrington 2339)
Open: bar: Mon-Sat 11am-2.15pm, 6.30-10pm, Sun 12noon-1.45pm, 6.30-10pm. Restaurant: Mon-Sun 12noon-2pm, 7.30-9pm

Magnificent views over the Torridge Valley and the hills beyond can be enjoyed from the garden of this delightful old hotel. A wide range of snacks is available in the bar, including a hot dish of the day such as curry, cottage pie or pork chops. The table d'hôte three-course lunch, served in the restaurant, is only around £2.75, with four or five choices of starter, three hot main courses – a roast and fish dish are always included – and a salad. There is also a generous selection of sweets from the trolley. Cheaper portions are available for children. The extensive evening à la carte menu features grills of all descriptions, and a three-course meal can be achieved for around £5.

Totnes

CASA DORO, 67 Fore Street (Totnes 863932)
Open: Mon-Sat 12noon-2.30pm, 7-11pm

[C] [S]

Catch the distinct Spanish flavour of this small restaurant on the ground floor of a three-storey listed building. Heliodoro Lopez runs the place with the aid of his wife and mother-in-law, and together they produce a marvellous list of goodies. Tasty starters such as 'tropicanas' (layers of grilled ham, cheese and pineapple served on bread) or barquitas de apio (celery boats filled with tuna fish, peppers and olives) make interesting appetisers, with paella, a Spanish omelette or a host of imaginative, cosmopolitan main courses to follow. Vegetables of the day are included in the price. Sweets, including delicious figs in brandy, are under or around £1.

THE COTT INN✕ Dartington (Totnes 863777)
Open: Mon-Sun normal licensing hours

[C] [P]

A charming 14th-century building – long, low and warmly lit. The split-level, stone floor and timbered ceiling create a fine, olde-worlde atmosphere. Meals here nowadays are all home-made and presented buffet-style. Examples from the excellent daily spread are pâté (80p), highly-recommended steak and kidney pie (£1.50) and gâteau (55p). So successful has the operation become, that owner Mr Shortman has recently added an extension to accommodate the growing number of diners. It's a free house, so you can drink whatever you wish, including French house wine at around 50p a glass.

CRANKS HEALTH FOOD RESTAURANT, Dartington Cider Press Centre, Shinners Bridge, Dartington (Totnes 862388)
Open: Mon-Sat 10am-5pm

[P] [S]

Cranks have made a name for themselves by serving appetising whole foods while at the same time encouraging crafts by displaying specially-commissioned articles and equipping their restaurants with craftsman-made furniture and pottery. This branch, in the interesting Cider Press Centre, which is dedicated to the encouragement and display of traditional crafts, is run on the usual Cranks lines with a buffet service counter serving soups, salads, and vegetable-based savouries, the accent being on compost-grown vegetables and unchemicalised (their word!) ingredients. All food, including wholemeat bread, is baked on the premises. A substantial three-course meal with a glass of wine (about 50p) and coffee is unlikely to cost more than £4 or so, and includes soup, a hot savoury such as spaghetti or carrot and parsnip soufflé, a sweet and coffee. There's outside seating for thirty in the summer.

JACKY'S BISTRO, 2 Fore Street (Totnes 864271)
Open: summer: Mon-Sun 7.30am-11pm, winter: Mon-Thu 9am-5.30pm, Fri-Sat 9am-11pm

[C] [♫] [P] [S] [♧]

With a French proprietress, Jackie Scarr, and a French chef de cuisine, food at this small bistro should be (and is) very good. The décor in browns and tans, with large stripped-pine tables, raffia place mats and pottery dishes, is warm and welcoming, and Jackie personally looks after her customers. The all-day menu includes home-made soup with roll and butter, spaghetti bolognese, goulash, or stuffed marrow. Salads are priced from about £1.45 to £2.20, steak with chips, mushrooms and peas at around £3.45; gâteau and cheesecake are around 55p. In the evening, the list is augmented by a number of starters such as salade niçoise, and main courses (at about £2.50 to £3.45) include poulet à la crème, sole à la bonne femme, steaks and veal escalope – all with fresh vegetables. A glass of the French Chambernade wine costs about 50p.

THE SEA TROUT INN★★ Staverton (Staverton 274)
Open: Mon-Sun 12noon-2pm, 7-10pm

[C] [♫] [P] [♧]

The à la carte menu is rather expensive and would surely take you beyond our

£5 limit, but you need not deny yourself the pleasure of eating in this attractive old inn, for they also serve a comprehensive listof bar meals. A typical meal would be grapefruit cocktail, home-made quiche Lorraine with chips and veg, gâteau or cheesecake and coffee for around £4. The bar occupies the original part of the building, and with oak furniture, white-washed walls, beamed ceiling and stone fireplace it retains a certain 'olde worlde' look. Bar meals are limited on Sundays when a full lunch is provided in the restaurant, and in fine weather meals can be taken on the patio. Note to parents: there is also a special children's room available.

Truro

GORTON'S RESTAURANT, 10 Pydar Street (Truro 79140)
Open: Mon-Thu, Sun 10am-10pm, Fri-Sat 10am-11.30pm

[♧]

Close to Truro Cathedral is this intimate new restaurant which is growing in popularity by the minute. An unbeatable-value three-course lunch menu brings together soup of the day or fruit juice, followed by home-made steak and kidney pie, a 'roast of the week' or a quarter roast chicken with fresh potatoes and vegetables, rounded off with home-made fruit pie or peaches and cream at only £2. À la carte eating is also possible, with the Chef's special chili con carne a firm favourite at £2.25.

Veryan

POLSUE MANOR HOTEL★★
Ruanhighlanes (Veryan 270)
Open: Etr-Oct: Mon-Sun 7.30-8.30pm

[P]

Dinner at this spacious, elegant manor house, secluded beyond a tree-lined drive, is a peaceful and enjoyable experience. You'll find it midway between Tregony and St Mawes on the A3078. Rex and Diana Dufty will make you very welcome in the gracious, country house-style restaurant. A typical table d'hôte three-course meal of home-produced, quality cuisine could include mushrooms with garlic mayonnaise, followed by roast duckling with orange and apple stuffing, rounded off with meringues served with strawberries and Cornish cream. Such a meal costs about £5. French wine by the glass costs around 50p.

Washford

HOSPICE BAR ★★ CHAPEL CLEEVE MANOR HOTEL, Chapel Cleeve (Washford 202)
Open: Mon-Sat 10.30am-2.20pm, 7-10pm

[C] [P]

This most attractive bar lies in the oldest part of the manor, and dates in part from 1399. Furnished in keeping with its historic character, the Hospice is a charming eating place in which to enjoy the somewhat simple three-course meal at very reasonable cost. Soup with roll and butter is the only starter, followed by a choice of six main dishes, of which barbecued spare ribs and rice, cottage pie, beef curry and rice, steak and kidney pie and ham salad are examples. Sherry trifle or chocolate mousse and a cup of coffee completes the meal, for which you need not pay more than £3.25. A glass of house wine costs about 55p.

Watchet

RALEGH'S CROSS INN, Brendon Hills, Watchet (Washford 343)
Open: summer: Mon-Sat 10.30am-11pm, Sun 11am-10.30pm, winter: restricted
P

Following recent full-scale alterations, this old Exmoor inn now has one large bar (which serves a variety of snacks and light meals), and a charming olde worlde restaurant for the discerning diner. Nearly everything is home-made, including soup served with a wheatmeal roll for around 80p, and liver pâté at about £1.40. Ham with egg and French fries costs around £2.50, while Brendon Hill Bobtails (rabbit casserole) and local pheasant casserole are about £2.75 and £3.40 respectively. Very nicely prepared desserts, all costing about 85p, include peach cheesecake, lemon soufflé and coffee gâteau. A large glass of house wine is around 40p. Somewhat beyond our budget is the Cordon Bleu Restaurant.

Wellington

BEAM BRIDGE HOTEL★★ Sampford Arundel (Greenham 672223)

Open: Bar snacks: Mon-Sat 10.30am-2pm, 6.30-10pm, Sun 12noon-2pm, 7-10pm, Restaurant: Mon-Sat 12noon-2pm, 7.30-9.30pm, Sun 12noon-2pm

C P

This small hotel on the A38 is an ideal stopping off place for the motorist. If you are in a hurry, the bar snacks are the thing – smoked mackerel at 90p or tuna fish salad at 95p are tasty examples. Bill of fare in the peaceful restaurant offers a very wide choice, with over a dozen starters. Deep fried breaded mushrooms with tartare sauce are delicious and cost less than £1. Pork fillets sautéed with peppers and onions or lambs kidneys with bacon are interesting main courses. A host of sweets include crême caramel, black cherry and kirsch ice cream and walnut gâteau which cost between 40p-70p. A glass of Spanish house wine is around 50p.

Wells

REGENCY HOTEL, New Street (Wells 75471)
Open: Coffee Room: Mon-Sun 10am-2.15pm, Bar Snacks: Mon-Sun 12noon-2.15pm, Restaurant: Mon-Sun 12noon-2.15pm, 7-10pm (closed Feb)

C P

This attractive Regency house on the northern outskirts of Wells is owned and run by Mr and Mrs Hall, who assure you of their personal attention. Mr Hall junior is a craftsman in copper and much of his work is displayed in the adjoining building. Snacks on offer at midday include farmer's, ploughman's or fisherman's lunch, all at under £1. Soup and a roll, followed by a quarter chicken with chips and salad will cost you about £3. On the à la carte menu, you'll need to stick to two courses (such as king-size scampi and Viennese cream toffee) to keep within the budget. A glass of Charbonnier is about 65p.

RIVERSIDE RESTAURANT, Coxley (Wells 72411)
3m south of Wells on the A39
Open: summer: Mon-Sun 9am-11pm, winter: Mon-Sun 11am-2.30pm, 6-10.30pm

P

This ten-year-old family-run restaurant was originally an 18th-century cottage which housed the local wheelwright in an adjoining barn. Nestling alongside the River Sheppey, it has retained its simple charm, not least because it is run very much as a family concern with Mrs

Gorizia Reina looking after the kitchen, daughter Lucy the restaurant, and her father Angelo Reina supervising the business as a whole. Children are particularly welcome with a menu to suit their tastes; dishes like egg and chips or sausage and chips cost around 80p. Main courses offer two house specialities: pollo alla cacciatora (chicken with a sauce of wine, tomato, mushrooms and pimento) at about £3 and bistecca alla Siciliana (rump steak in a slightly hot red wine sauce) at around £4.25 – all include boiled, creamed or chipped potatoes plus vegetable of the day or mixed salad. Coffees include a rum, coffee and fresh cream concoction, and a generous glass of Chianti or Valpolicella wine costs only about 50p. Any dishes on the menu may be taken away at slightly less than the normal charge.

Weston-super-Mare

THE REGENT STEAK HOUSE, 8 Alexander Parade (Weston-super-Mare 23481)
Open: Mon-Sun 12noon-2pm, 6-11.30pm

C P S

The Regent Steak House is a small, attractive, fully-licensed eating place with sixteen tables in polished dark wood, red/gold-patterned upholstered chairs with matching carpet and red curtains, all of which add warmth to the room. Charcoal-grilled steaks are the house speciality, but, as these are priced at around £3.50 (including French fries and peas), care must be taken when choosing accompanying courses. The 'chef's specialities' are more ambitious creations with tempting sauces, but these are likely to be outside our budget. For that grand finalé there are six special coffees, including monk's coffee with Benedictine liqueur.

Winscombe

SIDCOT HOTEL ★★ Sidcot (Winscombe 2271)
Open: Tue 7.30-9pm, Wed-Sat 12.30-2pm, 7.30-9pm, Sun 7.30-9pm

P

Set high in its own grounds, this imposing stone-built mansion has a pleasant dining room offering excellent-value table d'hôte lunches and dinners to non-residents. Home-made soups are one of a choice of starters for both meals. Six main courses are served at lunchtime, including carbonnade of beef or prawn curry. Dinner often has roast beef and Yorkshire puddings as one main course. Home-made desserts are served with fresh cream. Lunch is about £3.50, dinner around £3.75 and a glass of Spanish house wine is only about 40p.

Wiveliscombe

COUNTRY FARE, 4 High Street (Wiveliscombe 23231)
Open: Mon-Wed and Fri 9am-5.30pm, Sat 9am-5pm, 7.30-10pm, Sun 12noon-2pm

P

Use Wiveliscombe's free parking and stroll down the High Street to Country Fare! This small family restaurant has an extensive range of good, fresh basic food, including home-made cakes and pastries. The Pasking family regard the comfort and satisfaction of their guests as of prime importance; home cooking is prepared and served to high professional standards. Two beefburgers and chips will set you back only £1, ham, egg and chips £1.30. A set lunch for under £3 might include soup, pork chops in cider (locally-brewed, naturally) or a roast, followed by fruit pie and cream.

Yeovil

THE PEN MILL HOTEL, Sherborne Road (Yeovil 23081)
Open: Restaurant: Mon-Sat 12noon-2pm, 7-10pm, Buttery: Mon-Sun 12noon-2pm, 7-10pm

C P S

Situated near Yeovil's old Great Western Railway station, the Pen Mill Hotel, built in the 19th century of hamstone, was probably a station hotel originally. It retains its Victorian solidarity but cleanliness and a friendly staff give an air of comfort. Very popular is the cold buffet available at lunchtime from Monday to Friday. This consists of cold meats or pie with a selection of help-yourself salads from £1.65 or so. There is a hot daily special at about £1.50. Other bar meals include sausage, egg and chips at around £1 to sirloin steak with all the trimmings at about £3.75. Any of these meals when served in the evening include a free glass of wine. The restaurant serves a table d'hôte three-course meal for around £4.50 with a limited but good choice for all courses. The à la carte menu includes many tempting items which come within our budget.

Wessex and the Isle of Wight

The Anglo-Saxon kingdom of Wessex is steeped in a wealth of literary and romantic history, from its mythical connections with King Arthur and the Knights of the Round Table (many believe that Winchester – ancient capital of Hampshire and England – is in fact, Camelot) to the stark and haunting prehistoric monument of Salisbury Plain. Wessex's most famous writers, Thomas Hardy and Jane Austen, also did their bit to put this region on the map. Hardy's dramatic tales of the Dorset people and countryside are set in the days when good farming and corn-growing were as important to man as life itself. Still a mainstay of this region, high quality beef, lamb, pork and other farm produce can always be found in the well-stocked butchers and they form the basis of many local dishes.

Apart from its great historical traditions, this region is among the most beautiful in the country, attractive to foreign visitors and holiday-makers for its unspoilt open countryside, sandy coastline and the rugged beauty of the New Forest. Across the water, the Isle of Wight remains an immensely popular resort and an unchallenged holder of the sunshine league record – a climate ideal for yielding rich crops of soft fruit, vegetables (particularly succulent

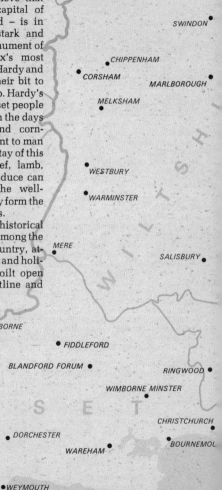

sweetcorn) and flourishing vineyards. Fresh fish and seafood such as lobster, crab, clams and oysters are plentiful in the waters off the Island, but the traditional dish – vectis pudding – is only for the very sweet-toothed.

The hearty shouts of the 'Lord of the Manor' and his entourage still resound over Hampshire's rolling green fields, where once the landed gentry regularly left their grand manor houses to take part in large-scale shooting, fishing and hunting parties. Throughout this area game is a particularly popular dish with pheasant, jugged hare with redcurrant jelly and New Forest venison in a rich red wine sauce among the list of favourite dishes. They are complemented by the marvellous strawberries and grapes and the superb crop of watercress, crayfish and fresh-water salmon that thrive in the crystal-clear local streams.

The following pages include many local inns and restaurants reflecting the rich traditions of bygone days in their menus, with dishes to tempt the most discerning country squire!

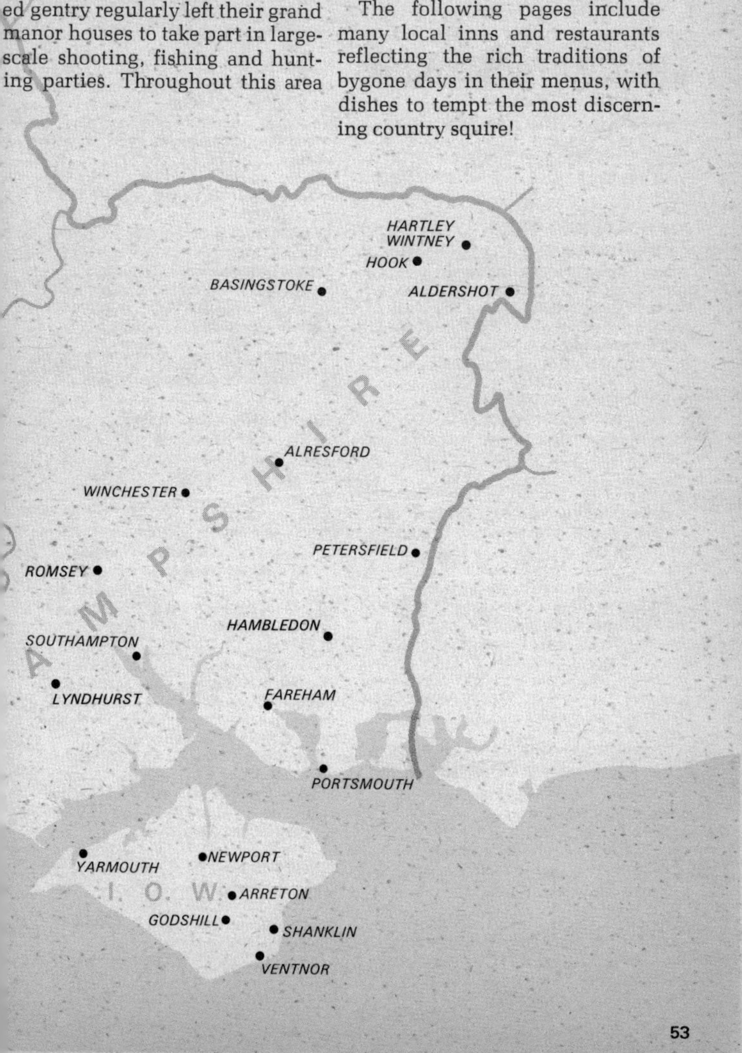

Aldershot

JOHNNIE GURKHA'S, 54 Station Road (Aldershot 277366)
Open: Mon-Sat 12.30-2pm, 5.30-11.30pm

[S]

Aldershot is better known as 'Home of the British Army' rather than a hunting ground for gourmets, but when engineer Hari Karki left the Gurkhas three years ago, where better to start his own restaurant than . . . Aldershot. He and his wife Meera have not only introduced the town to the rarities of genuine Napalese food but have attracted much praise from '999' readers. Behind its unpretentious exterior in the 'downtown' area the restaurant is decorated with trinkets from Nepal, photographs of the Himalayas, Gurkha regimental memorablia and a standard of service of which Kipling himself would have been proud. First-time visitors hardly need to move from the 'Nepali Special Thal' at £4.50 for three courses including a starter of mamocha – a soup with meat filled dumpling – well worth the twenty-five minutes it takes to prepare. Evening booking really is advisable. To go with the meal, no Nepalese wines but an own label French selection at £2.90 a bottle and draft Lowenbrau at 70p a pint.

Alresford

THE BODEGA, 32 Broad Street (Alresford 2468)
Open: Mon-Sat 10.30am-2pm, 7-10.30pm (11pm Fri & Sat)

[♫] [P] [S]

The Bodega is a smart and sophisticated wine bar in picturesque Alresford – a small town which with its quaint shops, steam engine and watercress beds, attracts tourists from all parts of the globe. Interior décor is unobtrusive, with cream-painted panels and dark wood tables and chairs. Candles in brass holders and a burnt orange carpet add warmth and colour. Start your meal with a home-made soup of the day (65p) and move on to a tasty Dutch speciality known as saté – a kebab of grilled pork in a piquante sauce, served on a wooden skewer at under £2. Sweets change daily, but could consist of chocolate mousse or ice cream with Grand Marnier. Specialities are chalked on a blackboard. All kinds of wines are available by the glass.

Basingstoke

THE BISTRO, 1 New Street (Basingstoke 57758)
Open: Tue-Fri 12noon-2pm, 7-10pm, Sat 7-10pm

[P] [S]

Doug and Suzy Palmer's homely little restaurant has deservedly acquired a very good local reputation in the few years since its conversion from a one-time doctors' surgery. Simple décor and furnishing create a typical bistro atmosphere. The lunchtime menu offers a choice of three or four main courses at competitive prices. For example, soup followed by roast lamb with orange and mint stuffing, plus peaches for dessert costs as little as £3. Alas, the majority of the evening menu (including daily specials chalked up on a blackboard) is beyond the budget, but this is one place where the excellent food and service warrants breaking the bank.

BURLINGTONS COFFEE SHOP AND WINE BAR, Seal House, Seal Road (Basingstoke 66266)
Open: Mon-Sat 10am-4.30pm, lunch11.30am-2.30pm

[♫] [S]

Nothing but the best is available at

Burlingtons departmental store and lunch is no exception. A trellis-work ceiling with wicker-globed lighting and subtle exposed brickwork behind the serving counter complete a décor which is both relaxed and tasteful. A tempting array of food awaits you. Start with nourishing ham soup at 35p, then choose from a wide selection of cold dishes, or a hot dish of the day such as chicken fricasée with peppers served on a bed of rice (this costs less than £2). Cold meat salads, including beef, chicken or ham are priced a little more, but the choice of salads is excellent – one example is rice with walnuts and sultanas. Delicious desserts such as feathery-light Black Forest gâteau or blackcurrant cheesecake are only around 50p. A glass of wine costs 60p.

CORKS FOOD AND WINE BAR
25 London Street (Basingstoke 52622)
Open: Mon-Sat 10am-2.30pm, 6-10.30pm, Sun 7-10.30pm

[♫] [S]

Situated on Basingstoke's busy pedestrian precinct, 'Corks' goes continental in the summer when customers can 'take a pew' on the paved area outside the shop, beside a blackboard menu – strategically placed to tempt passers-by. Inside, behind a screen of brown half-curtains, is a dark and mellow eating place with soft music playing. Church pews make unexpectedly comfortable and intimate seating, and fine engravings decorate walls which are either white-washed or cork covered. Pots of leafy green plants and a large basket of beautifully-arranged fresh flowers add a splash of colour, and the overall atmosphere is conducive to good eating. Starters such as burgundy pâté or smoked mackerel for under £1, plus hot casserole-type main courses with rice and potato at £2.35 are always available. There are three or more scrumptious puds to choose from (all under £1) and an excellent array of cold meat salads (at less than £3). In addition to the standard wine list (good-range), look out for the two 'wines of the week' and a 'drink of the week' (such as 'Cherry Sparkler' – Asti Spumante and cherries).

THE LIGHT OF SHAHZALAL
11 New Street, Joice's Yard (Basingstoke 3509)
Open: Mon-Sun 12noon-2.30pm, 6-12mdnt

[C] [P] [S] [✆]

Tucked away in an older part of the town, this Indian restaurant offers a wide range of food at surprisingly low prices. Embossed flock-paper adorns the walls and the thick carpeting creates a warm and cosy atmosphere. Service is the keynote here, with all staff genuinely anxious that you should enjoy your meal. A plethora of curries (marked hot, medium and mild on the menu to avoid burnt palates!) are available from £1.50-£2, whilst meat dhansak (hot sweet and sour) is around £1.70. Of the other specialities, chicken tikka with salad is heartily recommended at £2.30. For the less adventurous, English dishes, such as steak with mushrooms and chips at £2.50, are excellent value. Starters range from 50p-£1.30, with desserts (including jilaries, a delicious dough-based fritter) all priced at under 80p. Hungarian carafino house wine is 65p per glass, but there are many other drinks available from the well-stocked corner bar.

TUNDOOR MAHAL RESTAURANT
4 Winchester Street (Basingstoke 3795)
Open: Mon-Sun 12noon-3pm, 6pm-12mdnt

[♫] [S]

Once the Midland Bank, this listed building retains its original stately exterior while the inside is transformed into a smart restaurant with warm red décor, wood-effect walls, Indian-style arches and nicely-positioned alcoves with hanging lights. Fresh flowers, candle-lit tables and soft background music complete the pleasant atmosphere. Cuisine is basically Bangladesh and Indian specialities with some Malayan, Persian and English dishes. A special three-course lunch costs around £1.50, with three choices for the main course including prawn, meat or chicken pillau. The à la carte menu includes a selection of original dishes – dhal soup with orange (around 30p) and beef Bangla curry served with fresh cream are worth sampling (at under £3). Sweets are fairly standard Indian dishes.

Blandford Forum

ANVIL HOTEL AND RESTAURANT ★★
Pimperne (Blandford 53431)
Open: Mon-Thu 12noon-2.30pm, 6-10.30pm, Fri-Sat 12noon-2.30pm, 6-11pm, Sun 12noon-2.30pm

[P]

The only restaurant between Blandford and Salisbury is housed in a beautiful, thatched 16th-century building, reputed to have originated as an Elizabethan farmhouse. Satisfying snacks may be taken in the newly extended and cleverly restored bar. Home-made fare such as lasagne or cottage pie (both £1.20), coquille St Jaques (made from fresh local scallops – £1.50) or beef curry with rice at £1.60 are the order of the day. Salads, soup, pâté and basket meals are also available. The beamed restaurant, with its brick floor has an à la carte menu which could easily break the budget. Soup, chicken à la crème (poached in a white wine and mushroom sauce) and a sweet is just within the limit.

Bournemouth

ANN'S PANTRY, 129 Belle Vue Road, Southbourne (Bournemouth 426178)
Open: summer: Tue-Sat 10.30am-2pm, 6-9pm, Sun 10.30am-2pm, winter: Fri-Sat 10.30am-2pm, 6-9pm

[S] [ ]

This corner-sited restaurant, only 100 yards from the sea-front, has an exterior reminiscent of a superior Victorian pub. At lunchtime there is an extremely reasonable à la carte menu with starters below 30p, and main courses, including home-made cottage pie and gammon with pineapple, range from £2-£3. Children's choices at around 60p include the well-loved bangers, beans and chips. A three-course set lunch is priced by the main dish – starting at about £1.30 for Cornish pasty to around £1.70 for roast beef and Yorkshire pud. A three-course Sunday roast lunch costs less than £2. Excellent table d'hôte three-course dinners are also served for around £3.50, and there is a slightly more expensive à la carte evening menu. A glass of wine is about 50p.

FORTES, The Square (Bournemouth 24916)
Open: Florentine Restaurant: Mon-Sun 12noon-10.30pm, Coffee Shop: Mon-Sun: 8am-10pm (4.30pm winter), Self Service Restaurant: Mon-Sun 9.30pm-11pm (6pm winter)

[C] [♫] [P] [S] [ ]

This is a typical Trusthouse Forte operation, providing everything from takeaway snacks for the beach to three-course à la carte dinners in an elegant setting, at prices that represent very good value for money. The ground floor self-service restaurant serves an excellent lunch, high tea or supper at prices from little more than £1-£2, as well as cakes and pastries, sandwiches, ice creams and beverages. The Coffee Shop serves hot snacks and grills throughout the day, with soup, hotdogs, hamburgers, bowls of mixed salad and pizzas as just some of its attractions. The Florentine offers a choice of three-course lunches at prices from about £2.95 to just under £5, including various Italian dishes and a traditional weekend lunch at around £4.50. The à la carte menu is also reasonably priced. A half-litre of the house wine costs about £2.

LONG'S, 77 Old Christchurch Road (Bournemouth 20002)
Open: during normal licensing hours. Restaurant: Mon-Sat 12noon-2.15pm, 6.30-10.30pm

[S]

Long's is 250 yards or so up from The Square, on the left-hand side of Old Christchurch Road. It comprises a first-floor Brasserie restaurant, two ground-floor bars and a cellar bar complete with water fountains. The Brasserie's à la carte cuisine is largely French, but reasonably priced. Its table d'hôte lunch menu has a more English bias and is very good value at about £3.25 for four courses. Food in the Spanish, Granville and Cellar bars is excellent, with cottage pie or ravioli at around 70p, chili con carne at 90p or so and chicken and vegetable curry at about £1.10 among the hot favourites. There's a superb selection of wines, for both consumption on the premises and takeaway. A large glass of the French house wine costs around 50p.

THE OLD ENGLAND, 74 Poole Road, Westbourne (Bournemouth 766475)
Open: Tue-Fri 9.30am-3pm, 6-10.30pm Sat 6-10.30pm, Sun 12noon-3pm

[C] [♬] [P] [S] [&]

A warm welcome awaits you at this delightful olde worlde restaurant. Cuisine, though, is 20th-century and well-cooked with fresh vegetables. A set three-course meal costs £4.25 (with big reductions for children), alternatively an extensive à la carte menu includes a range of starters from chilled tomato juice at 35p, to crab cocktail at around £1.40. Numerous main dishes are available, typical options being Dorset chicken (£3.50) and pan-fried gammon with pineapple (£3.70). Steak, unfortunately, should be avoided if you're to stay within the budget. Tempting home-made desserts such as crème caramel or fruit crumble cost around 70p. Standard house wine is on hand at about 60p a glass, but the would-be connoisseur should try the newly-opened Dickens Wine Cellar directly below the restaurant. Enter by a separate door and here you can sup from a wide range of red, white and rosé, whilst partaking of a snack or light salad.

PLANTERS, 514 Christchurch Road, Boscombe (Bournemouth 302228)
Open: Mon-Sat 6.30-11.30pm

[♬] [S]

This modern restaurant with its Hollywood movie theme and lively background music boasts a list of cocktails as long as your arm. Most expensive of these is Carter's comfort (£1.80), a colourful concoction of southern comfort, orange juice and orgeat. The food is as expected, hamburger-based, with a few specials such as chargrilled steak, pork slice and gammon and pineapple. A quiche and mixed salad costs around £1.25. For dessert there is an all-American line up of spiced apple pie, chocolate fudge cake, hot waffle with maple syrup and fresh cream and various sundaes for under £1. A glass of wine adds 55p.

THE SALAD CENTRE, Post Office Road (Bournemouth 21720)
Open: Mon-Fri 10am-5pm, Sat 10am-2.30pm

[C] [P] [S] [&]

This family-owned-and-run Salad Centre encourages and caters for sensible health-food, vegetarian-style, eating. Patrons are invited to refrain from smoking and family pets are definitely not admitted. The décor is clean and bright, if a little spartan, and the staff charming and most helpful. Everything is home cooked and made of the freshest, purest ingredients, with no artificial additives of any kind. There is a brave display daily of more than a dozen different salads, with quiches, nut roasts, savouries and – in the winter – various hot dishes. Fruit juices include apple, lemon, grapefruit and beetroot and there is a good range of beverages, though the Salad Centre is unlicensed.

TRATTORIA TOSCA, 12 Richmond Hill (Bournemouth 23034)
Open: Mon-Sun 12noon-2.30pm, 6-11.30pm

[C] [♬] [P] [S] [&]

The cuisine at Edward Cobelli's charmingly informal Trattoria Tosca in The Square is, not surprisingly, Italian, but not expensively so. There is a good range of starters at prices from 40p-£1.85, spaghetti dishes at about £1.25-£1.70, and Italian specialities, including the romantically named filleto Casanova, at around £2.50-£5. A half litre of vino costs just around £2 and by the glass about 55p. Service is friendly, willing and speedy, but do book at the weekend if you want to be sure of a table.

Bridport

BISTRO LAUTREC ✕ 53 East Street
(Bridport 56549)
Open: Mon-Fri 12noon-2pm,
Mon-Sat 7-10pm

[S]

Food and environment go together in this typical French-style bistro. Candles in bottles, check tablecloths, Lautrec posters and chalked-up menus make just the right setting in which to enjoy a lunch of terrine provençale at about £1, followed, perhaps, by stuffed green pepper with vegetables or salad for just over £1. Evening meals, in a more sophisticated yet still informal atmosphere, cost over or around £5. You can buy a glass of wine here for about 50p, but if you feel like a treat, the palatable house wine is around £3.50 per litre.

BULL HOTEL 34 East Street
(Bridport 22878)
Open: Mon-Sat 12noon-2pm,
7.15-9.15pm, Sun 7.15-9.15pm

[P]

The Terleski family are in the process of restoring their 16th-century coaching inn. They are keen to offer good hospitality at a very reasonable price – and succeed. There's a wide range of bar meals, including a choice from the daily speciality menu costing between £2.25 and £3.25 for three courses, and hot or cold snacks from 50p-£3. It can all be washed down with a glass of real ale. The daily speciality choice offers unfussy dishes such as roast belly of pork and vegetables, and the usual range of grills is available. For dessert try crème caramel or apple strudel.

Burbage

THE SAVERNAKE FOREST HOTEL ★★
Savernake (Burbage 810206)
Open: Mon-Thu, Sun 12noon-2pm,
7-9pm, Fri-Sat 12noon-2pm 7-10pm

[C] [P]

On the fringe of the beautiful Savernake Forest, this charming old hotel specialises in home-prepared dishes. The Buttery Grill menu offers soup (65p) or pâté (£1) as starters. Main course prices include chips, vegetables, salad garnish, roll and butter and a choice of ice creams or cheese and biscuits – a steak or scampi are over £4 and pork or lamb chop are around £3.60. A large pizza is about £1.50. An ambitious à la carte menu in the restaurant offers trout usquebach – a traditional 18th-century Scottish recipe, or smothered duck (a 17th-century delicacy cooked slowly in honey and served with a wine sauce, dates and currants). Unfortunately most of the prices are a little beyond our budget here.

Chippenham

THE ROWDEN ARMS, Bath Road
(Chippenham 3870)
Open: Mon-Thu 12noon-2pm, 7-10pm,
Fri-Sat 12noon-2pm, 7-10.30pm,
summer only: Sun 7-10pm

[C] [P]

On the main Bath Road out of Chippenham is this attractive, modern pub with a low rake, chalet-style roof and a colourful painted farmhouse wagon in the forecourt. You can sip cocktails in the comfortable lounge bar while surveying the very extensive menu offering freshly-prepared food. A selection of fourteen starters ranges from soup of the day for about 40p to smoked salmon at around £1.45. Fish dishes, grills, salads and specialities, such as loin of pork Marsala (at £3.30) and rump steak (around £4), are available for the main course and there is an impressive choice of sweets at a variety of prices. Among the more expensive (around 50p) are banana split and rum baba. A tulip glass of wine costs about 40p.

WHITE HART INN, Ford
(Castle Combe 782213)
Off A420 Bristol/Chippenham on slip road to Colerne
Open: Mon-Sun 12noon-2pm, 7.30-9.30pm

[P]

Idyllically situated beside a trout stream and overlooking the lush Weavern valley, this 16th-century stone-built pub is the epitome of Olde Englande. Low, beamed ceilings, log fires and suits of armour set the scene, while Ken Gardner, Fleet Street journalist and writer, personally attends to the food preparation. Home-cooked ham-on-the-bone or braised beef, served with vegetables cost around £1.50 in the bar, while £2 will get you an individually baked steak and kidney pie and for less than £3 you can sample locally-caught trout. Some dishes from the à la carte menu could be sampled within the budget, but fresh trout stuffed with aubergines, spinach and walnuts costs around £4, so you would have to forego a course. A glass of wine costs about 45p.

Christchurch

SOMERFORD HOTEL, Lyndhurst Road, Somerford (Christchurch 482610)
Open: Mon-Sat 12noon-2pm, 7-9.30pm

[C] [P]

Lunch in the attractive dining area and bar of this impressive Tudor-style hotel is superb value. The table d'hôte menu offers three courses, including chicken and locally caught fish dishes and a good selection of sweets for about £3. The 'English Table' menu with roast is around £4, but with fresh Christchurch salmon is over £5. There is an excellent cold buffet and a variety of bar snacks is available. Children are specially catered for in the summer with a pets' corner and their own play area and bar, and they are equally welcome in the dining area. The à la carte dinner menu includes an abundance of local fish and seafood as well as grills and roasts, but you could break the bank by selecting without care.

Corsham

METHUEN ARMS HOTEL★★
(Corsham 712239)
Open: Mon-Thu, Sat 12noon-2pm, 6-10.30pm, Fri 12noon-2.30pm, 6-11pm, Sun 12noon-2pm, 7-10.30pm

[P]

Situated midway between Chippenham and Bath on the A4, the hotel is in close proximity to Corsham Manor, the country seat of Lord Methuen, whose heraldic arms are displayed above the entrance portico. In fact, the building is steeped in history and Winter's Court, where lunch and dinner are served, retains the oak beams and Cotswold stone of a grandiose bygone age. A midday four-course businessperson's meal is a bargain at £3.30 (especially as minute steak is on the menu), but unfortunately the candlelit dinners are just beyond our range. However, there are further options in the Long Bar such as sandwiches, basket meals, and a cold table, all reasonably priced. A goblet of house wine is about 60p.

Dorchester

LA GONDOLA, 45 High East Street
(Dorchester 67368)

Open: Tue-Sat, 12noon-2pm, 7-10pm

[P] [S]

Suzy and Gian-Piero Curioni's La Gondola, at the bottom of High East Street, is very popular with the locals for its family atmosphere and good North Italian cuisine at unpretentious prices. La Gondola offers fifteen or sixteen starters at around 50p-£1 and at least as many main dishes at prices from about £1.50-£3. Spaghetti bolognese (under £1) and veal cooked with Marsala wine sauce (about £2) are particularly enjoyable. The zabaglione sweet is a rare treat. A glass of the Italian house wine costs around 60p.

JUDGE JEFFREYS' RESTAURANT
High West Street (Dorchester 4369)
Open: Mon-Sun 9am-5.30pm, summer: Mon-Sun 7-11pm

[♫] [S] [🍷]

Viewed as a building, Pam and Brian Bean's Judge Jeffreys' restaurant is of great historical and architectural interest. It was sympathetically restored and put to its present use in 1928, but had been first monastery property and

then a private house for something like five centuries before. Judge Jeffreys lodged here in 1685 while making his mark in the town with orders for seventy-four executions. Today, the restaurant which bears his name is a friendly place, full of atmosphere, providing morning coffees, bar snacks, lunches, afternoon teas and dinners at prices which could hardly be accounted a trial to anyone. You can buy a substantial lunch for about £3 or eat à la carte for very little more. The evening à la carte menu is very English, listing scampi, haddock, plaice and scallops, all reasonably priced, with £4.75-£6 the average price for a dinner. Children's half portions are available from the main menus at half price and there is a special children's menu with dishes costing around £1.

Fareham

GABBIES, 30-32 West Street (Fareham 284853)
Open: Mon-Sat 12noon-2.30pm, 7.30-11.30pm

[C] [♫] [P] [S]

This smart hamburger restaurant in the older pedestrian shopping area boasts far more than weighty burgers on its menu. You can enjoy a good three-course meal here, choosing from seven starters and a number of tasty main courses such as seafood platter or chicken Maryland. Sweets include flans, gâteaux, cheesecakes, and speciality ice creams. Wine is available by the glass at around 45p. If you have a taste and appetite for burgers, Gabbies special is excellent – a $\frac{1}{4}$lb or $\frac{1}{2}$lb lean beefburger topped with mushrooms, peppers, tomato and melted cheese served in a toasted roll with French fries or salad for around £2.50 or £3.10.

Fiddleford

FIDDLEFORD INN
(Sturminster Newton 72489)

Open: Mon-Sat 12noon-2pm, 7-10.30pm, Sun 12noon-1.30pm, 7-10pm

[P] [♧]

This creeper-clad inn makes a welcome stopping-place on the beautiful, but remote A357 – the Sturminster Newton/Blandford road. Informality is the keynote and your hosts Geoffrey and Jill Fish ensure that there's a warm and cosy atmosphere. A lunchtime blackboard menu offers regularly changing speciality dishes, whilst an example of standard fare would be duck pâté (£1), chicken curry (£1.80) or flan salad (1.30) and apple tart (60p). Wine is 50p a goblet, making for a very economical meal. In the evening, though, unless you avoid steak the budget will be exceeded.

Hambledon

THE BAT AND BALL INN
Broadhalfpenny Down, Hambledon Road, Clanfield (Hambledon 692)
Open: Mon-Sat 12noon-2.15pm, 7-10.30pm (10pm winter), Sun 12noon-1.45pm, 7.30-10pm

[♫] [P]

Even in the mid-18th century, when the cricket club at Hambledon became the strongest team in England and turned a rustic pastime into a national sport, the Bat and Ball was a hit with the locals. The inn overlooked the pitch on Broadhalfpenny Down and the players (wise chaps) would repair to it after, and sometimes even during, a match to indulge in 'high feasting'. Today the inn is even more popular despite being way out in the country, so it's always advisable to book a table. Hosts Frank and Katherine Rendle (Katherine does the cooking) have retained a cricketing atmosphere in the front bar; curved cricket bats, two-stump wickets and all, while the other bar is decorated in the more traditional beams-and-brass style. Order food at the bar and eat here if you like, or have your meal waitress-served in the cosy restaurant which overlooks an attractive garden. You really have to be something of a glutton to bust our £5 budget because prices are very reasonable. All five starters (from soup to a generous prawn cocktail) are under £1 and eight main courses range from about 90p for a Jumbo sausage, through mouth-watering meat pies (around £1.30) to grilled sirloin steak at about £3.70 – great value, considering that all the main dishes are served with chips, peas, mushrooms, onions and salad garni. Salads and ploughman's are also available except on Mondays and Tuesdays, when a limited menu operates. If you're not stumped when it comes to the sweet course, try an apple pie (40p) or gâteau (70p) top-heavy with naughty-but-nice fresh cream; or finish off with cheese and biscuits. A glass of house wine costs 45p or so but half bottles are also available. No children or dogs allowed except on the front patio.

Hartley Wintney

WHYTE LYON (Hartley Wintney 2037)
Open: Mon-Sat 10.30am-2.30pm, 6-10.30pm, Sun 12noon-2pm, 7-10.30pm

[C] [P] [♧]

East of the picturesque village of Hartley Wintney, nestling in a hollow beside the A30, is the rambling, historic one-time coaching inn now owned by Schooner Inns. Peter Cole, who assists the manager, claims that part of the building dates back to the 14th century. At present two grill bars, heavily beamed and partitioned in the usual Schooner manner, offer a range of old favourites at competitive prices. The Portcullis Restaurant has a salad counter from which you can serve-yourself to as much side salad as you want. Ice creams or cheeses are included in the price of the main course, which could be rump steak (nearly £5), half a roast chicken in barbecue sauce (nearly £4) or plaice and lemon (about £3.50). A starter and a glass of wine will add between £1-£1.50 to your bill. Apart from a bigger selection of starters, Dover sole and duckling, the Cromwell Bar boasts the ghost of a girl who hanged herself in that very room – the rope is still there to remind us! So popular is the Whyte Lyon with the locals that a third restaurant – the Hartford Grill has been opened upstairs.

Hook

WHITE HART, London Road (Hook 2462)
Open: Tue-Sat 12noon-2pm, 7-10pm (10.30pm Fri & Sat)

[♫] [P] [♧]

On the old coach road from London to Exeter stands the White Hart, one of the oldest pubs in the country. Entrance from the car park is through an out-of-the-past courtyard, by a row of old cottages which were once the stable boys' quarters. The dining room, with its dark-wood fittings and a lattice work of beams, has one wall etched with the ghostly outline of a coachman and his horses. A special lunch at £4.50 gives a choice of fruit juice, pâté or soup followed by a choice of steak – sirloin or rump – or an enormous 14oz pork chop, all served with chips or new potatoes and the vegetable of the day. A sweet such as apple pie and cream or cheese and biscuits completes the meal. Bar snacks are of a high standard, and a three-course meal of cream of chicken soup, beef Stroganoff and strawberry gâteau can cost as little as £2.50.

Lyndhurst

THE BOW WINDOWS RESTAURANT
65 High Street (Lyndhurst 2463)
Open: summer: Mon-Sun 10am-10pm, winter: Mon-Wed 10am-6pm, Thu-Sun 10am-10pm

P S

The little town of Lyndhurst is on a major holiday route in the heart of the New Forest . . . and gets very busy in the tourist season. With this in mind, Bow Windows is particularly conveniently placed opposite a large free car park. Behind those bow windows is an interior decorated with mirror tiles and large murals of forest scenes. The menu is extensive and conventional. Good value table d'hôte choices at lunch and dinner will cost about £5 with coffee, and may include a roast, fish, or curry dish. Tread carefully as far as the à la carte is concerned; the cheapest dishes, such as steak and kidney pie or omelette will cost about £3.

Marlborough

ATTILIO'S WINE BAR, 13 New Road (Marlborough 52969)
Open: Mon-Wed, Fri-Sat 12noon-2pm, 6.30-11pm

A cheerful aura of Italy in a corner of rural Wiltshire, Attilio's interior is simple and attractive, with an emphasis on natural textures – rush, cane, brick and wood. The excellent pizzas – with fresh tomatoes – can form a filling base for a within-the-budget three-course meal. Lunchtime meals and snacks range in price from 60p-£3. You'll need a bit of mental juggling to keep the price of an à la carte selection down, however.

Melksham

THE WEST END, Semington Road (Melksham 703057)
Open: Mon-Sun 12noon-2pm, (Sun 1.30pm) 7-10pm

C P

This attractive mellow stone and tile hostelry has an interior with a farmhouse look – beamed ceiling, open-stone fireplace and scrubbed table tops. A limited menu offers simple but well-prepared dishes with emphasis on succulent steaks, all with interesting names. You may wrap your lips around the 'Farmer's Daughter' (a 5oz sirloin for around £3) or perhaps you'd prefer a Ploughboy's rump or Hungry Horse? Three courses including a village pâté for starter and Emmerdale apple pie with cream will cost between £5 and £6 with coffee. For a cheaper meal try the hot platter of the day or salad for under £2. House wine comes at around 50p per glass.

Mere

PESTLE AND MORTAR, The Square (Mere 860263)
Open: Mon-Fri 10.30am-5.30pm, Sat 10.30am-5.30pm, 7.30-10pm, Sun 12noon-5.30pm

[P] [S] [⚘]

This restaurant bears a very apt name as the stone townhouse in which it is housed was originally the apothecary's, dating back to the 17th century. The comfortably-modernised and tastefully-decorated interior boasts an attractive restaurant with aperitif bar/coffee lounge plus a smaller separate area for morning coffee and afternoon snacks. Personal attention awaits all visitors by owners Wendy and Jerry Anderson. Wendy is to be seen 'out front' while husband Jerry prepares food in the kitchen. A newly introduced Countryman range comprises various home-made pies and pastries, all below £2. An evening à la carte menu is also available at proportionately higher prices which are still within the limit if chosen with care. Try 'Taste of England' dishes here.

Petersfield

THE PUNCH AND JUDY RESTAURANT, High Street (Petersfield 2214)
Open: Mon-Sun 8.30am-5.15pm

[S]

This attractive olde-worlde building dating from 1613 has plenty of charm and combines a bakery, coffee shop and small restaurant. A set menu of good basic English fare includes starters such as sardine salad (around £1.05), smoked mackerel (about £1.10), salads in the £1.80-£3 range, fish dishes such as rainbow trout at around £3.50, grills from just over £2.50-£4.75 and a

selection of desserts from 60p-£1.20. There is also a dish of the day on offer such as roast loin of pork served with a good selection of well-prepared vegetables for around £2.50. A large glass of French house wine is about 50p.

Portsmouth

THE HUNGRY ONE, 15 Arundel Way, Arundel Street (Portsmouth 817114)
Open: Mon-Sat 9.30am-5pm

[♫] [P] [S] [⚘]

For the very best kind of snack bar, in clean, comfortable, purpose-built surroundings, try Michael See's Hungry One. Fresh salads are a speciality of the house and range, in price, from Cheddar cheese at just over £1 to red salmon at around £2. There is a good selection of substantial meals from about £1.50 for chicken or plaice and chips to nearly £2 for scampi and chips. There is a range of delicious desserts from around 50p. No alcohol, but finish with the locally-esteemed coffee.

Ringwood

PEPPERCORNS RESTAURANT
9 Meeting House Lane
(Ringwood 78364/4361)
Open: Tue-Thu 10am-2.30pm, Fri-Sat 10am-2.30pm, 7.30-11.30pm, Sun 12.30-2.30pm

[P] [S] [⚘]

Hanging flower baskets, bright against the whitewashed walls, pick out Peppercorns. Beams, white walls and hunting prints create a relaxed atmosphere, enhanced by displays of fresh flowers. Appetisers range in price from soup of the day at 45p to prawn cocktail at £1.10. Main courses, served with vegetables of the day, include a variety of omelettes from 95p-£1.25, lamb chops with redcurrant jelly at £1.75 and trout meuniere at £2.25. Cold buffet items cost from £1.45-£2 – home-cooked ham, roast beef and chicken included. Daily specials such as chicken curry (£1.35) or braised liver and onions (£1.40) change every day. Desserts, for example, Bakewell tart, fruit salad or Black Forest gâteau are in the 55p-65p range. A glass of wine costs 55p. Sunday lunch is a special feature, with a choice of four starters, two roasts or fish, two hot sweets or a selection of desserts from the trolley.

Romsey

THE WHITE HORSE, Ampfield (Braishfield 68356)
Open: lunchtime licensing hours

[♬] [P] [♧]

Nestling at the foot of a wide curve of the A31 is the welcoming sight of the picturesque, black-and-white-timbered White Horse pub. Inside, the large lounge bar is all beams and comfort, with a cavernous brick fireplace. Cindy and Ron Bagley offer astonishingly good bar lunches and you will find it difficult to spend as much as £5 for three courses, wine and coffee. Cindy does all the cooking and even the generous cottage pie, which comes in an individual dish, is full of surprises – with peppers and sweetcorn it only costs 50p! Beef curry, chicken supreme or sweet and sour pork are all under £1, and salads are available. Start with pâté and finish with delicious, light Black Forest gâteau or fruit flan bursting with fruit – both served with cream and costing just 60p. Ron has plans to open a children's garden, which will make The White Horse an ideal place for a satisfying family lunch.

Salisbury

THE BARON OF BEEF, Endless Street (Salisbury 28937)
Open: during normal licensing hours. Mon-Sun 12noon-2pm, 6-10.30pm

[C] [♬] [P] [S]

The Baron of Beef, opened in February 1978, is a timber and brick transformation of a much older pub. Its lunchtime bar menu includes lamb stew with vegetables at around £1 and braised beef with vegetables and trimmings at about £1.50, as well as home-made cold dishes such as egg, cheese and onion flan for £1.25 and prawn salad for under £2. A ploughman's lunch costs around 65p. The main menu includes excellent home-made soup or pâté as appetisers. Plaice, chicken, lamb or gammon are typical main courses, served with vegetables and trimmings, all at around £2.30 each. Steak dishes are between £3.25 and £4.25. Most desserts are around 60p. The Spanish house wines are about 50p a glass.

CLAIRE'S RESTAURANT AND COFFEE HOUSE 7-9 The Market Place (Salisbury 3118)
Open: Restaurant: Mon-Sat 11.45am-2.30pm (all year), 6-10pm (Jun-Sep), Wed-Sat 6-10pm (Sep-Jun). Coffee House: Mon-Sat 9.30am-5pm

[C] [♬] [P] [S] [♧]

Very handy for shoppers, this is a pleasant rendezvous for a quick break or a substantial lunch. Claire's offers good food at very reasonable prices and (with its children's meals offering two courses including fish fingers or beefburgers at under £1) is excellent for families. Evening dishes include veal provençal (£3.25) and chicken tikka (£2.95). House wine sells at around 50p a glass.

THE CROSS KEYS HOTEL, Shaftesbury Road, Fovant (Fovant 284)
Open: Mon-Tue, Thu-Sun 12noon-2pm, 7.45-9pm, Wed 7.45-9pm

[P]

The famous highwayman Jack Rattenbury enjoyed the victuals prepared at the Cross Keys. This charming, stone-built hostelry was built around 1485, and can be found in the heart of beautiful countryside. The

20th-century fare is English roasts and home-made sweets, though Elsie and Wendy Thompson have a flair for preparing more exotic dishes such as moussaka. Snacks available in the Buttery Bar include curry or chicken and chips for between £1 and £3, and very modestly-priced ploughman's lunches and freshly-cut sandwiches. A Paris goblet of house wine costs about 50p.

MICHAEL SNELL, 8 St Thomas's Square (Salisbury 6037)
Open: Mon-Sat 9am-5.30pm

[P] [S] [♧]

No-one should go to Salisbury without

trying Michael Snell's superb Black Forest gâteau. In these old, part mill-house premises, the Swiss-trained Mr Snell makes and sells his own chocolate and cakes, besides specialising in the sale of fine teas, coffees, jams, chutneys and local honey. His light lunch menu contains a great variety of dishes, all at under £2, including smoked mackerel fillet with carrot and coleslaw, and cheese flan or home-made pizza with salad. Appetisers include soup, French bread and butter for about 30p, and a selection of torten and pastries or speciality sorbets completes a satisfying three-course meal for around £3. Michael Snell is unlicensed.

Sherborne

HOUSE OF STEPS, Half Moon Street (Sherborne 2455)
Open: Mon-Sun 9am-5pm

[C] [♫] [P] [S]

Situated close to Sherborne Abbey, the mellow, stone-built House of Steps provides a reasonably-priced selection of snacks and more substantial meals. Home-made favourites such as steak and kidney pie and beef casserole with dumplings appear on the menu under 'Enticing Entrées . . .'. Accompany them with draught Somerset cider, Dorset mead or spiced elderberry wine at around 50p per glass. Afternoon cream teas are available at £1 or thereabouts. A three-course meal at the cold carvery can be had on a Saturday night for under £5.

SWAN INN, Cheap Street (Sherborne 4129)
Open: Mon-Sun 12noon-2pm, 6.30-10pm

[G] [P] [S]

The Swan Inn is to be found through an archway from a pedestrian short cut, leading from the main car park close to the town centre. This quaint hostelry offers a selection of satisfying grills, including scampi (£2.20), half duck and rump steak (both at £4.50), all served with garni and French fries. Grills may be supplemented with appetising starters (60p-£1) such as pâté, whitebait and prawn cocktail, and sweets such as home-made apple pie. Spanish house wine is about 55p for a 5oz glass.

Southampton

GOLDEN PALACE ✕ 17 Above Bar Street (Southampton 26636)
Open: Mon-Sat 11.45am-12mdnt,

Sun 12noon-12mdnt

[C] [P] [S]

Slap in the middle of Southampton's modern shopping area, this colourful Chinese restaurant oozes Eastern calm. Prettily decked out with coloured lanterns, tiles, high archways and pillars to give a 'palatial' effect, it is immensely popular with the local orientals, and every encouragement is given to Western diners to use chopsticks. Dishes from the Tim Sum menu such as prawns Cheung Fun or meat rolls and duck's webs (available from 12noon-5pm only) prove to be the best loved and are all, unbelievably, around £1.50 each. A three-course à la carte dinner works out at about £5.

LA MARGHERITA, 4-6 Commercial Road (Southampton 22390)
Open: Mon-Sat 12noon-3pm, 6pm-12mdnt

[C] [♫] [P] [S]

A popular nightspot, particularly with theatre and cinema folk from the nearby Gaumont, is Franco Fantini's La Margherita. 'Let's go Marghereating' is the house motto, with a choice of starters ranging in price from about 35p for fresh orange juice to around £2 for Parma ham and melon. There are made-to-order pizzas, from £1.10 upwards, and main dishes such as fresh fish, a significant proportion of which, except sole Meunière, cost less than £3. The house wine costs about 50p a glass.

PICCOLO MONDO, 36 Windsor Terrace (Southampton 36890)
Open: Tue-Fri 10am-8pm, Sat-Mon 10am-7pm

[♫] [S]

Very handy for top-of-the-town shopping and the Hants and Dorset bus station, Saluatore la Gumina and Domenico Bibbo's Piccolo Mondo incorporates bakery and snack bar. A good cup of coffee costs about 20p, freshly-baked cheesecakes and cream cakes around 30p, and freshly-cut sandwiches are available. Hot snacks include home-made lasagne alla Romana at around £1.25 and the cooked-to-order pizzas are priced at about £1.40.

PIZZA-PAN, 28a Bedford Place (Southampton 23103)
Open: Mon-Sun 10am-3pm, 6pm-1am

[C] [♫] [P] [S]

The enterprising Signor Strologo's bistro-cum-restaurant has boldly-written outside menus and an eye-catching window display of bottles to tickle the palates of passers-by. Inside (where a personal welcome awaits you), Ercol-style tables and chairs, with check tablecloths, fill the large eating area, whilst attractive chandeliers and a big tank of (inedible!) fish complete the furnishings. Most appetisers here tend to be rather expensive (around £1.30), but this is compensated by the pizza prices (*eg*, cannelloni ripieni – £1.75, pizza Napolitana – £1.55). Many steak, fish and poultry dishes are on offer, but if you want a 65p glass of wine, you'll need to choose carefully to keep within the budget.

THE RED LION, 55 High Street (Southampton 22595)
Open: Mon-Sat 12noon-2pm. Bar snacks: during normal licensing hours

[♫] [P] [S]

Local tradition has it that, in 1415, Henry V put down a treacherous plot with a hastily-arranged trial in what is now known as the 'Court Room' of the Red Lion. True or not, the room is an impressive one, with its half-timbered walls and stone Tudor fireplace. Charles Waldman's two-course lunch specials for under £2 are an extremely good buy. For the rest, the menu offers good plain English cooking at prices hard to beat

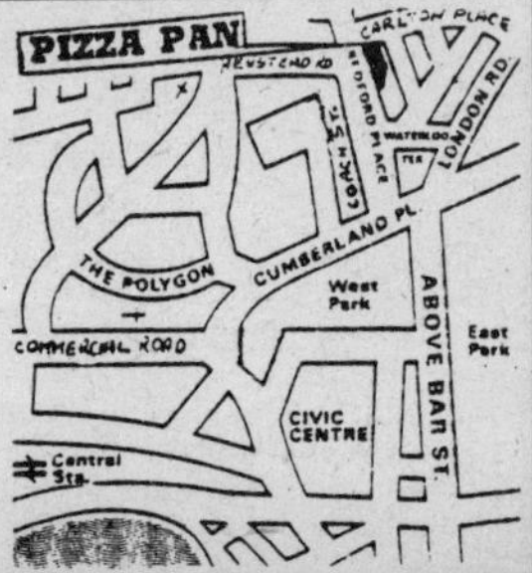

for value. The house wine is Spanish or Portuguese and costs about 45p a glass. The Red Lion is close to the Bargate.

SIMON'S WINE HOUSE, Vernon Walk, Carlton Place (Southampton 36372)
Open: Mon-Thu 11.30am-2.30pm, 7-10.30pm; Fri-Sat 11.30-3pm, 7-11pm, Sun 7-10.30pm

[♫] [S]

Mother and son hold court at this simple Simon wine house, with its dark wood,

bare bricks and bowls of shiny green palms. While Simon looks after the bar, his mother does the cooking. Dishes chalked on a blackboard include home-made pâté, chicken curry at only £1.25, and Simon's pie (a speciality of the house), with sweets such as gâteau, cheesecake and trifle all for around £1. Wines are served by the glass at about 70p each.

VEGIA ZENA, 49 Bedford Place (Southampton 31885)
Open: Mon-Sat 12noon-2.30pm, 7-11.30pm

[C] [♫] [P] [S]

An eye-catching red awning and brown-glass frontage proclaim the presence of this attractive little Italian restaurant. Inside, the décor is simple, with white, textured walls, low ceiling and red-tiled floor. Brightly-checked tablecloths and pictures of boating scenes add colour and interest. A cold cabinet displays seafood and other delicacies which can be found, in various forms, on the menu. Continental fish dishes are the speciality (at £3-£4), with such delights as fresh clams cooked in wine and herbs with croûtons, stuffed baked trout or fried rings of squid - all around £2-£3. Pasta and pizzas are priced from £2 to £2.50.

Swindon

SHERATON SUITE, East Street (Swindon 24114)
Open: Mon-Sat 12noon-2pm

[C] [P] [S]

If ornate surroundings are what you look for in a restaurant, you could do no better than to eat in the red and gold dining-room of the Sheraton Suite. Sit back amidst the chandeliers, velvet-upholstered chairs and flock wallpapers and enjoy the table d'hôte lunch, priced at about £3.50. This includes a starter of soup or fruit juice, and eight choices of main dishes such as roasts, steaks, chicken chasseur or fish plus a daily special such as devilled kidneys followed by cheese or a sweet from the trolley. You may, if you prefer, order from the à la carte menu; most dishes obviously fall outside our price range, but three courses such as melon, scampi and gâteau are still within reach. Snacks are available from the bar. Italian house wine is about 50p per glass.

Wareham

PRIORY HOTEL ★★★ Church Green (Wareham 2772)
Open: Mon-Sun 12.30-2pm

[P]

Formerly the 16th-century Priory of Lady St Mary this charming hotel retains much of its original character and enjoys a magnificent setting amid two acres of beautifully landscaped gardens on the banks of the River Frome. Lunch is served in the traditional dining room where a reasonable choice of high-class cuisine is available at around £5 for the full meal with wine and coffee. A sample three-course meal could include avocado 'lounge en ouche' (half avocado cooked in butter with bacon), breast of chicken Algerienne with vegetables of the day and a choice from the sweet selection. Evening meals, served in the Abbot's Cellar, are beyond the scope of this book.

RED LION HOTEL ★ The Square (Wareham 2843)
Open: Mon-Sat 12noon-2.15pm, Sun 12noon-2pm, 7-9.15pm

[C] [P] [S]

In the centre of this small country town, this brick hotel with dormer windows and colourful hanging flower baskets is a find for travellers en route to Bournemouth or Weymouth.

Interesting bar snacks are available from 40p-90p and a good table d'hôte three-course meal can be had in the restaurant for £3.75 at lunch-time or £5.25 in the evening. Choices for lunch could be spaghetti Bolognese, fricasée of veal à la crême and strawberry meringue. The dinner menu offers a more imaginative selection of desserts such as profiteroles. A wider choice is available on the à la carte menu, but three courses could break the budget. A glass of house wine costs 60p.

Warminster

CHINN'S CELEBRATED CHOPHOUSE
Market Place (Warminster 212245)
Open: Mon-Sat 12noon-2pm, 7-10.45pm (except mid-Oct)

♫ S

Rabbits, or rather the lack of them, are the reason that this charming little eating place exists today. The Pickford family had for many years carried on a Butchers' and Fish, Game and Poultry business in Warminster, and if it hadn't been for a devastating outbreak of myxomatosis in 1965, they would still be using these cellars for their once well-established trade in rabbits and rabbit skins which were graded and dispatched from here. Braving their misfortune the Pickfords decided to convert the cellars into a restaurant. So, today you will be welcomed by staff dressed in the traditional straw boaters and striped aprons of that original business. With their knowledge of meats, fish and poultry you are assured a good, reasonably-priced meal. Chops themselves cost around £2.50, whilst all steaks are English and, with the fresh fish, are bought whole to be made ready for the menu at prices ranging from about £2 for haddock to £4 or so for fillet or T-bone steak. Salmon, mackerel and herring, too, are smoked on the spot and all pâtés are home-made (sold as starters at 50-70p). House wine is about 50p per glass and Gaelic coffee (a speciality) at around 70p.

Westbury

THE CHEQUERED FLAG, Warminster Road (Westbury 822551)
Open: Tue-Sat 12noon-2pm, 7-10pm

S

Owner Kenneth Whitty and his charming wife Neida personally supervise this modern corner-sited restaurant at the end of a shopping complex. Napkins are black and white check – what else? – and to continue the motor racing theme, every meal begins on the 'starting grid' where the usual hors d'oeuvres (pâté, smoked mackerel, prawn cocktail) are served. Move on to the 'first lap' and a main course blow out chosen from a good variety of fish, poultry and meats, and then if you're still in the race, the second lap takes the form of a sweet from the trolley, home-made apple pie or various ices. Coffee and cream awaits you at the finishing line, of course. If you don't mind drinking and 'driving' there is wine by the glass at about 50p.

Weymouth

THE CLARENDON RESTAURANT
52/53 York Buildings, The Esplanade (Weymouth 786706)
Open: Mon-Sun 9am-11pm

C S ♧

A seafront restaurant near the shopping area which provides day-long refreshment for flagging shoppers and sunbathers. A variety of 'Shoppers' luncheons' includes cheese omelettes, sausage and egg or fillet of cod with French fries or shepherd's pie as a main course, costing around £1. Starters from around 35-65p and sweets for the same price complement the meal. Alternatively, a three-course lunch for about £2.20 offers a range of starters, grills, roasts and sweets – excellent value! A more ostentatious meal, 'The Clarendon Special' including prawn cocktail and steak, costs around £3.75. French house wine is always available. An ideal place to take a hungry family of holidaymakers.

Wimborne

HORTON INN, Horton
(Witchampton 840252)
Open: Mon-Sat 12noon-2pm, 7-10pm, Sun 12noon-2pm, 7.30pm-9.30pm

P

Good bar snacks are a feature of this attractive 18th-century free house. There's a paved patio where you can savour your food when the sun shines. Dorset pâté or smoked mackerel pâté are tasty snacks, both just over £1, and a range of attractive salads is available at around the £2 mark. The restaurant has an à la carte menu with an interesting selection of main dishes such as Somerset style pork at £3.80, but you may not be able to buy three courses for around £5. Wine by the glass is about 55p.

Winchester

BANNERS RESTAURANT, 18 Little Minster Street (Winchester 67212)
Open: Mon 12noon-2.15pm
Tue-Sat 12noon-2.15pm, 7-10.15pm

♫

Banners opened in December 1977. The décor is bistro-style with pine tables and chairs, and the atmosphere is warm and friendly. There is usually a choice of pâtés on offer for around 70p, with a tasty quiche or two in the region of £1.10, as well as salads and a good cold table which includes the likes of roast beef at about £2 and liver sausage (around £1.20). The modestly-priced hot dishes change from day to day and include such dishes as baked potato with cheese filling or chili con carne, both served with salad. Home-made puds are on offer at around 70p. The wine list is French and rather extensive, but includes palatable house wines at about 65p a glass of red, white or rosé. A feature of Banners is the special functions room where lively discos are frequently held and sumptuous buffets are prepared.

MOLES, 53 High Street (Winchester 4896)
Open: Mon-Sat 9.30am-5pm

S

'Moles' is a suitably subterranean name but the place is anything but boring. It's a cheekily imaginative little bistro, sited deep down below a Design and Craft basketware shop in part of what is reputed to have been an ancient tunnel that ran from the Cathedral, beneath the Royal Mint, and thence out of town. With its pine booths, green hessian-lined walls, flagstone floors and subdued lighting, Moles makes a pleasant and convenient meeting place for shoppers and visitors. Both pizza and quiche salads are available for under £2. A typical lunch includes a choice of lasagne at around £2.10 or chicken and mushroom pie with vegetables for about £2. The delicious fresh cream gâteau comes at around 50p. The Italian house wines are in the region of 50p a glass.

MR PITKIN'S WINE BAR & EATING HOUSE 4 Jewry Street (Winchester 69630)
Open: restaurant: Sun-Thu 12noon-2pm, 7-10pm, Fri-Sat 12noon-2pm, 7-10.15pm, bar: Mon-Thu 11am-2.30pm, 6-10.30pm, Fri-Sat 11am-2.30pm, 6-11pm, Sun 12noon-2.30pm, 6-10.30pm

C ♫ S

When Tony Pitkin left the hubbub of Fleet Street advertising, he brought a little of the London life to Winchester with him. His wine bar is now one of the busiest rendezvous in the city, with live music (often jazz) five nights a week and a pleasantly trendy, Edwardian-style atmosphere. The long, narrow bar has gas-lamp-style fittings and enlarged prints of wine labels; Mr Pitkin blends into the atmosphere well with his bow tie and tweedy waistcoat. Three courses from the appetising slabs of cold meat and smoked fish, hot dishes of the day (about £1.60) and good range of starters and sweets will cost £3-£4. A chef presides over the bar's Sunday roast and Yorkshire pudding (about £2.50). The upstairs restaurant, elegant and intimate with its marble fireplace and russet walls, serves a daily lunch for around £5, but beware of the enticing items with a budget-breaking surcharge in brackets. The portions are generous, the food rich, although we found the vegetables a little over-done.

SPLINTERS ✕✕ 9 Great Minster Street (Winchester 64004)
Open: Mon-Sat 11am-2.30pm

C S

Mike and Fiona Stenets' tastefully Victorian restaurant, with its dark gold wallpaper and 'ball' lights, offers predominently French cuisine – its à la carte lunches are mainly outside our price range, but it earns a well-deserved place in the guide for the excellent-value lunches served in the brasserie, where soup of the day plus roll and butter is about 70p, quiche lorraine with salad is around £1.20 and a tasty hot dish or two, such as moussaka, crab au gratin, or globe artichokes with butter, is a little over £1.30. Desserts are from around 70p. If the ground floor is full, you can order the brasserie menu upstairs in the restaurant. The house wines, French or German, cost around 60p a 6oz glass.

THE WYKEHAM ARMS, 75 Kingsgate Street (Winchester 3834)
Open: restaurant: Mon 12noon-2.30pm, Tue-Thu 12noon-2.30pm, 7-9.45pm, Fri-Sat 12noon-2.30pm, 7-10.15pm, Sun 12noon-2pm, bar: Mon-Sat 10am-2.30pm, Sun 12noon-2pm

[P]

Stroll from the city centre through Cathedral Close to this pub in the shadow of Winchester College. In the bars, the stripped pine, country house atmosphere is complemented by customers from the college, cathedral and cricket pitch. The newly-opened restaurant (à la carte lunch £5 or under, dinner little over £6) is pleasantly like a private living room. The warm welcome from Stanley and Mary Wright adds to this impression. Diners are surprised by a free bowl of salad between starter and main course. Good, solid food is elevated from the ordinary – steak and kidney pie, prepared with Guinness or poacher's pie (rabbit and venison in cider). In the bar, try the excellent value nourishing soup (55p), herby cottage pie (90p) or hot tuna and sweetcorn quiche (£1.30). Sweets range from bread pudding (25p) to chocolate gâteau or cheesecake (70p).

Isle of Wight

Arreton

THE FIGHTING COCKS
(Arreton 254/328)
Open: Mon 12noon-2pm, Tue-Sun 12noon-2pm, 7-9.30pm

[P]

Built on the site of an inn that had stood for three centuries, and using much of the original stone, The Fighting Cocks boasts a smart restaurant specialising in grills and seafood, but also offers pork chop or grilled gammon at about £3.80. Bar snacks feature soup at 40p or so, hot dishes at around £1.50 and cold meat salads starting at around £1.90. A glass of Spanish wine costs about 50p.

Godshill

ESSEX COTTAGE RESTAURANT
High Street (Godshill 232)
Open: Etr-Oct: Tue-Sat (out of season Sat and Sun only) 12.30-5.30pm, 7.30-9pm

[C] [P] [S]

Godshill is cream tea country with more tea gardens to the square inch, probably, than any other part of the British Isles. The Essex Cottage does a very good cream tea at under £1, as well as an excellent table d'hôte lunch at around £3. Dinner, though, is out of our range. The lunch menu is basic English fare including roast pork or lamb, and cherry pie and cream. The premises are now licensed.

Newport

BUGLE HOTEL, 117 High Street (Newport 522800)
Open: during normal licensing hours

[P] [S]

The origins of the Bugle Hotel are a little obscure. It served as the Parliamentary headquarters for the Island meeting between Charles I and the Parliamentary Commissioners. Table d'hôte lunches are around £3.50, a three-course table d'hôte dinner at about £4.20 and a four-course one at around £5, which could include mushrooms au gratin, followed by fillet of sole bonne femme, roast lamb and a selection of sweets from the trolley served in the oak-panelled dining room. A three-course, bar buffet lunch costs as little as £1.50. Corrida house wine is around 60p a glass.

Shanklin

CLIFF TOPS HOTEL ★★★ Park Road (Shanklin 3262/3)
Open: Restaurant: Mon-Sun 1-2pm, 7-9pm. Coffee Shop: Mon-Sun 10am-6pm (summer only)

[C] [P] [S]

Cliff Tops calls itself the 'good food' hotel and takes great pride in its English and French cuisine. The three-course table d'hôte lunch here costs around £4, the four-course dinner about £5.50, both prices inclusive of service. For dinner, choose from six starters including avocado pear vinaigrette or asparagus in hot butter. A soup course includes consommé and rice. The main course offers hot and cold dishes, a particular delicacy being sweetbreads Valencia with Patna rice. There is an excellent choice of sweets from the trolley. A variety of cold salads are served in the Coffee Shop at prices from £1.50-£3. The Hungarian house wine (Soproni) is around 60p a glass.

THE TUDOR ROSE RESTAURANT
59 High Street (Shanklin 2814)
Open: Tue-Sun 10am-9pm

[S]

A long, mock-Tudor building, originally a bakery and tea-rooms, in which proceedings are supervised by proprietor John Barrymore Simpson. Lunchtime fare consists of a popular 'buffet lunch' with fresh salmon, cold meats and flans tantalisingly on display, followed by a choice from the sweet trolley. With a starter such as pâté or home-made soup, the whole meal is excellent value at less than £4. Wine costs about 50p a glass.

Ventnor

THE ROYAL HOTEL ★★★ Belgrave Road (Ventnor 852186)
Open: Mon-Sun 8-9.30am, 12.30-2pm, 7-9pm

[C] [P] [🍷]

The Royal does a limited but reasonably priced à la carte menu, a three-course table d'hôte lunch at around £4 and a four-course table d'hôte dinner at about £4.75, as well as the standard Trusthouse Forte platters at around £5 and a menu of children's favourites priced below £1. Dinner is a particularly appetising affair, with such dishes as smoked eels or egg Mornay for a starter followed by guinea fowl in Montmorency sauce and then perhaps fresh strawberries for dessert. A quarter bottle of the Arc de Triomphe house wine costs about £1.

Yarmouth

THE BUGLE HOTEL ★★ St James' Square (Yarmouth 760272)
Open: Mon-Sun 12.15-2pm, 7.15-9.30pm

[C] [P] [S] [🍷]

The 300-year-old Bugle, with its panelled dining room, complete with ancient stone fireplace, has a great deal of character and charm. The cuisine is international and the menu table d'hôte,

with a three-course lunch at about £4 and dinner at around £5.25. Dinner is an excellent meal, offering a good choice of dishes including dressed crab as a starter, followed by lamb's kidneys bourguignon with delicious Black Forest gâteau as dessert. The recently-enlarged Galleon Bar, with décor on a nautical theme, has cold meat salads and various snacks available from 50p-£2.

THE GEORGE HOTEL ★★ Quay Street (Yarmouth 760331)
Open: Mon-Sun 8.30-10am, 12.30-2.15pm, 7.30-9.15pm

[C] [P] [🍷]

Built by the Governor of the Island, during the reign of Charles II, the George is now a comfortable family-owned and run hotel, popular with yachties and locals. A table d'hôte lunch in the panelled dining room costs around £4.20, but dinner is now a little above our budget. The food is English traditional, with fresh vegetables and is very good. For lunch you can enjoy cucumber salad, nutty fillet of plaice, and apricot trifle. Bar snacks include hot dishes ranging in price from £1.20 for sausage and chips to about £3.80 for steak and salad. Sandwiches and lighter snacks are also available. A large glass of French wine costs around 60p.

The South East

Edged by the south-eastern coastline, and dominated by that belle of seaside resorts, Brighton, the superb unspoilt countryside of the North and South Downs and the richly-wooded Weald of Kent offer the motorist a haven of peace and tranquillity, just a short drive from London. Over the centuries the warm climate and lush fertile lands of Kent, Surrey and Sussex have yielded abundant fruit and vegetable crops. Today products of these crops may be sampled throughout the region at the inns and hostelries of ancient market towns and attractive villages or in the less rustic eateries of lively seaside resorts and modern towns.

Kent, 'the garden of England', where the blossoms of the cherry and apple orchards colour the landscape, has been associated with fruit-growing since the Middle Ages, when the gardens of large manor houses first bore the fruits of a rich soil. Then, in the 16th-century, immigrant French farmers introduced the idea of market gardens. Cherries were a particular favourite with the fruit growers, evident in the number of local dishes that are still around today, such as the light-crusted cherry pie and a special cherry batter thought to have been introduced by the Normans. Other cherry products that grace the nation's tables are the rich and dark Morello cherry jam and that warming liqueur cherry brandy.

Apple orchards bulge with the crispy green Bramley apples, the country's most popular cooking apple, and other fruits include pears, plums, strawberries and gooseberries. Kent is also renowned for its mutton from the

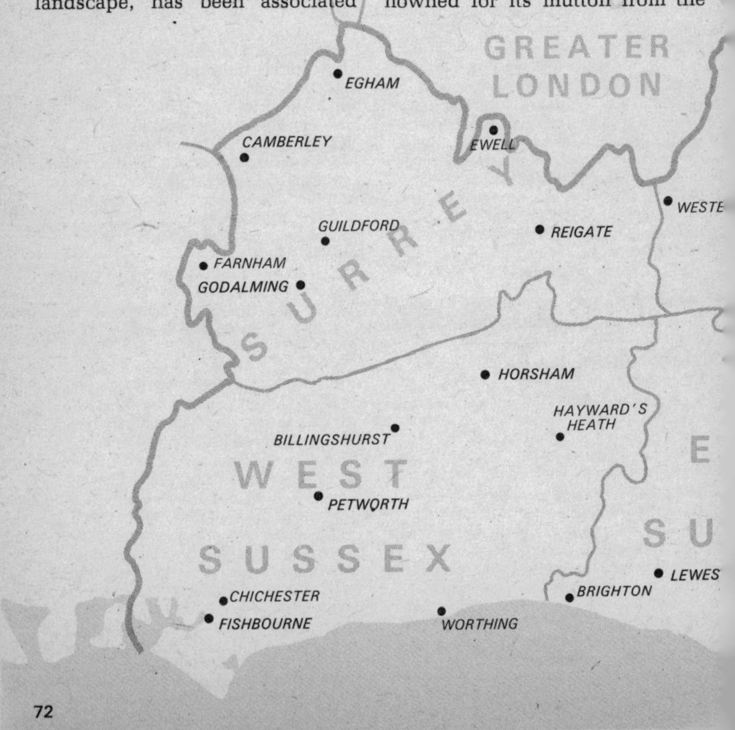

sturdy Romney Marsh sheep. This succulent meat is used as a base for a local broth and in a Kentish version of shepherd's pie.

The chalky reaches of the South Downs in neighbouring Sussex are the grazing grounds for sheep which produce the best lamb in the region. These lambs have their tails cut off when they are very young and a dish of lamb's tail pie was once a local delicacy. Sussex also has its share of fruit tarts, pies and puddings and a sweet fruit scone known by the unlikely name of Sussex heavy, but there are also many more savoury dishes in this area. Game dishes have always been a favourite here with Ashdown Forest partridge pie and Sussex rabbit the most popular. Other savouries include brawn, sausages and pork pies – all going down well with the local ale, brewed from the abundant hops grown in the area, or the locally-produced cider. Another local speciality is steak and kidney pie laced with a few oysters.

Oysters are not the only seafoods around the South East, for the rugged coastline is rich in fruits of the sea. Fish is sold fresh on the beaches of some south-eastern towns such as Hastings and Brighton. The crabs of Selsey, oysters of Whitstable, plaice and dabs of Deal, sole and other flat fish of Dover form the basis of many delicious local dishes. These and many other native delights may be sampled in some of the eating places found within the following pages.

Billingshurst

THE KING'S HEAD, High Street (Billingshurst 2921)
Open: Mon-Wed, Sun 12noon-2pm, Thu-Sat 12noon-2pm, 7-10pm

[P] [♨]

This delightful 500-year-old coaching inn in the centre of the village boasts a restaurant extension with a separate entrance from the bar – though you can partake of the cold buffet or snacks there if you are in a hurry. Fresh, home-made fare is the hallmark of the restaurant, where you could start with soup at 45p or pâté at 55p. Main dishes include steak and kidney pie for around £1.75 or lamb chops for just over £2. Good old treacle pudding is 45p, or if you prefer a lighter 'ending', try cheesecake at 55p.

OLD HOUSE, Adversane (Billingshurst 2186)
Open: Mon-Sun 10am-6pm

[P] [♨]

Mrs Baxter serves food throughout the day in this quaint, 14th-century restaurant, its two rooms with low oak-beamed ceilings displaying an abundance of antiques – some for sale. Basic English fare includes a special lunch served between 12noon-3pm for around £2.50. Soup of the day, home-made steak and kidney pie and a sweet of the day – fruit pie, ice cream or fruit salad – is a typical menu. The à la carte menu includes grills at about £2.25.

Brighton

THE CYPRIANA STEAK HOUSE AND GREEK RESTAURANT, 22 Preston Street (Brighton 202661)
Open: Mon-Sun 12noon-3pm, 6pm-1am

[C] [♫] [P] [S] [♨]

This small, intimate restaurant specialises in Scotch beef and authentic Greek food. English dishes consist of about eleven appetisers, fish, poultry, grills, flambés and omelettes. Greek specialities include as appetisers houmous or taramasalata, both at around £1. Main courses such as moussaka or stifado (beef cooked with shallots and served with rice and potatoes) cost about £3.40. Sweets from the trolley are around 75p. For a real treat, try a Meze – 'a full two-course meal consisting of fourteen delicious Greek dishes to satisfy the most discerning palate'. This is served for two or more people and costs around £4.50 per person.

DANSKE HUS, 163 Western Road (Brighton 202803)
Open: Mon-Sat 9.30am-6pm

[C] [S] [♨]

The Danes seem to be renowned in this country for open sandwiches and pastries. You'll find both here, at reasonable prices. It is time to throw your misconceptions about sandwiches being mere snacks to the wind. Try a Dane's delight for around £1 and bite through layers of roast pork, red cabbage, pickled cucumber, orange twist, prune, lettuce and rye bread! Alternatively, for between £2.50 and £4, you can linger over your selection from the Danish smørgasbrød. In addition there is an interesting international menu including baked potatoes or crêpes, stuffed with enticing fillings for about £2, and various hot meals. Apart from the selection of cakes and pastries, melt-in-the-mouth waffles with various accompaniments for around £1 will threaten your waistline.

MEETING HOUSE, Meeting House Lane (Brighton 24817)
Open: summer: Mon-Sun 8am-5.30pm, winter: Mon-Sat 8am-5.30pm

Tom and Sean Wall preside over their modern coffee shop-cum-snack bar with its wooden tables and bench seats, bright décor and counter service. Hot and cold dishes are available, including quiche lorraine and salad or steak and kidney pie at around £2, and there is also a good selection of cold meats. Starters include minestrone or French onion soup for about 30p and you can finish with a delicious Danish pastry or a slice of apple pie 70p.

TUREEN RESTAURANT, Upper North Street (Brighton 28939)
Open: Tue-Sat 12noon-2pm, 7-9pm, Sun 12noon-2pm

[C] [♫] [♨]

This unpretentious bistro-style restaurant features a large Japanese tureen in the window and floral-patterned banquettes along the walls. Cuisine is basically French and the à la carte menu offers a host of delights. Appetisers include crudités with garlic mayonnaise around £1.10, main courses to tempt you include sweetbreads in white wine, cream and mushroom sauce at about £3, and Mexican fillet steak for a little more. Desserts may cost from about £1 and a large glass of wine around 70p. A special table d'hôte menu for lunch and dinner is superb value: home-made soup, pork fillet baked in cider and sweet costs just over £3.50.

Broadstairs

THE MAD CHEF'S BISTRO, The Harbour (Thanet 65304)
Open: summer: Mon-Sun 10am-12mdnt, winter: Mon 10am-12mdnt, Wed-Sun 10am-12mdnt

[C] [P] [⚘]

Paul Ward is the Mad Chef at this little bistro on the harbour at Broadstairs. The emphasis here is on freshly caught fish and seafood. Lobster and turbot can be expensive but sample the lunchtime Quickies menu which includes crab or cockle and mussel omelettes for around £1.20. The à la carte menu offers other specialities such as pheasant and turkey pie or mixed meat kebabs, both at around £4. Starters include gazpacho, and there is a huge list of tempting sweets. Lovers of Dickensian memorabilia will be interested to note that the Mad Chef's is situated between Dickens' House Museum and Bleak House.

Camberley

ROBBO'S WINE BAR, 125 London Road (Camberley 21096)
Open: Tue-Thu 10.30am-2.30pm,

5.30-10.30pm, Fri-Sat 10.30am-2.30pm, 5.30-11pm, Sun 7-10.30pm

[♫] [P] [S]

Peter and Maggie Robinson sailed dozens of times around the world as pursers on cruise liners before berthing with their own 'Robbo's Wine Bar' at the top of the High Street. Signs of their travels are the cosmopolitan selection of wines including exotic 'specials' such as Tuscany Vernacchia 1977 at £3.50 which Petter dispenses from a grand oak bar. House wines include three whites – a dry Loire, a medium Liebfraumilch and a sweet Premieres Côtes de Bordeaux – a Côtes du Rhone and a Rose D'anjou – around £2.80 a bottle or 50p a glass. From the galley-type kitchen Maggie produces starters which include egg mimosa and grapefruit New Yorker, with dinner dishes at under £3 which range from a traditional herby boeuf bourguignon to tangy kidneys in mustard sauce. As befits a wine bar opposite gates of the Army Staff College, locals mix easily with future Field Marshals resplendent in their blazers and cavalry twills. And, if you feel like sampling the mystique of the east, ask Peter for shut-the-box, an undiscovered board game from India.

Canterbury

ALBERRY'S WINE AND FOOD BAR
38 St Margarets Street
(Canterbury 52378)
Open: Mon-Thu 11.30am-2.30pm, 6-10.30pm, Fri-Sat 11.30-2.30pm, 6-11pm, Sun 6-10.30pm

[C] [♫] [P] [S]

A genuine Roman pavement in the basement bar is the talking point of this establishment, where for the price of a steak sandwich you buy a whole evening of entertainment. Jazz, rock and folk musicians often play beneath the arched ceilings. A good selection of wholesome food includes quiche and salad for around £2 and the very popular steak sandwiches served with salad for about £3, with a variety of fresh fruit (such as pineapple and mangoes) for a nourishing last course.

CANTERBURY SHELL FISH CENTRE
78 Broad Street, (Canterbury 65442)
Open: summer: Tue-Fri 6-10pm, Sat 12noon-2.30pm, 6-10pm

[C] [♫] [P] [S] [🍷]

Located over the shellfish shop, this small and simple restaurant can justifiably claim to enjoy a reputation for its fresh fish. Besides the more usual seafood dishes, bass, eel, salmon, mullet and oysters are available in season and there are several 'non-fish' dishes to add variety to the menu. A fixed-menu is good value at a little under £4 for three courses and coffee, with a glass of house wine extra at about 50p.

TUO E MIO, 16 The Borough
(Canterbury 61471)
Open: Wed-Sun 12noon-2pm, Tue-Sun 7-11pm

[C] [♫] [P] [S] [🍷]

This cosy Italian restaurant is run by energetic proprietors Raffaele and Patricia Greggio. Unusual dishes such as quails, guinea fowl and pigeon are available on the à la carte menu for about £4 including potatoes, as well as the more predictable veal, chicken and pasta selection – all at around the £3 mark. Desserts are all about 70p and a half carafe of house wine costs £1.50.

Chichester

THE COFFEE HOUSE, 4 West Street
(Chichester 784799)
Open: Mon-Sat 10am-5.30pm
(half-day Thu during winter months)

[S]

Emphasis here is upon simple, no-nonsense food made from fresh ingredients and cooked on the premises. Plats du jour, including shrimp or chicken salads cost from £1.10 upwards. Three-egg plain omelettes are also available, as is Welsh rarebit at around 55p. The licensed restaurant menu is restricted but it's excellent value, particularly the cold buffet dishes at around £1-£1.75. House wines sell at about 45p a glass.

JASON'S BISTRO, Cooper Street, off South Street (Chichester 783158)
Open: Mon-Sun 12noon-2pm, 7.30-10.30pm

[♫] [S]

Keith Privett serves bistro-style lunches and dinners in this spacious and imaginatively-modernised old outhouse building. Starters, including home-made soup with hot garlic bread range from about 50p to £1.30. The 'Chef's Dish of the Day' is usually an excellent buy at around £1; other main courses cost between £1.25 and £2.50, including vegetables.

Deal

HARE AND HOUNDS, The Street,

Northbourne (Deal 65429)
Open: Mon-Sun 12noon-2.30pm, 7-11pm

[C] [P]

You can enjoy an excellent steak and kidney pie for around £1.50 at this charming country pub. Alternatively, you can sample one of the large variety of home-made quiches. Delicious soups are also home-made. A glass of wine costs about 55p.

Eastbourne

NEW LOUNGE, 4 Cornfield Terrace (Eastbourne 31309)
Open: Tue-Sun 11.45am-2pm

[P] [🍷]

Joyce Ellis prepares good, plain English fare in this family-run restaurant. A table d'hôte lunch offers a choice of soup or fruit juice followed by fish, roasts, steak and kidney pie, liver and bacon or cold buffet. Puddings include home-made fruit pie and custard or orange mousse for an all-inclusive price of around £2.25. A glass of house wine costs about 50p.

Egham

MAGGIE'S WINE BAR, 2 St Judes Road, Englefield Green (Egham 37397)
Open: Mon-Thu 11am-2.30pm 7-10.30pm, Fri-Sat 11am-2.30pm, 7-11pm, Sun 12noon-2pm, 7-10.30pm

[C] [♫] [P] [S] [🍷]

If you are energetic enough you can 'do' the Runnymede Memorial, the Kennedy Memorial, the RAF Memorial, and still be in time for Sunday brunch at Maggie's. If you wrongly feel that Sunday brunch at under £2 is not filling enough, enjoy a traditional three-course roast meal with a free glass of wine at under £4. Afterwards you can watch Prince Charles play polo at nearby Windsor Great Park, or you could stay with the Sunday papers that are provided. Sue de Barra, a Cordon Bleu cook, creates daily menus which include unusual soups such as egg and prawn at around 70p, home-made pâtés at around 90p, moussaka and lasagne at around £2, speciality creole and paella dishes, and for the trencherman, an English sirloin steak platter at £4.60. Partner Bob Grahamshaw shares the cooking even after a hard day in London selling an exotic brand of Swedish motor car.

Ewell

THE GRAPE VINE, 2 Cheam Road (01-393 8522)
Open: Mon-Sat 10.30am-2.30pm, 5.30-10.30pm

[♫] [P]

This stylish wine bar is a hub of activity in this suburban Surrey village. One attraction is the dazzling array of bargain-priced food – game pie and salad at only around £1, a selection of home-made quiches with salad also about £1 and lasagne at around £1.40. Cheesecakes, gâteaux or home-made apple pie are all about 60p. Wines by the glass start at around 60p.

Farnham

SEVENS, 7 The Borough (Farnham 715345)
Open: Mon-Sat 12noon-2.30pm, 6.30-10.30pm, (Fri-Sat 11pm)

[C] [♫] [S]

Sevens has an intimate atmosphere – from the crowded wine bar at the front to the low-ceilinged bistro at the rear and on the first floor. Starters range from about 60p-£1.30 and include a delicious mushroom pâté. Main courses start at around £2.40 for lasagne or chili con carne to about £4 for rump steak with dishes like coq au vin, barbecued beef and sweet and sour pork in between at around £3.50. Sweets and cheeses are all about 85p and there is a good choice of wine by the glass from around 60p.

Faversham

CHIMNEY BOY, Preston Street (Faversham 2007)
Open: Mon-Sat 11am-3pm, 5.30-11pm, Sun 12noon-2pm, 6-10pm

[P]

Husband-and-wife team Jackie and Tony Richards run this pub-cum-restaurant built on a Roman burial ground. They offer eight starters and a selection of about twelve main courses of the traditional type – steak, chicken, scampi and salads. A three-course set lunch will cost about £2.50, but be warned – portions are gigantic!

THE RECREATION TAVERN RESTAURANT, 16 East Street (Faversham 6033)
Open: Mon-Sun 12noon-2pm, 7-10pm

[C] [♫] [P] [S] [🍷]

Once a 17th-century, square oast house, this small tavern has been tastefully restored by the present owner. You can choose from a dozen salads or various quiches accompanied by salad plus

coffee for around £1.50. You may also be tempted by one of Graham's delectable sweets. Interesting hot dishes are always available at around £5 with vegetables.

Fishbourne

THE BLACK BOY (Bosham 572076)
Open: Mon-Thu 12noon-2.15pm, 6.30-9.30pm, Fri-Sat 12noon-2.15pm, 6.30-10.30pm, Sun 12noon-2.15pm

P ☘

This charming 17th-century inn is sited on the A27 just west of Chichester. Dark beams and gleaming brass and copper set the scene in the bar and small restaurant. Hot and cold snacks are served in the bar, where in addition to the usual ploughman's and sandwiches, three courses may be enjoyed. Starters include prawn cocktail or whitebait – both at 85p. Most main courses come complete with French fries and peas. They range from fillet steak at £3.95 to pizza at just over £1. Particularly good value dishes are chicken at £1.55, pork chop at £1.70 and scampi, plaice or gammon for £1.75. Cheesecake is around 45p and a glass of wine costs 55p.

Folkestone

PULLMAN WINE BAR, 7 Church Street (Folkestone 52524)
Open: Tue-Sat 12noon-2pm, 7-9.30pm

♫ P S ☘

The Tudor-style building housing Kim and Pamela Pardoe's wine bar is thought by some to be the most beautiful in Folkestone. Hot and cold dishes are presented buffet style. Soup is around 60p and a main dish, such as chicken with cider and calvados costs about £2.75. Sweets are about 90p and French wine is around 50p a glass. In fine weather, meals may be enjoyed in the attractive garden.

Godalming

MAIGRETS BISTRO, 78 High Street (Godalming 29191)
Open: Mon-Fri 12.30-2.30pm, 7.30-10pm, Sat 7.30-10pm

C ♫ S ☘

You won't find any trench-coated French police inspector in this quaint olde-worlde restaurant. Maigret, in this case, is the name of the pleasant lady owner and cook, Maigret Bricusse. The interior is a cosy low-ceilinged, beamed and half-panelled room which is all the more romantic in the evening, by candlelight. Bay windows overlook the main shopping street of Godalming. A blackboard menu offers a selection of well-cooked dishes at reasonable cost. A sample meal might include starters of avocado viniagrette or taramasalata at around 75p, main dishes such as chicken Somerset cooked in cider with celery and vegetables for about £2 or a selection of salads with prices starting at £1.55. Sweets cost 65p and there's as much coffee as you can drink for 35p. With wine at 60p per glass you should manage a meal here for less than £5.

Guildford

THE CASTLE RESTAURANT, 2 South Hill (Guildford 63729)
Open: Mon-Sat 12noon-2pm, 5.30-11.30pm (last orders 9.30pm) Sun 12noon-2pm

P

The older part of this restaurant blends well with the garden effect of the extension, with its stone floor and brick walls. Table d'hôte lunches cost around £4 for two courses or £4.50 for three courses. Seafood pancake is one of eight interesting starters on offer, and of eleven main courses, kidneys with mushrooms in red wine sauce is recommended. The list of sweets is impressive, chestnut ice cream sundae being one of the more unusual examples. Dinner is around £1 extra.

PEWS WINE BAR, 21 Chapel Street (Guildford 35012)
Open Mon-Sat 11.45am-2.30pm, 6.30-11.30pm (Fri-Sat 12mdnt)

♫ S ☘

David Allen runs Pews with flair and a

friendly smile. Formerly an old ale house, the building's split-level rooms have dark beams and wood panelling, but are bright with log fires in their proper season and fresh flowers all the year round. The blackboard menu has a choice of hot dishes, from around £1.80, for example chicken Portugaise and chili con carne and a variety of curries.

YVONNE ARNAUD RESTAURANT
Millbrook (Guildford 69334)
Open: Mon-Sat 12.30-2pm, 6.15-11pm

[C] [P] [S]

You won't go far in Guildford without seeing mention of the Yvonne Arnaud Theatre. A set lunch in the curved Theatre Restaurant costs about £4 for two courses and around £4.50 for three. The menu is constantly changing, as a high percentage of patrons are regular play-goers. Evening meals are excellent, but alas, out of our league.

Hastings

CROSSWAYS, Lower Pett Road, Fairlight (Pett 2356)
Open: Tue-Sun 12.30-2.30pm, 7.30-10pm

[P]

Well-prepared, good-value English cooking is the keynote of this small restaurant, looking very like a modern village home at the crossroads in Fairlight. A three-course lunch costs only about £2.50 and offers such old favourites as home-made steak and kidney or chicken and mushroom pies, roast beef with Yorkshire pud or roast chicken. Sweets, also home-made, include blackcurrant and apple pie or rhubarb crumble. The dinner menu is à la carte and more exotic fare such as rainbow trout with almonds (around £2.30) is available. With starters ranging from 25p for soup of the day to 80p for prawn cocktail and desserts from 40p, you will easily be able to afford a glass of house wine at 55p.

Hayward's Heath

COUNTRY AND WINE, 124 South Road (Haywards Heath 58040)
Open: Mon-Sat 10am-8.30pm

[C] [♫] [P] [S]

This modern bistro specialises in home-cooked fresh food and choice wines. Décor is unpretentious, with blue and white checked tablecloths, benches and simple wooden chairs. The menu includes various cold meat salads and a hot dish such as chicken casserole at about £2.50. Home-made soup and pâté are tasty starters at around 90p and sweets include gâteaux.

Herne Bay

LA CHANDELLE, Charles Street (Herne Bay 61126)
Open: Tue-Sat 12noon-2pm, 7-10.30pm, Sun 12noon-2pm

[C] [♫] [P]

This French restaurant provides informal eating in the downstairs quiche bar, where various flans are served with fresh salad at about £1.25. Sweets include chocolate brandy cake at around 80p. In the main restaurant the table d'hôte lunch includes avocado and prawns, grilled pork cutlets, a sweet and coffee for about £3.50.

Horsham

MERRYTHOUGHT RESTAURANT
5 Bishopric (Horsham 4894)
Open: Mon-Sat 9.30am-5pm, Sat 12noon-2.30pm

Michael and Margaret Bance welcome

you to their small Victorian-style restaurant where snacks are served all day and a comprehensive lunch menu operates from 12noon to 2.30pm. A three-course meal for *two* people may be savoured here for around £5. Soup is only around 25p and main dishes such as boiled ham, beef curry or salads are about £1.50. Puddings such as fruit salad vary in price from 40p-50p. Merrythought is unlicensed, so you will have to wash down your meal with a cup of steaming coffee at 30p.

Lewes

BARBICAN, High Street (Lewes 5996)
Open: Mon-Sat 12noon-2.30pm, 7-10.30pm

[symbol]

This 17th-century building in the centre of town has a restaurant on the ground floor and a snack bar in the basement. Proprietor David Fuller supervises and snacks are served all day, separate menus operating for lunch and dinner. Lunch is a meal to suit all pockets, with prices ranging from below 30p for fruit juice to around £5 for fillet steak. Starters include soup of the day (40p) and corn on the cob (65p). Cottage pie, steak and kidney pie, chicken curry, lasagne and moussaka are all well below £2 and a selection of nine salads are offered, eight of which are also below £2. Fish fingers, peas and chips or sausages and chips are children's lunches available for less than £1. A good selection of puddings such as lemon meringue pie, fresh cream trifle or cheesecake are around 60p. The dinner menu is more sophisticated in both selection and price, but it is possible to enjoy a meal such as white-bait, chili con carne and lemon sorbet for around £5. A glass of house wine costs 55p.

PAUL'S WINE BAR, 53 High Street (Lewes 4676)
Open: summer: Mon-Thu 12noon-2.30pm, 6-10.30pm, Fri-Sat 12noon-2.30pm, 6-11pm, winter: Sat 6-10pm

[♫] [P]

Original oak beams in this 400-year-old building lend atmosphere to this wine bar which operates on two floors. The printed menu offers budget grills – sirloin or rump steak is only about £2.50 and lamb cutlets £2. The cold buffet includes smoked mackerel or turkey at 90p. Chef's Daily Specials are highly recommended and veal and mushroom pie at around £1 or beef goulash at £1.20 are examples. Gâteaux (50p), fruit salad (45p) and ice cream (35p) are some of the sweets available. A glass of house wine is 55p. In the evening you may savour your food to the sound of the guitar.

Petworth

THE LICKFOLD INN, Lodsworth, 3 miles west of Petworth off A272 (Lodsworth 285)
Open: normal licensing hours

[P]

Real ale fanatics will feel at home at this old hostelry and free house, serving a wide selection of beer from the wood. To soak up their liquid intake, they might also be interested in the lunchtime menu of home-made steak and kidney pie, moussaka and other hot dishes, plus a good range of snacks and sandwiches for under £2. Evening meals include Mexican lamb cutlets, halibut mornay and mignon of beef chasseur, all around £3.60. Add a starter (whitebait?) and a sweet such as chocolate rum crunch to make a really memorable meal. House wine is about 55p a glass.

Reigate

PEER GYNT, Church Street (Reigate 21286)
Open: Mon 10.30am-2.30pm, Tue-Sat 10.30am-2.30pm, 7-10pm

[C] [P] [S] [symbol]

The delightful originality of this Norwegian restaurant is well worth a lunch-time visit (although open in the evening, the set price is around £10). Even the illustrated guide round the smørgasbrød is a veritable adventure in menus. And don't be put off by the hideous trolls staring out of the windows; inside, wood-panelled walls, wooden lampshades and Norwegian fabrics make a pleasant atmosphere. The lunch-time smørgasbrød at around £4 includes soup and as much as you can eat from the array of meat, fish, vegetables, fruits and desserts. There may be an opportunity to try roast leg of reindeer, or a selection of Norwegian smoked fish. Alternatively, a three-course meal for around £3 is available at lunch-time, with a central hot dish such as Scandinavian meatballs.

Sandwich

16TH CENTURY TEA HOUSE, 9 Cattle Market (Sandwich 612392)

Open: Mon-Sun 9am-6pm, 7-11pm

P S

Set in the market square of the picturesque old town is this historic 16th-century building with a quaint, beamed restaurant. A three-course lunch is served here for around £3.20. Appetisers include Normandy pâté with toast or hors d'oeuvres. Home-made steak and kidney pie or sweet and

sour chicken with special fried rice are two of the five main courses on offer, and desserts such as chocolate nut sundae or baked lemon curd roll complete the meal. A suggested evening dish is grilled gammon steak Hawiian style which, with starter and sweet costs around £4.30.

Tunbridge Wells

BRUINS, 5 London Road (Tunbridge Wells 35757)
Open: Mon-Sat 12noon-3pm, 7-11pm

C ♫ P S

Good food, good wine, good ale and great company are what Randy and Gill Brown, owners of Bruin's, view as life's *'bear necessities'*. All three are taken care of in this split-level bistro-style restaurant, decorated in shades of brown and adorned with an assortment of teddy bears that give the restaurant its name. Choices from the long and varied menu include starters such as home-made French onion soup at around 60p, and main courses like whole baby chicken provençale (around £3.95) or Bruin's casserole at about £3. Dessert choices for around 75p include pancakes, apple crumble and ices. Bruins burgers (100% beef) make a cheap and satisfying main course at around £2, including French fries, salad and relish. A range of bar snacks are available on the first-floor bar.

Westerham

THE HENRY WILKINSON, 26 Market Square (Westerham 64245)
Open: Mon-Thu 11.30am-3pm, 6.30-10.30pm, Fri-Sat 11.30am-3pm, 7-11pm

S

This small wine bar has a cellar restaurant with pine tables and a good choice of home-made casseroles and soups, fresh salads, savoury flans and pies. The blackboard menu displays the special hot dish of the day for lunch and supper, which is usually served with potatoes or rice and a green salad. Desserts include meringue glacée and a pudding of the day for around 75p. With a glass of one of the many wines on offer, a three-course meal costs from £4 upwards.

Worthing

HAPPY CHEESE, Liverpool Buildings, Liverpool Road (Worthing 201074)
Open: Mon-Sat 8am-5.30pm

♫ S

Two floors are devoted to this modern eating place and bar. A wallboard menu offers such dishes as home-made soup, roast chicken with vegetables, pizzas and salads. A three-course meal with coffee and wine need not cost more than £5.

Cotswolds and Chilterns

The hilly Cotswold landscape abounds with honey-coloured stone villages and a generous sprinkling of some of the finest old churches in England. Built in the days of the 16th and 17th centuries, when the West Country wool trade formed the basis of Britain's prosperity, these places of worship have become known as the 'wool churches' and are renowned for their architecture. All this, combined with the solemn beauty of the neighbouring Chiltern hills, makes this a region with plenty to arrest the eye, while its fertile soil yields many wholesome foods to tempt the taste buds.

Running through the region are two majestic rivers: the Thames and the Severn, which combined with the clear, small trout streams provide a delicate diet of fresh fish for all who desire it. Every spring sees shoals of tiny eels making their way up river against the current, where they are quickly caught and relished by the local fishermen. Succulent salmon is also plentiful here; it is claimed that Severn salmon is moister than that from the River Wye because of its longer spell in tidal waters. Marvellous specimens of the fish can be seen on display in local fish shops, whereas many local restaurants serve them fresh and lightly

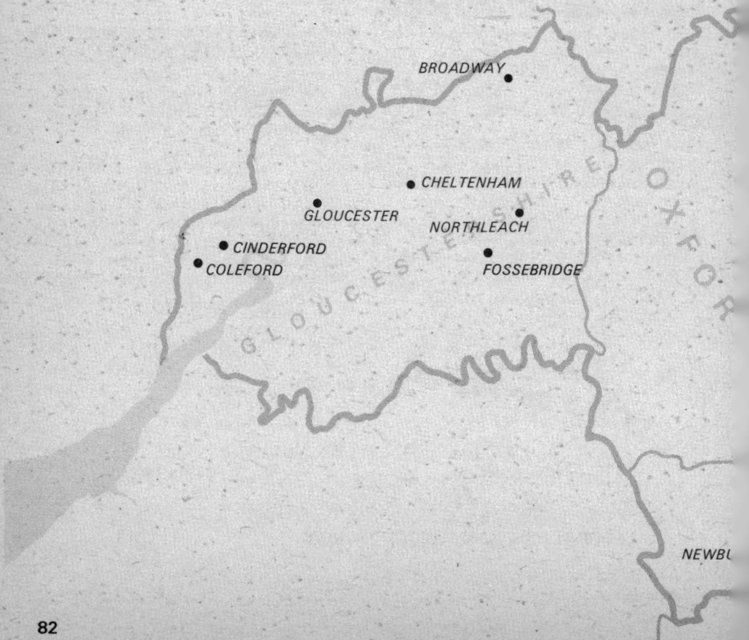

poached, with glorious sauces.

Plenty of attractions exist in this part of the country, embracing as it does so many world-famous places. Some have a royal and regal flavour, such as Windsor, second home of the Royal Family. A local speciality which is, indeed, fit for a Queen, is the rich Brown Windsor soup with a dash of Madeira. For those who enjoy the sporting life, there is Ascot, where that renowned race course will always draw the crowds, or the annual regatta at Henley-on-Thames. Oxford, the beautiful and most historic university town, has one or two local specialities to its name. Highly-seasoned marrow bones served with toast, or sweet Oxford sauce – delicious with Aylesbury duckling.

Gloucestershire cheese-making stems from very early days and developed into a cottage industry during the 17th century. Single Gloucester cheese has become extinct, but the orange-coloured Double Gloucester remains very popular and is used in many local dishes. Another delicacy of this region is Gloucester sauce, made from mayonnaise flavoured with cayenne pepper, chopped chives, a dash of lemon juice, Worcestershire sauce and a little sour cream. It is usually served as a tasty accompaniment to meat salads.

In short, the Cotswold and Chilterns region offers a wealth of famous places and tasty food.

4

Amersham

BEAR PIT BAR AND BISTRO
Whielden Street (Amersham 21958)
Open: Mon-Sun 12noon-2.30pm; Sun-Thu 7-10.30pm; Fri-Sat 7-11pm

[C]

A bear-baiting pit can still be seen inside this delightful, period bistro which is almost concealed in the courtyard of the 16th-century Saracen's Head pub. The raftered ceiling is emphasised by whitewashed brick walls and glowing dark furniture. The room is a perfect blend of antiquity and comfort. Proprietor David Short has arranged a comprehensive and interesting menu. 'Beginnings' include 'Bloody Mary' soup (70° proof – B. marvellous!) or grilled smoked mackerel, both under £1. Main courses are from around £2. Particularly recommended is a spicy chili con carne served with a crisp salad and hot pitta bread. The French dressing is outstanding. Alternatives include marinated beef kebab, gammon, trout, steak, crab salad Louis or Bear Pit Burgers. 'Endings' offer a good choice and chocolate gâteau with whipped cream is about £1. A glass of wine costs around 60p.

THE ELEPHANT AND CASTLE, High Street (Amersham 6410)
Open: summer: Mon-Sun 12noon-2pm, 7-9.30pm

[C] [P] [♧]

This historic pub, covered with climbing roses, offers good-value, well-prepared meals for the hungry public. Steak pie and two veg or Spanish omelette are popular choices costing around £2 and £2.25 respectively. You can take lunch in any part of the low-beamed, olde-worlde pub that takes your fancy, and in addition, there's a small-budget à la carte menu offering mostly grills. French house wine costs around 50p a glass. Children are welcome in the pleasant beer garden.

THE HIT OR MISS INN, Penn Street Village (High Wycombe 713109)
Open: Mon-Sun 12noon-2pm, 6.30-10pm. Closed: last week in Jul, first week in Aug

[P]

Within range of six from its own cricket ground across the road – any customer can join its own club and play – this aptly-named wisteria-covered 17th-century inn is a big hit with the locals and visitors alike. In the Cricketers Bar, they can also enjoy an excellent selection of home-cooked fare available every day for lunch or dinner. Chef's pâté and toast is about 95p, spaghetti bolognese around £1.70, and strawberries when in season about 45p, or try a 'steak butty' – sirloin steak grilled with onion and garlic, sandwiched in French bread and costing around £1.90. In addition, the restaurant serves an excellent three-course budget menu at lunchtime for about £5. Choice is wide – prawn and tomato medley, sauté of beef paprika and peach fool is a good example.

PAUPERS, 11 Market Square (Amersham 7221)
Open: Mon-Sun 12noon-2pm, 7-10pm

[C] [P] [♧]

Situated close to the parish church of St Marys, Paupers is housed in an attractive cottage with its black and white Tudor-style exterior gaily decorated with brass coach lamps and striped awnings. Inside is a warm 17th-century room which retains much of the period atmosphere with an inglenook fireplace, exposed beams, polished oak tables and pew seating. The menu offers two set dinners, two courses for less than £5 and three courses for nearly £6. Appetisers include mushroom pâté or prawn salad with seafood sauce and a choice of six main dishes includes lemon chicken or baked bream. You may finish with an excellent home-made sweet from the trolley.

Aylesbury

THE BODEGA WINE BAR, The Market Square (Aylesbury 27582)
Open: Mon-Thu 11am-2.30pm, 6.30-10.30pm, Fri-Sat 11am-2.30pm,

6.30-10.30pm, Sun 7-10.30pm

[P] [S]

The Bodega from the 18th century, is all that remains from the days of the historic George Hotel, which boasts a tunnel, used by Roundheads, under the Market Square. This sophisticated, well-decorated wine bar offers food cooked to perfection. A blackboard lists several delicious French pâtés or taramasalata at around £1, topside of beef for about £2.50 (including kous-kous or coleslaw) and American cheesecake for around 65p. The 1981 menu will include some German dishes.

THE HEN AND CHICKENS AT AYLESBURY, Oxford Road (Aylesbury 82193)
Open: Mon-Sat 12noon-2pm, Tue-Wed 7-10pm, Fri-Sat 7-11pm

[P]

This popular pub with its attractive ship-boarding stands on the Oxford Road roundabout close to the original 'Aylesbury duck' pond. Norman Haggan, the genial landlord welcomes you to the pleasant restaurant, tastefully furnished with pinewood tables and dresser and adorned by candles on the tables. The well-prepared food is very good value for money and Nicki, the chef, will be pleased to tell you about the recipes. Starters include delicious smoked mackerel (about 80p) and among the interesting main courses are pork chops in honey sauce at around £2.70, Aylesbury duckling at about £4 and speciality mixed grill (around £3), Traditional English Pudding of the Day costs about 60p and a glass of French wine 50p.

Bedford

GREEK VILLAGER RESTAURANT
36 St Peters Street (Bedford 41798)
Open: Mon-Tue 6pm-1am, Wed-Sat 6pm-2am, Sun 6-11.30pm; Closed: first two weeks in Aug

[♫] [P] [S]

Bursting with authentic atmosphere and cuisine, this taverna is a fun restaurant not to be missed. Mock Tudor beams and wagon wheel lighting make an attractive décor in the restaurant. As well as the usual taramasalata, tsatsiki and houmous, starters include delicious horiatiki salata topped with crumbly fetta cheese and olives (about 90p). You are spoiled for choice with main dishes. Dolmades for around £3 is particularly full of flavour. Greek sweets include baklava, siamali and kateifi and are about 70p each. A glass of Greek wine is around £1.

THE WINE BAR, 28 Harpur Street (Bedford 50606)
Open: Mon-Sat 11.30am-2.30pm

[C] [♫] [S] [♣]

This new wine bar is pleasantly decorated in the modern style on the ground floor of L'escalier club. Lunches only are served here, since the club takes over by night. Carved lamb and beef are highly recommended, as are daily specials such as liver and onions or deep fried chicken, both around £2. A help-yourself buffet which includes salad costs about £2.

Berkhamsted

PATRICIA'S RESTAURANT
40a Lower Kings Road
(Berkhamsted 2048)
Open: Mon-Sun 12noon-2.30pm, 3-5.30pm (teas), 7-9pm Closed: Wed

[♫] [P]

This warm, friendly and comfortable restaurant is a family-run business with father and daughter doing the cooking and Patricia attending to the diners' needs in the restaurant. Emphasis is on

English food, and table d'hôte lunch and dinner menus are offered from as little as £2. Traditional Sunday lunch is available. The à la carte menu offers all the good basic meat and fish dishes. Prices range from around £2 for roast beef or pork to about £5 for mixed grill. Sorry, no children under fourteen years.

Bishop's Stortford

THE SWAN RESTAURANT
88 South Street
(Bishop's Stortford 52007/59439)
Open: Mon-Sat 9am-9.30pm,
Sun 12noon-2.30pm

C ♫ P S

A delightful Regency-style frontage with attractive half curtains on brass rails tempts you to explore further into this restaurant. Once inside you will not be disappointed; a bright, modern and comfortable eating place with a menu of good wholesome dishes, awaits your approval. On the à la carte menu, the home-made soups and selection of omelettes are to be recommended, although more exotic dishes such as melon liqueur and Porterhouse steak garni are offered at prices coming close to our limit. A daily lunch menu costs around £3 for three courses plus coffee, with Sunday lunch at around £4.50 for adults, half price for children.

Broadway

COTSWOLD CAFE AND RESTAURANT, The Green
(Broadway 853395)
Open: summer: Mon-Fri 10am-6pm, Sat-Sun 10am-8pm, winter: Mon-Sat 10am-5.30pm, Sun 10am-6pm

The Cotswold Cafe and Restaurant has counted amongst its customers John Wayne and the pop group Genesis. Perhaps they were attracted by the servery at the front of this quaint Cotswold-stone building where delicious home-made ice creams are for sale, a speciality of Mrs Susan Webb's family since 1945. The restaurant serves snacks and three-course à la carte meals throughout the day, with prices varying from about £2.50 for cod and chips to around £5 for fillet steak.

THE GALLERY RESTAURANT
North Street (Broadway 853555)
Open: Tue-Sun 11am-9pm. Closed: Jan

P

James Hunt and Jody Scheckter competed with former racing driver Geddes Yeates in the Formula 3 racing circuits – as photographs in Geddes' charming restaurant show. A former

16th-century coach house, the white-painted interior has a wealth of black timbers supporting the barn-type ceiling and a minstrel's gallery at the far end. A special three-course lunch includes fresh orange juice, roast beef and Yorkshire pudding and a choice of desserts such as lemon meringue pie, sherry trifle or gâteaux for around £2.50. Lunchtime specials offered include home-made steak and kidney pie, fried chicken or cod – all for around £1.25, and a children's menu is available. The à la carte menu provides mainly grills, from about £1.40-£4.50.

GOBLETS WINE BAR, High Street (Broadway 852258)
Open: summer: Mon-Sun 12noon-1.45pm, 7-9.30pm, winter: Mon-Fri 11.30am-2.30pm, 6-10.30pm, Sat 6-11pm, Sun 12noon-2pm, 7-11pm

[C] [♫] [P] [S]

Dating back to 1631, this stone-built one-time inn is now a thriving wine bar. A stone-flagged floor with scatter rugs, and black and white half-timbered walls adorned by tapestry panels make an ideal setting for the numerous antiques. Imaginative home cooking by Gill Gillet and a warm welcome from Jane Noble have made Goblets very popular with the locals. Appetisers include home-made mackerel and apple pâté at around 90p and Andulusian gazpacho (chilled tomato soup with garlic, onions and peppers) at around 85p. Chicken à la Indienne (strips of chicken in mild curry and peach sauce) is about £2.50, with honeyed pork or beef and prune casserole in the same price bracket. Desserts include Goblets gâteau (about 75p). A glass of very good house wine costs around 55p.

Buckingham

THE OLD MARKET HOUSE
The High Street (Buckingham 2385)
Open: Mon-Sun 12noon-2.15pm, 7-9.15pm. Closed: Sun and Mon pm

[♫] [P] [S] [&]

The delightful, beautifully restored 14th-century half-timbered building immediately commands attention. The superb restaurant offers outstanding value for money. Table d'hôte lunch is from £2.50 and dinner (from £2.75) includes a starter, fish course, main course and sweet, with coffee extra at around 25p. The à la carte menu is also extremely reasonable with an exciting choice for all courses. Potted shrimps, trout in almonds and orange surprise will cost around £4.50. A glass of Spanish wine is only about 50p. As a bonus, Bernard the chef will tell you a tale or two, and you can treat yourself to a box of chocs from the adjoining shop.

Cheltenham

COTSWOLD HOTEL, 17 Portland Street (Cheltenham 23998)
Open: Mon-Sat: Bar snacks: 12noon-2pm

[C] [P] [S] [&]

What the Cotswold would be like without Con Carroll is anybody's guess. For fifteen years he has presided over this ground floor bar, earning it an enviable name for superb lunchtime bar snacks.
Centrepiece of the lunch operation is the carvery, offering hot roast beef, turkey and home-cooked ham with

salad or vegetables, as well as smoked or fresh salmon with salad. A selection of starters and sweets are available and a satisfying three-course meal can be enjoyed for around £5.

FORREST'S WINE HOUSE
Imperial Lane (Cheltenham 38001)
Open: Mon-Sat 10.30am-2.30pm, 6-10.30pm

[♫] [P] [S]

Forrest's is tucked away in Imperial Lane just behind Habitat and is a useful venue at lunchtime or during the evening with the cinema nearby. The large, high-ceilinged ground-floor premises was formerly a bakery but has been cleverly adapted, with low-slung pendant lights and intimate eating areas cordoned off by waist-high walls. There are over twenty wines sold by the glass here at prices from about 55p to 75p. The menu changes daily but a typical one might well include a choice of soups at around 45p, a Continental ploughman's (with sausages) or a pizza with tossed salad, both at about £1 and a choice of three enticing plats du jour such as beef casserole with red wine and mushrooms, or grilled rump steak from just £2 to around £3.

MISTER TSANG ✕ 63 Winchcombe Street (Cheltenham 38727)
Open: Mon-Sun 11.30am-2.30pm, 6-11.30pm

[C] [S] [🍷]

Food 'to indulge the palate and encourage good health' is what Mister Tsang and his family aim to provide. The authentic Cantonese cuisine and seafood specialities on which the restaurant prides itself are prepared so that the maximum nutritious value, taste and colour are retained. We were impressed by the house hors d'oeuvres at about £1.60, beef in black bean sauce (around £2.70) and king prawns with ginger and spring onions. To keep within the budget and do justice to the extensive menu, go with a friend or three! The seafood pot (a secret recipe, costing about £4.50) serves two, and Mister Tsang's 'Introduction to True Cantonese Cuisine' for two or more people works out at about £3.20 a head for a good variety. Desserts include Chinese toffee apples and are £1 or less.

MONTPELLIER WINE BAR AND BISTRO, Bayshill Lodge, Montpellier Street (Cheltenham 27774)
Open: Mon-Sat 12noon-2.30pm, 6-10.30pm, Sun 12noon-2pm

[♫] [P] [S] [🍷]

This imposing Regency building behind the Montpellier Rotunda has been converted from a long-established grocer's shop into a ground-floor wine bar and cellar bistro. You can buy ten or so wines by the glass for about 50p upwards. Notice boards display the daily menu, which includes hot soup at around 50p among the dozen or so starters, a hot speciality dish of the day, a variety of pies, smoked meats and fish from around £1.50 to £2.50, interesting salads, and tempting sweets from 65p.

Cinderford

THE WHITE HART HOTEL AND RESTAURANT, St White's Road, Ruspidge (Cinderford 23139)
Open: Mon-Sun 12.15-2pm, 7.30-9.45pm

[C] [P] [♧]

Recent changes to this restaurant include the lounge bar's transformation into a cocktail saloon, and the one-time skittle-alley's conversion to a friendly little bistro. An extensive à la carte menu features the popular Forester's Grill for around £3.30. Dishes such as pork tenderloin, steaks and chicken Kiev are about £4.50, so if you want a starter and a sweet you will have to choose carefully to stay around £5. The cold table in the lounge has meats and interesting salads which you serve yourself – as much as you want for around £1.80-£2. A snack menu includes Californian salad (chicken, sweetcorn and home-cooked ham with lightly curried mayonnaise) at about £2.20 and hot dishes such as chili con carne at £1.50. Traditional Sunday lunch is served at just under £5.

Coleford

WHITE HORSE INN, Staunton (Dean 33387)
Open: Mon-Sat 12noon-2pm, 7-10pm, Sun 12noon-1.15pm, 7-10pm

[P]

This early Victorian pub, strategically sited 'twixt Coleford and Monmouth on the A4136 in the beautiful Forest of Dean, was built on top of a much older hostelry which now forms the inn's Cellar Restaurant. Prices are a little above our limit here, but the Saddle Room Grill, complete with beams and stable paraphernalia, offers well-prepared food which is both economical and interesting. Home-made liver pâté is about £1 and home-made soup 50p. Smoked mackerel or local trout served with vegetables are both around £3. Dish of the day could be lasagne, coq au vin or game pie. Desserts include Black Forest gâteau at 85p.

THE WYNDHAM ARMS ✕ Clearwell (Dean 33666)
Open: Tue-Sat 12noon-2pm, 7-10pm, Sun 12noon-2pm, 7-9.30pm

[C] [P]

Built in 1340, in the centre of the ancient Dean Forest village of Clearwell, this picturesque inn has long been renowned for the excellence of food served in the à la carte restaurant. The Wyndham Arms has also gained an enviable reputation for satisfying bar snacks and for appetising meals in the Grill Room, soused herring salad or mushrooms tartare cost about £1.20 in the bar, while egg and prawn mayonnaise or chicken liver pâté are a few pence more. An extensive range of grills includes fresh local trout, pork chop, gammon steak and fillet steak, served with all the trimmings and costing from around £3-£6. Home-made desserts at 95p are very tempting.

Eton

THE ETON BUTTERY, 73 High Street (Windsor 54479)
Open: Mon-Sun 9.30am-7pm

[C] [♫] [S] [♧]

Alongside the Thames and next to the bridge joining Windsor to Eton is this bright, modern buttery with its smart French cane chairs and elegant pot plants. Take a tray and make your choice from the cool and colourful salads, cold meats and poultry on display, or try a hot dish such as chicken and ham vol au vent at around £2.50. You will want to linger over your sweet and pot of fresh coffee, so find a window seat and watch the boats on the river below, with Windsor Castle in the background.

ETON WINE BAR, 82-83 High Street (Windsor 55182/54921)
Open: Mon-Thu 11.30am-2.30pm, 6-10.30pm, Fri-Sat 11.30am-2.30pm, 6-11pm, Sun 12noon-2pm, 7-10.30pm

[S]

Within earshot of the famous College, this attractive wine bar is the place to go for good wholesome food and a folksy atmosphere. Décor is simple, with scrubbed wooden floors, church-pew seating and stripped-pine furniture. Alternatively you can sit out in the small garden. Mike and Bill Gilbey and their wives do the cooking, producing such delights as pâté village au poivre vert at around £1, chicken liver, bacon and egg mousse at £1.20 and chili pork at less than £3. Desserts include Victorian Brown Bread ice cream. A selection of wines is available from 60p a glass.

Fossebridge

FOSSEBRIDGE INN★★ Northleach (Fossebridge 310)
Open: Mon-Sun 12noon-2pm (Sun 1.30pm), 7-9.30pm

[P]

Ideally-placed in a wooded valley and beside a small river is this part-Georgian, part-Tudor inn, with its roaring log fires, stone walls and beautiful antiques. At around £1 you can sample starters such as mushrooms à la Grecque or spicy crab pâté, and a main course of home-made cottage pie or fresh local trout costs from £1.75 upwards. The selection of home-made sweets may include a light and fluffy lemon meringue pie or a crispy bread and butter pudding. A glass of house wine at 55p, and a cup of filtered coffee provide the liquid accompaniments to an enjoyable yet inexpensive meal.

Gloucester

THE COMFY PEW, College Street (Gloucester 20739)
Open: Mon-Sat 9am-5.30pm

[S]

On the main approach to the cathedral, The Comfy Pew lives up to its name with some entirely appropriate seating. Michael Edgington's food is home-cooked and wholesome; it's reasonably priced, too, with soup, roll and butter at around 50p, a variety of meat or fish salad platters from £1.50, pâtés with salad and toast, curried prawns with toast and snacks on toast all under £1.50.

TASTERS WINE BAR, 22 London Road (Gloucester 417556)
Open: Mon-Thu 12noon-2.30pm, 7-10.30pm, Fri-Sat 12noon-2.30pm, 7-11pm

[P] [S]

This cheerfully decorated bar, close to the city centre features mainly cold dishes such as Stilton and spring onion quiche or mackerel pâté (at about 75p) but cider-baked gammon or Normandy pork may be the hot dish of the day, both at around £2 and extremely tasty. Crisp, fresh salads are in demand and sweets cost 60p-£1.

Hemel Hempstead

THE OLD BELL HOTEL, High Street (Hemel Hempstead 52867)
Open: Mon 12noon-2pm, Tue-Thu 12noon-2pm, 7-9pm, Fri-Sat 12noon-2pm, 7-10pm

[C] [P] [S]

Built in 1580, and an inn since 1603, the Old Bell is a fine example of a 17th-century hostelry. Here you can dine by candlelight in the original Tudor dining room with its intriguing 19th-century French wallpaper. Appetisers include melon with orange segments and curaçao for just over £1. Main courses include lamb kebab at around £2.50 or pepper steak, cooked in butter and finished with brandy and cream at about £4. A sweet from the trolley costs around 80p.

Leighton Buzzard

THE CROSS KEYS ★ The Market Square (Leighton Buzzard 373033)
Open: Mon 10.30am-2.30pm, Tue-Sat 10.30am-2.30pm, 7-10pm, Sun 10.30am-2.30pm

[C] [P] [S] [☘]

Opposite the famous 15th-century Market Cross, this pub food bar serves a selection of hot and cold snacks at budget prices. On fine days you can bring the children and enjoy food on the paved forecourt. A special children's menu operates – including egg salad at 50p to half-portion scampi and chips at about 70p. Hot snacks for adults are either served with chips or vegetables and potatoes – plaice, curried chicken, veal escalopes or Hot Dish of the Day such as hot-pot or beef stew are examples, all in the £1-£1.50 range. Cold buffet meats, fish, pâtés and salads are reasonably priced and desserts such as gâteaux with fresh cream cost around 60p. A large glass of house wine is about 50p.

Little Chalfont

THE COPPER KETTLE, Cokes Lane (Little Chalfont 3144)
Open: Tue-Sat 9.30am-5pm

[P]

Simplicity is the keynote here, with polished tables and wheel-backed chairs for about twenty people. The lunch is home-cooked, just as mother used to make it and, astonishingly, below £2 for three courses. Soups or fruit juices are offered as appetisers for

20p. Main dishes served with a variety of fresh vegetables include steak or chicken and mushroom casseroles, roast pork and apple sauce or home-baked pies or flans – all at £1.30. Cherry and apple sponge and custard or fruit cocktail and ice cream are just two of the sweets available at 36p. Delicious coffee is about 20p.

Luton

OLIVER'S, 3 Crawley Road
(Luton 22592)
Open: Mon-Sun 12.30-2pm,
7.30-10.30pm

[C] [♫] [P] [S] [♣]

Owner John Booth has taken a leaf from Oliver Twist and makes a feature of offering second helpings, though there is enough first time round to satisfy the keenest appetites. A lunchtime meal such as fricassée, two other courses and a glass of wine will only cost about £1.75! For around £5.60 there is also a three-course table d'hôte meal with a choice of eight starters including smoked mackerel, whitebait or turkey and ham vol-au-vents. From the carvery comes roast beef or pork with a selection of vegetables. Sweets include oranges in Grand Marnier, and coffee with sweetmeats is included in the price.

Maidenhead

THE BACCHUS WINE BAR AND RESTAURANT, St Mary's Walk
(Maidenhead 36683)
Open: Mon 10.30am-2.30pm, Tue-Sat 10.30am-2.30pm, 7-10.30pm

[C] [♫] [P] [S] [♣]

If you are after something completely different, sample a Swiss cheese fondue in this tasteful wine bar, with its brick walls, stone floor, chunky wooden tables and candlelight. Slightly more expensive, at £3.50, are almond or mushroom cheese fondues. They are all served with a fresh potato dish of the day and a natural salad. Meat fondues are £5, so if you are an inveterate meat-eater you will have to forego the other courses. Starters include delicious taramasalata at £2, seafood platter and avocado Bacchus, both £1.25. Desserts include Swiss chocolates and petits fours for 85p. If fondues are not your style, there is an excellent snack menu.

Marlow

BURGERS, The Causeway
(Marlow 3389)
Open: Mon 9am-12noon,
Tue-Sat 9am-5.45pm

[P] [S] [♣]

Opposite Marlow Park, this 17th-century building has been in the Burger family since 1942. The restaurant is on two levels. A simple, homely menu offers well-cooked food at very reasonable prices. Dishes include liver pâté or egg mayonnaise as a starter, steak and kidney pie or chicken and ham vol-au-vents with potatoes and vegetables, plus walnut torten or Black Forest gâteau and cream to finish. A three-course meal costs around £2.50 with coffee.

SHELLEY'S, The Marlow Wine Bar,
2 Chapel Street (Marlow 73932)
Open: Mon-Sat 12noon-2.15pm,
7-12mdnt, Sun 7-12mdnt

[C] [♫] [P] [S] [♣]

Shelley's enjoys an ideal location, close enough for visitors to the Henley Regatta and just right for anyone having a day out by the river. The interior has an olde worlde air. French cuisine is dominant, with many exciting dishes such as pasta Fifini, savoury crêpes and lamb and beef blanquette. Vegetarian dishes are also available with curried

The Hatchet

**Market Place, Newbury.
Telephone: 47352**

The building is nearly 200 years old, and situated in the market place in the centre of Newbury. Comfortable bar, with seating in stalls along one side.

Restaurant has an old world effect, with rustic ceiling and old cartwheels for centre lighting.

There is a function room with a separate bar, for large parties.

squidgy (a stew-based dish using mixed vegetables, nuts, sesame seeds and lentils) as just one interesting example. An open-fire grill serves as an indoor barbecue, tempting customers with sizzling steaks. Three courses with coffee and wine costs around £5.

Newbury

THE HATCHET, Market Place
(Newbury 47352)
Open: Mon-Sat 12.30-1.45pm,
6.30-9.45pm, Sun 7.30-9.45pm
Newbury Race Days: 12noon

⑤

By the Corn Exchange in this attractive market town, you'll discover this interesting restaurant, with its unique ceiling of wattle sheep-pen fencing. Emphasis is on grills and roasts at competitive prices. Rump steak is around £3.75, lamb cutlets or shallow-fried rainbow trout about £3. A good selection of starters includes seafood cocktail and there are tempting sweets from the trolley to complete the meal.

THE SAPIENT PIG, 29 Oxford Street
(Newbury 44867)
Open: Lunch: Mon-Fri 12.30-2pm;
Dinner: Tue-Sat 7.30-10pm

Ⓒ🎵Ⓟ⑤◎

This sophisticated bistro is steeped in Laura Ashley. The cosy atmosphere is an ideal setting for the delicious home-cooked fare. Hot dish of the day is under £3 and could be anything from sauté of pork provençale to Olde English steak and kidney pie – both served with three vegetables. Coronation chicken is an appetising cold dish costing only £1.20 and salads are available from 40p. Desserts, including such delights as strawberry Pavlova or sherry trifle cost around 75p. A glass of French or Italian wine is about 65p. On fine days you can enjoy your meal in the garden.

Northleach

COUNTRY FRIENDS ★ Market Place
(Northleach 421)
Open: Tue-Sat 12.30-2pm, 7-9.30pm,
Sun 12.30-2pm

Ⓒ Ⓟ

The table d'hôte at this charming Cotswold-stone restaurant is excellent. For around £4.50 on weekdays, about £5.75 on Sundays, you can enjoy an imaginative meal which offers a choice of starters – a soup, perhaps a fish pâté – and a main course served with potatoes and a fresh vegetable or salad. On Sunday the choice of main course includes a roast, and weekday menus include such things as gingered pork chops, or seafood pancake; sweets might include chocolate roulade or Calvados and apple mousse.

Olney

THE OLNEY WINE BAR, 9 High Street
South (Bedford 711112)
Open: Mon-Sat 12noon-2pm,
7-10.30pm (Fri-Sat 11pm)

Ⓟ

The charming Georgian shop front of this wine bar leads into a room with an attractive open fireplace. The original bakehouse ovens are still to be seen in the back room. Bill of fare is on a blackboard and includes pâté and taramasalata, both at around £1, and Swedish chicken for just over £1. Pork fillets in tarragon and mushroom sauce and Westmorland tart are specialities.

Oxford

**BURLINGTON BERTIE'S
RESTAURANT AND COFFEE HOUSE**
9a High Street (Oxford 723342)
Open: Mon-Sun 11am-12mdnt

Look above the Jean Machine in Oxford High Street, and there's Bertie's – all plants, pub mirrors, cane-bottomed chairs and highly-polished tables with wrought-iron pedestals. You can get a meal or any kind of drink here at any time. The cuisine is English and Continental, the service fast and efficient, the welcome warm and friendly. Salads are priced at under £3, spaghetti and risotto dishes at under £2.50, and meat and fish main courses at under £4. Sandwiches toasted or plain, cost under £1.75, and come with salad. Desserts include 'specials' such as toffee coffee crunch for around £1. A glass of French table wine costs about 60p.

MAXWELL'S, 36 Queen Street
(Oxford 42192)
Open: Mon-Sun 11.30am-12mdnt

[♬] [S] [🍷]

A bright and breezy first-floor restaurant where the high ceiling, iron girders and steel supports give an aircraft-hangar effect. American-style food is efficiently served in an informal atmosphere. Specialities such as T-bone steak, lamb kebab, chili and chicken (around £3.75) supplement the hamburgers, which come with French fries, tossed salad and a choice of dressings. Ice cream sodas and milk shakes continue the American theme.

THE NOSEBAG, 6-8 St Michaels Street
(Oxford 721033)
Open: Mon-Sat 10am-5.30pm
(Fri-Sat 7-11pm), Sun 12noon-5.30pm

[♬] [S]

Inelegant its name may be, but this upstairs, split-level restaurant, with its oak-beamed ceiling and bright and homely décor, has a certain charm all of its own. The lunchtime hot dish of the day for around £1.60, is likely to be moussaka, chicken à la crème or herrings in oatmeal. A tempting choice of original salads (as much as you like) costs around 80p. With soup at about 60p and hot garlic bread at about 40p, the three-course lunch must be a bargain, even after ordering delicious home-made ice cream or sorbets. And on Friday and Saturday evenings the Nosebag offers an excellent three-course meal for just over £5 with exciting main courses such as mackerel with gooseberry sauce.

OPIUM DEN ✕ 79 George Street
(Oxford 48680)
Open: Mon-Sat 12noon-2.30pm,
6-12mdnt, Sun 1-2.30pm, 6-12mdnt
[C] [♬] [P] [S]

Don't let the name discourage you, the only addictive thing sold at the Opium Den is the food. The interior of this Chinese restaurant is as sinister as its name suggests, with black walls and ceiling and subdued lighting. However, the welcome is sincere and the food good. Mainly Cantonese with a few Pekinese dishes, the specialities of the house are the sizzling dishes brought piping hot to your table on wooden platters. Lunchtimes are always busy, with a table d'hôte menu available at around £2.50. The à la carte is extensive, with prices to suit all pockets. Set dinners are particularly reasonable at around £6-£7 for two people.

Reading

BEADLES WINE BAR, 83 Broad Street
(Reading 53162)
Open: Mon-Sat 10.30am-2.30pm,
5.30-10.30pm

[♬] [S]

This popular basement wine bar is situated on the one-time site of Simmonds Brewery and the original globe lights are still a splendid feature. An interesting selection of food includes 'snacks for the peckish or starters for the starving' such as egg mayonnaise and salami (80p), taramasalata (95p) or large hors d'oeuvres – roll mop, smoked ham, egg mayonnaise, prawns, salami, gherkins and pâté for £2.50. Main courses served with salad could be roast beef, turkey, chicken, dressed crab or prawns, depending on their availability. Delicious home-made speciality desserts are particularly tempting – try Benja – individual choc and fudge topped with fresh cream for a mere 45p. French or Italian wine is 55p a glass.

THE GEORGE HOTEL ★★ King Street
(Reading 53445)
Open: Mon-Sun 12noon-2.30pm,
6-11.30pm (Sun 7-11pm)

[S] [🍷]

The historic, timbered George Hotel complete with cobbled courtyard and stagecoach has obscure origins, but appears in a rent roll dated 1578. Today it boasts four steak bars of distinctive character. The Cocked Hat, Pickwickian and Cavalier Grills and Rib Room offer an excellent selection of grills and roasts. Half a roast duckling with apple sauce and jacket potatoes is very good value at around £5 – this includes a choice of sweets or cheeses. Rib of beef, served with jacket potatoes with sour cream and chives, plus a selection of serve-yourself salad, costs about £5. The price includes ice cream or cheese to follow.

HEELAS RESTAURANT, Broad Street (Reading 559555)
Open: Tue-Sat 9.45am-5pm (10am Thu)

P S

Still a haven in one of Reading's most popular department stores, but now relocated and newly built on the second floor, Heelas' new restaurant offers a relaxing break from the hustle of a busy day's shopping. Predominantly green and white décor with lots of leafy green plants is complemented by the classy contemporary prints which line the walls. Smart waitresses provide swift service and the food tastes all the better for being served on modern Wedgwood bone china. There are meals to suit the whole family from a half portion of fish and chips for Junior and a Danish open sandwich, piled high with meat or cheese and salad, for Mum, to the Chef's choice roast beef and Yorkshire pud for Dad. Dad's meal is the most expensive but even with three courses, coffee and a glass of house wine for around 56p, he could still have change back from £5.

MAMA MIA, 11 St Mary's Butts (Reading 581357)
Open: Mon-Sat, 12noon-2.30pm, 6-9.30pm, Sun 11am-2pm

S

Mirco Rado's Trattoria Mama Mia serves only Italian food and wines in an almost operatic setting of rough-cast, white-painted walls, crowned by rafters hung with clusters of Chianti bottles and strings of onions and other vegetables. Home-made soups at around 50p, pastas and pizzas from around £1.25, offer excellent value, although penny- and weight-watchers are advised to resist the entrées.

SWEENEY AND TODD, 10 Castle Street (Reading 586466)
Open: Mon-Sat 8.30am-2.30pm, 5.30-10.30pm

P

Through the Victorian pie shop, up sawdust-strewn steps, is this small saloon-type restaurant, with church pew seating, copper rail curtains and gilt globe lighting. Lunchtime specials such as roast sucking pig cost around £2.20, with fresh vegetables at 40p. Imaginative home-made pies (about £1.10-£1.40) include steak and oyster, kidney and fennel and poachers (mixed game). 'Vicars' lunches consist of a plate of cold meat with French bread, pickles and salad and they set you back around £2. Cheesecake, gâteaux or flans are some of the home-made desserts on offer for 65p-80p. Wine is 55p a glass. On sunny days, children can eat in the garden to the rear.

TRUNKWELL HOUSE, Beech Hill (Reading 883754)
Open: Mon-Sat 12.30-2.30pm, 7.30-10.30pm (Fri-Sat 7.30-11pm), Sun 12noon-2pm, 7.30-10pm

C P

Hard to find, but well worth the effort, this imposing Victorian house is hidden 300 yards down a single-vehicle-width road. Owner Isidro Rodriguez does the cooking, while his all-male Spanish staff wait at table. The food is superb, with a businessperson's lunch of chicken, veal, pork chop, steak (all in gorgeous sauces) or an enormous trout with crisp vegetables, starter, sweet and coffee for about £4. On summer days a cold buffet with smoked salmon or cold meats is served in the garden for £2.

Redbourn

AUBREY PARK HOTEL ☆☆☆
Hemel Hempstead Lane, Redbourn, St Albans (Redbourn 2105)
Open: Ostler's Room: Sun-Sat

12.30-2pm, 7-10pm, (Sat 7-10.30pm)

[P]

The warmly-glowing Ostler's room, with its glazed brickwork and low-beamed ceilings, is dedicated to the serving of traditional English dishes in an atmosphere of medieval jollity. A wholesome three-course meal can be picked from a choice of Welsh cawl or Ostler's seafood (prawns, apple and celery in a cocktail sauce), followed by deep dish steak and kidney pie, braised beef in stout, or turkey Victoria and finishing with pastries and puddings from the cook's pantry.

Rickmansworth

THE CHEQUERS RESTAURANT
21 Church Street
(Rickmansworth 72287)
Open: Mon-Sun 12noon-2pm, 7-10.30pm

[C]

The Chequers Restaurant, built in 1580, is the oldest building in this old town, and here you can have a delicious meal either in the attractive restaurant or, weather permitting, in the garden. This is another Four Pillars Group venture and the menu and prices are comparable with those at the Barnet restaurant, though during any particular week the actual dishes available are different. There is a separate, more expensive steak menu. A table d'hôte lunch is available at about £2 a head.

St Albans

BLACK LION HOTEL, Fishpool Street, St Michaels Village
(St Albans 51786/64916)
Open: Mon-Fri 12noon-2pm, 7-10pm, Sat 12noon-2pm, 7-10.30pm, Sun 12noon-2.30pm

[C] [P]

Dormer windows and mellow brickwork characterise this attractive 18th-century inn situated at the lower end of picturesque Fishpool Street. Modernisation has not stripped the interior of its character and old beams and brickwork abound. In the bar an impressive cold buffet is on display for £2.50 and a hot dish of the day such as Irish stew costs around £2. A table d'hôte menu in the restaurant is priced by the main dish – from about £5 for lamb sweetbreads with banana or fillet of plaice bonne femme to nearly £6 for escalope of chicken Viennoise or roast pork. Appetisers include corn on the cob, ham and cottage cheese coronet and a selection of home-made soups. Choice from the sweet trolley is good.

TUDOR TAVERN, 28 George Street
(St Albans 53233)
Open: Mon-Sun 12noon-2.30pm, 6-11.30pm

[C] [P] [S]

The special thing about Berni is that it restores and preserves some of this country's most attractive old buildings. The Tudor Tavern is the oldest complete half-timbered building in the ancient city of St Albans. Many main-dish prices here include tomato soup to start, roll and butter, and ice cream or cheese and biscuits to follow, so an 8oz rump steak with chips, tomato and peas at about £4.50 leaves some change for a glass of wine.

Slough

ZORBA'S WINE BAR, 105 High Street
(Slough 35234)
Open: Mon-Sat 12noon-3pm, 7pm-1am

[C] [S]

This interesting wine bar has an original open stone wall, exposed beams and an array of gifts from foreign lands (such as Thai parasols) brought by regulars on their return from holidays. The menu is similarly cosmopolitan, though the emphasis is on Greek cuisine. Starters such as taramasalata or houmous, followed by moussaka, kleftiko, dolmades or tava (Greek casserole) and a dish of green figs make an all-Greek meal for around £3.50. Italian or Greek wines cost about 60p a glass.

Sunningdale

THE IN-BETWEEN RESTAURANT
Station Parade (Ascot 21215)

[C] [♫] [☙]

Located on the busy A30, this friendly, relaxed restaurant is a find for the passing motorist. A touch of Spain is evoked in the Spanish arches, dark wood polished tables and burnished copper pendant lights. A three-course table d'hôte lunch for around £2.50 is excellent value, offering a choice of dishes which could include moussaka, followed by freshly roasted pork, apple sauce and a variety of vegetables and sherry trifle. A choice of international wines by the glass costs 55p. Portions for children are half price. A more expensive 'executive' lunch offers more exotic main courses, and the à la carte menu is staggeringly comprehensive, including speciality dishes from every part of the globe – you need a little more than our budget to do justice to this fare!

Thame

THE COFFEE HOUSE, 3 Buttermarket (Thame 2407)
Open: Mon-Sat 10am-5pm

[☙]

This charmingly decorated restaurant with its pine furniture, white walls, large open fireplace and green plants was opened in 1979. Appetisers include home-made pâté with brandy, served with French bread (the most expensive starter at around £1), main courses include spaghetti bolognese made with wine, pizza salads and a daily special such as cottage pie or chicken and ham pie all for around £1.75. Desserts include chocolate rum mousse for around 75p.

Waltham Cross

SOUR GRAPES, 41b High Street (Lea Valley 718633)
Open: Mon-Thu 11am-2.30pm, 7-10.30pm, Fri-Sat 11am-2.30pm, 7-11pm, Sun 7.30-10.30pm

[P] [S]

Situated close to the 'cross', this attractive wine bar has maps of French vineyards on the walls and distinctive wooden tables and chairs making it a relaxed and casual rendezvous for lunch or dinner. The blackboard menu offers a hot 'dish of the day' for around £1.50, pizzas at about £1, salads at around £1.70 and apple pie and ice cream for about 60p. There is a good choice of wines by the glass at about 60-65p. Service is friendly and efficient and in fine weather you can enjoy your food in the peaceful gardens at the rear.

Welwyn Garden City

TOBY FOOD AND WINE BAR
49 Wigmores North
(Welwyn Garden City 26663)
Open: Mon-Thu 11.30am-2.30pm, 6.30-10.30pm, Fri-Sat 6.30-11pm

[P]

Striking artwork and an attractive brown awning identify Toby's, where Eric and Elsie Norris both do the cooking for their popular wine bar. Dishes may include smoked mackerel at about £1, beef casserole for around £2 and home-made apple pie and fresh cream for about 75p. The Victorian décor of this first-floor, split-level bar, with its genuine mahogany bar front is an ideal background for enjoyment of both food and excellent wine. Downstairs, the Toby Grill serves breakfasts, snacks, salads and grills.

Windsor

THE DRURY HOUSE RESTAURANT
4 Church Street (Windsor 63734)
Open: Tue-Sun 12noon-5.30pm

[☙]

In this charming 17th-century setting, within a stone's throw of the guardsmen at the gate of the Castle, Joan Hearne serves good, plain English food at no-nonsense prices, with a choice of salads from around £2.50 and of main dishes from £2, for grilled lamb's liver and bacon, to around £4.50 for three courses. Omelettes cost around £1.50. Home-made gâteaux are on sale.

JETHRO'S WINE BAR
18a The Passage, off Thames Street (Windsor 54814)
Open: Mon-Sat 12noon-2.30pm, Tue-Sat 6-10pm

[C] [♫] [P]

Jethro Tull (1674-1741), agriculturalist and inventor, is reputed to have lived in the house of which this attractive basement premises forms a part. Church pews and pine stools give a certain character to the pleasant décor. Try the chili on rice for about £1.75, or terrine and French bread for around £1. Cold ham or beef salad costs between £2.40 and £2.50. There is a good choice of wines, many of which are sold by the glass, the cheaper ones at around 50p.

LONDON STEAK HOUSE
10 Thames Street (Windsor 66437)
Open: Mon-Sat 12noon-3pm, 6-11pm, Sun 12.30-3pm, 6.30-10.30pm

[C] [S] [♧]

Handily placed for a visit to Windsor Castle, this busy restaurant, although small, has refreshingly uncluttered floor space. Traditional-style wall-lights interspersed with framed prints make for a pleasant enough décor. A well-cooked meal such as consommé printanier (55p), lamb cutlets (£2.60) and ice-cream (50p) sounds reasonable, but you'll need to add about £1 for your two vegetables. Wine is a little expensive at 85p per goblet.

Wingfield

THE PLOUGH INN
On the A5120 near Toddington (Wingfield 3077)
Open: Mon-Sat 12noon-2pm, 6-10.30pm, Sun 12noon-2pm, 7-10.30pm

[♫] [♧]

A good place to stop when the weather's good, this Whitbread pub dating from the early 17th century, is in pleasant countryside between Dunstable and Ampthill, and has a garden. A fairly conventional choice of lunches is available (roasts, steak, fish, etc), but excellent value. Apart from peas, only fresh, local vegetables are served. Snacks are available in the evenings and on Sundays, with interesting specialities such as humble pie (country herb sausage meat, cheese, tomato, potato) or hot ploughman's pie (potato base with cheese and onions) for about 50p. The friendly, pipe-smoking landlord, Les Pope and his wife, Betty complete the welcoming atmosphere of the Plough.

Winslow

THE BELL HOTEL, Market Square (Winslow 2741)
Open: Mon-Sun 11.30am-2.15pm, 6-10.15pm (Sun 7-10.15pm)

[C] [♫] [P] [S]

Musical church bells provide an authentic background to the peaceful, historic atmosphere of the heavily-timbered and balustraded Claydon Restaurant of this 17th-century hotel. The lower part of the restaurant has the old stone walls of the original brewing room. The table d'hôte menu in the restaurant offers three courses plus coffee for less than £5. Tournedos Val Prais is an enterprising main course, and fresh strawberries and cream are served as a dessert when in season. The Wineslai Bar serves a good selection of grills including steak garni at about £3 or lamb chop, pork chop or plaice for around £2. French fries and chips are included. A lunch special with vegetables of the day costs about £1.50.

Wokingham

SETTERS FOOD AND WINE BAR
49 Peach Street (Wokingham 788893)
Open: Mon-Sat 12noon-2pm, Mon-Thu 7-10.15pm, Fri-Sat 7-10.30pm

[♫] [P]

This wine bar, with its stripped-pine furniture and wooden floor boards, is an ideal haunt for business people at lunchtime. Candles and pop music transform the scene in the evening into a romantic haven for couples. The blackboard menu shows the daily special which may be beef in red wine or in beer, and costs around £2.50. Cream of spinach soup at about 70p, smoked mackerel pâté at around £1 and gooseberry fresh cream fool at about 80p, make a delicious meal.

Woolhampton

THE ROWBARGE ✕ Station Road (Woolhampton 2213)
Open: Mon-Sun 12noon-2pm, 7-9pm

[♫] [P] [♧]

Character actor Lawrence Naismith presides over this low-ceilinged, beamed and wood-panelled inn. Business people and others from far and wide fill the place to capacity in order to enjoy the substantial and imaginative bar lunches. The menu changes every day, but excellent examples are home-made rissoles in wine gravy with sauté potatoes at about £1.45 or haddock Monte Carlo (served with parsley and egg sauce, poached egg and sauté potatoes) at around £2.20. Also on offer is cheese and bacon flan at about £1.80.

Greater London

For those with open minds and adventurous spirits, eating-out in London gives scope for a full-scale exploration of style, flavour and atmosphere.

By using the pages that follow to your best advantage, you can turn a five pound note into a kind of international passport to the world's most exotic cuisine – London's range of eating places is nothing if not cosmopolitan! In some parts you can be leaving the musky aromas of the Lebanon one minute and be surrounded by the fiery smells of Mexico the next, sampling not only hitherto-unknown cuisine, but acquiring the taste for a whole new culture and lifestyle.

However, those with more conventional tastes need not despair, for next to the most exotic eating houses in the metropolis are the long-standing traditional restaurants, as English as the plain, wholesome food they serve – often with elegant simplicity.

Many of the eateries offer live entertainment, and don't mind if you linger over your meal. Many others prefer to specialise in good value, quick service orders, catering mainly for theatre-goers and

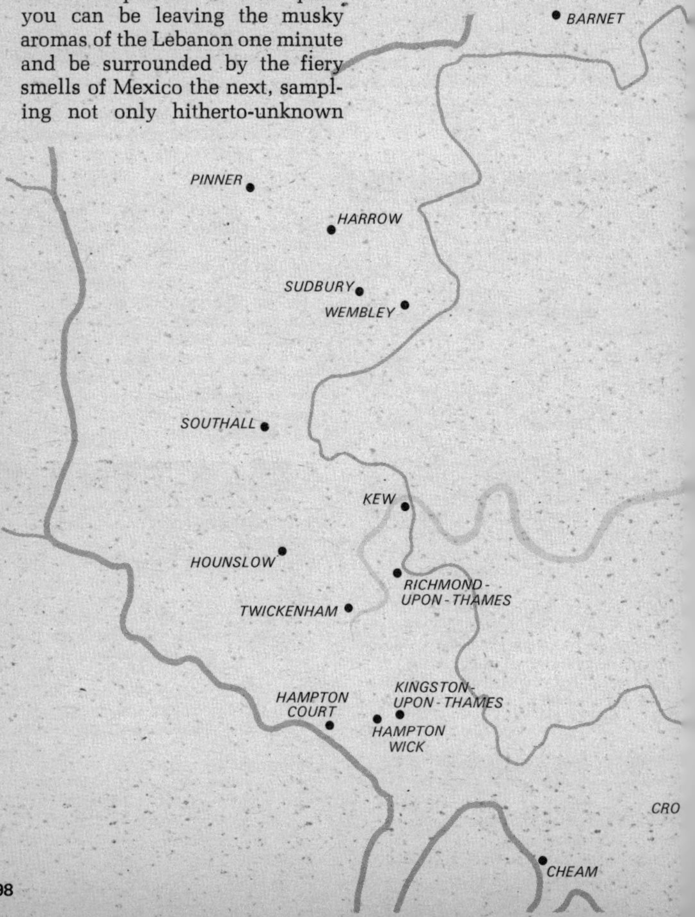

day-trippers. All those figure prominently here.

To make things easier, London has been divided into two areas: Greater London (the area administered by the GLC) and Inner London (in order of postal areas).

In recent years, London has seen the arrival of a relatively new concept in eating out – the wine bar. Appealing mainly to the younger set, many of these places regard the selling of speciality wines as their first priority, but all those featured in this book offer a good selection of hot and cold dishes as well. Add to these the chic bistros (mostly of French origin) with their checked tablecloths and candles in bottles, historical pubs with sawdust-strewn floorboards, the butteries and grill rooms of grand hotels and all the brasseries, tavernas, trattorias, pizzerias and thousands of conventional restaurants and you have some idea of what the capital city has to offer.

Although London boasts some of the best hotels and restaurants in the world, it *is* possible to eat cheaply here, providing you know where to look. Browse through the following pages and you will not be lost for a choice of some of the best traditional food that London can offer – from a Sunday-style roast joint to the East Ender speciality: cockles, winkles, eels and mussels.

5

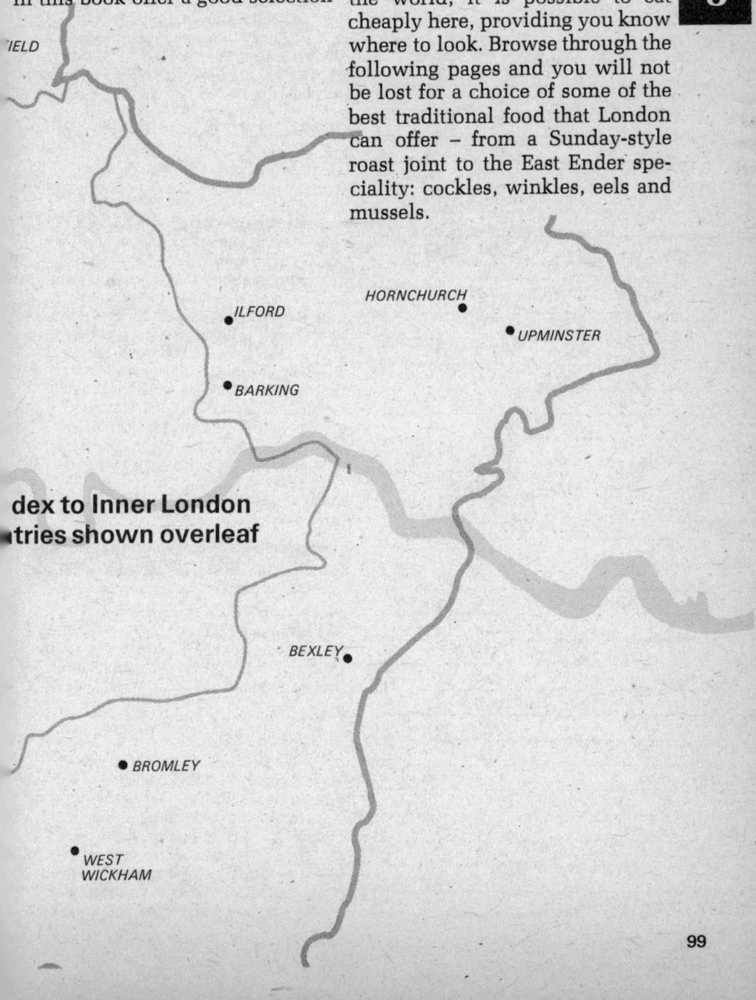

Greater London Index

E1

DICKENS INN, St Catherine's Way, St Catherine's Dock (01-488 2208)
Open: Tavern Room: during normal licensing hours, Pickwick Room and Dickens Room: 12.30-1.45pm, 7.30-10pm

This old brewery dates back to around 1780 and the fact that the building was at one time moved several hundred feet is reflected in the huge oak pillars and beams supporting it. The Tavern Room on the first floor offers a good cold collation including cockles at about 50p, prawns for around £1.20, ploughman's at around £1.25 and cold meat salad for about £2.20. The recently opened Dickens Room, a fish restaurant, offers cockles and mussels for about £2.20, stargazy pie for around £3 and an intoxicating sherry trifle.

GRAPESHOTS, 2-3 Artillery Passage (01-247 8215)
Open: Mon-Fri 11am-3pm, 5-7pm

[C] [P] [S]

For a wine bar in Artillery Passage, Grapeshots is an appropriate name, but put out of your mind the fact that grapeshot was produced by dropping lead from a height into water – the grapes here are of a more fruity variety. This Davys of London wine bar, on the ground and basement floors of a building round the corner from Petticoat Lane, is rather on the small side but with an intimate, relaxed atmosphere. The menu is limited and largely cold but good value at around £2 for an enormous helping of cold meat, with a mixed salad at 60p. Game, salmon and strawberries are sold in their proper seasons.

E2

THE VENUS STEAK HOUSE
368 Bethnal Green Road (01-739 2650)
Open: Mon-Fri 12noon-3pm, 6pm-1am (Fri 6pm-2.30am), Sat 12noon-2.30am, Sun 6pm-1am

[C] [♫] [S] [♲]

A delight for business people, this is a place where one can get a high grade meal in a very civilised, slightly formal atmosphere without paying through the nose for it. George Zachovia, the proprietor, will greet you at the door and lead you to the bar for an aperitif, or to your table. Black-jacketed waiters hover on the sidelines to see that your glass is never empty. Prime Scotch steaks are the house speciality, but the menu offers a host of enterprising dishes at down to earth prices, such as kebab à la Greque for around £3. The set lunch also at about £3 is excellent value. Rump steak, with a selection of fourteen vegetables costs less than £4.

E7

CORINTHIA RESTAURANT
278 Romford Road, Forest Gate, (01-534 3719)
Open: Mon-Sat 12noon-3pm, 6pm-12mdnt (Fri-Sat 6pm-1am)

[P] [S]

Andreas has run this attractive Greek restaurant for over twenty-four years and you will find a warm welcome awaiting you. His wife Louise directs the kitchen, which is renowned for its excellent Greek 'specialities of the house'. Afelia is particularly recommended – a generous portion is around £3. If you don't want to eat Greek, there is a range of English and French cuisine to titillate your palate.

E8

THE GLOBE, 20 Morning Lane, Hackney (01-985 6455)
Open: Mon-Sun 11am-2.30pm

[P]

Sunday lunch in this well decorated pub is traditional East End help-yourself to cockles, winkles and baked potatoes. Weekday lunches are more varied, with an impressive display of cold food such as cold meat pâté at about £1 or pizza and French bread for around 80p. Recommended hot dishes include steak and kidney or chicken and mushroom pies at around 75p. The grill at the far end of the bar produces gammon, ham, pork chops or scampi for about £1.20-£1.80 and sirloin steak for around £2.50. Vegetables are extra. Sweets with cream average about 50p, the price of a glass of Spanish wine.

EC1

THE COFFEE SHOP AT THE WHITBREAD BREWERY
Chiswell Street (01-606 4455)
Open: Mon-Fri 8.30am-5.30pm, Sat 9am-4pm

The large brewery complex houses this bright little restaurant with its country-kitchen atmosphere and quaint cobbled courtyard. Simple food is served here, with at least one hot dish such as chicken à la king (around £1) available daily to supplement the many salads, which cost between £1-£1.30. Finish with a no-nonsense pud such as jam roly-poly and a cup of very fresh coffee.

EC2

BALLS BROS, 6-8 Cheapside (01-248 2708)
Open: Mon-Fri 11.30am-3pm, 5-7pm

[P] [S]

This is a typical Balls Bros City outlet, with food at lunchtimes only, but an excellent wine list including some very reasonable half-bottles. The ground floor bar serves satisfying snacks and sandwiches, while the basement restaurant offers a range of good salads and one hot dish daily, all from around £2-£2.50. This is a friendly and comfortable little bar, with a faithful following among City and business folk.

BALLS BROS, Moor House, London Wall (01-628 3944)
Open: Mon-Fri 11.30am-3pm, 5-7.30pm

[C] [P]

Don't look for an evening meal here,

because you won't find it. The lunchtime menu is a typical one for the Balls Bros chain, with hot and cold dishes from around £2.75, as well as sandwiches, and house wines from about 60p a glass. Portions are generous, and service excellent, and the atmosphere very friendly. As with all the BB outlets, the long-staying staff know their customers and it's nothing to see a City gent waiting for 'his own' waitress to be free to serve him rather than defect to another.

BALLS BROS, 42 Threadneedle Street (01-283 6701)
Open: Mon-Fri 11.30am-3pm, 5-7pm

This is the smallest Balls Bros wine bar and (at the time of writing, at least) the only licensed premises in Threadneedle Street. Very popular with stockbrokers, this intimate little wine bar has only sixteen covers and offers a very limited menu and sandwiches, but excellent BB wines are available at prices ranging from 60p a glass. Again, you'll only get food here at lunchtime.

THE CITY BOOT, 7 Moorfields High Walk (01-588 4766)
Open: Mon-Fri 11.30am-3pm, 5-8.30pm

[C]

You can buy extremely fine sandwiches here from around 85p, as well as the usual range of Davys of London salads and cold meats for about £2.50 a sizeable portion. The food side of the operation (lunchtime only) is small and simple but very good. One Davy's treat is the serving of grouse, partridge, pheasant and Scotch salmon when in season. Polished wood and candles help to create a serene atmosphere in which to enjoy a glass of the French wine – around 80p a glass.

THE GEORGE AND VULTURE
3 Castle Street (01-626 9710)
Open: Mon-Fri 12noon-3pm

[C] [🍇]

Charles Dickens stayed at The George and Vulture and made it famous in his 'Pickwick Papers'. But even without Dickens it has a claim to fame as probably the oldest tavern in the world, for it is known to have existed in 1175 although only one wall remains of the old structure. The present building retains the Pickwickian aura and is almost a museum in its own right. You can't stay there now, but you can have a substantial lunch at a very reasonable price. There is a good selection of starters, most of them around 85p. Fish and main courses (a good mixed grill, for example) are from £2.50, with vegetables extra at about 45p a portion. For a sweet there is, in season, fresh stawberry flan, and a variety of other items at 60p or so. Stilton cheese is recommended, but there is plenty of choice from the cheese board. A French house wine is about 75p a glass. The restaurant is available in the evening for private functions.

EC3

CITY FLOGGER, 120 Fenchurch Street (01-623 3251)
Open: Mon-Fri 11.30am-3pm, 5-7pm

[C]

Although it is in the basement of a modern office development, this Davys of London wine bar next door to Mappin & Webb has the Group's usual 19th-century décor, with sawdust on the floor, hessian-covered walls and wood panelling. A special plate of prawns at £1 is particularly recommended as are seasonal game dishes. There are French-bottled house wines from 80p or so a glass. Don't just turn up and expect to get in, for the place is usually jam-packed with people from Lloyds and the City banks.

EC4

BOW WINE VAULTS, 10 Bow Churchyard (01-248 1121)
Open: Restaurant: Mon-Fri 12noon-3pm, Wine bar: Mon-Fri 11.30am-3pm, 5-7pm

The minimum charge of £4 for lunch at the Bow Wine Vaults would buy you baked Scotch salmon with mayonnaise, or perhaps you would prefer smoked chicken salad for around £2. Starters are priced from 80p for chilled watercress soup to £1.50 for smoked salmon mousse. Main courses include daily specials at around £2.90-£3.90 (vegetables add about 40p), and for a sweet you might choose chocolate truffle or strawberry fool, at 85p or so. The restaurant is a converted warehouse with whitewashed walls, but a Victorian atmosphere is created by the furnishings and bric-à-brac. The wine list is extensive. The French house wine costs about 60p a glass.

CORTS, 33 Old Bailey (01-236 2101)
Open: Mon-Fri 11.30am-3pm, 5-8pm

[C] [S]

Rub shoulders with lawyers (and possibly criminals too!) in this comfortable wine bar near the Central Criminal Court. Maybe, though, you'd be more interested in the young and pretty waitresses. Food at lunchtime is straightforward and enjoyable, with soup at about 65p, a selection of quiches, pies and cold meats for around £2 (potatoes and salad could add about £1.20), and cheesecake, chocolate gâteau or apple pie at 70p or so.

MOTHER BUNCH'S WINE HOUSE
Old Seacoal Lane (01-236 5317)
Open: Mon-Fri 11am-3pm, 5.30-8.30pm

C P S

Under the railway arches in Old Seacoal Lane, hard by Ludgate Circus, this Davys of London wine bar does a nice line in Buck's Fizz at £2.50 a tankard. But if you're counting the pennies, stick to your guns and call for a glass of house wine at around 90p a quarter-bottle helping. Food (do book for the place is extremely popular) is mostly cold but very tasty and good value. A generous plate of finest ham off the bone or game pie with mixed salad or hot potatoes can be had for under £2.50. Seafood is a speciality here.

OODLES, 31 Cathedral Place
(01-248 2559)
Open: Mon-Fri 11.30am-5.30pm
(7pm summer months)

Although it's in a new building, this Oodles has succeeded in retaining the character of all the others, even though this branch is unlicensed. See under Marble Arch W2 for full description.

OODLES, 3 Fetter Lane, Fleet Street
(01-353 1984)
Open: Mon-Fri 11.30am-3pm

In the heart of the newspaper world, this Oodles offers identical menu and atmosphere to the branch described under Marble Arch W2. But it's open for only 17½ hours in the week.

SLENDERS WHOLEFOOD RESTAURANT AND JUICE BAR
41 Cathedral Place (01-236 5974)
Open: Mon-Fri 8.30am-6.15pm

♫ P S

Situated in a quiet backwater of the City, and with an equally quiet décor of natural brick, wood and hessian, Slenders is tremendously popular. There is seating for over 100 in separate booths. At lunchtime it is incredibly busy. The menu is vegetarian and you can obtain a good wholesome meal for about £1.80. Everything is prepared on the premises, including the wholemeal bread. A good mixed salad or a hot dish such as vegetable and cheese flan or stuffed peppers costs about 90p for a portion, and sweets – chocolate mousse or fresh fruit salad are around 65p each.

N1

GRAPES WINE BAR, Angel Arcade, Camden Passage, Islington
(01-359 5223)
Open: Mon-Tue, Thu-Fri 12noon-3pm, 6-12mdnt, Wed and Sat 12noon-12mdnt

♫ P

This sophisticated basement wine bar, with subtle décor including cushioned 'milk churns' is a most original haunt. On Saturday evenings you can enjoy live folk music or even a Noel Coward evening! Original dishes include aubergine Charlotte at around £2, chili con carne garnished with fresh apple for about £2, home-made desserts such as cheesecake and summer pudding. A glass of house wine costs around 75p.

N6

DRAGON SEED RESTAURANT
66 Highgate High Street, Highgate Village (01-348 6160)
Open: Mon-Thu 12noon-2.30pm,

5.30-11.30pm, Fri-Sun 12noon-12mdnt

[S]

Just up the hill from Waterloo park, where tame squirrels will take food from your hand, is Highgate Village which boasts a Chinese restaurant amongst the 18th-century façade of the small row of interesting shops. Inside, soft carpet, upholstered chairs and an all-pervading dragon motif transport you East. Here you will find courteous, unobtrusive service and delicious food which is remarkably good value for money. A meal of sliced meat soup, Peking duck with vegetables and rice and banana ball fritters in golden syrup plus a glass of house wine costs about £5 – just one selection from a menu which lists over 100 dishes, few of which exceed £3. Specials include fried whole lobster with ginger and spring onion or whole suckling pig in sauce (24hrs notice required).

THE FLASK TAVERN, 77 Highgate West Hill, Highgate Village (01-340 3969)
Open: normal licensing hours

[C] [P] [S] [garden]

Built in 1663, The Flask Tavern has been the haunt of many interesting characters, including the legendary highwayman Dick Turpin and distinguished painters Hogarth, Morlane and Cruickshank. During the summer the natural wood tables, set out in the large stone courtyard, are constantly in use. You may eat a snack in one of the three popular bars, but if something more substantial is preferred, a good three-course meal can be had in one of the bars for around £3. Starters include soup or grapefruit, main course sauté kidneys, fried plaice, fried rock salmon or cod and shrimp Mornay. Dessert is a choice of ice creams or banana fritters. Wine is about 50p.

N8

LA CRESTA RESTAURANT, 18 Crouch End Hill (01-340 4539)
Open: Mon-Fri 12noon-3pm, 5.30-11.30pm, Sat 5.30-11.30pm

[P]

A family-owned-and-run restaurant, where a warm welcome is assured. The menu is mainly Italian, with a few English fish and steak dishes thrown in for good measure. Highly recommended is the house speciality of veal escalope valdostana – a marvellous concoction of ham, cheese, spaghetti and veal at about £3, and the freshly-baked poppy seed bread (around 45p). An international wine list is available.

NW1

FAMAGUSTA TAVERN, 3 Camden High Street (01-387 3391)
Open: Mon-Sun 12noon-3pm, 6pm-12.30am

[S]

Be sure to have plenty of room under your belt when you visit Famagusta, for the delicious Greek cuisine, produced by proprietor Ioannas Louca, is served in very generous portions. On weekdays there is a choice of two or three 'Famagusta Specials', main courses served with potatoes or rice, and salad; and all but one are around £2.50. Hors d'oeuvres start at 60p with a choice of ten interesting Greek dishes such as kalamari – squid cooked in a wine sauce. Charcoal grills are also reasonably priced – try quails at about £2 each. Three courses, such as hors d'oeuvres, kebabs and sweet, plus coffee and wine, may only cost around £4. The simple but effective décor is conducive to good eating, particularly in the evening when candlelit tables reflect a warm glow from the red tablecloths. Reproduction carriage lamps are the main form of lighting.

MUSTOE BISTRO, 73 Regent's Park Road (01-586 0901)
Open: Tue-Fri 6.30-11.15pm, Sat-Sun 1-3pm, 6.30-11.15pm

[P] [S] [garden]

Edward Mustoe personally supervises this one of his two bistros, with its wooden partitions, banquettes and interesting old prints. Food is basic English fare, with starters of home-made soup (around 45p) or pâté (about 70p) and main dishes including kidneys in Worcester sauce or beef in beer, both around £2.30. A selection of cold meats with salads is also available for the same price and a sweet costs about 65p. House wine by the glass is around 55p.

SEA SHELL, 33-35 Lisson Grove (01-723 8703)
Open: Tue-Sat 12noon-2.30pm, 5.30-11pm

Here is a fresh fish restaurant par excellence, where portion control has been abandoned in favour of customer satisfaction. A Rolls-Royce parked outside while its owner queues for a take-away cod and chips, or enjoys a quick sit-down meal in the small restaurant, is not an uncommon sight.

Apart from the fried chicken, the menu is devoted entirely to fish such as plaice, cod, halibut, skate, lemon sole and Dover sole. An extremely satisfying meal can be had for around £3.50, including soup and sweet.

SUNWHEEL, 3 Chalk Farm Road
(01-267 8116)
Open: Sun-Thu 12noon-9pm,
Fri-Sat 12noon-10pm

[C] [♫] [P] [S]

'Eat no evil – we don't monkey around with your food', says the menu. The meals at this natural food restaurant are guaranteed free of adulterating chemicals. Split cane lampshades hanging low over attractive checked tablecloths and high ladder-backed chairs add to the natural atmosphere. Starters include chickpea dishes such as houmous or falafal, for around £1.20-£1.50. There's no meat on the menu, but there is fish – either fish tempura (fried in egg-free batter) with vegetables at about £3.30, or fish special of the day for around £3.50. Wholegrain pasta such as vegetable-fried noodles or tofu dishes (freshly-made soya bean curd) are about £2. Tofu cream cake is one of the interesting selection of desserts which range from around 75p-90p. Natural wholewheat bread, baked daily and served with sesame seed butter is delicious. You can try your hand here with Japanese chopsticks. A large glass of house wine is about 60p.

NW3

PEACHEY'S, 205 Haverstock Hill
(01-435 6744)
Open: Mon-Sat 11am-3pm,
5.30pm-12mdnt, Sun 12noon-3pm

[C] [P]

Down the road from the Post House and directly opposite Belsize Park tube station is this small wine bar. Unusual décor features cigarette card sets in frames, Victorian prints, stuffed pike and trout in glass cases, a stag's head and numerous other exotic items of bric-à-brac. Ferns in hanging baskets add warmth to the scene. The food selection, chalked up on a wallboard, changes daily. Starters such as kalamari are about £1.20. Hot dish of the day is from £2.50-£4 and a particularly delicious example is thinly sliced fried liver, covered with avocado slices and pieces of gammon. Chicken curry with peaches and rice is about £3. Vegetables are extra, so you could exceed the limit if you also sample a glass of house wine at about 55p.

PIPPIN RESTAURANT
83-84 Hampstead High Street
(01-435 6434)
Open: Mon-Sun 11am-12mdnt

[C] [P]

An enticing selection of vegetarian specialities in the shop window draws you into this interesting restaurant. Self-service operates – just collect a tray and have it laden with your choice from the list of items displayed on the wall menu. Everything is reasonably priced – salads, hot risotto and cauliflower cheese are all about £1.10, delicious nut roast around £1 and fresh fruit salad about 75p. Wine costs about 60p a glass.

NW5

EDWARD'S BISTRO, 323 Kentish Town Road, (01-267 6956)
Open: Mon-Fri 12.30-2.30pm,
6.30-11pm, Sat 6.30-11pm

[P] [S]

Edward's Bistro was built around an old shop and the old shop front has been preserved inside the entrance. Wood panelled walls hung with paintings, a dark ceiling and gingham-covered lamps hanging over each table complete the effect. Lunch starters include mushrooms in yoghurt at around 50p, and the main course has quiche and salad at around £1.30, chicken korma, spinach crêpe and steak and kidney pudding at a little over £1. All desserts are served with cream. Dinner is more pricey, but still excellent value, including specialities such as pork and pineapple kebabs, ragoût of beef and pepper or garlic steak. An imaginative three-course dinner with wine by the glass or carafe can be enjoyed for about £5.

SE1

THE BOOT AND FLOGGER
10-20 Redcross Way (01-407 1184)
Open: Mon-Fri 11am-3pm, 5.30-8.30pm

Just off Southwark Street is an old ham-curing warehouse, part of which is the John Davy Free Vintner wine bar. One of the smaller Davy outlets, it offers one of the finest wine lists in the whole of London, including vintage ports going back to 1837. Dark wood, glazed partitions and comfortable seating lend a cosy air, and the bill of fare includes game pie at around £2 and plates of cold meats at around £1.80; a 'special' is a dish of prawns at about £1.20. There is an excellent cheesecake or you may care to finish with a couple of toasted fingers with anchovy or sardine.

ROYAL FESTIVAL HALL CAFETERIA
South Bank
(01-928 3246/2829)
Open: Mon-Sun 12noon-2.30pm, 5-10.30pm

♫ P

Good places to eat are few and far between once you're south of the river, so it's worth knowing that you can use the Festival Hall cafeteria whether you're attending a performance or not. Quite near to Waterloo Station and not far from Waterloo Bridge, the South Bank complex is aesthetically pleasing even to those who are not too keen on modern architecture. The uncrowded cafeteria overlooks the busy and perennially interesting Thames, and provides a pleasant place to relax and enjoy a meal. Each day there are two hot dishes costing around £2.50 as well as cold meats and salads, and home-made sweets and good coffee are served. A glass of house wine comes at about 65p.

RSJ, 13A Coin Street (01-928 4554)
Open: Mon-Fri 12noon-3pm, 6-10.45pm, Sat 6-10.45pm

C S

Once a stable but for the last thirty years a cycle warehouse, this newly-converted restaurant occupies prime position near to the West End and Covent Garden. Decorated in smart brown and white, it is deservedly popular with business-people from the nearby offices. Starters include watercress soup and haddock mousse (under £1) and main courses offer cold salmon-trout and calf's liver with avocado at around £2.75. Dutch apple pie, strawberries and cream and various sorbets provide the basis of the sweet selection. House wine costs 60p a glass.

SKINKERS, 40-42 Tooley Street
(01-407 9189)
Open: Mon-Fri 11am-3pm, 5.30-8.30pm

C

Built into the railway arches under London Bridge, next door to the London Dungeons horror museum, Skinkers is beautifully cool in summer, very spacious and relaxed, and enormously popular with City folk and local business people. Décor, menu and wine list are in Davy tradition. The buffet offers starters from about £1, a plate of finest smoked ham, roast beef or game pie (all at around £2), with a mixed salad at 60p or so. House wine starts at about 80p a glass. If you're going on the off-chance, get there early.

SE3

THE BARCAVE WINE BAR
7-9 Montpelier Road, Blackheath
(01-852 0492)
Open: Mon-Sat 11am-3pm, 5.30-11pm, (Fri-Sat 12mdnt) Sun 12noon-2pm, 7-10.30pm

Special feature of this wine bar is the pretty walled terrace garden on two levels with fountains, a fish pond and hanging plants – very restful on a summer evening. Listed on a blackboard are Today's Specials such as moussaka at about £1.90 and beef Stroganoff, curry or cold chicken and salad at around £2.90. A printed menu offers a choice of eight starters from soup (about 60p) to rainbow trout (about £1.70). Cold buffet includes excellent rare roast beef for around £1.50. Quiche or lasagne are examples from the hot buffet at about £1.50. Cheesecakes, gâteaux, trifles or fresh fruit salad are served, and cost from 80p.

KATE 2 BISTRO, 121 Lee Road
(01-852 3610)
Open: Tue-Sat 7-10.30pm

The food at this simple bistro presided over by Kate Lee and Diana Willis was described as the 'most enjoyable meal tasted in over thirty years of eating out' by one of our inspectors. A varied menu includes mackerel fillets in sherry sauce as an appetiser at about £1, home-made quiche and mixed salad for around £2.80, mussels stuffed with garlic butter at about £3.50 or steak pizzaiola at around £4.30 as main courses, and a selection of delicious desserts which change daily as shown on the blackboard. Special portions are offered for children.

SE9

BISTRO 22, 1 West Park, Mottingham
(01-851 2233)
Open: Tue-Sun 7-11.30pm

C ♫ P

French posters, bright tablecloths and candles lend an authentic air to this unpretentious bistro, where the menus are written in French and English. A host of interesting dishes are on offer, but care will be needed if you are to pick three courses for around £5, since vegetables are individually priced. Try prawn cocktail at less than £1, hot garlic bread (only about 20p), cocktail de fruits de mer – seafood in wine and cheese – around £3.60 *with* vegetables and syllabub au citron – about 65p. A large glass of house wine costs around 65p.

MELLINS WINE AND FOOD, 90 Eltham High Street, Eltham (01-850 4462)
Open: Mon-Sat 12noon-2.30pm, 7-11pm, Sun 7-10.30pm

Mellins the apothecary stood here for about 200 years and the wine bar has retained the signs, labels and display cases. An interesting menu offers hot or cold platters such as ham ratatouille or kipper kedgeree for around £1.30, lasagne or chili con carne for about £1.90, and goulash, navarin of lamb or pork 'n peppers for close on £3. Banana mousse is one of the many tasty desserts always available from about 65p. A glass of house wine costs around 55p.

SE10

BAR DU MUSÉE, 17 Nelson Road, Greenwich (01-858 4710)
Open: Mon-Sat 12noon-3pm, 6.30-11pm, Sun 12noon-2pm, 7-10.30pm

This wine bar is on two levels with a cellar bar reached by a spiral staircase. Coats of arms and Dickensian prints enhance the décor. There's a good choice of starters but try the soup of the day, with French bread, at around 65p. Hot dishes such as pizza and salad (around £1.70) or gammon and pineapple (about £2.50) are recommended and there is a choice of ten salads. Beef or ham salads at around £2.60 are particularly good. Desserts include cheesecakes, gâteaux and profiteroles – in the 75p-£1 range.

DAVY'S WINE VAULTS
165 Greenwich High Road
(01-858 7204)
Open: Mon-Fri 11.30am-3pm, Mon-Thu 5.30-10.30pm, Fri 5.30-11pm, Sat 12noon-3pm, 7-11pm
[C] [P]

Under Davy & Co's head office building in Greenwich the old wine cellar is now used as a wine bar and eating house. Victorian touches add to the out-of-the-past aura and help to make this a most popular place. Davy's offer 'fine foreign wines' and 'rare ports of the finest vintages' to wash down their specialities such as avocado pear with prawns at just over £1.25, cold chicken cooked in red wine and spices at about £3.60, or the tempting fresh salmon salad at around £5.80. If you're looking for something slightly less expensive, why not try the cold buffet?

DIKS, 8 Nelson Road, Greenwich (01-858 8588)
Open: Mon, Wed-Sat 12noon-2pm, 7-11pm, Sun 12.30-3pm

Value for money is guaranteed at this delightful restaurant. Proprietor Richard Evans cooks all the food, even the bread rolls and mint fudge served with the coffee. The soup and pâté are served in terrines from which you help yourself to as much as you like. At lunch, three courses are priced by the main dish – veal scaloppini Viennoise with fruit juice and meringue glacé around £3. A three-course dinner offering turkey with mushrooms in white wine is still under £6.

GREENWICH COFFEE HOUSE
269 Greek Road, Greenwich
(01-853 4461)
Open: Sun-Mon, Wed 10am-6pm, Thu 10am-6pm, 7-9.45pm, Fri-Sat 10.30am-5pm, 7-10pm
[♫] [S]

Young chef/proprietor Marc Garchon-Dyer says his cooking has been greatly influenced by his French mother, and he produces a Cordon Bleu Chef's Special (such as kidney sautéd in wine with fresh vegetables) every day to prove it. In fact, this quaint little coffee house, with its bright pine furniture,

caters for the majority of tastes by offering a selection of pastries and salads (about £1.50) to supplement the substantial hot meals, such as farmhouse mixed grill and chicken vol-au-vent.

THE SOURCE, 106, Blackheath Road (01-691 1010)
Open: Sun-Mon 12noon-3pm, Tue-Sat 12noon-3pm, 7.30-11.30pm

[♫] [🍷]

Enthusiastic vegetarians, Keith and Norma Perry ensure that you enjoy wholesome, unadulterated food in pleasant surroundings – pine tables, a Welsh dresser and an old kitchen range set the scene for a gastronomic experience in healthy eating. Appetisers include beanshoot salad and stuffed vine leaves, both at 85p, or minted grapefruit and orange for around 60p. The list of main dishes is no less interesting, with ratatouille Niçoise costing about £1.90 or asparagus quiche at around £1. All the desserts, such as cinnamon apple cake, are under £1 and are served with fresh cream or yoghurt.

SE19

JOANNA'S 56a Westow Hill, Upper Norwood (01-670 4052)
Open: Mon-Fri 12noon-2pm, 6-11.15pm, Sat 6-11.15pm

[♫] [P] [S] [🍷]

Very appealing décor, with hanging plants, large photographs of film stars and smart check tablecloths, is complemented by an atmosphere kept fresh by two huge ceiling fans. Burgers are a speciality of the house – 100% beef served in a toasted sesame bun plus potatoes and fresh salad. There are eight varieties – 'Gourmet' is dressed in wine and mushroom sauce plus melted cheese. You can have a ¼lb burger for around £2.30, or an enormous ½lb one for about £2.60. Grills and dishes such as chili con carne (served with side salad and hot pitta bread for about £2.50) are also on offer as are starters and delicious desserts such as 'Joanna's Special' – a hot waffle with maple syrup and whipped cream or chocolate fudge cake both about 90p. A large glass of house wine is around 60p.

SE27

SAU LEE CHINESE RESTAURANT
479 Norwood Road, West Norwood (01-670 5053)
Open: Mon-Thu 12noon-2.30pm, 5.30pm-12mdnt, Fri-Sat 12noon-12mdnt, Sun 12noon-2pm, 5.30pm-12mdnt

[C]

Choose carefully from the long and varied menu here and you can enjoy a banquet on a budget. Special set lunches start at only around £1.50 – a choice of seven Chinese dishes and one English dish. Special Peking dinner for two to four persons is a feast for about £4.20 – seven courses with prawns, chicken, beef and duck in various guises. The à la carte menu lists 132 savoury items, all very reasonably priced. A special dish is toasted prawns with sesame seeds (about £1.80). Nine desserts include chow chow or gum quats, both around 50p. A glass of wine costs about 55p.

SW1

BEN'S OF WESTMINSTER, 29 Victoria Street (01-222 0424)
Open: Mon-Sun 12noon-3.30pm, 5.30pm-11pm

Ben's 'Upper Chamber' à la carte dishes could easily add up to a goodly sum, but there is a set lunch at around £5.50. This offers a choice of three starters, a main dish such as grilled trout or roast lamb, with potatoes and two other vegetables, a sweet or cheese, and coffee. The 'Lobby' food, with soup or quiche for a starter, a hot dish, cheese, bread and butter, coffee and a glass of wine, plus 10% service charge, would set you back about £4.50 or so. A bottle of house wine costs £3 or thereabouts. Even if you don't know London you will have guessed by now that Ben's is quite near the Houses of Parliament and within the sound of its big namesake. The 'Upper' and 'Main' chambers are sedate and opulent-looking, while the 'Lobby' atmosphere is more relaxed and informal.

THE GREEN MAN, Harrods, Knightsbridge (01-730 1234)
Open: Mon-Sat 11.30am-3pm

[P] [S]

They say that there's nothing you can't buy at Harrods – at a price, and that's true even when it comes to finding a tasty meal. Located next to the Men's Department, the air is distinctly pubby and masculine in the Green Man restaurant. Pleasant and fast service is one bonus to the excellent food, with seafood platter at around £5 the most expensive item on the menu. A cold buffet displays a choice of salads, cold

meats and a very good game pie for about £2. Apple pie or cheesecake are examples of desserts. A glass of house wine costs about 65p.

MOTCOMB'S, 26 Motcomb Street (01-235 6382)
Open: Mon-Fri 12noon-3pm, 7-11pm, Wine bar: Mon-Fri 11.30am-3pm, 5.30-11pm

[C] [♬] [S]

It is, perhaps, appropriate that this popular wine bar faces Sotheby's saleroom, for it combines the antique with efficiency and *chic* in a most enchanting way. Food is out of the ordinary too, though luckily the accent is on freshness rather than antiquity. Although it would be all too easy to exceed the £5 limit when dining in the restaurant, a more economical meal is possible. There are several starters at prices around £1.25, most main dishes are in the region of £3.50 – bouillabaisse Marseilles, loin of pork in wine and chicken with a whisky sauce, for instance. A sweet or cheese costs around £1 with wine at about 60p.

THE SCALLOP RESTAURANT
Central Hall, Westminster (01-222 3222)
Open: Mon-Sat 12noon-2.30pm, 3.15-5.30pm

Occupying the whole of the basement under the vast Central Hall, The Scallop caters for large numbers yet manages to present well-cooked, appetising food at modest prices. The à la carte menu includes grills and omelettes, all (except steak) priced around £2, fish and chips or salad for under £1.75, and a selection of sweets priced around 50p. The special lunchtime menu offers soup or fruit juice at around 30p, a choice of five main courses such as a roast, steak and kidney pie or a pasta dish (costing in the region of £1.55), and a sweet at about 40p. There is also a three-course set lunch for around £2.75 which is very good value.

STRIKES, 124 Victoria Street (01-834 0644)
Open: Mon-Sun 12noon-11.30pm

[C] [♬]

Just why a group of American-style eating houses should be named after a British general strike is hard to fathom, but arrive at Victoria Station feeling hungry and you may be glad to see a Strikes restaurant opposite the main exit. Inside you'll find a long narrow room with tables along one side, decorated with pictures of the 1926 strike, and there's a staircase twisting down to a second dining area. Starters vary from soup at 40p to avocado pear and prawns at £1.25 and you may choose a main course from a wide selection of hamburgers (£1.35 – £2.60), platters (fish and chips at £1.40 to minute steak, egg, baked beans and chips at £2.85), steaks (up to £4.25), salads (£1.85 for tuna, or cottage cheese with whole peach, or prawn). Whichever you choose you'll be offered a choice of relishes and sauces at your table. Desserts are all variations on the theme of ice cream, and magnificent concoctions some of them are – as they should be when they cost up to £1.75! The house wine is 65p a glass, and amongst other beverages are Strikes Shakes at 65p.

SW3

BISTRO D'AGRAN, 1a Beauchamp Place, Chelsea (01-589 3982)
Open: Mon-Sat 12noon-2.45pm, 7-11.30pm

[C] [S]

If you are looking for a good place for an inexpensive meal and a glass of wine then the Bistro d'Agran is the place for you. This French-style bistro has pink walls and mahogany booths made from benches from an 1840s coffee house. The lunch menu includes a number of low-priced main dishes such as liver cooked in butter, onions and red wine, at about £2.20 or spaghetti bolognese at a little over £1. Even steak Diane is only about £3.75, as is salmon steak Danoise. Prices include vegetables, but you might like to add hot garlic bread at 35p. Starters average about 75p, sweets cost from around 50p for cream caramel to 70p for banana split. There is a minimum charge for dinner of £2.60, which would buy you fried chicken Southern style.

LE BOUZY ROUGE, 221 King's Road Chelsea (01-351 1607)
Open: Mon-Sat 11.30am-3pm, 5.30-11pm, Sun 7-10.30pm

[♬] [S]

A wine and spirits shop on the ground floor and a wine bar in the basement is an excellent combination, and a useful place to find a few yards from Chelsea Antique Market (if you've any money left). Simple foods, such as pork sausage and butter beans and navarin of lamb, are served in ample portions for around £1.80, and salads are available, too. There is a good variety of wines, of course, with the house wine costing from 50p a glass. Large bags hanging from brass rods provide comfortable backrests to the bench seating. A welcome change is the background of classical music – piped, certainly, but nevertheless a soothing change from the roar of London's traffic.

CARAVELA, 11 Beauchamp Place, Chelsea (01-581 2366)
Open: Tue-Sat 12noon-2.30pm, Tue-Sun 7pm-1am

[C] [♫] [P] [S] [🍷]

Delicious squid is served at this simple, semi-basement Portuguese restaurant, so if you're adventurous – or Portuguese – you'll enjoy such novel dishes as grilled squid or highly spiced pork chops, each for about £3. But there are less exotic dishes to choose from in a warm cosy atmosphere, with varnished wood slats cladding the ceiling, walls and arched alcoves. A fine model galleon on the bar, and pictures, continue the theme of ships and the sea. Victorian gentlemen would have loved the continually-changing view through the window, which is at ankle-level to the street. Watch the prices, too – vegetables are sometimes charged extra and there's a cover charge of 50p – but it's not expensive for this part of London and it may be useful to know somewhere which is open until 1am every day of the week.

CHEYNE WALK WINE BAR, Pier House, 31 Cheyne Walk (01-352 4989)
Open: Mon-Sat 11.30am-3pm, 6.30-11pm, Sun 12noon-2pm

[C] [♫]

Behind the graceful statue of David Wynn's 'Boy on a Dolphin' is a wine bar where you can eat until late evening (and drink until midnight) to the accompaniment of live piano music. The Victorian-style interior in shades of brown and hung with carriage lamps and old prints overlooks a splendidly romantic night view of the illuminated Albert Bridge. Two Cordon Bleu cooks provide tantalising starters such as tuna fish parcels or pâté-stuffed mushrooms for £1 or under; main courses of steak and kidney or chicken and mushroom pie with vegetables for under £3, a range of salads and cold meats, and at the higher end of the price scale, fresh Dover sole for £4.50.

SW6

HAFEZ, 45 Fulham High Street, Putney (01-731 2787)
Open: Mon-Sun 12noon-3pm, 5-11pm

[C] [P]

London, we are told, can now boast the most authentic Middle Eastern restaurants in Europe, so the opening of a new Persian restaurant was of particular interest some two years ago. Now Putney residents can enjoy something more sophisticated than conventional Indian and Chinese food. And at a modest price, it fulfils this need admirably, serving starters from 60p, and kebabs with exotic names like chelo and jujeh for around £2. And what about estanboli polo, a mixture of rice and meat, or a spicy stew rejoicing in the name of koresht ghormh? One attractive feature is that its proprietor, Ahmad Dabierzadeh, waits personally at table, and explains the mysteries of the menu.

SW7

DAQUISE, 20 Thurloe Street, South Kensington (01-589 6117)
Open: Mon-Sun 10am-12mdnt

[S]

Full meals can be obtained here at any time between midday and midnight, so if you fancy goulash for tea you can have it. You can buy a selection of other dishes at this Polish restaurant, from Russian zrazy at £1.80 to chicken à la

Vienna at £2, as well as straightforward salads and omelettes costing around £1. Vegetables will add another 50p or so, and soup will cost about 40p. Ice cream and pastries are available if you want a sweet to finish the meal. From noon until 3pm, set-price two-course lunches are served. Soup, followed by meatballs kasza or stuffed aubergine, for instance, costs around £1.80. Desserts are mainly gâteaux (from 30p-50p), whilst house wine is around 45p per glass. Downstairs there is a small licensed restaurant where the atmosphere is cosily intimate.

SW8

ATUCHACLASS, 24 Queenstown Road
Open: Mon-Sat 6.30-11.30pm

[♫] [P] [S]

An offshoot of the up-market 'Alonso's' (next-door-but-one), this intimate bistro certainly has a touch of class, from its quarry-tiled floor and subdued lighting to its imaginative international cuisine and the excellence of its fresh vegetables. The prices are just about within our limit, which for this type of establishment is surprising in itself. How about this for a meal: chicken liver pâté with herbs, spinach and chutney; Indonesian lamb in pastry (pieces of lamb, prawns, rice, raisins, mushrooms, chutney, light curry sauce) served with a selection of fresh vegetables; raspberry sorbet, coffee and a glass of wine? That adds up to just over a fiver.

SW11

ANGELA AND PETER, 300 Battersea Park Road (01-228 6133)
Open: Mon-Sat 12noon-3pm, 7-11pm

[♫] [S] [🍷]

The décor of this wine bar-cum-bistro is enhanced by interesting relics from the former antique shop. Excellent home-made fare includes cream of cucumber soup (about 60p) or tuna pâté (around £1.25) as starters, chicken with almonds in white wine and cream sauce (around £3), lamb cooked in white wine sauce with garlic (about £3.50) or rump steak (around £4) as main courses, and delicious sherry syllabub at around £1.

FROGG'S LEGS WINE BAR
264 Battersea Park Road (01-223 0825)
Open: Mon-Sat 11am-3pm, 5.20-11pm, Sun 11am-3pm, 7-10.30pm

Proprietor Jan-Michel Gautier has created a very French atmosphere in his small wine bar where one may linger over a lazy Sunday coffee with a choice of French or English newspapers to keep you informed. The menu is written on a blackboard listing interesting French dishes and also large hamburgers and pork chops, all dishes around £2. Unusual provincial French wines are on sale in the restaurant.

JUST WILLIAMS, 6a Battersea Rise (01-223 6890)
Open: Mon-Sat 12noon-3pm, 5.30-11pm, Sun 12noon-2pm, 5.30-10.30pm

[C] [♫] [P] [S] [🍷]

This intimate wine bar, with its pine display counter, colourful check tablecloths and interesting bric-à-brac, is enthusiastically managed by John Rush. The blackboard menu lists interesting Greek starters such as houmous and taramasalata, all served with pitta bread for about £1.50. Three hot dishes always available are chicken fricassée, goulash and lasagne, all at around £2.75. Desserts include cheesecakes and gâteaux such as passioncake – a delicious fantasy of walnuts, apples and cream – about 75p. Fifteen wines are available by the glass from around 60-80p.

TOAD HALL, 62 Battersea Bridge Road (01-228 8380)
Open: Mon-Sat 8-11pm

[♫] [P] [🍷]

There are no willows down by the Thames at Battersea now and Kenneth Grahame would be surprised at this version of Toad Hall. Mole, Ratty and the others are depicted in murals and the menu is as zany as anything Toad could have invented. In fact, you need Manager David Scott-Bradbury to interpret items like 'Lady C' or 'A Leek in Bed' (which are starters) and 'Desperate Dan's Cow Pie' or 'Greek Tragedy' (main courses). There are 'puds' too, and coffee, all for about £5. A service charge is added. A *tumbler* of house wine costs around 85p, after which you'll be fit to fight the weasels and stoats and very likely win into the bargain.

SW15

LA FORCHETTA, 3 Putney Hill (01-785 6749)
Open: Mon-Thu 12noon-2.45pm, 6.30-11.15pm, Fri-Sat 6.30-11.30pm

[C] [♫] [P] [🍷]

You'll find this bright little Italian restaurant at the bottom of Putney Hill. You can buy a cheap pasta dish here for around £1.50. A more elaborate meal could exceed budget but won't if you take care. Starters range from soup at about 80p to Parma ham and melon at around £2.20. Similarly, you could choose scampi alla provinciale at about £4 or piccatina al Marsala (veal escalope in Marsala) at about £3, or steak dishes at £3.50 or so. Vegetables add about 60p, and you can choose a sweet from the trolley or try zabaglione al Marsala – good value at around 90p. A glass of the Italian house wine costs just over 60p. There is a cover charge of 40p. A good place for a tête-à-tête dinner.

MR MICAWBER'S, 147 Upper Richmond Road, Putney (01-788 2429)
Open: Mon-Fri 12noon-3pm, 5.30-11pm, Sat 12noon-3pm, Sun 12noon-2pm, 7-10.30pm

♫ S ♧

There's sometimes a queue for food, but you won't have to wait too long for something to turn up in Mr Micawber's wine bar. You should be able to heed Mr Micawber's maxim about annual expenditure too, for food is very reasonably priced and you can buy a glass of house wine for about 50p. Choice of food is limited, but there are hot casseroles, chili con carne and quiches as well as cold meats, pies and salads.

SW16

MR BUNBURY'S BISTRO, 1154 London Road, Norbury (01-764 3939)
Open: Tue-Sat 12noon-2.30pm, 7-11pm (Sat 11.30pm)

A small bistro with Victorian décor and a cosy atmosphere enhanced by the oil lamps and old photographs and prints. Susan Williams looks after the diners while husband Kenneth keeps busy in the kitchen preparing such delights as Bunbury pie (a large individual pie filled with lean chunks of beef, mushrooms, onions, and carrots topped with flaky puff pastry). The set lunch at under £4 is excellent value. Vegetables are plentiful and served in separate earthenware dishes; the puddings (always generous helpings) are home-made.

RINO'S RESTAURANT, 84 Streatham High Road, Streatham (01-769 7916)
Open: Mon-Sun 12noon-3pm, 6pm-12mdnt

C ♫ S ♧

A large regular clientele haunts this very busy Italian trattoria – and not just because Salvatore Polumba, one of the proprietors, otherwise known as Rino, is always chatting with the diners. The menu is very extensive – fourteen starters and five soups offer an interesting choice including snails, tunny fish and Italian hors d'oeuvres. Pastas, pizzas and omelettes are around £1.50 and Rino's specialities, served with two vegetables of the day, include pollo principessa (chicken with white wine, cream and asparagus tips) or piccatina al Marsala (veal escalopes cooked in butter and Marsala wine) priced from around £2.80. Sweets such as zabaglione al Marsala (about £1), crêpes Suzette (around £2) or lemon sorbet (about £1), complete a substantial meal. A glass of house wine costs around 70p.

SW19

THE CROOKED BILLET, 15 Crooked Billet, Wimbledon Common (01-946 4942)
Open: Mon-Thu, Sun 12noon-2.30pm, 7.30-10pm, Fri-Sat 12noon-2.30pm, 7.30-10.30pm

C ♧

A building which started life as a barn way back in the 15th century, is now an olde worlde restaurant, retaining some of the bygone features such as timbered beams and pillars. Fare is varied and at sensible prices. Starters range from 40p-£1.20, featuring egg mayonnaise and Swedish herring. Of the main dishes, rainbow trout and beef Lyonnaise are both good value at under £3, whilst huge salads are a snip at around £2. Home-made apple pie and Black Forest gâteau make delicious desserts at 75p, whilst St André is the house wine and costs 50p a glass.

DOWNS WINE BAR, 40 Wimbledon Hill Road (01-946 3246)
Open: Mon-Sun 12noon-3pm, 7pm-2am

C ♫ S ♧

Unobtrusive décor gives an atmosphere of intimacy and informality, both in the cosy cellar bar, with its alcoves and dance floor, and in the ground floor bar, where one can take a quieter meal. The menu is changed daily, but there's always a good selection of both hot and cold dishes. Pâtés such as duck with cognac and chicken liver with brandy come at around £1, while a variety of quiches and cold meat salads cost slightly more. Hot dishes, such as burgundy beef, pork paprika or tarragon chicken in cream and lemon sauce are around £2, but extremely tasty. House special is seafood chowder served with garlic bread at around £3.

W1

L'ARTISTE MUSCLE, 1 Shepherd Market (01-493 6150)
Open: Mon-Sat 12noon-3pm, 5.30pm-12mdnt, Sun 7-11pm

[♫] [S]

In the heart of the Shepherd Market lies L'Artiste Musclé, a French wine-bar-cum-bistro in a 19th-century building which at first sight appears to be a well-populated junk shop. Closer inspection discloses that people are actually eating and drinking inside, though with a minimum of ceremony as they rub shoulders with anything from old chests to chamber-pots while doing so. The menu is short, but has a real French-peasantish flavour, with items such as jambon and quiche. Typical prices are about £2.25 for côte de porc or ragout d'agneau. The French house wine is around 50p a glass.

BISTRO 42, 42 Crawford Street (01-262 6582)
Open: Mon-Sun 12noon-3pm, 6pm-12mdnt

[C] [♫] [P] [S] [♧]

Dark-panelled walls and ceiling, tables lit by low hanging lanterns, framed prints of Paris and advertisement posters lend to this unobtrusive little restaurant an unmistakably French atmosphere. The extensive menu is in French with English translations and offers a particularly mouth-watering selection, such as champignons frits sauce tartare (mushrooms fried in breadcrumbs with tartar sauce) followed by brochette d'agneau Cardinal avec riz (fillets of lamb with bacon on a skewer served with barbecue sauce on rice). Main courses start at around £3 with an additional charge for vegetables, but portions are so generous and sauces so rich and satisfying as to make any extras almost unnecessary.

BON APPETIT II, 14 Albemarle Street (01-499 5317)
Open: Mon-Fri 7am-5pm, Sat 7am-2.30pm

[S]

In elegant Albemarle Street this small restaurant-cum-sandwich bar is a bit of a surprise. But if you work in the area, and particularly if you enjoy Italian pasta dishes, it's a useful place to know. Ravioli, spaghetti, lasagne or risotto cost around £1 and there's a big variety of snack dishes such as ham, egg and chips in the same price range. Sweets cost from about 25p to 40p and the house wine is around 50p a glass. If the place is full there's a sister restaurant across the road.

THE CASSEROLE, 67 Tottenham Court Road (01-636 1099)
Open: Mon-Sat 8.30-11am, 12noon-3pm, 5.30pm-12mdnt, Sun8.30-11am, 12noon-3pm, 6-11pm

[S] [♧]

Proprietor Philip Towe is also chef in this cheerful basement restaurant with a hand-painted mural of jolly little animals frolicking in the woods. The menu is extensive and includes snacks as well as special main courses such as pork Normandy (fillet of pork with wine, mushrooms, brandy and parsley, served with rice and salad) at about £3.80 or beef Stroganoff at around £3.50. Extra vegetables cost in the region of 30p a portion. At the cheaper end you can choose from items such as lamb curry, beef casserole or moussaka at prices in the £1.80-£2.50 range. Sweets are priced from about 70p, with cheesecake or gâteau at around 70p. A goblet of house wine costs about 70p.

THE CHICAGO PIZZA PIE FACTORY
17 Hanover Square (01-629 2669)
Open: Mon-Sat 11.45am-11.30pm

[C] [♫] [P] [S] [♧]

This popular pizza restaurant has a very formal atmosphere, the walls lavishly decorated with Chicago memorabilia. The deep-dish Chicago-style pizza is new to this country: it has a thick crust and rich filling based on mozzarella cheese. Don't go alone however, as the smallest serves two – and is priced accordingly (around £3.50). If you think you can tackle more than a pizza, start with savoury stuffed mushrooms with sherry and garlic and finish with a delicious cheesecake. Owner Bob Payton's great passion, second after pizzas, is music and a sophisticated stereo system keeps his customers entertained while they wait the customary thirty minutes for their culinary masterpiece to appear from the kitchen.

DOWNS WINE BAR, 5 Down Street (01-491 3810)
Open: Mon-Sat 12noon-3pm, 5.30pm-1am, Sun 12noon-3pm, 7-12.30am

[C] [♫] [P] [S] [♧]

A wine bar situated in an 18th-century

backwater of Mayfair might be expected to price itself into the millionaires-only class, so it is a pleasant surprise to find that a dinner for £5 is eminently possible at Down's. True, one could choose a more expensive meal, but with a starter of smoked mackerel at about 95p or rough country pâté (same price), a daily special (chicken chasseur for instance) at around £2.95, or trout or lamb kebab costing about £3 with vegetables and a sweet such as cherry cheesecake averaging 85p, even the addition of the 10% service charge does not take us over the top. There is also a well-stocked 'downstairs' cold table. There is quite a range of wines by the glass, priced from around 70p.

GARFUNKELS, 57/61 Duke Street (01-499 5000)
Open: Mon-Sun 11am-11pm

[♣]

Shopping in Oxford Street needn't be a chore when you have the pleasure of a meal at Phillip and Reginald Kaye's luxurious restaurant to look forward to. The soft brown, beige, cream and amber interior and the profusion of palms and other greenery provides a restful haven just far enough from the milling crowds. For a light refresher you might choose the salad bar where you can help yourself to heaps of fresh salad from £2 for a main course, or you might prefer a hot meal such as chicken farmer style (off the bone) served with a mixture of diced bacon, onions, carrots, peas and potatoes for just under £2 or, at the same price, chili con carne with baked potato. A starter of vegetable soup at 50p, a dish of Garfunkel's American ice cream at 65p for dessert, coffee at 30p plus a 65p glass of house wine will provide a substantial meal for £4, day or evening.

GRANARY, 39 Albemarle Street (01-493 2978)
Open: Mon-Fri 11am-6.50pm,
Sat 11am-2.30pm

[♫] [S]

Baskets of ferns and air-conditioning create a fresh, cool atmosphere in which to enjoy your meal in this delightful restaurant. Choose what you fancy from the tempting array of food on display, and one of the heart-throb waiters will carry it to your table. The menu is chalked up and is sure to include a choice of nine main dishes, all at around £1.80. Salads are less than £1, and there is a really delicious array of sweets priced at about 75p. The Spanish house wine is around 60p a glass.

IKAROS, 36 Baker Street (01-935 7821)
Open: Mon-Sat 12noon-3pm,
6pm-12mdnt

[C] [♫] [S] [♣]

This small Greek restaurant has an authentic air. The charcoal grill wafts the most delicious smells to the diner and gives a flavour to the food not found in normal cooking. An interesting Greek starter such as taramasalata or longaniko sausage costs around 85p, and main dishes include doner kebab at around £2.50 and moussaka at £2.60. Vegetables cost about 60p a portion and sweets come from 60p. A large glass of house wine costs around 70p. This is another restaurant where it would be all too easy to exceed the £5 limit, but for central London the prices are not unreasonable.

KNIGHTSBRIDGE SPAGHETTI HOUSE, 77 Knightsbridge (01-235 6987)
Open: Mon 12noon-3pm,
Tue-Fri 12noon-3pm, 5.30-10.30pm,
Sat 12noon-3pm, 5.30-11pm

[♫] [P] [S] [♣]

This is the most famous of the Spaghetti Houses – six Italian restaurants specialising in pasta dishes. The menu is nearly the same throughout the group, with all the pastas and pizzas costing around £1.20 a portion. Also on the menu are fish and meat dishes, served with potatoes and another vegetable, or spaghetti, or rice, or salad. With the exception of fillet steak, none of these dishes is priced over £3.60. There's a good selection of starters, sweets and cheeses. A glass of house wine is around 65p.

LORD BYRON TAVERNA, 41 Beak Street (01-734 0316)
Open: Mon-Sat 12noon-3pm,
6pm-3.30am (closed Sat lunch)

[C] [♫] [S]

'You have to kiss a helluva lot of frogs before you find Prince Charming'. This is just one of the thousands of comments that decorate the walls and ceiling of this Greek taverna. Hardly Byronic, but most of the graffiti are quite amusing, and if you can think up something better you are welcome to add you piece. The restaurant premises were once lived in by Caneletto, the Venetian painter, and there is a blue plaque to commemorate this above the entrance. Food is almost entirely Greek, starters including a special variety of taramasalata and avgolemono (chicken soup with egg, lemon juice and rice), either costing about 70p. Most of the main course dishes are priced around £2 but salad and other vegetables are charged extra and may add £1 or so. Desserts are from 60p.

RASA SAYANG, 10 Frith Street (01-734 8720)
Open: Mon-Fri 12noon-3pm, 6pm-12mdnt, Sat 6pm-1am

[C] [♫] [S]

Attentive waiters at this cool, airy South East Asian restaurant, with its tasteful wood and wicker décor, will help you to select dishes from the intriguing menu. Starters include a variety of soups and a host of main courses are offered – seafood, chicken, beef, pork and vegetarian dishes. Speciality of the house is 'satay' – tender skewers of chicken and beef marinated in Malaysian spices, gently grilled and served with fresh cucumber, rice cakes and a rich savoury peanut-based sauce – all this for around £2. Desserts costing from 80p-£1 include kolak pisang – banana slices in coconut milk sweetened with brown sugar or seasonal fresh fruits. Side dishes are extra, so you will have to select with care to remain within the budget. A very large glass of wine is 85p, but half a pint of lager complements this cuisine well and will only set you back 45p.

RISTORANTE ALPINO, 42 Marylebone High Street (01-935 4640)
Open: Mon-Sat 12noon-11.30pm

[C] [♫] [S] [🍷]

A typical Alpino this, with décor in the chalet style; skis on the wall, and the standard Alpino menu including chicken Kiev and escalopes of veal cooked in Marsala, both at just over £2.55. A very friendly little restaurant, managed with Italian flair and Italian charm. An accordionist plays light music to aid the digestion of the supper trade. Madame Tussaud's is close by.

RISTORANTE ALPINO, 102 Wigmore Street (01-935 4181)
Open: Mon-Sat 12noon-11.30pm, Sun 7-11.30pm

[C] [♫] [P] [S] [🍷]

This is the Alpino for Oxford Street shoppers, with a small front section for afternoon teas, a main restaurant of about sixty covers and a side rear room with fifty more. The gâteaux for all the Alpinos are made in the patisserie beneath this particular restaurant and very good they are. 'My Black Forest Gâteau is the best in London' the pastry cook has been known to boast, and no one – but no one – argues with a Sicilian pastry cook.

THE ROSE RESTAURANT, Dickins and Jones, Regent Street (01-734 7070)
Open: Mon-Sat 11.30am-3pm, 3.15-5.15pm

[C] [♫] [S] [🍷]

Judging by the starched linen tablecloths, heavy cutlery, thick carpets and cool, green plants hanging in baskets from the elegant supporting pillars, Dickins and Jones work hard to maintain the old traditions. There is both a cold carvers table at around £5.25, and a hot carvers table for a little over £5.50 at lunch-time. Ask your waitress for a voucher, and choose what you fancy from roast rib of beef and veg, fish and salads. In addition, there are the hot dishes of the day such as spaghetti bolognese at about £2.50, fillet of plaice with French fried potatoes for around £3.40, and saddle of lamb marechella served with sauté potatoes and whole beans (around £4.40), or a choice of grills such as Scotch entrecôte or lamb cutlets, with a mouth-watering selection of gâteaux, trifles and pastries on the buffet, and a good range of ice cream-based sweets – none more than £1.10. Wine by the glass is 65p.

SWISS CENTRE RESTAURANT
10 Wardour Street (01-734 1291)
Open: Mon-Sun 11.30am-12mdnt

[C] [♫] [P] [S] [🍷]

There are four separate restaurants at the Swiss Centre, each with its own décor and menu. Of these only The Chesa prices itself out of this book. The other three are predominantly Swiss in style from the three different regions and all offer regional specialities, most of which are well within our price-range. Of special interest are the fondues, hors-d'oeuvre (which may be ordered either as an appetiser or as a main dish) and herrings or brill cooked in a number of intriguing ways. The speciality of the house is the range of sausage meats, bread, ice cream, gâteaux and chocolates, all freshly-made on the premises. Rum sponge with marzipan at around 50p and Matterhorn Ice Firn (sponge, ice cream, curaçao soufflé and candied fruits made into an ice pie and glazed in the oven) at about 80p are just two of these.

UEMA, 160 New Cavendish Street (01-637 8339)
Open: Mon-Sun 12noon-3.30pm, 6-12mdnt

[C] [♫] [P] [S] [🍷]

The subdued lighting in this small restaurant, just around the corner from the BBC, helps to convey an Indian atmosphere. Those not wishing to cauterise their insides with a burning curry can eat here in safety! Many of the dishes are delicately spiced but you can, if you want, have curry that will really burn. You can get a good, satisfying meal here for around £4.

W2

THE GYNGLEBOY, 27 Spring Street (01-723 3351)
Open: Mon-Fri 11am-3pm, 5.30-9pm

C S

The 'Gyngleboy' was a leather bottle, or black jack, lined with silver and ornamented with little silver bells 'to ring peales of drunkeness'. So now you know. Conveniently close to Paddington Station, this is a very superior wine bar offering a substantial choice of cold dishes – even the game pie is cold. So are the smoked chicken and smoked eel specials, as well as the home-baked apple pies and puddings. But try the soup – that's piping hot. The cellar is extensive and there's a sophisticated range of château bottled vintages.

OODLES, 128 Edgware Road, Marble Arch (01-723 7548)
Open: Mon-Sat 11am-9pm, Sun 12noon-8pm

S

You've got to hand it to Oodles Ltd. The name over its restaurants conjuries up visions of plenty. And that's just what it offers – large helpings of nourishing country-style dishes, just like Mother used to make them. Casseroles, beef stew, chicken curries, steak pie, are all under £1.95, which with a modestly priced wholesome sweets selection and a glass of wine will keep the bill to under £5. This Oodles is the most recently opened of the five branches in London, and each has the same simple décor – rough wooden tables, bench seats, white stucco walls, hung with wooden advertising plates such as used to be seen on horse-drawn delivery carts. See also listing under EC4 and WC1.

TAORMINA, 19 Craven Terrace (01-262 2090)
Open: Mon-Sun 12noon-1am

C

As in most London restaurants, you have to choose rather carefully when ordering your meal here. The Taormina's motif is a wheel, the window area being taken up by two large cart wheels, with the theme repeated on the cover of the menu. White stucco walls relieved by paintings and ornaments, and a false ceiling of polished beams make the interior light and pleasant. Food is authentically Italian, with soups at about 70p, freshly-made pizzas (you'll have to wait while yours is cooked), pasta and rice dishes from £1. And then there's squid (around £4) which is cooked in tomato purée with garlic and parsley – delicious. Sweets start at 40p or so. A glass of house wine is about 60p.

W3

NORTH CHINA, 305 Uxbridge Road, Acton (01-992 9183)
Open: Mon-Thu, Sun 12noon-2pm, 5.30-11.30pm, Fri-Sat 12noon-2pm, 5.30-12mdnt

Proprietor Lawrence Lou specialises in Peking cuisine – particularly in Peking Crispy Aromatic Duck – a rare delight which can be enjoyed whole (around £10) or in portions (the smallest is about £3.50). Special dinners are on offer for two people at around £5 each – mixed hors d'oeuvres, spare ribs, Peking duck, prawns in chili sauce or sweet and sour sauce, shredded beef, diced chicken with cashew nuts in yellow bean sauce and Chinese-style toffee apple or banana is one example. The usual baffling à la carte menu with hundreds of dishes is also astonishingly reasonable. A glass of wine costs 75p.

W4

FOUBERTS WINE BAR, 162 Chiswick High Road (01-994 5202)
Open: Mon-Thu 12noon-3pm, 7-10.30pm, Fri-Sat 12noon-3pm, 7-11pm

S

This is a small basement wine bar which uses both wooden and cast-iron furniture to give a slightly Bohemian air. Italian dishes such as lasagne (about £1.50) are good here, or if you prefer English no-frills food you can get a steak for around £3.50. Soup with roll and butter costs 40p or so. A large selection of wines includes several which can be bought by the glass for around 55p.

W5

CRISPINS WINE BAR, 46-47 The Mall, Ealing (01-567 8966)
Open: normal licensing hours. Food

available: 12noon-2.30pm, 6-8pm

The unusual exterior is reminiscent of an old railway station, with its cast-iron-and-glass portico forming a protected area where ironwork tables and chairs are available for patrons. There is a similarly-equipped garden at the back for rain-free days. The bar itself is reputed to be the largest in London, stretching almost the full depth of the premises, with cast iron tables and chairs arranged along one side. In spite of its size it gets very crowded on Friday and Saturday evenings. The interior is French bistro-style, the décor somewhat barn-like with natural wood beams and panels and a quarry-tiled floor. Food is cheap and good. At lunchtime a little over £1.50 buys a hot dish such as moussaka, curry or hotpot with accompanying vegetables, and cold food such as quiche with salad is available at lunchtime or in the evening at similar prices. Desserts are about 50p a portion. House wines cost in the region of 50p a glass. There is another Crispins at 14 The Green.

CRUSTS GAFF, 17 The Green, Ealing (01-579 2788)
Open: Mon-Thu 12noon-11.30pm, Fri-Sat 12noon-12mdnt, Sun 12noon-10.30pm

[♫] [P]

An abundance of natural wood comes in handy for hanging numerous knick-knacks including a spinning wheel, steel helmets and statues. Walls covered with old prints and mirrors complete the individual décor of this popular bistro. Emphasis is on good, wholesome food. Starters include soup at around 75p or pâté at about £1. Main dish specialities such as barbecued chicken are on offer at around £3.50, spare ribs at about £2. Meat and cheeseburgers are rock bottom budget items and there is a selection of competitively-priced salads. Sweets include apple pie and crème caramel for around 80p-£1. A glass of house wine costs in the region of £1.

W6

CAPRI, 2-2a Holcombe Street (01-748 5000)
Open: Mon-Sat 12noon-3pm, 6pm-12mdnt

[C] [♫] [S] [🍷]

Just a few paces off Hammersmith's King Street, this small restaurant has a genuine Italian atmosphere. Rough plastered walls are decorated with unusual pictures painted on copper, and at the end of the restaurant brick arches form alcoves for plants. The heavy wooden chairs with rushwork seats are comfortable. Soups are priced from around 50p and pâté is about 90p, but most of the other starters are rather too highly-priced for us. A number of main course dishes are out of reach too, and vegetables will add about 45p or so to the prices quoted. Items in the right price bracket include trout or pork chop at around £2.25, veal escalope with asparagus and cheese costing about £2.80, or boneless chicken with tomatoes and mozzarella at about £3, as well as items such as omelettes and salads which cost in the £1.25 to £1.75 range. Sweets are priced from about 65p and house wine is 55p or so a glass. There is a cover charge of 40p.

W8

THE ARK RESTAURANT, 122 Palace Gardens Terrace (01-229 4024)
Open: Mon-Sat 12noon-3pm, 6.30-11.30pm

[C] [S]

You won't need to walk into The Ark two by two, but it is advisable not to arrive with a large family party unannounced. The Ark is a small, intimate bistro in the true French tradition. It has plain tables and a warm, friendly staff. The plat du jour, though not entirely French, ranges from crevettes rosés (a shrimp concoction at around 90p), to moules marinières at about £1.25 for starters. For the main course, coq au vin (only around £2.50) or foie de veau à l'ail (calf's liver with garlic) linger in the memory – and on the palate. Follow on with profiteroles, or a gigantic portion of sorbet, wash it all down with a large glass of respectable house wine and, surprise, surprise, at lunchtime you may still have some change from your £5 note.

PENTHOUSE RESTAURANT
Barker's Department Store, Kensington High Street (01-937 5432)
Open: Mon-Sat 11.45am-2.15pm (last orders)

[P] [S] [🍷]

The light and roomy Penthouse Restaurant is not only five floors up from London's frenetic pavements, but judging by its stately décor, it almost belongs to a past age. Praise be, Barkers is one of the few remaining department stores which still provides an attentive and efficient waitress service, a welcome alternative to self-service trays and long queues. A wholesome three-course meal can be had for around £3, the set lunch providing a choice of no fewer than six main courses. Be careful though; if you have a sweet from the trolley you have to pay extra for it. And if your fancy is for salad, you can eat as much as you like from the cold table – all for under £3. Wine by the glass costs between 70p and 90p.

YANGTZE, Troy Court, 222 Kensington High Street (01-937 1030)
Open: Mon-Sat 12noon-11.30pm, Sun 12noon-11pm

[C] [♫] [P] [S]

This light and airy restaurant next to the Commonwealth Institute offers both Pekinese and Cantonese cooking. There is a comprehensive selection of fish, poultry and meat dishes. You can get a full meal here for a little over £4, or you can, by ordering in advance, have something a bit special such as fried crab with ginger and onion at about £6.50. The restaurant is fully licensed and a large glass of wine costs 65p or so.

W9

ELGIN LOKANTA, 239 Elgin Avenue (01-328 6400)
Open: Mon-Sun 12noon-12mdnt

[C] [S]

The grill-kitchen of this Turkish restaurant is at the front and takeaway kebabs are a favourite of the locals. Mezeler (starters) include deliciously flavoured calves' livers at about 80p and there are over twenty more starters on the menu. Main courses are from around £2-£3.50 and are all served with pilaf rice. Try one of the lamb specialities such as sis saslik (skewered lamb with mushrooms and onion slices). Honey and walnut baklava (60p) is a tempting dessert from the trolley with which to complete your meal. There is a nominal cover charge for which you receive butter, hot pitta and black olives. House wine costs £1.50 for a half carafe, or 60p by the glass.

W11

FINCH'S WINE BAR, 120 Kensington Park Road (01-229 9545)
Open: Mon-Sat 11am-3pm, 6-11pm

[C] [P] [S]

Only a stone's throw from the Portobello Road antique market is this neat little basement premises, with its plain white walls and pillars forming intimate alcoves. Hot dishes include a quiche or pie from £1.75, while the cold collation offers such tempting delicacies as avocado pear filled with prawns (in a marvellous cocktail sauce) for around £1.40, pâté (about £1.20), dressed crab or chicken, around £1.20, and many others. The wine list is varied and (good news!) they won't run out – the wine shop is directly above.

KLEFTIKO, 186 Holland Park Avenue, Holland Park (01-603 0807)
Open: Mon-Sat 12noon-3pm, 6-11.30pm

[C] [♫] [P] [&]

Michael Hagisoteri opened the Kleftiko as an offshoot of his nearby hairdressing establishment on the Holland Park Avenue corner of Shepherds Bush roundabout. And very bright and cheerful it is, with natural brick walls, trellis-work ceiling, red and white cloths and fresh flowers. If you really want to go to town, book in advance and order Meze – a six-course evening meal at about £5 a head during which you can sample authentic Greek dishes. Starters cost about 90p and include houmous, taramasalata and tambouli. Main dishes are served with rice and salad and include kleftedes at £2.10 and the lamb speciality kleftiko or afelia, either of these costing around £3. Any two or three items may be combined and they then cost about £3 a helping. Sweets are about 60p, fresh fruits in season around 85p. The Greek house wine is 75p or so a glass, Greek coffee is about 35p.

TOOTSIES, 120 Holland Park Avenue (01-229 8567)
Open: Mon-Sun 12noon-12mdnt (Sun 11.30pm)

[♫] [S] [&]

Although Tootsies does not open until midday, the menu offers 'Eye Openers': orange juice with raw egg 'for those who did and wish they hadn't' and a full English breakfast 'for those who didn't and wish they had'. This is primarily a hamburger house – a dozen varieties are listed costing from about £1.30 to about £1.80, all prices including chips (except in the case of the 'calorie counter' version, where bun and chips are replaced by pineapple and cottage cheese) and a selection of relishes. You can get a number of other dishes here – steaks, salads, quiches, for example, at very reasonable prices, and there are delectable cakes and ice-cream specialities.

W12

SHIREEN TANDOORI ✕
270 Uxbridge Road (01-749 5927)

Open: Mon-Sat 12noon-3pm, 6-11.30pm, Sun 6-11.30pm

[C] [♫] [P] [S] [♣]

You can drink an aperitif and nibble spicy Indian nuts at the bar and seating area at the far end of this smart little restaurant, just ten minutes' walk from Shepherds Bush roundabout. Attractive Indian prints are displayed against matt black walls, and the natural wood of the ceiling is echoed in the herringbone-patterned latticework which screens diners from the main road. Main course prices range from about £2.45 (for Tandoori chicken) to a little over £4.30 (for Jhinga tandoori, a prawn speciality), the addition of vegetables (about £1.15), coffee (around 45p) and wine (bottles only) could bring the total over £5 even without a sweet. But if you appreciate the art of Tandoori cooking and subtle spicing you will enjoy a meal here.

WC1

THE BUNG HOLE, 57 High Holborn (01-242 4318)
Open: Mon-Fri 11.30am-3pm, 5.30-8.30pm

[C] [S]

The Bung Hole seats 140 on three floors. It has a cool, attractive cellar bar, a busy ground floor, and an upstairs pine-panelled restaurant suitable for larger bookings and popular for evening parties and champagne shindigs. The décor is typical of a Davys of London wine bar, with good solid, mainly oak furniture, the usual large number of 'Smokers' chairs and interesting Victorian and earlier bric-à-brac. The menu is largely one of cold dishes at around £1.80, including game pie, plate of roast beef or plate of tongue. Grouse, partridge, pheasant and Scotch salmon are served in season as are stawberries and raspberries. An excellent glass of wine costs about 85p.

OODLES, 113 High Holborn (01-405 3838)
Open: Mon-Fri 11.30am-9pm, Sat: 11.30am-2.30pm

[S]

Apart from staying open more hours in the week than the others, this branch of Oodles is no different from any other, but catch the flavour of its menus by reading the description in the entry under W2.

OODLES, 42 New Oxford Street (01-580 3762)
Open: Mon-Sat 11am-8pm, Sun 12noon-7pm

[S]

The frontage may be reminiscent of 'Ye Olde Tea Shoppe', but inside this eating house is unmistakably Oodles. No time to linger over evening meals, but a glass of wine can be had here. See under W2 for menu details.

WC2

CORTS, 84-86 Chancery Lane (01-405 3349)
Open: Mon-Fri 11am-3pm, 5.30-8pm

[C] [S] [♫]

You are less likely to meet criminals here than in the Old Bailey Corts, but lawyers abound as the wine bar is handy for the Strand Law Courts and is not far from the various Inns of Court. Here you will find an air-conditioned basement self-service bar and a ground-floor restaurant in which olive green and red blend with polished wood to create a warm *ambience* which is matched by the pleasant and helpful waitresses. Food is on the same lines as the original Corts (see under EC4) and starters include items such as smoked mackerel or avocado pear vinaigrette at around £1.25. A carafe of wine costs about £3, or you can buy a glass of French house wine which costs around 70p depending on its region of origin. Food is served at lunchtime only.

HAPPY GARDEN, 47-49 Charing Cross Road (01-437 7472)
Open: Mon-Sun 12noon-12mdnt

[C] [S] [♣]

The best way to judge an ethnic restaurant is to see who eats there, and Europeans are a very small minority of diners at this busy Chinese restaurant in the heart of theatreland. You can choose from a fine selection of Cantonese dishes. Golden roast ducks line the window and you can see what's cooking as you pass; let yourself be enticed in and you can get a good three-course meal for around £5 (set meal £3.20). The restaurant is licensed.

PLUMMER'S RESTAURANT, 10a James Street, Covent Garden (01-240 2534)
Open: Mon-Sat 12noon-3pm, 5.30pm-12mdnt

Victoriana epitomised by old photographs, prints and large mirrors, characterises this eating house, one of the original of the 'new wave' of restaurants in Covent Garden. Dishes include home-made steak and kidney pie, Californian chili served with Chef's salad (both around £3) and Plummer's Superburgers (8oz 100% pure Scottish beefburger topped with bacon, egg and melted cheese).

PORTERS RESTAURANT, 17 Henrietta Street, Covent Garden
(01-836 646)
Open: Mon-Sat 12noon-3pm, 6-11.30pm (Sun 10.30pm)

C P 🍷

Bang up to date, this fashionable restaurant is perhaps the only one in the country to equip its waitresses with 'bleeps' so that they are in constant contact with the kitchens. There's even a VDU on the checkout! By way of a contrast, food is traditional and all home-made, consisting of dishes such as Billingsgate pie, cockie leekie and ramekin of meats (all under £2), which conjure up the old market-place flavour of Covent Garden. Good old-fashioned puddings include bread and butter pudding, Henrietta's chocolate pot and delicious water ices.

SOLANGE'S WINE BAR, 11 St Martin's Court (01-240 0245)
Open: Mon-Sat 11am-3pm, 5.30-11pm

C ♫

A great attraction of this large, unpretentious wine bar is the excellent food, which is prepared in the famed neighbouring two knife and fork restaurant, Chez Solange. The four rooms can accommodate 200 people, and when it isn't raining, there is room for even more on the white-painted garden furniture outside. The menu changes daily, and is written on a blackboard. As an appetiser you could sample one of about a dozen cold dishes – champignons à la Greque at 65p, pâté maison or ratatouille at 85p are tasty examples. Hot dishes of the day cost less than £2 and might include coq au vin, veal or spare ribs – delicious with a serving of cauliflower cheese at 45p. Desserts such as fruit salad or cheesecake are in the 65p-80p range. A glass of house wine will cost about 60p. Handy for a meal before or after a visit to nearby Wyndhams Theatre.

SPAGHETTI HOUSE, Cranbourne Street (01-836 8168)
Open: Mon-Sat 12noon-3pm, 5-11pm

P S 🍷

Cranbourne Street, which intersects Charing Cross Road at Leicester Square underground station, is handy for theatreland and the art galleries around Trafalgar Square. Made-to-measure pine tables enable sixty people to be seated in comfort in the Spaghetti House and food is more varied than the restaurant's name implies. Apart from the expected pasta dishes (at prices around £1.30 per portion) there is a good selection of main meat and vegetable courses, from pasticcio di pollo (sliced chicken and mushrooms baked in cream sauce and served with mashed potatoes) at about £1.60 to entrecôte alla pizzaiola at something over £3.90. There is a selection of salads, too, at prices around £1.60. Starters include items such as avocado vinaigrette at about 75p, salami at around 85p, smoked ham with melon in the region of £1.95, and four different soups priced around 52p. The house-speciality sweet is Torta san Gennaro. Zabaglione is available only in the evening and costs about £1.20.

TUTTONS, 11-12 Russell Street
(01-836 1167)
Open: Mon-Fri 9am-12mdnt, Sat 11am-12mdnt, Sun 12noon-10.30pm

C S 🍷

This cream-decorated brasserie with plain pine furniture offers a good range of snacks and salads, and some unusual main dishes such as vegetables and spices wrapped in pastry and baked at around £2.70 or smoked chicken and avocado salad at about £3. You are welcome to drop in for a late breakfast, or perhaps just a coffee, and in fine weather you may sit outside beneath the awning and eat while you watch the world go by.

VECCHIA PARMA, 149 Strand
(01-836 3730)
Open: Mon-Sat 12noon-3pm, 5.30-11pm

C ♫ P S 🍷

In the best traditions of Italian restaurateurs, the Ronchetti family do a grand job in running this restaurant close to London's theatreland – Signor Ronchetti is the barman and his wife is also behind the bar. Of their two sons, Sergio cooks and Silvano produces the 'service with a smile' of which they are so proud. Apart from the usual pasta and pizza dishes, mostly around £1.20, there are several tasty grills, omelettes, fish and salad choices, many of them costing not much more than £2.50 and served with potatoes and vegetables. Desserts include fruit trifle, cassata and peach melba all for around 60p. Finish with a glass of respectable house wine.

Barking

THE SPOTTED DOG, 15 Longbridge Road (01-594 0228)
Open: Mon-Sun normal licensing hours

[C] [S]

Genuine East London atmosphere abounds in the Spotted Dog, one of Davy & Co's original enterprises (near Barking tube). The ground floor 'doghouse' offers good old steak and kidney pudding with vegetables and potatoes for around £2.50, but a steak or a mixed grill will be more pricey (around £4.50). Bar snacks such as sandwiches, filled rolls and toasted fingers are also available. An enormous fireplace, on the vast mantelpiece of which is an antique plough, dominates the room. Downstairs, you find yourself in the 'clink' – a dungeon-like place complete with an ill-looking skeleton. No bread and water here, but plaice or scampi and chips at around £3.10.

Barnet

CHIKAKO'S JAPANESE RESTAURANT, 86 High Street (01-441 3003)
Open: Mon-Sun 6.30-11pm (lunch by prior appointment only)

[S]

Opposite the Church in High Barnet is a surprise indeed, be careful or you may walk past it. But once inside you'll know you're in for a treat as you sit down at the traditional Japanese table and a hot lemon towel is placed in your hands. An excellent five-course table d'hôte meal comprising appetiser, soup, main course, dessert and Japanese tea or coffee costs around £5 depending on the choice of main dish. All meals are traditional Japanese recipes with exotic names such as beef teriyaki, pork tonkatsu and shabu shabu (Japanese-style fondue). Chikako will explain the dishes.

FRANCO AND GIANNI, 45 High Street (01-449 8300)
Open: Tue-Sat 12noon-3pm

[C] [S]

This attractive little Italian restaurant is somewhat out of our league in the evenings but at lunchtimes a typically Italian table d'hôte menu prevails, offering such dishes as cannelloni or lasagne for starters, medaglioni di manzo (thin fillet steak in red wine and mushroom sauce) with cauliflower and potato to follow, gâteau of the day plus coffee – all for around £4.50.

THE TWO BREWERS, 64 Hadley Highstone (01-449 3558)
Open: Mon-Thu 10.30am-2.30pm, Fri-Sat 10.30am-2.30pm, 5.30-11pm, Sun 12noon-2pm, 7-10.30pm

[P]

A one-time 'Pub of the Year'; this superb Tudor-style building is well-known to the locals, and they take full advantage of the high standard of cooking. Meals are eaten in the restaurant which echoes the Tudor theme, with warm red curtains and carpet. A daily-changing menu offers traditional Old English dishes such as grilled gammon and pineapple, cod and chips or home-made steak, kidney and mushroom pie all around £3. With starters, sweet, coffee and wine you will feast for around £5.

Bexley

HARPER'S FERRY, 82 High Street (Crayford 527494)
Open: Wed-Thu 6.30-11.30pm, Fri-Sat 6.30-12mdnt

[S]

A Civil War theme is rampant in this small American-style restaurant in the

High Street. Main dishes include the extravagantly-named 'chicken Carolina' (a chargrilled quarter of chicken, served with sweetcorn and French fries), the 'President', the 'Democrat' and the 'Gettysburger' (ground beef on a toasted sesame seed bun, topped with sweetcorn relish and pickled cucumber and a mountain of mixed salad and French fries). Apple pie, pancakes and ice cream with various syrup toppings make suitably American desserts and you can buy a bumper glass of wine for about £1.

Bromley

HOLLYWOOD BOWL, 5 Market Parade, East Street (01-460 2346)
Open: Mon-Thu 11.30am-2.45pm, 6-11.15pm (Fri-Sat 6-11.45pm), Sun 6-11pm

[♫] [S] [♣]

Old enamelled bill posters and hanging plants decorate this popular hamburger restaurant. There are nine burgers to choose from, all with interesting names; for example, the 'hen house' has a fried egg topping and the 'Bronx boiger' is 'overflowing with spicy baked beans'. The star of this show is 'Hollywood Bowl's de-luxe cheeseburger' – a hunky half-pounder with a generous topping of melted cheese, lettuce, tomato and pickles smothered in thick mayonnaise. All of them are served in a toasted sesame bun with French fries. A rump steak at around £3.75 with a choice of three salads around £1.75 each are alternative main courses. Fresh home-made apple pie is a tasty dessert at around 55p.

Cheam

BRASSERIE, 50 High Street (01-642 0573)
Open: Mon-Sat 12noon-3pm, 6.30-11pm

[S]

Victoria and Michael Kouroghli have just opened this bright French brasserie with its pine tables and church-pew seating. They present an extensive menu specialising in crêpes and seafood, so not surprisingly, one of the most popular items is a combination of both (seafood pancake – about £2.25). Large and varied salads (under £2), seafood au gratin, boeuf bourguignon and chicken florentine (around £3) make tasty meals for lunch or dinner. Follow them up with a home-made sweet such as chocolate mousse, cheesecake or chocolate gâteau at around 70p. A glass of wine costs 70p.

Croydon

FUSTO D'ORO PIZZERIA, Leon House, 237-239 High Street (01-688 4869)
Open: Mon-Sat 11am-3pm, 6pm-12mdnt

[C] [♫] [P] [S]

If pizza's your dish you'll be quite spoiled for choice at this popular Italian pizzeria in the heart of Croydon. There are twenty-two varieties. For the quickie meal, eat your pizza in the busier section of the restaurant where the décor is simple, with formica-topped tables. When you want to linger and enjoy a more romantic atmosphere, dine by candlelight in the other section. Wherever you eat the food is the same, with pizzas from the basic margherita to an elaborate Mediterraneo with seafood and tomatoes, pasta dishes, salads and steaks. For dessert there's a choice of either 'dolci', including such tempters as rum baba, zabaglione or cheesecake.

SNIFTERS WINE BAR, 71 High Street (01-686 8480)
Open: Mon-Thu 11am-3pm, 5.30-10.30pm, Fri 11am-3pm, 5.30-11pm, Sat 11am-3pm, 7-11pm

[C] [♫] [P] [S]

Art nouveau décor and a mezzanine floor with balcony are unique features of this attractive wine bar. The menu is excellent, with a choice of seven interesting appetisers such as egg mayonnaise with anchovy at about 70p and pâté with wholemeal bread for around 90p. Cold buffet offers fine ham off the bone or roast beef (both about £1.50), quiche (around 95p) or smoked mackerel (about £1.20). Hot buffet includes pastas at around £1.25 and veal escalopes for about £1.85. Additionally, the blackboard lists daily specials such as lamb cutlet in rosemary or chicken supreme for around £1.75. An excellent choice of desserts such as home-made apple pie and cream (about 70p) makes the three-course meal complete. A good selection of wines by the glass ranges in price from around 60p-75p and you are spoiled for choice.

THE WINE VAULTS, 122-126 North End (01-680 2419)
Open: Mon-Sat 11am-2.30pm, Mon-Thu 5.30-10.30pm, Fri 5.30-11pm, Sat 7-11pm

[C] [P] [S] [♣]

Another Davy & Co outlet this, with

solidly Victorian décor and sawdust on the floor in true Davy fashion, in basement premises on Croydon's busy High Street close to the railway station and next door to Marks & Spencer. Toasted fingers cost about 20p each here, or 90p for a plate of six, but otherwise the menu and prices are fairly typical of the company. A glass of house wine costs around 95p a glass, and there are some interesting end-of-bin wines listed on the blackboard.

Enfield

DIVERS WINE BAR, 29 Silver Street (01-367 2549)
Open: Tue-Fri 12noon-2.30pm, Mon-Sun 7.30-10.30pm (11pm Fri and Sat)

[♫] [P] [S]

The smart brown awning of this little wine bar picks it out in the tree-lined street. The black-board menu offers daily specialities such as chili con carne, goulash or roast chicken. Portions are very generous and a Divers salad, which hosts Nick and Graham will make up for you, is excellent value at about £1. Pizzas, quiches and Ploughman's are always available for less than £1 and desserts include a delicious chocolate cherry gâteau for around 75p. A dazzling selection of wines and good background music make this a popular mealtime haunt. Summer visitors may like to eat in the sheltered, paved garden.

Hampton Court

CARDINAL WOLSEY, The Green (01-979 1458)
Open: Mon-Sun 12.30-3pm, 7-10.30pm

[C] [P] [♧]

This charming inn, pleasantly sited close to Hampton Court, offers sound home-made English fare for the footsore and famished foreign tourist's enjoyment – and British visitors are equally welcome. A three-course table d'hôte meal, changed daily, but always providing interesting choices, costs around £5. Portions are very generous and old favourites frequently featured include Chef's stock pot soup, home-made pâté, roast beef and Yorkshire pud, steak and kidney pud, apple pie and peach Melba. A glass of house wine is about 60p.

Hampton Wick

GENZIANI RESTAURANT
35 High Street (01-977 4895)
Open: Mon-Thu 12noon-2.30pm, 6.30-10.30pm, Fri-Sat 12noon-2.30pm, 6.30-11pm

[C] [P]

The Genziani family run this intimate Italian restaurant – Dino prepares the food and his wife Dora attends to the needs of the diners. Apart from conventional Italian cuisine, fish, omelettes, salads and grills are also served. Hors d'oeuvres include home-made pâté at around 60p and antipasta della casa for about £1. Minestrone soup, home-made and thick, with fresh vegetables is a meal in itself for around 75p. Spaghetti della casa is a speciality – a version of bolognese with sliced ham and melted cheese – and is yours for about £2.50. A selection of desserts includes hot zabaglione – a serving for two people costs around £1.47. House wine is about 60p a glass.

Harrow

PLATO'S, 294 Preston Road (01-904 8326)
Open: Mon-Sat 12noon-3pm, 6-11pm

[S]

This Greek restaurant is furnished in the modern style and specialises in French and English as well as Greek cuisine. Theo Vazanias is always on hand to ensure your enjoyment of his food. The à la carte menu offers a dazzling choice of over twenty starters, more than thirty main courses and about twenty sweets. You could break the bank by going for all the most expensive items, but there is still a wide choice awaiting you. An all-Greek meal could include tsatsiki as an appetiser at around 65p, with dolmades or afelia as your main dish for about £2.50 and baklava or kateifi as delicious desserts at around 65p. Vegetables are extra and there is a cover charge for bread and butter.

Hornchurch

URASWAMY'S, 17 High Street (Hornchurch 43235)
Open: Mon-Thu 12noon-2.30pm 6-11.30pm, Fri-Sat 12noon-2.30pm 6pm-12mdnt, Sun 12noon-2.30pm, 6-11.30pm

[C] [S]

Traditional Indian cuisine, with a good selection of specialities from the Tandoori ovens, sets this restaurant apart. Chicken or lamb pasanda cooked in red wine and cream and costing about £3.15 are both tasty dishes which will not fail to please. Hot, medium and mild curries, for under £2.25, can be enjoyed in the comfort of tasteful orange décor, cooled after a vindaloo by a large ceiling fan! Cool desserts include mango, lychee or pineapple for under 90p. A glass of French house wine will cost around 60p.

Hounslow

THE TRAVELLERS FRIEND
480 Bath Road (01-897 8847)
Open: Mon-Fri 12noon-2.30pm,
Fri-Sat 7-9.30pm

[C] [P]

Tudor architecture is reflected in the oak beams, pillars, plain brick and stone walls and olde worlde furnishings of the charming restaurant in this hostelry. Cuisine is basically English with the odd French dish to vary the pace. Starters include soup at around 50p, pâté maison at about 80p and prawn cocktail for around £1. Main courses include fish (from £2.50-£4.50), grills (from £2.20 for pork chop to £5 for fillet or T-bone steak) and entrées such as coq au vin (about £3.20), escalope of veal cordon bleu (around £3) and duck à l'orange (about £3.50). Vegetables are 50p extra. Various gâteaux cost around 60p and a large glass of Italian house wine is about 60p.

Ilford

HART'S, 545 Cranbrook Road,
Gants Hill (01-554 5000)
Open: Mon-Thu 12noon-3pm,
6-10.30pm, Fri-Sat 12noon-3pm,
6-11pm, Sun 7-10.30pm

[C] [♫]

Leonard and Allan Hart's wine bar specialises in good home-made cooking ideal for businessmen and travellers alike. Start with home-made cabbage soup (about 70p) or hot grapefruit in port wine (around 70p), then sample lasagne (about £1.80). Freshly caught trout from Hanningford or Australian Pacific prawns cooked with garlic may stretch the budget but are good value. Hard-to-resist desserts include hot black cherries with port and ice cream (about £1). There is a formidable selection of wines to be had by the glass and in fine weather you can enjoy your meal on the tree-lined terrace to the rear.

Kew

LE PROVENCE, 14 Station Parade,
Kew Gardens (01-940 6777)
Open: Tue-Sat 6pm-9.15pm,
Fri-Sat 12noon-3pm

[P]

This traditional French restaurant, tucked away under the oak tree-lined parade at Kew Gardens, offers honest French cooking at no-nonsense prices. Daily specials are excellent value – fresh artichoke vinaigrette is around £1.20, risotto du chef just over £1 and foie saute à la Venitienne (sliced liver cooked in butter with sherry and sliced onions, served with a selection of vegetables) at about £2.70 are typical examples. Main courses, all served with vegetables, range in price from around £1.50 to nearly £3.50. The desserts are a delight – real fruit sorbet (usually raspberry) or meringue glacé Chantilly (around 90p) are both superb. There is one drawback – being unlicensed, Le Provence cannot serve wine – unless you bring your own. But the place is very popular with the locals and booking really is essential!

Kingston-upon-Thames

CLOUDS, 6-8 Kingston Hill
(01-546 0559)
Open: Mon-Sun 12noon-2.30pm,
6-11pm

[P] [S]

This busy, friendly restaurant operates on two floors. The first floor is a Crêpery (pancake) and Cocktail Bar, where very thin pancakes made from buckwheat flour may be filled with exotic savoury or sweet fillings. A filling of prawns and asparagus laced with wine costs less than £2 and for £1.50 you can sample a Gypsy Paprikash – a savoury filling with beef, green peppers, tomatoes, paprika and sour cream. Dessert crêpes include Chantilly crêpe – fresh banana slices in brown sugar topped with whipped cream or Grand Marnier crêpe – laced with the luscious liqueur – both at less than £1. The ground floor menu offers stuffed mushrooms among other appetisers, quiches, spaghettis, hamburgers, spare ribs or salads as a main course (from £2-£3) and gâteaux, cheesecakes or fantastic ice creams for dessert. A glass of house wine costs 60p.

COUNTRY KITCHEN RESTAURANT
20 Vicarage Road (01-549 4774)
Open: Mon-Fri 9.30am-5pm,
Sat 9.30am-6pm

[P] [S] [♿]

Decorated in the style of a country kitchen, this small restaurant has white-painted walls, red tile-patterned floor and scrubbed wood tables and chairs. Hanging baskets and green potted plants add to the rustic atmosphere. Good, basic food is available all day, from fried 'brekkers' for around £1.10 to a three-course lunch or early dinner. Home-made soup of the day, dish of the day such as chicken casserole served with spring greens and new potatoes and lemon meringue pie will cost around £2.30. There is a huge range of snack food available including a daily 'supa-snack' such as sardines with tomato and onion salad at about 80p. Lemonade shandy is the nearest you'll get to alcohol, since the Country Kitchen is at present unlicensed, though this may be rectified soon!

STONEWALL, 14 Kingston Hill
(01-549 5984)
Open: Mon-Sun 12.30-2.30pm, 7-11pm

C P

There is a continental air about the rustic wood-and-house-plant décor of this restaurant. Its windows overlook the wide tree-lined pavement of Kingston Hill, on the outskirts of an old market town which is now almost part of London. Food is imaginative and not overpriced though one could exceed the limit when choosing from the à la carte menu. Mushroom Dijonaise followed by chicken fricassée and Grand Marnier pancakes comes to around £5 and there is a 40p cover charge. House wine is about 65p a glass. A traditional three-course Sunday roast costs £3.50.

Pinner

THE OLD OAK, 11 High Street
(01-866 0286)
Open: Mon-Fri 12noon-2pm, 7-10.30pm, Sat 12noon-2pm, 7-11pm, Sun 12.30-2.30pm, 7.30-10pm

C

The set price for a three-course lunch is only about £2.50 here, including service charge. Businessperson's lunch starters include delicacies such as avocado and grapefruit salad, Waldorf salad (apple, celery and walnuts in sour cream) or crevettes aioli (peel-yourself prawns and garlic mayonnaise). There is a wide choice of main dishes: meat which could be pork in an apple, sage, cider and cream sauce, or a spicy dish such as chili con carne or curry de volaille aux bananes. To finish a satisfying repast, sweets include rum and coffee mousse and Old English flummery, or you might prefer Brie or Camembert to keep the meal memorably Continental.

The restaurant is licensed, a glass of house wine costing around 60p.

Richmond-upon-Thames

MRS BEETON'S, Hill Rise
(01-948 2787)
Open: Mon-Sun 10am-5.30pm, Wed-Sun 6.30pm-12mdnt

This village-style restaurant has a craft shop in the basement selling local crafts and kitchen items. The informal restaurant is run by a co-operative of housewives who are allocated a day to prepare and serve the food, which is home-made and excellent value for money. Starters include minted cucumber soup of liver pâté for around 50p. Cheese and courgette quiche is about 70p, fricassée of chicken and mushrooms with rice or lasagne are both around £1.75. A huge choice of desserts includes a very light chocolate layer cake – a very large portion costs about 60p.

Southall

MAHARAJA TANDOORI RESTAURANT, 171-175 The Broadway
(01-574 4564/571 1189)
Open: Mon-Sun 12noon-3pm, 6-11.30pm

C P S

A place that lays claim to be the only Indian restaurant in the heart of the Indian community must be something out of the ordinary. And indeed it is. In the softly-lit, unpretentious, U-shaped room you can find the elusive art of curry cuisine practised at its best. The menu explains in simple language (and grammatical English!) the origin of Tandoori and invites you, as much as the all-pervading smell of spices and herbs does, to partake of a limited but comprehensive menu of 'Maharaja Specialities'. Don't fail to try the boti kebab, an outstanding delicacy of lamb chunks dipped in herbs and grilled Tandoori way, for around £2.70, and combine it for your partner with an irresistable extravagance of Tandoori boneless chicken pieces curried in sweet and sour sauce for about £3. The portions are enormous, so don't over-order. With spiced poppadams or nan and one fair-sized portion of pillau Basmati rice you should still have enough funds for one of the Maharaja's Indian sweets dishes at around 80p. And if you can resist the wine list, you can keep well within your budget with a salty or sweet Lassi (yoghurt drink) for another 80p. There is a 25p cover charge and a 10% service charge.

Sudbury

TERRY'S RESTAURANT AND BANQUETING SUITE, 763-765 Harrow Road (01-904 4409)
Open: Mon-Fri 12noon-2pm

[P] [🍷]

The main operation here is catering for large parties, but on weekday lunchtimes the reception area is utilised for serving what could be one of the cheapest three-course lunches in London. For around £1.50 you get a choice of starters which include items such as melon cocktail and egg mayonnaise, a choice of four main dishes such as roast or meat pie with appropriate vegetables, omelette, or cold meat salad, and a choice of four sweets or cheese and biscuits. Very popular and undoubtedly good value.

Twickenham

SCOTTY'S, 59 York Street (01-892 4789)
Open: Mon-Tue 11.30am-2.30pm, Wed-Sat 11.30am-2.30pm, 7-11pm, Sun 12noon-2.30pm

Victorian country kitchen décor sets the scene in this small restaurant where good, home-cooked English fare is served. Dishes are displayed on a blackboard, with such items as steak and kidney pie or Shepherd's pie with two fresh vegetables for around £1.30. Sunday lunch is excellent value, with a choice of three starters including Mother's soup at about 35p, several main courses such as roast beef and Yorkshire pud for around £1.70 and home-made desserts including treacle tart or apple pie costing about 55p. The evening menu is more expensive, but portions are larger and the choice is wider. Try corn-on-the-cob (about 65p), followed by escalope of veal Holstein (around £3), Mother's Surprise Pud (about £1) and endless coffee (around 40p). Scotty's is unlicensed, so bring your own wine.

Upminster

ROOMES RESTAURANT, Station Road (Upminster 50080)
Open: Tue-Thu 9am-5pm (Fri-Sat 5.30pm)
[S] [🍷]

This attractive restaurant, with hanging Spanish brass lights is on the second floor of Roomes department store. Service is personal and friendly and good, no-nonsense food is excellent value for money. The menu changes every day, but particularly recommended is the home-made steak pie, bursting with meat and served with two veg. With a starter and sweet, the meal is likely to cost about £2.50. Wine is available by the glass for around 50p. Children's portions cost about 50p to £1. Don't miss the fabulous display of Elsenham preserves and pâté de foie Perigord for sale.

Wembley

PEKING CASTLE RESTAURANT
379 High Road (01-902 3605)
Open: Mon-Sun 12noon-2.30pm, 6-11.30pm

[S]

Apart from the à la carte menu, this quiet haven from the rush of the High Road traffic, where hanging Chinese lanterns and a dragon motif evoke the East, offers special dinners for two or more people at about £4.50 a head for seven items or around £5.50 a head for nine items. If you fancy a meal composed of soup, crispy duck, chicken in yellow-bean sauce, prawns in chili sauce, vegetables, fried rice and toffee apple, £4.50 is not overmuch to pay for it. The main menu includes the usual array of fish, poultry and meat dishes, the cuisine is the upper-class Peking style.

West Wickham

MISTINGUETT WINE BAR
95 High Street (01-777 6223)
Open: Mon-Thu 12noon-2.30pm, 7pm-12mdnt, Fri-Sat 12noon-2.30pm, 7pm-12mdnt

[C] [♫] [P] [S]

A French atmosphere predominates in this friendly wine bar with its dark wood tables, French posters, oil lamps and candles. A blackboard displays a list of the food served – a wide range from soup of the day at around 55p to fillet steak at about £4.20. Pizzas and spaghetti bolognese are around £1, scampi or chicken with French fries just over £2 and chicken Kiev under £4.50 (with vegetables). Sweets include cheesecake or apple pie and cream for about 75p. A good selection of wines from all over Europe are available for around 65p a glass.

East Anglia

Whipped by the wind, this expansive plain of England, with its flat, fertile fens, has struggled against the sea for centuries. Decorative windmills and watermills bear witness to man's harnessing of the elements, while the sea is kept at bay by dykes or marram grass planted amongst the sand dunes. The sandy beaches and shimmering Broads attract bathers and boating enthusiasts by the thousand, while devotees of Constable discover the real Flatford Mill and Dedham Vale with its fields of beet and barley. Ancient woodframe houses, a legacy of the Flemish weavers, noble churches and stately homes abound throughout the region and Cambridge boasts unsurpassed architecture in her magnificent colleges.

The shores of Norfolk, Suffolk and Essex yield seafood and fish of exceptional variety. From the 12th century the locals have depended on fish as the mainstay of their diet. Great Yarmouth fishermen were known to consume ten herrings apiece for breakfast – sufficient to charge their batteries for a day of wrestling with the nets. Such was the enthusiasm for the nutritious herring that it has all but disappeared from the North Sea, but Yarmouth bloaters can still be enjoyed at a price and delicious alternatives are skate or sea trout.

Cromer crabs and Wells whelks are famed throughout England, while Stewky Blues – grey-blue cockles from Stiffkey are reputed to be the best in the world. Mussel beds are profuse, and moules marinières à l'anglaise are served in many restaurants. When there is an 'r' in the month, you can sample the succulent native oysters of Brightlingsea – prized since the 12th century.

The brooding, brackish marshes between land and shore are the source of a variety of unique edible plants. Most famed is samphire – a succulent plant with fleshy leaves eaten either as a vegetable – tasty with mutton, lamb or dab, or as a satisfying dish on its own. If you haven't the time to hunt for samphire, try Fakenham market or even one of the roadside stalls. Seakale, wild spinach, fennel and wild shoreline asparagus are abundant and lend spice and flavour to many a local dish.

Conventional agriculture also has a part to play, Norfolk turkeys and Suffolk hams are raised on the

fat of the land and Norwich and Ipswich are renowned for their breweries which prosper on the excellent local malting barley.

Traditional eating places featured in the ensuing pages are almost bound to serve Suffolk home-cured bacon – steeped in a mixture of brown sugar or treacle and beer, it looks almost black on the outside, but tastes delicious. If you are lucky, you may even be able to sample an East Anglican crazy combination – such as herrings with dumplings or cockles and bacon.

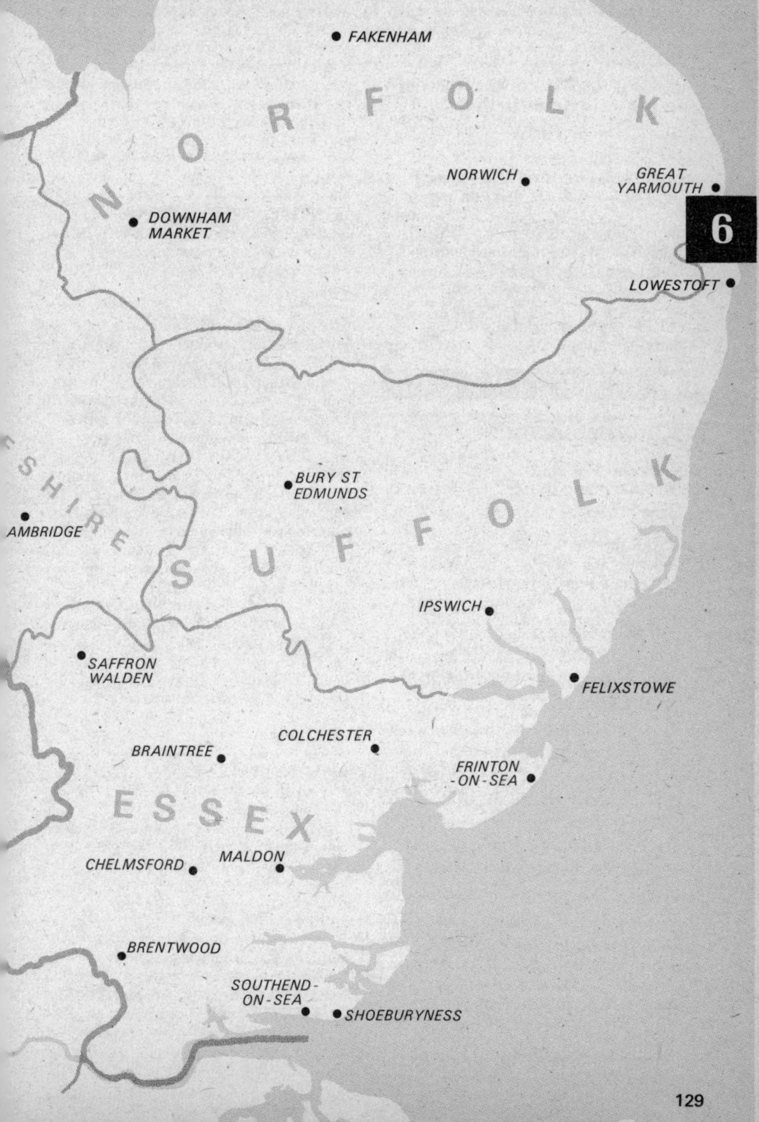

6

Braintree

TUDOR ROSE, Little Square
(Braintree 45349)
Open: Mon 12noon-2.30pm,
Tue-Thu 12noon-2.30pm, 7-10.30pm,
Fri-Sat 12noon-2.30pm, 7-11pm,
Sun 12noon-3pm

This attractive 17th-century restaurant is situated in the oldest part of town, in a particularly historic area with 'Cromwell's Court' nearby. Original beams, inglenook fireplace and wooden wheelback chairs give the room an atmosphere of history. A full à la carte menu is available, but for the budget-conscious the set three-course lunch offers an excellent choice of dishes at around £2.50 each. A 'specials' menu offers pâté Tudor Rose, beef Stroganoff with saffron rice, dessert and coffee for around £4 and a three-course meal including lasagne or other 'special' pasta dishes will be about £3.50. A three-course traditional roast lunch is about £4 – try the roast duck with 'heavenly' sauce.

Brentwood

THE EAGLE AND CHILD
13 Chelmsford Road, Shenfield
(Brentwood 210155)
Open: Mon-Sun 12noon-2pm, 7-10pm

[♫] [P]

This popular Tudor-style pub houses a carvery restaurant which has wood-panelled décor reminiscent of a private club. Value for money is self-evident with modestly priced starters such as pâté at about 80p, followed by a choice of meats carved to your liking. Fresh roast legs of lamb and pork, topside of beef and whole turkeys are on display and James or Keith, the waiters, will only stop filling up your plate when you say so. All this plus generous portions of vegetables for about £3.50. Alternative main courses include home-made steak pie or salad selection for £2. A choice of sweets is also included in the price. Spanish wine is about 55p a glass. On fine days, a salad bar operates in the attractive garden and if you're lucky you may see a display of Morris dancing.

Bury St Edmunds

THE BEEFEATER STEAK HOUSE
27 Angel Hill (Bury St Edmunds 4224)
Open: Tue-Sun 12noon-2.30pm,
6-12mdnt

[C] [♫] [P] [S] [♣]

Don't let the name mislead you, this is a Greek restaurant typical of any to be found on the Greek islands – the weather being the only difference! However, you'll hardly miss the sun as you sit amidst the fishing nets and Greek bric-à-brac enjoying the traditional moussaka, kleftiko or dolmadakia. The cost of a three-course meal is a bit over the budget at £6.25, but qualifies, as a glass of wine is included. Go for a Greek dish such as fresh squid or octopus with rice and salad, rounding off with the traditional Greek coffee. The less adventurous may have to pay more for the conventional English dishes (about £6.70); the charcoal-grilled steaks are a credit to proprietor Andreas Kyriakou and his family.

CHARLIE'S RESTAURANT
32 Angel Hill (Bury St Edmunds 5824)
Open: Mon-Sat 12noon-2.30pm,
7pm-12mdnt, Sun 7pm-12mdnt

[C] [♫] [P] [S] [♣]

Sitting on the south east corner of Angel Hill, between the Cathedral and Abbey is this modern hamburger restaurant. Appealing particularly to the young at heart, the décor is simple and the music loud. The theme is Charlie Chaplin, with large blow-ups of his photographs decorating the walls and film clips on the menu. Char-grilled hamburgers are the speciality with a choice of exciting toppers such as barbecue sauce, blue cheese or mushrooms in a creamy sauce. All are served on a freshly baked sesame bun, sprinkled with herbs and spices, accompanied by French fries and a salad garnish, and constitute a tasty meal for under £2.50. For something a little more substantial you may prefer the chef's special steaks although these will add a further £1.50 or so on to your bill. Wine is available, but you may find a cool glass of American lager more appropriate.

PEGGOTTY'S CARVING ROOM
30 Guildhall Street
(Bury St Edmunds 5444)
Open: Tue-Fri 12noon-2pm, 6.45-10pm,
Sat 12noon-2pm, 6.30-10.30pm,
Sun 12noon-2.30pm

[C] [S] [♣]

Notice the Dickensian-type exterior with eye-catching red canopies over the windows. Inside, the heavy wooden tables, tapestry-upholstered chairs, brick pillars and sand-coloured walls lined with prints create a cottage-like atmosphere. Starters are served to your table, then, in the carvery style, you take your pick from an array of hot or cold roasts, carved for you by the chef, or proprietor Luigi, and add to this your own selection of vegetables or salad. Roll and butter and sweet are included in the price of the main course with starters and coffee additional, totalling only around £4.

Cambridge

EROS, 25 Petty Cury (Cambridge 63420)
Open: Mon-Fri 12noon-3pm, 5.30-11pm, Sat-Sun 12noon-11pm

[S]

Eros has the atmosphere of a taverna, complete with Greek music, despite very English décor with college arms on panelled walls. The menu is enormous, with fish, omelettes, roasts, grills, salads and a formidable variety of steaks, not to mention Greek, Cypriot and Italian dishes by the dozen. For a satisfying three-course Greek meal, start with taramasalata, followed by sousoukakia and round it off with Grecian-style gâteau and a glass of wine – all this for around £4!

PEKING ✕ 21 Burleigh Street (Cambridge 54755)
Open: Tue-Sun 12noon-2.15pm, 6-10.45pm

[P] [S]

At lunchtime a set menu offers a substantial meal for around £2! In the evening an extensive à la carte menu of delicious dishes operates for which the Peking is renowned locally. Some delicacies are beyond the £5 limit, but with care one can enjoy a feast of original food. Start with asparagus and chicken soup (around 65p), then sample diced chicken in oyster sauce or sliced pork with leeks and garlic (both just over £2) and finish with Chinese toffee apples (about £1.60 for two people). Rice and service are extra. Chinese wine is about 90p a glass.

THE PENTAGON, The Arts Theatre, 6 St Edwards Passage (Cambridge 355246)
Open: Mon-Sat 12noon-2pm, 6-11.30pm

[C] [♫] [S]

The majority of the dishes are chosen from an attractively displayed buffet of turkey, ham, beef, salmon, quiche and assorted salads. A daily menu of at least three hot dishes such as steak and kidney pie, pork chops or fillet of

plaice meunière at around £2.45 is also available. A large glass of French house wine costs around 60p. A special theatre-and-supper deal is offered to parties of ten or more.

THE ROOF GARDEN, The Arts Theatre, 6 St Edwards Passage (Cambridge 359302)
Open: Mon-Sat 9.30am-8pm

[C] [S]

This 200-seater self-service restaurant over the Arts Theatre is one of the busiest rendezvous in the city. The main dining area is light and airy but in fine weather many customers prefer to sit outside on the roof. You can eat here from early morning when a full English breakfast is served, through to the 'theatre supper' of hefty ploughman's, cottage pie, fried chicken in a basket and the like. A three-course lunch of melon, Chef's Special dish and home-made sweet with coffee and wine will cost around £3.50. A special item is a two-course lunch for about £1.50, the courses changing every day.

UNIVERSITY ARMS HOTEL ★★★★
Regent Street, (Cambridge 51241)
Open: Mon-Sun 12.30-2pm, 7-9pm

[C] [P]

Close to the centre of Cambridge, and overlooking Parker's Piece – a 25-acre park – stands this imposing hostelry which has been the leading hotel here since 1831. It has been owned by the Bradford family since 1891. The large ground-floor restaurant overlooks the park through windows which depict the arms of the colleges in stained glass. Only by sticking to the three-course table d'hôte menu will you be safe on the budget as an à la carte meal plus wine would be well over £5. For about £4.95 you can choose from a menu of traditional dishes such as fried lemon sole, roast leg of pork with apple sauce, or cold ham salad plus starter, sweet and coffee. A simpler lunch may be chosen from the buffet set up in Parker's Lounge for around £2.20.

VARSITY RESTAURANT
35 St Andrew's Street
(Cambridge 56060)
Open: Mon-Sun 12noon-3pm, 5.30-11pm

This two-storey Greek restaurant is housed in one of Cambridge's many listed buildings in one of the city centre's not-so-busy streets. The atmosphere is very authentic, with Greek pictures scattered on white-washed walls, an effect which is emphasised by black wooden beams and doors. A good three-course meal, including wine and coffee, can be enjoyed for around £3. Food is basically Greek with some French and English dishes. Kebab of the house – two skewers of tenderloin, served with Greek salad and fetta cheese, is one of four speciality dishes. Service is quick and friendly despite the fact that the restaurant seats 105.

WILSON'S RESTAURANTS
14 Trinity Street (Cambridge 356845)
Open: The Carvery: Mon-Thu 12noon-3pm, 6-11pm, Fri-Sat 12noon-3pm, 6pm-12mdnt
The Granary: Mon-Sat 10.30am-10.30pm, Sun 10.30am-6pm

[P]

Wilson's is a fine black and white, 16th-century building housing three restaurants. The Carvery, on the first floor, retains the Tudor style. There is a good choice of starters and desserts served by waitresses, but the interesting feature is the help-yourself carvery table, where the chef will carve beef, roast pork or poultry to your choice and you select your own vegetables. Three courses and a glass of house wine will cost around £5. For a quicker, less expensive meal, try The Granary. A separate entrance takes you into the original cellars and here up to ten hot dishes are on display. Beef casserole, curried chicken and sweet and sour pork are all about £1.80, while a selection of hot quiches are on offer for around £1. Fresh cream desserts are available for about 80p. Trinity Street Restaurant on the second floor offers a more traditional à la carte menu which is a little above our limit.

Chelmsford

CORKS, 34a Moulsham Street (Chelmsford 58733)
Open: Mon-Sat 12noon-2.30pm, 6-11pm, Sun 7-10.30pm

[C] [♫] [P] [S]

Situated opposite the AA office, this trendy wine bar is a popular place for a good meal or informal drink and chat. A brown-painted window front and the Tudor beams beyond entice you over the threshold, where a tempting menu chalked on the ubiquitous plât du jour blackboard announces moussaka and salad, at around £1.75, or turkey pie and pâté (about £1). The competent staff is led by Michael Dunbar who is always on hand to extend a friendly welcome to his guests. Wine is about 50p a glass.

PIZZA AND PASTA, 44 Moulsham Road (Chelmsford 352245)
Open: Mon-Sat 12noon-2.30pm, 6-10.30pm

[C] [icon]

A decorative brown awning and Venetian blinds adorn this highly original-looking Italian restaurant and garden terrace. The simple but appetising menu specialises in the pizzas and pastas anticipated. Starters include Spanish gazpacho for around 95p and minestrone at about 80p. An imaginative pizza is napoletana, with mozzarella cheese, tomatoes, capers, anchovies and olives for around £1.95. Pastas include delicious fetuccine matriciana (noodles with tomato, onion and bacon) at about £1.85. Selection of sweets is good with home-made cheesecake and strudel at around £1.

Colchester

BISTRO 9, 9 North Hill (Colchester 76466)
Open: Tue-Sat 12noon-1.45pm, 7-10.45pm

This small bistro has a short menu of home-made dishes served with fresh vegetables and home-made bread. It will be easier to keep within the £5 limit in the basement, where substantial 'snacks' are served. Home-made soup and bread, the hot dish of the day (such as moussaka or chili con carne), and a pudding from the à la carte menu – try the brown bread ice cream – will cost about £3.50. With quiche and salad as a main course, you'll spend less than £3. The Bistro always offers a vegetarian dish of the day at around £2.70 and a set lunch of two courses and coffee for £3.50. The service by friendly waitresses is guaranteed to please, as is the pleasantly informal atmosphere, the large refectory tables (you may have to share), and pretty country décor.

Wm SCRAGG'S ✕✕ 2 North Hill (Colchester 41111)
Open: Mon-Sat 12noon-2.15pm, 7-10.30pm

[C]

This elegant seafood restaurant bears the name of the journeyman bricklayer who bought the premises in 1832, and lived there peacefully until the ripe old age of seventy-eight. Many of the appetising dishes come dangerously near to our limit, a couple of the cheaper ones being sole lasserre and trout du garve, both around £3.80. However, a fine selection of bar snacks is available; smoked trout pâté at £1.50, seafood flan with salad or whole smoked mackerel at around £2.50, and a good choice of inexpensive sandwiches such as prawn and lettuce or fish pâté and cucumber. A sweet may be chosen for about £1, and there are many varied wines, sold by the glass costing from 55p.

Downham Market

CROWN STABLES, CROWN HOTEL (Downham Market 2322)
Open: Mon and Wed-Sun 10am-10pm

[C] [P] [icon]

This 300-year-old coaching inn has always been a popular haunt of locals in the quiet town of Downham Market. However, since the spring of 1980, the old stables have been converted into a slick grill room and buttery with natural wood tables, tiled floor, brick walls and horsey bric-à-brac creating a clean and simple atmosphere. Here, a very reasonably-priced cold buffet comprises home-cooked cold meats and hand-raised pies, quiches, pâtés and flans with a selection of salads at under £2. Charcoal grill steaks or kebabs will push up the price, but Ploughman's platter, pizza or a steak sandwich are tasty alternatives at the other end of the price-scale. Home-made gâteaux and flans are around 75p.

Fakenham

THE CROWN HOTEL ★ Market Place (Fakenham 2010)
Open: bars: Mon-Wed, Fri-Sun, licensing hours, Thu 10.30am-4.30pm, 5.30-11pm, restaurant: Mon-Sat 12.15-2pm, 7.15-9.15pm, Sun 12.15-2pm

[C] [icon] [P] [S]

Ancient and modern is the theme here. The building, with its balustraded entry is 15th century and the enthusiastic manager, Gary Jamison, must be the youngest in the business. In the restaurant, dark oak beams and panelling are offset by starched white tablecloths and napkins, a red carpet and red-globed oil table lamps. A three course table d'hôte lunch is only around £3.50 and offers a good choice for all courses. Sardine and tomato salad, Florida cocktail or ravioli are examples of starters, Norfolk game pie, roast chicken or omelette with a filling of your choice are some main course dishes and sweets from the trolley include cheesecake, fruit and cream or éclairs. A slightly extended menu operates for a three-course dinner at about £4.50. A four-course Sunday lunch for the same price, includes a fish course such as goujons of cod. The à la carte menu offers more exotic dishes – still reasonably priced; but you would have to select carefully to keep within our budget. Lobster rumaki is a tempting appetiser – a Japanese kebab-style offering with lobster, water chestnuts and bacon marinated in soy sauce and wine.

THE LIMES HOTEL, Bridge Street (Fakenham 2726)
Open: Mon-Fri 12noon-1.30pm, 7-9.30pm, Sat 12noon-1.30pm, 7-10pm, Sun 12noon-1.30pm

[P] [S]

This friendly free house was only created in 1975, but already it has an excellent reputation for fresh, home-cooked food. The 'Summer Special' three-course lunch costs £3, and the choice is good for each course – you could choose roll mop herring, minute sirloin steak and sherry trifle. The 'Winter Special' offers warming starters and sweets. A cold lunch buffet is on offer in the conservatory for £1.50 – and all the meats are home-cooked. À la carte dinner by candlelight offers a very wide selection, with a dozen appetisers, including whitebait at 90p or smoked salmon at £1. Entrées vary in price, but gammon steak with peaches or pineapple or deep fried southern style chicken, both served with vegetables of the day, are less than £3. Sweets such as sorbets are from 70p.

Felixstowe

BUTTERY BAR, ORWELL MOAT HOUSE ★★★★ Hamilton Road (Felixstowe 5511)
Open: Mon-Sat 12noon-2pm, 6-9.15pm (Sun 12noon-2pm summer only)

[C] [P] [♣]

This elegant buttery with its dark oak panels and richly-ornamented ceiling offers you all the comfort and luxury of a four-star hotel without the prices. Home-made soup of the day could be followed by smoked Scotch salmon, Norfolk turkey, ox tongue or other cold meats all served with salads, pickles, and a roll and butter. Finish with home-made fruit pie and cream and wash it all down with a glass of red, white or rosé house wine, and you'll still be within the budget. In the restaurant, table d'hôte lunch is around £5 and dinner about £5.50.

Frinton-on-Sea

ANNE'S, 36-38 Connaught Avenue (Frinton-on-Sea 2304)
Open: Mon-Sun 10am-5.30pm

[C] [♫] [P] [S] [♣]

Set in fashionable Connaught Avenue, this charming Georgian bay-windowed restaurant, with its many hanging potted plants, offers refreshment all day until 5.30pm. The lunch from 12noon-2pm may comprise soup of the day, tasty home-made steak and kidney pie served with potatoes and two vegetables and a sweet from the trolley for around £3. There is also a choice of roasts and grills. A glass of French wine costs about 40p. If you are too late for lunch, try a high tea of chicken or ham or plaice and chips, all around £2.50. Anne's Popular Special Sunday Roast, for around £4 always includes roast topside as one of a choice of three roasts.

Great Yarmouth

BRUINS RESTAURANT, 149 King Street (Great Yarmouth 2967)
Open: Mon-Sat 12noon-2pm, 6.30-10.30pm, Sun 12noon-1.30pm, 6.30-10.30pm

[C] [♫] [P] [♣]

Originally two merchants' houses, this modern grill restaurant features particularly attractive décor, with wood-clad walls, polished wood floor and tables, high-backed banquettes and pendant copper-shaded lamps over each table. The 'Daily Economiser' menu offers excellent value at around £2.25, all in – Tuesday offers gammon and pineapple, Wednesday, lamb cutlets, Thursday, chicken, plus sweet of the day. There is a good choice of starters, fish, salads, grills and sweets on the à la carte menu which qualify for this Guide. House wine costs about 60p.

Ipswich

CROWN & ANCHOR HOTEL ★★
Westgate Street (Ipswich 58506)
Open: Mon-Sun 12noon-3pm, 6pm-12mdnt

[C] [P] [S]

Behind an ornate gothic, stone façade, this Trusthouse Forte concern has been completely modernised and refurbished. There are two comfortable restaurants, the Grill and the Sherry Restaurant, the latter being slightly more expensive. Although described as 'Henekey's Steak Bars', plaice (about £3.50), Barnsley chop (about £4) and chicken cordon bleu (£4.20) are also available and the prices include sweet or cheese. Appetisers are around the £1 mark, and include whitebait and smoked mackerel. Children's portions of the main meals are half-price.

GREAT WHITE HORSE ★★
Tavern Street (Ipswich 56558)
Open: Buttery: Mon-Sat 10.30am-9.30pm Carving Table: Mon-Sun 12.30-2.15pm, 7-9.15pm

[C] [S]

A leading inn in Ipswich since the 16th century, the Great White Horse was once the haunt of Charles Dickens when the author was employed as a reporter on the Ipswich Chronicle and it was later to receive a mention in his *Pickwick Papers.* A wood-panelled buttery offers a wide range of food from toasted tea-cakes to omelettes and grills served all day at prices well within our budget (there is even a special menu for the under 12s). A more elegant meal may be enjoyed within the plush deep red and copper surrounds of the Carvery. The à la carte menu here is rather over the top, but an excellent table d'hôte Carving Table menu gives a choice of five starters including prawn cocktail; prime rib of beef, selected hot roasts with traditional accompaniments or cold roast with salad; sweet from the trolley or cheeses plus coffee with cream for an all-inclusive price of £5.50.

MARNO'S, 14 St Nicholas Street
(Ipswich 53106)
Open: summer: Mon-Wed 10am-2pm, Thu-Sat 10am-2pm, 7.30-10pm, winter: closed Wed pm

A vegetarian restaurant with dishes imaginative enough to tempt the most confirmed meat-eater. The lunch menu includes savoury flans, bean hotpot, nut rissoles, freshly-made salads and fruits for about £3.70. The much more extensive evening menu averages around £5.25 for three courses such as mushroom pâté, Cheshire cheese and herb pie, pashka (a Russian mixture of curd cheese, butter, cream, raisins and brown sugar), followed by herbal tea or a glass of house wine. Live music is provided by local folk musicians at weekends.

NOBLE ROMANS, 9 Buttermarket
(Ipswich 219376)
Open: Mon-Sat 10am-11pm, Sun 5.30-10.30pm

[S]

Claudius and Tiberius are among the fourteen noble Romans whose names are taken in vain for the pizzas in this trendy Italian restaurant. A 'Claudius' has mozzarella cheese with tomato and costs about £1.35 while a 'Tiberius', at the top of the range, has tuna, sardine, anchovy, onion, lemon, olives, capers, mozzarella and tomato for around £1.65. A full three-course meal here need only cost about £3, with appetisers such as melon for around 65p and most desserts costing around 70p – try Black Forest gâteau or lemon sorbet. A large glass of Italian house wine is about 55p – all this and décor in oatmeal, fawn and brown with basket-weave chairs has attracted a regular clientèle.

Lowestoft

VICTORIA BAR BUTTERY, VICTORIA HOTEL ★★★
Open: Mon-Sat 12noon-2pm, Mon-Fri 9-10.30pm

[C] [P]

A well-stocked cold buffet table holds roast Norfolk turkey, ox tongue, beef, ham and prawns in cocktail sauce, which with a serve-yourself salad average at about £2 a head. Hot meals often include grilled minute steak, breaded scampi or fillets of Lowestoft plaice, but the Chef's special (changed daily) is warmly recommended. At the cheap end of the scale are sandwiches, a Ploughman's lunch or hamburger with salad garnish. Sweet and a starter add around 50p and a glass of house wine about 60p.

Maldon

MANN'S BISTRO, 46 Market Hill
(Maldon 57752)
Open: Mon-Sat 7-10.30pm
(11pm Fri & Sat)

[♫] [S] [🍷]

Wooden tables and benches, bathed in candlelight and the live music of soft guitars (some evenings) enhances the bistro-like atmosphere at Mann's. Situated close to the boating yards and moorings, this intimate little haunt offers first-class respite for the sailing fraternity, and anyone else besides. The imaginative menu is changed regularly and leaves you spoiled for choice with such delights as pigeon pie, pork stuffed with apricots and prunes and ragout of liver. An unusual vegetarian dish is included in each menu at around £1.80 for sweet and sour red beans or Neapolitan quiche. With an appetiser such as grapefruit and mint and a sweet from the trolley, a most appetising meal with wine at 60p per glass and coffee should cost you less than £5.

WHEELER'S, 13 High Street
(Maldon 53647)
Open: Tue 12noon-1.30pm, 6-9.30pm, Thu-Sat 12noon-1.30pm, 6-9.30pm
Closed: mid Sep

[S]

Opened in 1979, this 300-year-old building, complete with old ship's timbers inside, contrasting with the rest of the décor, boasts an unusual fish restaurant. The house wine by the glass – Rheinhessen Niersteiner at 45p – is an excellent accompaniment for the fried haddock (around £1.50) or perhaps the lemon sole on the bone (about £2). All the fish is freshly delivered daily from Grimsby and George Wheeler and his son Ross buy only the best quality. Finish with a sweet from the trolley.

Norwich

LE BISTRO, 2a Exchange Street
(Norwich 24452)
Open: Mon 11.30am-2pm, Tue-Fri 11.30am-10pm, Sat 11.30am-2.30pm, 5-10pm

[C] [♫] [S] [🍷]

Table d'hôte at Le Bistro is very good value, an English lunch costing around £2 and dinner – with some French dishes – about £3.70. You could choose a good meal from the à la carte menu for less than £5.50, too. Veal Maison is a popular choice; other favourites include Sole Normandy and duck with orange sauce. The first and second floor restaurants are pleasant and comfortable (once the stairs are negotiated), with dried-flower arrangements set against brocade-patterned wallpaper and brown check cotton cloths.

MANO, 72 Prince of Wales Road
(Norwich 613143)
Open: Mon-Sat 7-11.30pm

The bright orange and white exterior of this bistro proclaims its presence on the corner of Prince of Wales Road and Cathedral Street. As a striking contrast the interior is a faithful reproduction of a Parisian café with dark red paintwork, red velvet café curtains on brass rails and French posters. Green and white tablecloths cover the ten cast-iron tables which provide seating capacity for 34 people. Contrary to appearances, owner Mano is in fact Turkish and his restaurant boasts a truly international menu. A meal of whitebait, followed by duck pilaff plus pears in burgundy wine and coffee will cost around £5, but the addition of a glass of wine may well exceed the limit. There are less expensive alternatives on offer.

THE PIZZA PLACE, 6 Pottergate
(not on telephone)
Open: Mon-Sat 11.30am-2.15pm, 6.30pm-12mdnt

[♫]

Part restaurant, part art gallery, Pizza Place has the work of local artists displayed on its white walls on sale at modest prices. Round pine tables with matching high-backed chairs complete the modern décor of this popular restaurant. Home-made pizzas are plate-sized, with a 'white' pizza (ie without tomatoes) and a seafood pizza adding a touch of originality to the usual list. Salads are available too, and there are speciality steaks such as steak à la creme and steak Milanese for around £3.40. Only three sweets are listed, but they include cheesecake and orange in Grand Marnier, so who would ask for more? The house wine is Torre Nova red.

REMBRANDT RESTAURANT, Easton
(Norwich 880241)
Open: Tue-Sat 12noon-2.15pm,

7-10.30pm, Sun 12noon-2.15pm

[C] [♫] [P] [♣]

Proprietors Bruno and Trudie Riccobena moved here from London five years ago and they have since introduced a wide range of menu styles to suit all tastes, including one for children. The restaurant also has facilities for invalids. Without careful selection, the à la carte can easily exceed our limited budget, but the special 'Business Lunch' and 'Holidaymaker's Lunch' at £3 and £2.50 or less are very good value. Main course might be gammon, calves' liver, plaice, omelette or salad, and two or three international dishes are available each day. Under the Rembrandt chef's 'Taste of England' series, steak and kidney pies, in particular, are selling like hot cakes!

SAVOY RESTAURANT ✕✕✕ 50 Prince of Wales Road (Norwich 20732)
Open: Mon-Sun 12noon-2.30pm, 6pm-1.30am

[C] [♫] [P]

The Athenian Room on the ground floor is elegantly green with chandeliers, Greek pictures and small booths. The windows overlook an enclosed patio with vines and plants galore. Downstairs is the Cellar Taverna, seating over 100 on two levels, complete with a small dance floor. Three-course table d'hôte lunch in the Athenian Room is about £2.50 on weekdays and £3.50 on Sundays. Main course choices are particularly good – roast beef or chicken, moussaka, kebabs, plaice or ham salad. The à la carte menu is very extensive, with Greek, English, Italian and French cuisine, but you will have to select a three-course meal carefully to stay around the £5 limit. A large glass of house wine costs 65p.

SMEDLEY'S ✕✕ Princes Street (Norwich 23193)
Open: Mon-Fri 12noon-3pm, 7-11pm, Sat 12noon-3pm, 7pm-12mdnt

[C] [S]

The ground floor lounge bar seats about forty around a brick-topped bar surface. Adjacent to this is a dining room where simple plated meals, roughly ranging from 80p-£2, are served. Items such as chicken casserole, whitebait and salad and dressed crab are available for both lunch and dinner. Upstairs is the main restaurant, pine-ceilinged with booths and hanging lights, where there is an extensive à la carte menu with a large price range and a three-course set menu.

Try a starter such as rich game soup, followed by (amongst other choices) rump steak, and then a sweet from the trolley for around £5.

TATLERS, 21 Tombland
(Norwich 21822)
Open: Mon-Sat 12noon-2.30pm, 6-11.30pm, Sun 12.30-2.30pm, 7-11pm

[S] [🍷]

You'll find Tatlers amongst the beautiful buildings of Tombland. A group of young people have converted an old house into this attractive restaurant, with a bar upstairs, and have succeeded in creating an air of Victorian opulence by the use of floral wallpaper, red curtains, Victoriana lamps, and mirrors. High-backed settles arranged around plain wooden tables provide a degree of privacy and seclusion. All food is prepared on the premises, the accent being on traditional Norfolk dishes prepared from local produce. Starters include soup (about 65p), pâté or smoked mackerel mousse (about £1.40) and main course dishes range in price from meat loaf at £2.50 to peppered fillet steak at £4.70. More unusual dishes include rabbit in mustard and rosemary (£2.40) or pigeon, duck and orange pie at about £2.60. Vegetables are likely to add about 50p-70p to these prices. Sweets (the list includes syllabub and chocolate fudge cake) cost an average of 70p. The house wine is about 65p a glass.

Saffron Walden

EIGHT BELLS, Bridge Street
(Saffron Walden 22790/22764)
Open: Restaurant: Mon-Sun 12noon-2pm, Mon-Thu 7-9.30pm, Fri-Sat 7-10pm, Bar food: Mon-Sat 12noon-2pm, 6-9.30pm, Sun 12noon-2pm, 7-9.30pm

[C] [P] [🍷]

Situated in a comfortable spot on the edge of town, like the noble old sentinel it is, this four hundred-year-old inn retains its original pub sign and a good deal of olde worlde charm. Both the budget lunches (with main courses such as jugged rabbit, spicy gammon casserole and beef curry from around £2), and the more pricey à la carte selection are of extremely high standard (including such delights as Saffron Veal at around £5.45 with appetisers, dessert and coffee with chocolate mints). There's a cold buffet served in the bar at around £1.25. Don't miss a delicious dessert from the sweet trolley.

Shoeburyness

SHORE HOUSE RESTAURANT
Ness Road (Shoeburyness 3408)
Open: Tue-Sat 12noon-2pm, 7-10pm, Sun 12noon-2pm

[C] [♫] [P] [🍷]

If the fresh air gives you an appetite you'll find this sea-front eating place a very tempting proposition. However, the plush restaurant with its warm red décor is likely to just tip our limit. Three courses from the interesting à la carte menu can cost from £4-£6 although a set three-course lunch with excellent choice of dishes is £3.95 plus service. You'll have to stick to the bar buttery if you want a real budget-priced meal. For about £3.50 you can have a very good two-course lunch such as egg mayonnaise, roast turkey with stuffing, new potatoes and fresh vegetables plus coffee. A glass of Spanish house wine is about 52p.

Southend-on-Sea

CAPRICE CARVING ROOM
96 The Ridgeway, Westcliff
(Southend-on-Sea 76417)
Open: Tue-Sat 12.30-2.30pm, 7-10.30pm, Sun 12.30-2.30pm

[🍷]

Two hundred yards from Chalkwell station on the north side of the railway, the Caprice enjoys quiet surroundings at the corner of a residential square. For around £3.50 the choice is yours from the hot or cold Carving Table, featuring such dishes as prime roast beef with fluffy Yorkshire pudding and roast leg of English pork with apple sauce. Vegetables and a choice from the sweet trolley, or cheese and biscuits, are included in the price, but even with extras such as home-made pâté, roll and butter, coffee and a glass of wine, the cost is only around £5. First-class service is a prime consideration here and you will probably want to linger over a speciality coffee, freshly brewed with a cream topping, chosen from the list of over a dozen. Children's portions are available at around £2.50, and there's a good selection of wines and spirits.

CHINATOWN, 28 York Street
(Southend-on-Sea 64888)
Open: Mon-Thu 12noon-2.30pm, 5pm-12mdnt, Fri-Sat 12noon-2.30pm, 5pm-1am, Sun 12noon-12mdnt

[P] [S]

This cosy Chinese restaurant close to the town centre offers an enormous choice of traditional Chinese and English dishes at budget prices. Well-cooked and pleasantly served by Ken, the owner's son, Wan Tun soup is extremely tasty and roast duck Hong Kong style, decorated with Chinese mushrooms and peppers and costing about £2.20 is highly recommended. Chop suey and chow mein dishes are excellent value for money. A special set dinner for one person, which includes coffee, costs less than or around £2.

CHRYSANTHEMUM CHINESE RESTAURANT, 202 Eastern Esplanade (Southend-on-Sea 582360)
Open: Mon-Sun 12noon-3pm, 6pm-12mdnt

[C] [♫] [P] [☘]

Southend's renowned Chinese restaurant is on the seafront road to Thorpe Bay. It enjoys great popularity built up over ten years, particularly for the Friday and Saturday night music and dancing sessions in the suitably-lit basement. Specialities such as roast Shanghai duck, Chrysanthemum fried chicken and barbecue spare ribs range in price from around £3.10 to £3.80 and are well worth trying, but the long menu gives tremendous choice. For the adventurous, the Chef recommends two set meals which include two appetisers such as crab claw and Chinese kebab, two meat dishes, two vegetable dishes, fried rice and coffee for around £5.

COTGROVE'S RESTAURANT, 11 High Street (Southend-on-Sea 338155)
Open: Mon-Thu 11.45am-9.15pm, Fri-Sat 11.45am-9.45pm, Sun 11.45am-9.15pm

[C] [♫] [P] [S] [☘]

David and John Cotgrove now run the successor to their grandfather Arthur's original High Street restaurant opened in 1896 – a modern 185-seater imaginatively adapted from a former supermarket building. The décor carries forward a family tradition of 'fish and ships' including a colourful tiled panel sculpted by a local student, and several drawings and oil-paintings executed by John himself. In the bar there is a fascinating display of sea-shells. Almost everything you could wish for is on the menu, from a roast with three vegetables at around £2.25 to home-made steak, kidney and mushroom pie for about £1.85 at lunchtime. Fish is, of course, a speciality starting with fried plaice (around £1.70) and rising to poached Scotch salmon with new potatoes and peas (about £4.95). Starters include egg mayonnaise or smoked mackerel for about 85p. Desserts such as cheesecake are in the region of 75p as is a glass of house wine.

FRANCO'S, 19 Alexandra Street (Southend-on-Sea 32889)
Open: Mon-Thu 12noon-2.30pm, 6.30-11pm, Fri-Sat 12noon-2.30pm, 6.30-11.30pm

[S]

From Schweizerhof, St Moritz, to Southend-on-Sea may sound an unlikely route to success, but owner Franco Ludovici swears by it. His intimate Italian restaurant (situated on the corner of Market Place and Alexandra Street, opposite the ABC) has always had a regular brand of late night diners, but recently he has extended his repertoire to include a businessman's lunch at around £3. Ribs of beef or ham on the bone with jacket potatoes make filling lunchtime fare at reasonable prices, though the à la carte menu offers plenty of alternatives.

THE PIPE OF PORT, 84 High Street (Southend-on-Sea 614606)
Open: Mon-Thu 11am-2.30pm, 6-10.30pm, Fri 11am-2.30pm, 6-11pm, Sat 11am-2.30pm, 7-11pm

[C] [P] [S]

This wine bar is situated just off the High Street in a basement premises underneath Greenfields. There is a good, if limited, menu with some interesting starters, such as the toasted fingers topped with anchovy, sardine or Stilton at around 80p for six. A three-course meal of soup, smoked mackerel (two fillets) with salad and fresh fruit salad can be had for around £3.50. One appealing entrée is the 12oz charcoal grilled rib of beef at around £3.30.

SPENCER'S, 20 High Street, Hadleigh (Southend-on-Sea 559209)
Open: Mon-Thu 10am-2.30pm, 6-10.30pm, Fri-Sat 10am-2.30pm, 6-11pm, Sun 10am-2.30pm, 6-10.30pm

[S]

This wine bar is easily spotted by the attractive pavement patio. Comfortable banquette seating and French cane-back chairs enable you to take your ease while absorbing the interesting reading on the walls. Chalkboards display the menu, offering plenty of choice. Pâté is about 85p, lasagne around £1 and beef curry about £1.20. The poppy seed French bread is very good as is the help yourself salad selection from around £1.50 and the chili con carne at about £1.20. Brian Spencer selects all his own wines and a glass of excellent French house wine costs around 60p.

CASTLETON
HATHERSAGE
CHESTERFIELD
FLAGG
BAKEWELL
DERBYSHIRE
ASHBOURNE
KIRK
LANGLEY
MICKLEOVER
DERBY
NOTTINGHAMSHIRE
OLLERTON
NOTTINGHAM
LINCOLN
LINCOLNSHI
SLEAFORD
BOSTON
GRANTHAM
MELTON
MOWBRAY
STAMFORD
LEICESTERSHIRE
LEICESTER
NORTHAMPTONSHIRE
NORTHAMPTON

East Midlands and the Peak District

Throughout the five counties that make up this region there is one common denominator – diversity! All offer something different and rewarding to the visitor, whether it is in the countryside or in the towns; the past or the present. Here nature includes amongst her charms the meadows and wolds of Lincolnshire and the rolling hunting lands of Leicestershire. To the west is Robin Hood's Sherwood Forest, with the Peaks of Derbyshire further west, and to the south the fertile hills of Northamptonshire. The county towns, rich in history yet modern in outlook, are handsome and prosperous, and throughout the counties there are numerous tiny villages that invite the passing stranger to stay a while and share in their tranquillity.

It's an invitation that should not be missed. The appeal of this area can only be hinted at, so too the delights of the local fare. The town of Melton Mowbray in Leicestershire has given us a selection of fine foods. There is the Melton Hunt Cake, a very dark, rich fruit cake fortified with rum, which has been a favourite of the gentlemen of the hunt for the past 120 years. There are Melton Mowbray pies, raised pork pies with a difference; the meat made slightly pink by the addition of a little anchovy sauce. If you don't fancy a pie try Melton Hunt Beef; the original spiced beef, it is rubbed with a mixture of salt, salt petre, sugar and herbs, left for 10 days, and then boiled in beer. It is normally served cold and is absolutely delicious!

For a snack you could try the potted meat of these parts, a beef or ham coarse paste which is delightful spread on toast or, even better, as a filling for baps. These large, flat and round rolls are ideal for whatever filling your fancy turns to.

Stilton, Sage Derby or Red Leicester; if you like cheese these are names to conjure with. Sample their individual delights with a slice of Mansfield gooseberry pie, or a couple of Nottingham Bramleys.

If you've still got room, or if your time is your own, the opportunities for gastronomic voyages of discovery are endless. The names alone are enough to tempt the curious: Hallaton Hare Pie Scrambling, Quorn Bacon Roll, Polony, these are just a few. You shouldn't have to search too hard to find these dishes and you will be continually amazed by the variety of traditional foods that this region offers. Make a good start by consulting the following entries; there's no better way to begin!

Ashbourne

THE ASHBURNIAN, Compton (Ashbourne 2798)
Open: Mon-Sat 12noon-2pm, 6-10pm, Sun 12noon-6pm

[C] [S]

The restaurant with its white rough-plaster walls and dark beams with reproduction brass lanterns, has a pleasantly olde worlde atmosphere. A comfortable cocktail bar adjoining has hessian-clad walls and copper-topped tables. The menu is very reasonably priced, with starters ranging from around 40p-95p – including prawn cocktail and a choice of seven main courses, all served with vegetables and including a sweet (such as apple tart with cream) in the listed price. Half a roast chicken is around £3.

SPENCER'S COFFEE HOUSE RESTAURANT, 37-41 Market Place (Ashbourne 3164)
Open: Mon-Sat 9am-2pm, 2.45-5.45pm

[P] [S] [♧]

This attractive little restaurant is housed in Georgian premises overlooking the cobbled market square of this historic town. A daily-changing lunch menu offers a good selection of traditional dishes, an example of which would be cream of leek soup with roll and butter, home-made steak and kidney pie with new potatoes and green peas, and apple and blackcurrant tart – all for around £4 with glass of wine.

Bakewell

THE BARN, Bath Street (Bakewell 2687)
Open: Mon-Sun 12noon-2pm, Fri 7.30-10pm

[♧]

Formerly an actual barn, these converted premises retain much of the original farmland character. The stone walls are painted white and decorated with numerous pot plants and items of equine bric-à-brac, whilst the barn door itself is now a large opening picture window, which looks out onto a pretty flower garden. Set lunches consist of fairly simple starters such as soup or fruit juice, followed by plaice or your favourite roasts (beef with Yorkshire pudding or leg of pork) served with new potatoes and fresh vegetables. Desserts include sherry trifle and gooseberry crumble, and with coffee the meal will cost £3.40-£4 depending on main course choice. The evening meal is just beyond our limit if you add the 55p for a glass of house wine.

MILFORD HOUSE ★ Mill Street (Bakewell 2130)
Open: Mon-Sun 1-1.30pm, 7-7.30pm

[P]

Situated on the ground floor of the Milford House Hotel, this pleasant ten-tabled dining room offers quality meals at sensible prices. The whole operation has been personally run by the Hunt family for many years and service is their keynote. Set lunches are £3.75 and feature roast chicken and grilled plaice. Evening meals are only slightly dearer (£4.25), with roast stuffed loin topping the bill. After tasting dessert specialities such as strawberry pie with cream and orange trifle, you'll surely agree that Bakewell is an apt location for the restaurant. Coffee is included in the price, whilst a glass of house wine will set you back about 65p. A word of warning – the short opening hours mean that advance booking is a must.

Boston

THE AUCTIONEERS' TEAROOM 43/44 Market Place (Boston 66600)
Open: Mon-Fri 9am-5.30pm, Sat 9am-5pm

[P] [S] [♧]

Close by an Estate Agents and up seventeen steps is this first-floor restaurant decked out like a country garden. A trellis supporting flowers and plants is suspended from the ceiling and green is the theme of the décor. There is even a song bird in one corner to complete the illusion! The three-course table d'hôte lunch is excellent value from around £1.50. Start with soup of the day, then choose from a selection of main courses served with chips – chicken, haddock and Cornish pasty are typical examples. Finish with fruit pie and custard. At this price, you could afford to splash out on a whole bottle of wine! The à la carte menu is more expensive, but with rump steak, rainbow trout or duckling à l'orange on offer, you could easily be tempted – and still stay within the budget.

THE CARVING ROOM, NEW ENGLAND HOTEL ★★ Wide Bargate (Boston 65255)
Open: Mon-Thu 12noon-2pm, 7-10pm, Fri-Sun 12noon-2pm, 7-10.30pm

[C] [P] [♧]

At the rear of the imposing New England Hotel is the elegant, Regency-style Carving Room, with white pillars, rich red-patterned carpet and green wallpaper, leather upholstery and tablecloths. Here you may eat a superb roast lunch or dinner. The carving table is bedecked with large roast joints, fresh vegetables and salads – you help yourself to as much as you want. This, together with the choice of a sweet from the trolley, will set you back £3.85. Appetisers are extra, but hardly necessary! Potted shrimps or avocado pear with prawns are the most expensive at around £1.50, but soup is only 60p. Children can help themselves and are charged the special price of £2.50. A glass of wine is around 55p.

Castleton

THE CASTLE HOTEL AND RESTAURANT (Hope Valley 20578)
Open: Mon-Thu, Sun 12noon-2pm, 7-10pm, Fri-Sat 12noon-2pm, 7-10.30pm

[C] [P]

Within the Peak District National Park and in the village centre, is this stone-built 17th-century coaching inn, its interior a wealth of exposed stonework and beams. Excellent table d'hôte menus operate for lunch and dinner – you are spoiled for choice. Lunch costs £4, with sixteen starters including avocado viniagrette, pâté-filled mushrooms in batter and smoked mackerel. Four roasts head the long list of main dishes. The roast beef with vegetables, ratatouille, horseradish sauce and Yorkshire pudding is particularly recommended. Fillet of pork à la crème, chicken chasseur and cider-baked ham with cinnamon peaches are other possibilities. A selection of sweets on the trolley are all served with fresh cream. Dinner is £4.50 and offers even more choices. Italian wine served in a one-glass bottle is remarkable value at 40p.

Chesterfield

BURLINGTON RESTAURANT
Church Way (Chesterfield 34735)
Open: Mon-Sat 11.45am-3pm, Grill Room: Mon-Sat 9am-5.30pm

[C] [S] [♧]

Here's a restaurant, almost in the shadow of Chesterfield's famous 'twisted spire', where food prices are straight as a die. Soup with roll and butter costs about 40p, hors d'oeuvres 65p, a main course with vegetables from £1.80 for a savoury omelette or pizza to fillet steak garni at around £4. The most expensive sweet is a portion of fresh cream gâteau which tops 60p.

THE OLD SPINNER RESTAURANT ✕
Sheffield Road, Sheepbridge (Chesterfield 450550)
Open: Mon 12noon-2pm, Tue-Thu 12noon-2pm, 7-10pm, Fri 12noon-2pm, 7-10pm, Sat 7-11pm

[C] [P] [♧]

This intimate restaurant is decorated in black and white Tudor style. A popular eating place with businessmen, it enjoys an excellent reputation as a restaurant of renown. The businessman's lunch offers a choice of five starters, five main courses, a choice from the sweet trolley, a glass of wine and coffee at around £3.75, though you don't have to be a businessman to enjoy it! An extensive à la carte menu offers more exotic International dishes, but watch your pocket.

Derby

BEN BOWERS, 13-15 Chapel Street (Derby 367688/365988)
Open: Mon-Fri 12noon-2pm, 7-11pm, Sat 7-11pm, Sun 12noon-2pm

[C] [♫] [P] [S] [♧]

Located above the Blessington Carriage public house is this long, rectangular restaurant, with seating for about sixty at polished wooden tables. A four-course lunch of (for instance) home-made soup of the day, grapefruit and orange cocktail, pizza Neapolitan (topped with anchovies and black olives) with salad and French fried potatoes and a sweet from the trolley costs about £3.75, with children's portions at around £2.25. The dinner menu features dishes from Russia, Mexico, Austria and the Caribbean and is on the pricey side. £5 would restrict your choice, but for £6 it's worth splashing out on one of the 'special' nights when a cabaret is provided.

Downstairs in Betty's Buffet Bar, excellent pub lunches include chili con carne or lasagne for less than £1.

THE CATHEDRAL RESTAURANT LTD
✕✕ 22 Iron Gate (Derby 368732)
Open: Mon-Wed, Fri 12noon-2pm, 7-10pm, Thu 12noon-2pm

[C] [♫] [P] [S] [♧]

In the shadow of Derby Cathedral, this elegant little restaurant with its low ceiling, exposed central beam and sparkling table tops, glassware and cutlery, is housed in a building dating back to 1530. Then a nunnery, it has since been a Ladies' club and a chartered accountants' office. At lunchtime a four-course table d'hôte menu is available at £4.50. Choice is good and dishes include salads, omelettes, pizza, spaghetti bolognese and steak, kidney and mushroom pie while shish kebab, grilled trout, chicken cathedral, sirloin steak and jumbo scampi are examples of the more pricey fare. A large glass of house wine costs about 60p. In the evening there is a similar, though slightly dearer table d'hôte dinner, and the à la carte menu, though tempting, is expensive.

THE FRENCH REVOLUTION, Friargate (Derby 40581)
Open: Mon-Thu 12noon-2pm, 7.30-10.30pm, Fri-Sat 12noon-2pm, 7.30-11pm

[C] [♫] [P]

A touch of France in the centre of Derby – this intimate little bistro with its French posters, prints, music and cuisine, checked tablecloths and generous glasses of French wine (only about 50p) is deservedly popular. Two table d'hôte lunch menus are particularly good value – one at around £2.50 offers French onion or a cream soup, lamb cutlets, loin of pork or chicken with vegetables and a sweet, while the Bonaparte Special at about £5 offers soup, prawn cocktail or fruit juice with a choice of sirloin steak served plain or in a red wine sauce and a choice of desserts. In the evenings, typically French table d'hôte dinners are served: three courses cost around £4 and four courses about £5.

LETTUCE LEAF, 21 Friar Gate (Derby 40307)
Open: Mon-Sat 10am-7.30pm

[P] [S]

Beyond the little craft shop selling handthrown pottery, woodcrafts and books on yoga and health food is this white-walled restaurant with its bright curtains, basket-work lamp shades, wooden tables and tasty vegetarian menu. Vegetable soup or fruit juice are inexpensive starters at around 25p. Omelettes, salads, savouries and snacks supplement a daily speciality such as marrow provençal, lasagne, gratin Dauphinois, pizza or celery hotpot. Most main dishes cost under or around £1.20, with sweets such as fresh fruit salad, yoghurt with honey or Lettuce Leaf muesli under 60p. Finish with a dandelion coffee – full of flavour – for about 30p. Spanish or Hungarian wines cost around 60p a glass.

RAMSDEN'S TAVERN, 35 Cornmarket (Derby 49375)
Open: Mon-Sat 12noon-3pm, 6-12mdnt, Sun 12noon-2.30pm, 7-11pm

[C] [S]

Ramsden's Tavern is a Victorian-style pub situated in the heart of the city, housing no fewer than three bars, a steak bar and a buttery. Various pictures, theatre posters, Victorian-style wall lighting and brassware decorate the white rough plaster walls of the steak bar which serves a standard grill-type menu of beef steak, gammon or fried fillet of plaice. Prices range from around £2.50 to £5 and included in the price of each main course is a choice of French fried potatoes or baked jacket potato, vegetables, roll and butter plus dessert or cheese and biscuits. Coffee and starter are extra but the average price of a three-course meal with wine is around £5. The Buttery, run in the same efficient manner, offers a few different cuts of steak such as T-bone and rib eye. A full meal with wine could take you just over £5 here, but a three-course speciality lunch including rib of beef only costs about £3.

Flagg

PLOUGH INN (Taddington 336/421)
Open: Mon-Sun 12noon-2pm, 7-10pm

[P]

You'll find this popular first floor restaurant above an 18th-century inn, tucked away in the little Peak District village of Flagg, six miles south-east of Buxton off the A515. There are pleasant rural views for diners from the refectory tables and prices here, as you'll discover, are exceptionally low. Good news, though, travels fast and it is necessary to book if you're not to be disappointed. A soup starter, plus, for instance, cheese and onion pie with chips and peas (one of over a dozen unpretentious main courses), with gâteau to finish, costs only £2.20. House wine is about 50p a glass, but at these prices you can easily afford a more adventurous hock or claret from the well-stocked cellar.

Grantham

BARKERS STEAK BAR, The Chequers, Market Place (Grantham 72566)
Open: Mon-Sat 12noon-2pm, 7-10pm

[P]

The building housing this smart steak bar is reputedly haunted by a faceless thing – possibly the ghost of one of the nuns who used to creep from this old nunnery along a tunnel to the church. However, there is nothing spectral about the food, which is very substantial. Rump, sirloin and fillet steak or scampi are all served with chips, peas and side salad, cheese and biscuits or fruit pie or ice cream are included in a price which ranges from around £3 for plaice up to our limit for fillet steak. As you sip your Spanish wine in the bar you will find it hard to imagine ghostly wails or clanking chains!

CATLIN'S, 11 High Street (Grantham 5428/9)
Open: Mon-Tue 9am-6pm, Wed 9am-2pm, Thu-Sat 9am-6pm

[S]

Steeped in history, the olde worlde grocery and confectionery shop of Catlin Bros Ltd, boasts a restaurant with wood-panelled walls, oak beams, pottery and bric-à-brac on the first floor. The property dates back to 1560 and its claims to fame include the 'discovery' of Grantham gingerbread and the ghost of one Captain Hamilton, a Royalist officer during the Civil War. Snacks are served throughout the day and a typical meal from the à la carte menu might be home-made soup (30p), pepper and salami pizza with salad (£1!) and raspberries with cream (60p). French house wine is very reasonable at 40p a glass, in fact for the buff there is an interesting range of wines from non-fashionable countries. Service is efficient and courteous.

Hathersage

BRADGATE BUTTERY, Main Road (Hope Valley 50665)
Open: Tue-Sun 11am-12mdnt

[P]

English cuisine is the order of the day at this attractive Tudor-style restaurant with its Minstrel's Gallery where fifty evening diners can enjoy a meal with a view. Entrees include lamb chops with mint sauce, salmon steak poached in butter with freshly ground black pepper and sea salt and spatchcock chicken (whole baby chicken with onions, garlic, black pepper, sea salt and other seasonings) and range in price from £2.30 to around £4. Together with farmhouse soup, roll and butter, home-made gâteau, coffee with cream and a 50p glass of French wine, the average meal costs around £4.75.

Kirk Langley

MEYNELL ARMS HOTEL ★★
Ashbourne Road (Kirk Langley 515/6)
Open: Bar meals: Mon-Fri 12noon-2.30pm, 6.30-10pm, Sat 6.30-8.30pm, Sun 12noon-2pm, 7-10.30pm, Restaurant: Mon-Sat 7-9pm

[C] [P]

An excellent stopping place en route for the Peak District, the lounge bar serves a range of wholesome dishes at lunchtime and in the evening. Three courses can easily be enjoyed for less than £3 – soup of the day, followed by chicken and chips or home-made steak and kidney pie and a sweet from the trolley is a typical example. A three-course table d'hôte dinner offers a good choice for just over £5. Main courses include roasts, escalope of veal, lemon sole or gammon and pineapple. A glass of house wine costs about 50p.

Leicester

DU CANN'S WINE BAR, 29 Market Street (Leicester 556877)
Open: Mon-Fri 11.30am-2.30pm, Sat 11.30am-3pm, Wed-Sat 7-11pm

[S]

In one of the city's many little side streets is this popular split-level wine bar. The attractive ground-floor room offers self-service selection of a variety of cold carvery items (turkey, ham, beef etc and some speciality seafood dishes) against a background of plain green walls, livened up by old prints, shelves of crock casks and old wine bottles. A varied three-course meal can be had for about £4. Below it is the white-walled cellar with its glimpses of original brick, where a full waitress service operates. In the evenings succulent steaks – around £6, chops and grilled trout – both about £4, supplement the cold selection. A comprehensive list of wines and vintage ports is available in both bars.

THE GOOD EARTH, 19 Free Lane (Leicester 538585)
Open: Mon-Thu 12noon-3pm, Fri 12noon-3pm, 7-11pm, Sat 12noon-6pm

[P] [S]

Tucked away in narrow Free Lane is this inviting first-floor wholefood restaurant. Inside all is natural wood, with displays of farming implements, hanging brass lanterns and a large farmhouse dresser with old plates and storage jars of preserved fruits, vegetables and grains. Help yourself to hot or cold dishes from the buffet display. A full meal will cost around £2.50, for which you choose from a selection of soups, hot savoury dishes or roasts, savoury rissoles, a variety of nourishing salads, home-made cakes, fresh fruit and natural goat's milk yoghurt. A small carafe of wine costs about £1.40. Parties of twenty or more can arrange to eat an evening meal on nights other than Friday. A sister restaurant in Churchgate is virtually identical – even in name – but is unlicensed.

THE HAYLOFT, HOLIDAY INN ☆☆☆☆
Nicholas Circle (Leicester 51161)
Open: Mon-Sun 11am-10.30pm

[C] [P]

In striking contrast to the modern hotel accommodation, the Hayloft restaurant has an old tithe barn atmosphere, with suitable décor of a hay cart, horse and oxen trappings, and enough room for 100 people. A satisfying three-course meal can be had here for around £4.90. Try the farmhouse soup (freshly made from the cauldron) followed by a 'good and wholesome salad' or baked mackerel with capers 'just like mother used to make', and parsley potatoes. To finish you may choose crème caramel or pie or gâteau from the pastry shop plus a cup of coffee (served from a bottomless pot for one charge). A special attraction on Sundays is the 'splosh and nosh' menu; for just over £5 (half-price for children) per person you can enjoy a swim in the hotel pool, followed by a three-course meal with coffee. The French house wine is 85p per goblet. If you find swimming a little too energetic, the regular weekend dinner dances might be just your thing.

THE POST HOUSE HOTEL ☆☆☆
Braunston Lane East (Leicester 896688)
Open: Barge Buttery: Mon-Sun 7am-10.30pm

[C] [P]

Longboat owners will feel very much at home in this bright and original buttery, where the ceiling is curved to resemble an abstract version of an upturned boat, and the walls sport a colourful mural of a bargee family and their craft. Red-and-blue paintwork and a scattering of water cans and kettles complete the canal-boat atmosphere. The imaginative menu gives excellent scope for a satisfying three-course meal for upwards of £4. Tasty starters and grills supplement the quick-and-easy hamburgers, salads and omelettes, most of which are around £2.50. A selection of 'filled fit to burst' sandwiches (toasted or otherwise) cost around £1. A children's menu is available on request.

A SPANISH PLACE, 38a Belvoir Street (Leicester 542830)
Open: Mon-Sat 9am-6pm

[S]

An orange awning and pot plants gives this small modern restaurant a continental flavour. Inside, the emphasis is on home-made cuisine and a friendly, hospitable atmosphere, heightened by the fresh posy of flowers on each table. Snack foods and main meals are available throughout the day. Sandwiches and toasted snacks are made from freshly baked bread and cost between 60p to £1.20. A tasty three-course meal could include a Spanish omelette as an appetiser (around 50p), fried chicken, peas and jacket potato (about £2) and home-made fruit pie with fresh cream for around 50p. Business lunch boxes are made up by Susan and Josef Anoyo, the proprietors, to suit individual customer's requirements. Unlicensed.

SWISS COTTAGE RESTAURANT
52-54 Charles Street (Leicester 56577)
Open: Mon-Sat 9.30am-7pm

[P] [S]

Opened about 16 years ago, this smart restaurant with attractive exposed brickwork, dark wood-effect tables, copper light shades and waitresses dressed as Swiss maids, was the first of six similar eateries which have sprung up in Leicester. Each site has been chosen for its ease of access for shoppers and business people in the city centre. At lunchtime, chops, steaks, home-made steak and kidney pie, chicken and gammon steak are served at prices ranging from around £2-£3.25. Soup is less than 40p and there is an excellent choice of home-made pies served with fresh cream for around 50p. Sister establishments are located in Churchgate, Lee Circle, Odeon Arcade and the Haymarket. The Swiss Cottage Garden, one of two places at the Haymarket, is the only licensed premises.

TOWER RESTAURANT, Lewis's, Humberstone Gate (Leicester 23241)
Open: Mon-Fri 11am-3pm, Sat 11am-5pm

[C] [P] [S]

The sleek, 137-foot tower of Lewis's store, topped with coloured lighting was the talk of Leicester and district in 1936, when it was built. The fourth floor restaurant takes its name from this and its interior décor is based on one of the Queen's ships of the Thirties – all turquoise, and gold with a rich, red patterned carpet. A special shopper's lunch costs just £2. The table d'hôte three-course lunch is also excellent value at just under £3. There is a choice for each course and a typical meal would be soup, followed by grilled ham and pineapple with sweet of the day to finish. The à la carte menu is extremely reasonable, with most main courses such as roasts around £3 and sweets from the trolley from 50p-70p. There is a special children's menu for under 11s. There is no service charge and VAT is included. Red, white or rosé wine by the glass costs about 50p.

Lincoln

CRUSTS, 46 Broadgate (Lincoln 40322)
Open: Mon-Sat 9.30am-2.30pm, 7pm-12mdnt

[C]

Only the name 'Crusts', printed in bold lettering on the window distinguishes this restaurant from the quaint little shops on either side of it. The building occupies the site of the original Roman wall which surrounded the city and, inside, the walls are decorated with framed bills and receipts dating from 1837 when an inn stood on this site. A cosy atmosphere is created within by the use of country-style furniture, whitewashed walls and dark beams, and a rich red carpet. This is a comfortable place in which to enjoy the good food and hospitality of proprietors Chris and Rita Barnes. Business lunch is a must for the budget-conscious as you can have soup of the day; southern fried chicken, peas and French fries; roll and butter, and a choice of cheesecake or ice cream for only £2.25. Carte du jour offers a selection of entrées with prices from £3.16 for fried North Sea cod to £5.70 for an 8oz prime fillet steak – half price for children. Unbelievably, this price includes soup or fruit juice, a special Crust salad, French fries, garden peas, roll and butter followed by home-made ice cream or a selection from the cheeseboard. A glass of Spanish or Hungarian wine comes at 50p per glass.

THE DUKE WILLIAM, 44 Bailgate (Lincoln 21351)
Open: Mon-Thu 11.30am-3pm, 6.45-10.30pm, Fri-Sat 11.30am-3pm, 6.45-11pm, Sun 12noon-2pm, 7-10.30pm

[P]

This charming 18th-century pub stands in the oldest part of the city, close to the famous cathedral. The simple décor of white-painted stone walls and beamed ceiling is complemented by tapestries and bric-à-brac which create an olde worlde atmosphere in keeping with the age and character of the building. Lunch here is a homely affair with dishes such as home-made steak and kidney pie, grilled plaice or ham salad, and the price of a three-course meal is around £3. For around £6, a fairly extensive dinner menu offers such dishes as fried whitebait, grilled trout with almonds or chicken à la crème. Coffee and wine are extra, so evenings can be rather expensive unless care is taken in selection.

HARVEY'S CATHEDRAL RESTAURANT, 1 Exchequer Gate, Castle Square (Lincoln 21886)
Open: Sun-Mon 12noon-2pm, Tue-Sat 12noon-2pm, 7pm-12mdnt. Closed: Mon Oct-Jun

[C] [P]

In the shadows of Lincoln Cathedral and Lincoln Castle is Bob and Adrianne Harvey's bright, split-level restaurant, housed in a historic building once a pub (complete with drunken ghoul). Lunch here any day and you will receive excellent value for money and a good choice of well-prepared food. On weekdays all the starters are about 50p-75p and a selection of salads, including fresh salmon trout range from around £2.25-£3.20. Daily special hot dishes are similarly priced and sweets cost about 75p. On Sundays the three-course lunch is priced by the main course which could be roast beef (around £3), or Taunton casserole of pork and apples in cider at around £2.75. Children's lunch portions are about half price and a glass of house wine costs around 60p. The five-course dinner is a little beyond the scope of this guide.

ZORBA'S RESTAURANT, 292-3 High Street (Lincoln 29360)
Open: Mon-Fri 11.45am-2.30pm, 6.30-11.30pm, Sat 11.45am-11.30pm

[C] [P] [S]

Modern décor with banquette seating and contemporary refectory tables recommends this city-centre first-floor restaurant where good wholesome English and Greek cuisine is served with speed and efficiency. A small adjoining bar with Mediterranean bric-à-brac completes the scene. You can enjoy a three-course special lunch from £3, with plenty of choice of English fare such as roast beef and Yorkshire, haddock and chips or farmhouse grill. The à la carte menu includes hors d'oeuvres from around 75p for spaghetti bolognese to about £1.25 for prawn cocktail. Roasts and grills vary from around £3 to £5. A dozen continental dishes are on offer as are some Greek specialities such as Cypriana meze – a selection of hot and cold Greek dishes for about £5. A glass of house wine costs around 50p.

Melton Mowbray

CERVINO RISTORANTE ITALIANO
1-3 Leicester Street
(Melton Mowbray 69828)
Open: Mon-Sat 12noon-2pm, 6.30-11pm (11.30pm Sat)

[C]

Unmistakably Italian, this pale pink restaurant is rich in memorabilia from the empty Chianti bottles that hang from the ceiling to the many picture postcards and posters of the home country which adorn the walls. The green gingham of the tablecloths provides a fresh contrast. An all-Italian menu offers such specialities as tonno e fagioli (tuna fish with bean salad) for 90p followed by pollo imperiale (chicken with cream, mushrooms and asparagus) at £2.50 including vegetables of the day and potatoes. Banana del Vesuvio is a mouth-watering Italian sweet of baked banana with cream, rum and sugar – a special treat at only 95p. Coffee in a glass with cream is 35p which, even with a glass of house wine at 55p, brings the bill to around £5.

Mickleover

NAG'S HEAD, 25 Uttoxeter Road (Derby 513104)
Open: Mon-Thu 12noon-2pm, 7-10pm, Fri-Sat 12noon-2pm, 7-10.30pm

[C] [P] [S]

1929 was a significant year for Mickleover, as it saw the opening of the Nag's Head on the crossroads in the village centre. In the same year a dining car was being constructed to form part of the historic 'Brighton Belle', a train that made daily journeys between London and Brighton until its retirement in 1972. Now renovated to her former glory, the coach has finally come to rest on new sidings attached to the Nag's Head. Original brass racks and fittings are complemented by a décor in warm shades of rust, and fifty-six diners are accommodated in booths seating two or four. The menu offers starters such as soup of the day (35p) or pâté (75p), and grills such as plaice, trout, gammon or steaks between £4 and £5 including sweet and coffee.

Northampton

COUNTRY KITCHEN, 1 St Giles Terrace (no telephone)
Open: Mon-Sat 9am-5.15pm

In the basement of an elegant terraced house, this small restaurant has the quiet simplicity of a farmhouse kitchen, with white walls and natural brickwork, but with needlecord carpet to add a touch of comfort, and blue and white crockery giving a touch of colour. Toasted sandwiches and a wide variety of cakes and pastries are available all day and lunch is so popular that you may have to wait for a place at one of the five tables. Emphasis is on good fresh produce and everything is home-made. Vegetarian dishes are available as well as such things as Cornish pasties and shepherd's pie, and a substantial three-course meal costs no more than £2.

THE VINEYARD ✕ 7 Derngate
(Northampton 33978)
Open: Mon-Fri 12noon-2pm,
Tue-Fri 7.30-10.30pm, Sat 7-10.30pm

[C] [♫]

A gaily striped canopy and half-curtained window give a continental-café look to this modern restaurant in Northampton's busy centre. Inside, the décor is simple and effective, one wall being clad in pine with illuminated niches displaying a variety of antiques and bric-à-brac. The short but imaginative menu is changed weekly and offers dishes of British, European and Middle Eastern origin. For a truly international meal you might choose taramasalata (a Greek dish with smoked cod's roe) as an appetiser followed by hare in walnut sauce, with dondurma kaymakli (an Egyptian ice-cream flavoured with mastic) for dessert.

Nottingham

BEN BOWERS, 128 Derby Road
(Nottingham 43288/47488)
Open: Mon-Fri 12noon-2pm

[C]

A sister to its namesake in Derby, this restaurant offers a good value three-course meal (*eg*, soup of the day, poached fillet of sole with parsley sauce and lemon meringue pie), plus coffee, for under £4. Below in the basement, Betty's Buffet Bar has a wide range of snacks (30p-£1) and cold meat salads (around £1.50). In 1980, an extension was added to the bar to cater for another thirty-eight patrons, and service is now 'American fast food' style. In either eaterie house wine is about 60p a glass.

LE BISTRO, 20 St James Street
(Nottingham 42993)
Open: Mon-Thu 12noon-2pm, 7-11pm,
Fri-Sat 12noon-2pm, 7-11.15pm, Sun
7-11pm

[C] [♫] [P] [S]

'Twixt Old Market Square and Maid Marion Way is this bow-windowed and brick-fronted restaurant. Inside, boothed seating, pine tables and fringed lampshades emphasise the intimate French atmosphere. Here excellent table d'hôte lunches are served: a two-course menu offers soup with French bread and a choice of lasagne or tuna salad for about £1.95, or try a three-course meal for around £3.50 which includes a good choice for all courses – including an inspired plat du jour. The à la carte menu offers a dazzling choice of French specialities but you will have to choose with care unless you feel like breaking the budget. A choice of house wines are available by the glass for around 65p.

EVIVA TAVERNA AND KEBAB HOUSE, 25 Victoria Street
(Nottingham 50243)
Open: Taverna: Mon-Sat 7pm-2am
Kebab House: Mon-Sat 10.30am-7pm

[C] [♫] [P] [S]

If you want to let off steam you can buy plates for smashing here. First, though, enjoy your meal in this basement restaurant transformed by white walls, vines, bunches of grapes and olive branches to a little bit of Greece in the heart of England. There are a few grills and roasts on the menu, but the chef's specialities – stifado (a rather special beef stew), kleftiko (lamb cooked with herbs) and dolmas (stuffed vine leaves) are particularly good and won't break the bank. Starters are priced from around 35p and most of the sweets (including baklava) cost in the 80p range. For two people dining together a half bottle of wine is provided free of charge, or you may choose from the list and have £1 knocked off the wine bill, which really is a worthwhile concession. Having enjoyed all this, listened to Greek music and watched Greek dancers in an adjoining room, you may feel like showing your appreciation by a bit of plate-smashing. Above the taverna is a kebab house run by the same proprietor, Mr Kozakis. This is a pleasant place to stop for a snack or for lunch, and the doner kebab, served with pitta bread and salad, is specially recommended.

GRANGE FARM RESTAURANT
Toton (Long Eaton 69426)
Open: Mon-Sat 12noon-2pm, 7-11pm

[P]

A much extended brick-built farmhouse dating back to 1691 is quite a find just two miles off the M1 (exit 25), especially if it offers generous portions of

wholesome English fare attractively presented, as this restaurant does. The dining room itself is in one of the oldest parts of the building, where oak beams and white brick abound, and there you can sample a quite superb table d'hôte lunch for around £4.75. A seemingly limitless choice of dishes is available – there are around nineteen starters including whitebait, lasagne, melon and pâté, twelve main dishes such as rainbow trout, rabbit pie or supreme of chicken Marengo, all served with two vegetables and both creamed and roast potatoes, and almost twenty different sweets, some rather unusual, like green figs with cream, ice cream with blackberry brandy or meringue Chantilly. Wine is about 55p a glass.

LA GRENOUILLE RESTAURANT✕
32 Lenton Boulevard
(Nottingham 411088)
Open: Mon-Fri 12.30-1.30pm, 7.30-9.30pm, Sat 7.30-9.30pm

[♫] [P] [⚱]

Imagine white-painted tables (only seven of them), white chairs with black cord upholstery, placed on black and white vinyl flooring against brick-red hessian walls highlighted with French posters; then add red tablecloths and matching table napkins. There you have La Grenouille – a little corner of France on the corner of a terrace of large Victorian houses. Young owner Yves Bouanchaud provides superb French food using mainly fresh products. Don't chance the à la carte menu if you're really hard up but it's worth going a bit over the £5 to enjoy a meal here if you can afford it. The table d'hôte menu offers a starter of home-made soup or terrine, a main dish such as boeuf bourguignon with vegetables and salad (this changes daily) and a sweet such as fruit salad or chocolate gâteau with cheese as an alternative, at around £4.40. Coffee and a glass of the French house wine will add about £1.

THE KINGFISHER, 127 Mansfield Road
(Nottingham 45449)
Open: Tue-Sat 12noon-2pm, 7-11.30pm

[P] [S] [♧]

Salmon steak, king prawns, skate and haddock are amongst the twenty main dishes available in this honest-to-goodness fish and chip shop on a busy road from the town centre. Although a roaring take-away service operates, the rear of the premises houses a functional dining room with plain wooden tables and curtain-divided booths in which to take your meal in comfort. Eight starters and sweets such as rum baba, fruit salad and apple pie with cream are available, all at around 60p. An ample wine list includes a popular French tipple at 50p per glass.

LDJ SWISS MILL RESTAURANT
48 Wollaton Road, Beeston
(Nottingham 259765)
Open: Wed 12noon-2.30pm,
Thu-Sat 12noon-2.30pm, 6-10pm,
Sun 11.30am-4pm

[P] [S]

Formerly the mill manager's cottage, this white-painted brick eaterie stands in the shadow of a large textile mill. Later a transport café, it is now a stylish restaurant, with black-painted exposed ceiling beams, white walls and olde worlde bric-à-brac. Basic English fare is served in generous portions in a relaxed, informal style. The menu offers a choice of starters from soup of the day at around 70p to smoked salmon at about £1.20. Grills are from around £3-£6, fish or salads around £2.60-£3.20 and a good selection of sweets such as peach meringue, gâteaux and home-made fruit pies all served with fresh cream are about £1. A special lunch menu offers a selection of roasts with vegetables and Yorkshire pudding for around £3. A glass of house wine costs about 60p.

MOULIN ROUGE ✕ 5 Trinity Square
(Nottingham 42845)
Open: Mon-Sun 12noon-2pm, 5.30-10.30pm

[C] [P] [S]

Not strictly a French restaurant but very much a Continental haunt, the Moulin Rouge is close to the Victoria shopping centre and the Theatre Royal. The sparkling restaurant has predominantly red décor, with crisp white table linen and banquettes. The à la carte menu includes appetisers, soups, fish, omelettes, entrées, poultry, curries, grills, salads and desserts, with a wide range of prices. A daily main course 'Special' costs £1.95, but three courses must be selected with care if you are to avoid going too much over £5. If you cannot find the meal you crave 'the menu is only a suggestion, our chef is at your command'. A large glass of house wine is around 60p.

THE PARAQUITO RESTAURANT
473 Mansfield Road
(Nottingham 609447)
Open: Tue-Sat 12noon-2pm, 7-10pm

Since taking over the Paraquito in 1976, Jan and Sheila Laskowski have been trying to live down the 'egg and chip' image it had acquired before they bought it, by now offering fine service and a good quality menu. Their three-course lunch, costing under £3 (including VAT) embraces four choices of starter, one of four main dishes such as roast pork, chicken chasseur or braised lambs liver, plus vegetables of the day and a choice of sweet or cheese. Alternatively, try the steak platter, which includes prawn cocktail, sirloin steak, a side salad, chips and all the trimmings with a dessert or cheese for under £6. In the evening, a four-course dinner is available, under £6, with main dish choices of trout, chicken, gammon and many more. There's a 10% service charge in the evenings only.

PASTRAMI'S, 6 Hurts Yard, Upper Parliament Street (Nottingham 46888)
Open: Mon-Sat 12noon-2.30pm

[C] [♫] [S] [♧]

Simple, good taste is the hallmark of this lunchtime diner, tucked away in a narrow alley dating back to Georgian times. Habitat furniture, posters, pictures and plants create a 'trendy' air. Food is cheap, home-made and varied. Starters include spare ribs in barbecue sauce (around £1), soup of the day (45p) and fresh melon chunks in blackcurrant syrup (60p). Pastrami's Specials such as chickebab (chicken pieces with herbs on a skewer served with French fries), Foot Long Dog ('12" of gastronomic decadence') or Pastrami on rye (pure lean beef, marinated with herbs, served on hot rye bread with salad) – are all around £1.50. 'Kidstuff' – from 65p-£1.20 includes juniorburger or spaghetti. Salads and hamburgers are also available – try a Lo-Cal burger – absolutely *no* bun or French fries, but enough salad to stuff a large rabbit! Super desserts such as hot waffles or hot fudge sundae will ruin any diet. A glass of wine costs around 60p.

RISTORANTE CASANOVA
16 St James Street (Nottingham 43448)

Open: Mon-Thu 12noon-2pm, 7-11pm, Fri 12noon-2pm, 7-11.15pm, Sat 7-11.15pm

[P] [S]

Below street level in pedestrianised St James Street is the cool, stylish, Casanova dining room with its arched ceiling, brightly-coloured Italian-tiled floor, Italianate antiques and tables made private by low dividing walls with velvet curtains hung from brass rails. The equally elegant cocktail bar is located down a further flight of stairs. Two very reasonably-priced lunch menus are available, one at around £1.75 offering two courses, including zucchini ripieni (courgettes stuffed with savoury meat sauce) as a main course. Three courses are available for about £3.25, with an excellent choice.

Scallopine al limone is recommended – veal fillets served with delicious lemon sauce. The à la carte menu is bristling with Italian specialities, but you may have to forgo a course to keep within our budget.

THE SAVOY HOTEL ★★★ Mansfield Road (Nottingham 602621)
Open: Colonial Restaurant Mon-Sat 12noon-2.15pm, 7-9.30pm, Sun 12noon-2.15pm, Steak Bars: Mon-Thu 12noon-2.15pm, 6.30-11pm, Fri-Sat 12noon-2.15pm, 6.30-11.30pm, Sun 12noon-2.15pm, 7-10.30pm, Salad Bar: Mon-Fri 12noon-2pm

[P] [♧]

One of the most popular eating out places in Nottingham, this large, luxurious hotel has a sumptuous restaurant and richly decorated steak bar on the ground floor. The lower ground floor houses a second steak bar with exposed stonework and a salad bar with exposed wall and ceiling timbers. Food is excellent value for money. The restaurant offers a three-course lunch with a vast choice for all three courses, from around £4.30. A five-course dinner with even more choice is about £5.70, some choices such as poached salmon steak with prawn sauce adding around 60p to the bill. The steak bars serve very good grills – T-bone steak with all the trimmings and a choice of dessert is only about £4.60. Children's portions at reduced prices are available on certain dishes. The Cromwell salad bar offers a selection of reasonably priced salads, filled rolls and gâteaux at less than 50p a portion. Wine by the glass can be sampled for around 55p.

SWISS COTTAGE, 18 Chapel Bar (Nottingham 411050)
Open: Mon-Sat 9.30am-7pm

[P] [S]

Peter and Bernard Morritt have made this modern, canopied premises in a cul-de-sac the seventh of their family chain of restaurants. Amidst the exposed brickwork and copper lighting it is possible to sample anything from the most simple sandwich (around 20p) to the tastiest rib steak (about £4.40, with all the trimmings, chips and vegetables) preceded by a choice of soups at around 35p. Finish with a delicious strawberry pancake topped with fresh whipped cream (at around 65p), home-made cherry pie or cheese and biscuits. The restaurant is unlicensed.

THE WATERFALL, 7-8 Hurt's Yard, Upper Parliament Street (Nottingham 42235)
Open: Mon-Thu 10am-2.30pm, 7-11pm, Fri 10am-2.30pm, 7-11.30pm, Sat 10am-5pm, 7-11.30pm

[S]

It's well worth the search for this interesting little restaurant nestling in the Georgian shopping centre, reached by means of a narrow flagstoned alleyway by the side of the Fox Inn. A wide bow window fronts the restaurant which seats about sixty within its three sections, each with a distinctive olde worlde atmosphere. The waterfall forms part of a cool and splashing grotto which provides an attractive focal point. The dark-wood tables take on a more sophisticated look in the evenings with the addition of Nottingham lace tablecloths and flickering candles. An interesting and reasonably-priced à la carte menu offers a traditional selection of dishes including minute steak at around £2. For the same price, a three-course business lunch offers such dishes as home-made soup, roast lamb or pork cutlet chasseur, sweet plus coffee. If your taste is for the more exotic, you may choose veal cordon bleu or fillet of sole Monte Carlo from the speciality à la carte menu – but beware, prices are higher and you'll have to be selective to stay within our limit.

Ollerton

ROSE COTTAGE, Rufford (Mansfield 822363)
Open: Mon-Tue 12noon-6.30pm, Wed-Fri, Sun 12noon-10pm, Sat 12noon-11pm

[P]

Two miles south of Ollerton on the A614 and almost opposite the entrance to Rufford Abbey is this quaint brick cottage with small leaded windows, surrounded by an immaculate garden. Inside is all wood panels and beams, with three separate areas for dining. A wide range of fare is available from midday throughout the week. A three-course table d'hôte lunch for around £3 could include minestrone soup, braised lamb chops and vegetables and ice cream gâteau. Also available are snack items such as plaice, chips and peas for £2 or minute steak for £4. Desserts at 75p include chocolate fudge gâteau or mandarin sundae. A more sophisticated menu is used in the evening, when care will be needed to avoid exceeding the budget. A glass of French or Spanish wine is about 60p.

Skegness

THE COPPER KETTLE, Lumley Road (Skegness 67298)
Open: summer: Mon-Sun 9.30am-9.30pm, winter: Mon-Wed, Fri-Sat 10am-5.30pm (closed Jan-Feb)

[S]

Set amongst the shops in one of the town's busiest streets, you could easily dismiss this brown, bow-windowed restaurant as yet another gift shop. However, once inside, you can forget the hurly-burly world of amusement arcades and trumpery, and relax in the peaceful atmosphere created by rich green carpeting with subtly contrasting white plaster and plain brick walls. Modern lights, masquerading as old-style oil lamps, hang from the ceiling at strategic points between the pine tables. The fare is limited, but will prove very good value for money. The three starters, including melon, cost between 50p-80p, whilst the dearest main course is rump steak with chips and peas at only £3.30. Home-made desserts are about 50p.

Sleaford

CARRE ARMS HOTEL★
(Sleaford 303156)
Open: 12noon-2pm, 6.30-8pm

[P]

The red-brick public house built in 1906 is on the edge of the town centre near a level crossing. The bright, well-maintained dining room offers a good selection of mainly grill and roast dishes at reasonable prices. Even if you do splash out on a steak, surrounded by a simple starter and sweet, you are unlikely to go far beyond £5, and a glass of wine is only 35p.

SWEET VIENNA, Southgate Shopping Centre (Sleaford 304055)
Open: Mon, Wed, Thu 11am-2.30pm, 7-11pm, Tue 11am-2.30pm, Fri-Sat 11am-2.30pm, 7-12mdnt, Sun 12noon-2pm

[P] [S]

As the name suggests, Mr Hrubesch's restaurant has a delightful Austrian flavour. There's even piped Strauss music to aid digestion in the white-walled restaurant with refectory tables and wooden benches, or the adjoining snack bar. However, amongst the Tyrolean sauces and Zigeuner gipsy schnitzel (about £3.50), lurk conventional grills and fish dishes, ranging from £2-£4. Snacks include American hamburgers (home-made like everything else here), pizza or goulash, costing between £1 and £2. Sweets are from 60p.

Stamford

THE BAY TREE COFFEE SHOP
10 St Pauls Street (Stamford 51219)
Open: summer: Tue-Sat 9am-5pm, Sun 12noon-5pm, winter: Tue-Sat 9am-5pm, Sun 2-5pm

[S]

This quaint, bow-windowed little coffee shop is located in one of Stamford's quieter streets, close to the main shopping area. Horse brasses displayed on dark beams and prints on the cream walls create a pleasant period atmosphere. Emphasis is on home-made fare and prices are astonishingly reasonable. Soup of the day plus roll and butter is 25p, main courses such as steak and kidney pie with two veg, lasagne or cheese and asparagus with side salad are just over £1 and a delicious dessert such as a fresh fruit Pavlova is only 35p! By 1981 you shall be able to enjoy a glass of wine with your meal – a license has been applied for.

YE OLDE BARN RESTAURANT
St Mary's Street (Stamford 3194)
Open: Mon-Sun 12noon-2pm, 6-10pm (closed Sun in winter)

[P] [S]

Step into the alleyway at the rear of Ye Olde Barn coffee shop and you will find this two-storey restaurant, crowded with fine antiques and gleaming with well-polished copper and brass. The upper floor seats sixty below the rafters of the fine timbered roof, where a small cocktail lounge is also to be found. Downstairs is a slightly smaller restaurant boasting the same low prices and excellent value for money. Gammon steak, pork chop, steak and mixed grills are served with vegetables and cost anything from £1 upwards, with warming dishes such as home-made steak and kidney pie served with jacket *and* creamed potatoes and a selection of vegetables at around £2.15. Cold meat salads are under £2.50. A sweet such as profiteroles with chocolate sauce rounds things off nicely, and sets you back under £1. House wine is 50p a glass.

Sutton-on-Sea

ANCHOR, 12 High Street (Sutton on Sea 41548)
Open: summer: Mon-Sun 10am-5.30pm, 7-10pm, winter: Mon, Fri-Sat 10am-5.30pm, 7-10pm, Tue-Wed, Sun 10am-5.30pm, Thu 7-10pm

[C]

A canopied doorway and bow windows pick out this country-style restaurant, converted from an old house reported to be a home of Alfred Lord Tennyson. Food to suit the pocket and palate of any poet is served here. For around £3 a three-course lunch including minute steak garni is yours, and for £4 a three-course dinner plus coffee could include melon, chicken escalope Holstein and a sweet from the trolley. The à la carte menu is also very reasonable, with a good choice of starters, roasts, fish dishes, salads, grills and desserts well within our budget. Half portions are available for children. A glass of wine costs 55p.

LEEK
NEWCASTLE-UNDER-LYME
WATERHOUSES
STOKE-ON-TRENT
ELLESMERE
STAFFORD
STAFFORDSHIRE
SHREWSBURY
SALOP
WOLVERHAMPTON
SUTTON COLDFIEL
WEST
CHURCH STRETTON
AFFCOT
BIRMINGHAM
STOURBRIDGE
MIDLAN
CLENT
LUDLOW
BROMSGROVE
LEINTWARDINE
STOURPORT-ON-SEVERN
WAR
DROITWICH
HENLEY-IN-ARDEN
WARWI
HEREFORD
STRATFORD-UPON-AVON
WORCESTER
CANON PYON
&
MALVERN
PERSHORE
WORCESTER
EVESHAM
HEREFORD
LEDBURY
UPTON-UPON-SEVERN

Heart of England

This is a land of contrasts. Truly the 'Heart of England' it holds within its borders Birmingham, Coventry, the Staffordshire Potteries and the 'Black Country', symbols of industrial wealth both past and present, and yet it includes some of our most beautiful and unspoiled countryside.

To the west are the Shropshire Hills, (an area of outstanding natural beauty), the Offa's Dyke Path, the orchards and grazing lands of Hereford; to the east lie Cannock Chase, Warwickshire's picturesque villages, the ancient Fosse Way and Shakespeare Country. Castles and great country houses abound, as do the thatched and half-timbered old-world cottages of this region. Whether your tastes are for the grand or for the simple you will find something here to please you. Make a point of venturing further afield, to the majestic Malvern Hills and discover rural beauty as yet untouched by tourism.

Wandering from the well-trodden path is always rewarding, particularly so when sampling the local fare. Hereford beef is famous all over the world, and can be enjoyed almost anywhere. Instead try a speciality of this area, perhaps Shrewsbury Lamb cutlets, which are baked, grilled in butter, then served in aspic; or Warwick Scones, which are baked with honey and then served hot with butter or, for the sweet-toothed, with yet more honey. Try Herefordshire pigeon pie, or nutmeg curd cakes; but don't just follow these suggestions, use the following entries to track down these and other delicious dishes of this area. Happy hunting!

Affcott

THE WHITE HOUSE, Church Stretton
(Marshbrook 202)
Open: Wed-Sun 12.15-2pm, Tue-Sun 7-9.30pm

[P] [♣]

Be sure to book in advance if you are planning an evening sortie to this tiny roadside restaurant, which once housed the village smithy. A typical country cottage, the décor is simple but effective, with white walls and black beams brightened by pot plants. The lunchtime menu often includes a tasty fresh mushroom soup or gazpacho, followed by roast loin of lamb, its stuffing rich with walnuts. Braised kidneys or fresh salmon are possible alternatives. A display of mouth-watering sweets could include delights such as grape and banana vacherin or hazelnut meringue. Sunday lunches are about £4, half price for children.

Birmingham

BLACK HORSE INN, Northfield
(021-475 1005)
Open: Mon-Fri 12noon-2pm, 7-10pm, Sat 12noon-2pm

[C] [♫] [P] [S] [♣]

The Barons' Bar Grill Room is upstairs in this impressive 'black and white' inn on the Bristol road. Overhead is the original raftered roof, but the barn-like aspect is counteracted by hessian-covered walls and the solidity of oak furniture. The menu is standard for Davenports inns, and the main dishes are those found in most grill rooms, the accent being on steaks for between £4-£5, with other dishes including plaice and gammon (both around £3), all prices including vegetables. Starters fall between 40p and £1, desserts from around 55p. With a glass of wine costing around 60p, choosing steak may entail the sacrifice of a third course.

THE CAPTAIN'S TABLE, HOLIDAY INN ☆☆☆☆ Holiday Street
(021-643 2766)
Open: Mon-Sun 7am-10.30pm

[C] [♫] [P] [S] [♣]

You could almost be at sea in this restaurant, with its rope ladders, and old sails draped from the ceiling. Meals 'from the tavern' are good value, with 'tempters' such as corn-on-the-cob or Chef's own country style pâté about £1.90. Mixed meat salad as a main dish is around £2 and a variety of pies, sweets and gâteaux, served with cream are just over £1. A very large glass of wine is about 80p. A novelty children's menu offers Batman's Supersonic Dinner (beefburger and chips) for around 90p and a host of other popular junior dishes including Uncle Orinoco's 'Afters' – various ice creams at about 50p. A pleasant three-course meal can be had at the Carvery Buffet, but the price is barely within our budget.

DANISH FOOD CENTRE
10 Stephenson Place (021-643 2837)
Open: Mon-Sat 9am-12mdnt

[C] [S]

Located on the access ramp to the New Street shopping centre, this pleasant Danish restaurant creates a bright, clean Scandinavian air in the large, split-level interior with attractive floral decorations, wood and brick walls, and green carpets. Waitresses in red-and-white checked uniforms complete the colourful scene. It comprises two eating places – the Danwich Bar which serves a delicious range of open sandwiches and the Copenhagen Room which offers a first-class set menu plus the famous self-service cold table, where soup, fish, poultry, meats, salads, cheese, sweets and fruits are attractively laid out at a set price of around £5 at lunchtime, though

the evening spread is just outside our limit. Gammon steak, French fries and peas, with a choice of either starter or sweet costs about £2.50. Sirloin steak plus the trimmings with a choice of either starter or sweet is very good value at about £4.

DELPHI KEBAB HOUSE, 63 New Street (021-643 6694)
Open: Mon-Fri 12noon-2.30pm, 5.30-11.30pm, Sat-Sun 12noon-11.30pm

[C] [♫] [S]

Of the many Greek specialities served at the Delphi, souvla – lamb on the spit grilled over charcoal, served with a Greek salad and pitta – is worth a special mention as it is very tasty, filling, and good value at around £3.70. With main courses like this you don't really need a starter but one of the 'dips' at about 75p may tempt you, or there are stuffed vine leaves costing a little more. If you've fallen for an hors d'oeuvre you'll need to look for a less-filling (and less-expensive) main course. There are a number to choose from with prices under £4 – kebab lamb or pork, two different sausage dishes, and fillet of sole served with chips and salad, are examples. A dessert will not add much more than 60p. Step out of busy New Street into the discreetly-illuminated interior of this restaurant and you can imagine yourself in Greece. Screens and paintings from the Mediterranean create an exotic atmosphere. It comes as a surprise when the oracle speaks with a Midlands accent.

THE FOUR SEASONS RESTAURANT
Lewis's, Bull Street (021-236 8251)
Open: Mon-Fri 11.45am-2.30pm, Sat 11.45am-2.30pm, 3.30-5.30pm

[C] [S]

The decorative theme is, appropriately, the four seasons of the year depicted in relief in four attractive fibre-glass murals. The à la carte menu offers a traditional list of grills, omelettes, salads etc. at reasonable prices and the table d'hôte menu with two daily specialities provides very good value at around £2.50 for three courses. A children's menu, cleverly designed in the form of a 'Wanted' poster entitled 'Big shots for small fry' offers a main course, ice cream and cold drink at prices to please any parent. There is even a bowl of assorted vegetables, potato and gravy plus a dish of custard for baby at half the children's price.

LA GALLERIA, Paradise Place (021-236 1006)
Open: Mon-Sat 11am-2.30pm, 5.30-10.30pm, Sun 7-10.30pm

[C] [P]

This modern wine bar and restaurant has small, old-fashioned pub-style tables and deep red mahogany woodwork. The display counter houses a range of cold meat salads and a blackboard menu above lists hot dishes. The emphasis is on Italian meals, with six varieties of pizzas from about £1.20-£1.80 and pasta dishes such as lasagne at around £1.80. Veal à la crème, chicken chasseur and various steaks come from £2.25 upwards. Starters include minestrone soup, mussels or home-made pâté and there is a choice of desserts for about 60p-80p.

GAYLORD ✕✕ 61 New Street (021-632 4500)
Open: Mon-Sat 12noon-5.30pm, 6-11.30pm, Sun 12noon-3pm, 6-11.30pm

[C] [S]

The mirror-lined hallway decorated with pot plants is a foretaste of the authentic Indian atmosphere in the spacious green restaurant above, where Tandoori cooking can be viewed through glass windows while you wait. The menu offers a wide range of dishes with a lunchtime 'eat as much as you like' menu for around £4.25. 'Tandoori mix' is a gourmet delight – a three-course meal for about £5. A special vegetarian meal is offered for around £3. Dishes on the à la carte menu are reasonably priced at lunchtime and chicken, lamb or fish delicacies flavoured with oriental spices abound.

GINO'S BELVEDERE RESTAURANT
East Mall Shopping Centre
(021-643 1957)
Open: Mon-Wed 12noon-11pm, Thu-Fri 12noon-11.15pm, Sat 12noon-11.30pm, Sun 12noon-10.30pm

[C] [♫] [P] [S]

Walls decorated with enlarged engravings of old Venice give an immediate Latin flavour to this popular, centrally-situated Italian restaurant. You can make do with just a pizza or omelette, or choose from the extensive à la carte menu at around £4 for three-courses and coffee. A special three-course lunch is available at an all-inclusive price of £2.50. After 7pm there is a speciality menu offering a selection of more sophisticated items which are a little more expensive.

THE GRAPE VINE, Units 2 and 3, Edgbaston Shopping Centre, Edgbaston
(021-454 0672)
Open: Mon-Sat 12noon-2.30pm, 5-9pm

[C] [♫] [P] [S]

Proprietor Peter Gully is a man with a mission. His aim is to lead people away from using processed foods – artificially flavoured, bleached or dyed, and preserved with chemicals; he is opposed to 'battery' farming too, and believes a sensible vegetarian diet can improve health as well as making inhumane production of animal proteins unnecessary. There are always home-made soups, hot flans and nut roasts, and main dishes use peas, beans, nuts, rice, free-range eggs and rennet-free cheeses to provide the necessary protein element. A representative three courses such as soup (60p), cashew nut roast (£1.50) and trifle (70p) gives some idea of what to expect.

HAPPY GATHERING ✕✕
54-56 Pershore Street
(021-622 2324/3092)
Open: Mon-Sun 12noon-12mdnt

[C] [P]

This successful Cantonese restaurant is situated on the outskirts of the main city centre. The interior is very clean and typically Chinese with red embossed wallpaper, wood panelling and brightly-painted oriental pictures. Food is authentic Cantonese and proprietor Mr Lai is particularly proud of the baked crab in black bean sauce and the duck in plum sauce. Businessperson's lunch costs around £1.25 and includes a choice of two starters, four main courses, boiled or fried rice and a pot of China tea. Because of the nature of Chinese eating, a choice from the à la carte menu can be as cheap or expensive as you like depending on the variety of dishes chosen. Chicken with lemon sauce is £2.40. There is a more formal set dinner at around the £4 mark.

HAWKINS CAFE-BAR, King Edward Building, 205-219 Corporation Street
(021-236 2001)
Open: Mon-Fri 8.30am-11pm, Sat 10am-11pm, Sun 5-11pm

[C] [♫] [S]

Situated close to the law courts and Aston University is this new concept in food and drink. The strong art nouveau décor proves an interesting blackcloth to the half-hour lighting extravaganzas on Friday and Saturday and occasional appearances of guest artists such as George Melly or Georgie Fame. On to the food – prices range from about 75p for home-made soup to around £2.50 for roast rib of beef with fresh salad. A dish of the day, filled baked potatoes and pizzas are also available.

HEAVEN BRIDGE ✕✕ 308 Bull Ring Centre, Smallbrook Ringway
(021-643 0033)
Open: Mon-Fri 12noon-11.30pm, Sat 12noon-12mdnt, Sun 12noon-11.30pm

[C] [P] [S]

The à la carte menu, in Cantonese and English, lists nearly 200 dishes. Hors d'oeuvres, from around 50p-65p include rice rolls, dumplings, croquettes and water-chestnut pâté and in addition twenty-four choices of soup are offered. Main courses, varying in price from about £1.50-£5 include an exciting array of dishes – seafoods such as cuttle-fish, crab, oyster and lobster, and meat and poultry in many guises. A large glass of che foo (Chinese sweet wine) costs around 55p.

HORTS WINE BAR AND BISTRO
Harborne Road, Edgbaston
(021-454 4672)
Open: Mon-Sat 12noon-2.30pm, 5.30-10.30pm, Sun 12noon-2pm, 7-10.30pm

[P] [S]

Easily recognised in fine weather by the

'overspill' of tables and chairs onto the wide pavement outside and the distinct French flavour in the simple brown-and-beige décor, this is a popular haunt of local business people. An assortment of nourishing English and Continental food is available, including a dish of the day such as risotto, pâté and various salads at around £1.65. Home-made soup is 50p, whilst desserts such as gâteau or American cheesecake are about 65p. With French house wine at 50p per glass, you should have plenty of change from £5. There's a small raised area at the rear, for the more intimate and quiet meal.

MAXWELL'S PLUM WINE BAR & BISTRO, 163 Broad Street, Fiveways (021-643 9453)
Open: Mon-Sat 11.30am-2.30pm, Mon-Fri 5.30-10.30pm, Sat-Sun 7-10.30pm

♫ P S

Plate glass windows and a gay striped awning distinguish this wine bar from its neighbours in the shopping area. A speciality worthy of note is the spicy Welsh sausage, served with fried potato, tomato and onions, but a good selection of quiches, flans and home-made sweets are available on the buffet. Daily hot dishes include prawn provençale, lamb curry, pork chop Milanese and cod Mornay. Tuesday and Sunday evenings are highlighted by the regular appearance of continental or folk musicians.

MICHELLE ✕ 182-184 High Street, Harborne (021-426 4133)
Open: Mon-Sat 12noon-2pm, 7-10pm (Closed Aug)

S

Step into Michelle's French restaurant and you move back in time – to the heyday of the small-time grocer's shop. Dark mahogany shelving, a tiled bacon area and large mirrors belonging to the original Co-op grocers shop it once was, form the basis of a most unusual décor. Of the typically French cuisine, the coq au vin and boeuf bourguignon are among the best French dishes to be had this side of the Channel. Even the à la carte dinner menu allows you to eat well for under £5 but, the one-choice-only table d'hôte at lunchtime is excellent value at only £3 including wine.

NEW HAPPY GATHERING ✕✕
43-45 Station Street (021-643 5247)
Open: Mon-Sun 12noon-12mdnt

C

Mr Henry Wong offers traditional Cantonese cuisine at this gracious and comfortable restaurant. A staggering menu boasts more than 100 dishes, the majority in the £2-£3 range. Portions are generous and you can choose from a variety of not-so-familiar dishes such as a steamed duck with plum sauce, water-chestnut pudding or braised duck's web in oyster sauce. Sweets include various fritters in syrup for around 70p and Chinese pastries cost about 35p. Set meals offer a good variety of savoury dishes from around £4.

PINOCCHIO ✕ Chad Square, Hawthorne Road, Harborne (021-454 8672)
Open: Mon-Sat 12.15-2pm, 6.30-10.30pm

P S

Tucked between a hairdresser's shop and a newsagent, in a tiny, modern shopping centre, close to the village of Harborne, this converted shop also acts as a sort of unofficial art gallery, for the restaurant exhibits and sells pictures by local artists. The menu is wide-ranging and tempts extravagance, but if you stick to the three-course table d'hôte lunch menu you'll be surprised at the amount of change you'll get from £5 a head.

RAJDOOT ✕✕ 12-22 Albert Road (021-643 8805)
Open: Mon-Sat 12noon-2.30pm, 6.30pm-12mdnt, Sun 6.30pm-12mdnt

C P S

Ornate brass, red silk and hessian walls and burning joss sticks complete the transition from West to East, in this authentic Indian restaurant offering Punjab and Tandoori cuisine. Excellent set lunches are available from Monday to Saturday at around £3. Dinners are à la carte, with an average meal coming just within our budget. Tandoori specialities (charcoal clay oven barbecues) include delicious rashmi kebab – chicken minced with onion, chillies, fresh mint, coriander and herbs and spices. A huge goblet of house wine costs 80p.

ROCK CANDY MOUNTAIN
High Street, Harborne (01-427 2481)
Open: Mon-Sat 12noon-2.30pm, 5.30-10.30pm, Sun 12noon-2pm, 7-10.30pm

♫ S

Bright, gaudy, garish but immaculate is the only way to describe this 'latest concept in wine bars – music – restaurants – meeting places and astral food'. Set in the centre of Harborne, it hums with activity and welcomes everyone. 'Kiddies' have their own special spaghetti-hamburger-ice cream menu. The comic-strip menu offers pizzas, salads, hamburgers, BBQ ribs, steak, kidney, mushroom and Guinness pie, chili con carne and steaks. Prices range from £1.25 to £3.75. Kick off with corn on the cob (75p) and finish with chocolate fudge cake with ice cream (65p) – one of a selection of way-out desserts.

SANDONIA, 509 Hagley Road, Bearwood (021-429 2622)
Open: Mon-Sat 11.45am-3pm, 6-11.30pm

[C] [S] [🍷]

Owner Mr Constantinou (known to his regulars as Mr Conn) comes from Cyprus and opened this restaurant over seventeen years ago. 'Regulars' include a couple who have dined at the same table every Thursday night for fifteen years – there's faithfulness for you! The table d'hôte lunch at around £1.50 consists of soup or fruit juice, a choice of items such as a roast or braised steak with vegetables, and ice cream or fruit pie with custard. A three-course lunch à la carte is likely to cost about £4: for this one might have soup; a main course of a roast or a 'fry-up' such as egg, sausages, chips and peas, an omelette or a fish dish. A sweet chosen from a long list is likely to cost around 45p. A glass of house wine (usually Cyprus) is about 55p. The dinner menu is more expensive but one could still make a choice within the £5. Grilled halibut or curried prawns, roast Norfolk turkey, a number of grills and kebab or chicken pilaf all at under £3 are examples, these prices including potatoes and two green vegetables. There is a good selection of starters at about 80p and sweets are priced from around 65p.

VALENTINO'S ✕ High Street, Harborne (021-427 2560)
Open: Mon-Sat 12.30-2pm, 7-10.30pm, Sun 12.30-2pm

[C] [♫] [P] [S] [🍷]

A smart little Italian eaterie, converted from one of the main street shops in which decoration is kept simple enough to have a relaxing effect. A table d'hôte lunch of egg mayonnaise, grilled sirloin steak and a piece of gâteau costs about £3.50 with coffee and wine extra, though the à la carte menu could tempt you over the limit if you have extravagant tastes. Coffee and cream is around 45p.

WHITE SWAN, Harborne Road, Edgbaston (021-454 2359)
Open: Mon-Fri 12.30-2.30pm, Tue-Sat 7.15-10pm

[C] [P]

When Ron and Norma Phillips took over this old established inn they were told that a ghost prowled around the upstairs area; so far they have no trace of the uninvited guest, but keep your eyes open just in case! Ghost or no ghost, the White Swan is a popular eating place, so booking is advisable. Steaks and grills are served in the restaurant at prices from around £3-£5. Appetisers range from about 50p-£1, sweets from 60p-70p. Wine is around 50p per glass.

Bromsgrove

ANDRÉS, 7 High Street (Bromsgrove 73163)
Open: Mon 11am-3pm, Tue, Fri-Sat 9.30am-11pm, Wed 11am-11pm, Thu 11am-3pm, 7-11pm

[♫] [🍷]

Gay brown and gold awnings tell you that you've arrived at Andrés, a modern Greek restaurant, tastefully decorated in pine with pottery lampshades and tiled floors. A daytime menu provides quick grills, salads and omelettes for shoppers and business people at less than £3 for three courses. During the evening Andrés exudes the atmosphere of a Greek taverna with authentic bouzouki music, a menu offering moussaka and kebabs at around £2.50 and Greek wines. These specialities are in addition to a more extensive selection of traditional English fare such as sirloin steak with trimmings at £3.15 and scampi at £2.25. A starter of melon at 60p and dessert of sweet pancake at around 50p is within our budget.

Canon Pyon

THE BARN RESTAURANT, Bush Bank (Canon Pyon 435)
Open: Tue-Sat 7-9.30pm,
Sun 12noon-2pm

[P]

In the heart of the Hereford countryside, just over a mile north east of Canon Pyon is this picturesque half-timbered converted barn. Once a drover's stopover between Wales and Hereford, the minstrel gallery and exposed beams are probably little different since those bygone days. Everything is cooked on the premises and the dinner menu is varied and wholesome. Some items are beyond the scope of this guide, but interesting starters such as tuna-stuffed tomatoes, grilled grapefruit with rum and borsch (beetroot) soup are all around 80p. A main dish such as chicken Alexander (in cream and white wine sauce with asparagus) costs about £4. A selection of home-made sweets such as poached peaches cost 85p. Sunday lunch at £4 offers a good choice for all four courses. Try ham and chicken pancake, followed by moussaka and a home-made dessert.

Church Stretton

THE STUDIO, 59 High Street (Church Stretton 722672)
Open: summer: Mon-Sat 12noon-2pm, 7.30-10pm, winter: Mon 7.30-10pm, Tue-Sat 12noon-2pm, 7.30-10pm

[C] [♫] [P] [S]

After housing a potter's studio earlier this century, part of this row of 300-year-old white-painted cottages has reverted to its former business of hospitality. For in the days when there were reputedly more pubs than houses in Church Stretton, the 'studio' was an inn. Inside is a small, cosy bar and a dining room with an atmosphere of clean simplicity. The standard lunch menu can easily keep within £3 for three courses, and sometimes features home-made pork pie. The more exciting dinner à la carte has tempting specialities together with more conventional dishes, but is likely to break the budget.

Clent

FOUR STONES, Adams Hill
(Hagley 883260)
Open: Tue-Sat 12.30-2.30pm, 7-11.30pm, Sun 12.30-2.30pm

[P] [🍷]

In the heart of the scenic Clent Hills, just south of the A456 'twixt Kidderminster and Halesowen, is this quaint little bow-window fronted cottage which has been converted into a country-style restaurant. Dark wooden beams, posts and horsebrasses complete the rural atmosphere. Here you may enjoy a set three-course lunch which could include soup of the day, a choice of roasts and a home-made dessert for less than £3. The à la carte menu is much more extensive, and provided you avoid the Chef's Specials, you should be able to have a feast within our budget. Appetisers range from 40p for soup to £1.50 for smoked trout, with prawn cocktail at less than £1. Two pork chops or half a chicken with vegetables and side salad are about £3.25. Desserts from the trolley are around 60p and are tempting examples of the home cooking here. With careful choice you will be able to afford a glass of French wine at 55p.

Coventry

CORKS WINE BAR, Whitefriars Street
(Coventry 23628)
Open: Mon-Fri 11am-2.30pm, 6-10.30pm, Sat 6-11pm, Sun 7-10.30pm

[♫] [P]

Dark green walls, a raftered ceiling, tiled floor and old tulip-shaped wall lights create a yester-year effect enhanced by cast-iron and refectory tables, old French street name plates, prints and mirrors. Two plat du jour blackboards list the range of cold and hot dishes available, these changing every day. Prices range from around 50p-£3. Soup of the day is about 40p, gâteaux 65p, pizzas about 90p, meals of the day such as spaghetti or boeuf bourguignon just over £1, meat salads £1.75 and steak at under £3. If you're feeling adventurous, escargots at £1.65 are an interesting alternative. House wine is 48p or 65p.

NELLO PIZZERIA, 8 City Arcade
(Coventry 23551)
Open: Mon-Thu 9.30am-11.30pm, Fri-Sat 9.30am-1am

[C] [P] [S]

An informal atmosphere and freshly-baked food have established the Nello as a popular eating place – ideal for weary shoppers and tourists alike. Pastas are listed as starters on the menu, though a plate of home-made lasagne or cannelloni is a tasty meal in itself. Pizzas include the Special Pizza Nello – a banquet of cheese, tomato, tuna, prawns, mushrooms, anchovies, egg, ham and olives – all this for around £2. Grills and roasts are also available, ranging in price from about £1.50 for sausages and chips to £3.50 for steak.

TREVI RESTAURANT
29 Warwick Row (Coventry 20671)
Open: Mon-Fri 12noon-2.30pm, Mon-Thu 7-11.30pm, Fri-Sat 7pm-1am

[♫] [P] [S]

Overlooking pleasant public gardens, this tiny Italian restaurant is personally managed by Sebastian Grasso from Sicily. A budget lunch could start with home-made minestrone at around 35p followed by lasagne (about £1) or sirloin steak (around £3) and finish with a home-made sweet from the trolley (about 60p). If you are dieting, try the delightful salads, which vary in price from around £1.20 for a cheese salad to £1.40 for a chicken salad. The à la carte menu is more expensive, but with careful choice you can enjoy a superb meal. A glass of Italian house wine costs about 45p. At weekends 'Enzo' sings continental tunes to the sound of his guitar.

Droitwich

THE SPINNING WHEEL RESTAURANT
13 St Andrews Street (Droitwich 2278)
Open: Mon-Sat 10am-5.30pm

[S] [🍷]

Popular with shoppers, tourists and local businesspeople, the Spinning Wheel enjoys a prime position in Droitwich's new shopping centre. Access to this attractive cottage-style restaurant is across a paved patio area complete with fish pond and garden furniture. Friendly waitresses will serve you from a comprehensive menu ranging from 'English Breakfast' to light snacks and more substantial grills, omelettes etc. A table d'hôte three-course meal consisting of soup of the day, roast pork and apple sauce with vegetables, plus sweet costs £2.10. Main dishes from the à la carte are also reasonably priced with pizza or steak and kidney pie at around £1.45 to beef curry on boiled rice with nuts and raisins or pork chop with pineapple, mushrooms and side salad at around £2.35. With starter, a fresh cream sherry trifle at 60p and coffee, the whole need cost no more than £3. Wine is sold in individual-sized bottles at 50p.

Ellesmere

THE BLACK LION, Scotland Street (Ellesmere 2418)
Open: Restaurant: Mon-Fri 6.30-9.30pm, Bar: Mon-Sat 11.30am-2pm, 6.30-9.30pm, Sun 12noon-1.30pm, 6.30-9.30pm

[C] [P] [S]

This early 16th-century inn stands in the centre of Ellesmere. In the dining room, with its exposed beams and simple décor, steak, chicken and scampi are supplemented by sole in prawn and mushroom sauce (one of the most expensive dishes at £4 plus), and lasagne (about £3). There's a wide range of standard bar meals. The special Black Lion Ploughman's for around £1 is guaranteed to satisfy the most ravenous ploughman, with its red and white Cheshire and Stilton cheeses.

Evesham

SMALL TALK, 58 Bridge Street
Open: Mon-Tue 9.30am-5.30pm, Wed-Sat 9.30am-2pm

[S]

White walls and exposed dark-wood beams are offset by a charming small floral print used for tablecloths and curtains in this convivial snack bar. Seating is on two floors and upstairs you have a bird's eye view of the town. Appetisers include grapefruit segments or soup of the day for around 35p. Steak and kidney pie with new potatoes and peas costs £1.50 and quiche Lorraine is even cheaper. Chicken and ham pie with salad is around £2. Desserts such as blackcurrant and apple pie with cream, lemon meringue pie or various fresh cream gâteaux are in the 55p-60p range. You will have to wash your meal down with a cup of excellent tea or coffee because Small Talk is unlicensed.

Henley-in-Arden

THE LITTLE FRENCH CAFE, 28 High Street (Henley-in-Arden 4322)
Open: Mon-Sat 10am-6.30pm, Sun 2.30-6.30pm

Stop at this pretty creeper-clad cottage with its heart-shaped sign in picturesque Henley-in-Arden for a snack or a well-prepared, home-cooked light lunch. Mike and Linda Parker have recently re-opened the cafe which is now convincingly Olde Worlde in style – whitewashed walls, exposed beams, stone-flagged floor, chintzy curtains and all. Start with home-made pâté, then decide between a selection of cold savoury flans with salad at around £1.60 or Hot Dish of the Day – such as kedgeree served with a selection of side salads at £1.75. A delicious home-made dessert costs about 45p. An assortment of drinks is available – none of which is alcoholic as the café is unlicensed.

Hereford

CATHEDRAL RESTAURANT
Church Street (Hereford 65233)
Open: summer: Mon-Sat 9.30am-7.30pm, winter: Mon-Wed 9.30-4pm, Fri-Sat 9.30am-4.30pm,

7-10.30pm. Closed: Thu-Sun

♫ S

As its name would suggest, this small restaurant is set close to the cathedral in a quiet street. The black beams and white walls typify the tourist's idea of Hereford. Proprietor, Mrs Ann Went and her daughter Julie work hard in the kitchen while son John serves at the tables. The lunch menu is very reasonably priced and a satisfying meal of home-made soup, a roast, boiled apple pudding and a glass of wine costs about £4.50

THE CITY WALLS, 67 St Owen Street (Hereford 67720/69134)
Open: Wed-Fri 12noon-2pm, Tue-Sun 7-11pm

♫ P S

This restaurant is built on part of the original city wall – at a point where taxes were collected in bygone days. Included in the price of the main dish (half roast duckling or chicken, for instance) is the vegetable of the day, French fries, home-made apple pie with cream or ice cream. With starter, coffee and wine (60p per glass) the £5 budget may just be exceeded.

THE OVEN DOOR COFFEE HOUSE St Peter's Close, Commercial Street (Hereford 2557)
Open: Mon-Sat 9am-5pm

This unusual restaurant nestles coyly in the shadow of St Peter's church. There's a paved patio area around the entrance where meals may be taken in summer, while the inside resembles a pine-built chalet. Hot lunch dishes include lasagne at about £2, and hot sausage roll platter or 'grilled cheesy' at around £1. Cold dishes include a ploughman's at about £1.10, pâtés and flans.

THE TASTE INN, 17 Bridge Street (Hereford 58964)
Open: Tue-Sat 10am-9pm, Sun 10am-7pm

C ♫ P S

A bright, glass-fronted, flower-decked restaurant with cheery checked tablecloths and signed pictures of celebrities adorning the walls. Delicious speciality dishes such as guinea fowl in red wine sauce, venison or coq au vin are served with chipped potatoes and petits pois and remain quite modestly-priced, while the more ordinary dishes such as plaice or chicken and chips and various grills, pies and fry-ups are terrific value at around £1.50. There is a choice of twenty-five house wines, all priced at just over 55p a glass.

TUDOR RESTAURANT
48 Broad Street (Hereford 58374)
Open: Mon-Sun 9.30am-5.30pm

[S]

This three-storey building in one of the busiest streets of Hereford dates back some 400 years. Proprietor Mrs Joan Edwards is an avid weight-watcher and, keen to dispel the myth of salad being an inferior substitute for a meal, she spends most of her time in the kitchen preparing nutritious creations such as continental salad with salami and olives, the Tudor Danwich (brown bread with lettuce, cheese, egg and tomato) and many others, plus the usual list of grills and pies. Children are given a particularly warm welcome.

Leamington Spa

THE ASHOKA, 22 Regent Street (Leamington Spa 28272)
Open: Mon-Thu 12noon-2.30pm, 6pm-12mdnt; Fri-Sat 12noon-2.30pm, 6pm-2am; Sun 12noon-2.30pm, 6.30pm-12mdnt

[C] [P]

'The Ajanta caves on a dull day' best describes the main room of this restaurant, with its authentic Indian light shades, wall paintings, candles and statues of nude goddesses. House specialities are Tandoori dishes cooked in clay ovens imported from India, biriani (served with vegetable curry), chicken tikka and Silver Jubilee special, prices vary from around £3-£4.50. Set meals are available from £3.25-£4.75 for three courses and coffee.

MANOR RESTAURANT, MANOR HOUSE HOTEL ★★★★ Avenue Road (Leamington Spa 23251)
Open: Mon-Sun 12.30-2pm, 7-9.30pm (closed Sat lunchtime)

[C] [P]

The Manor Restaurant is a very large and formal dining room befitting this elegant hotel. The à la carte menu far exceeds our limited budget, but the pleasure of dining here in style is not lost to you forever, as there is a versatile table d'hôte menu available for lunch and dinner. A lunch including prawn cocktail, lamb sweetbreads en croûte with sliced green beans, roast and minted new potatoes, and strawberry Melba will cost under £5 with coffee and wine. You may have to forgo the wine with dinner as the table d'hôte price is just over £5 with coffee. A separate 'Saddleroom Grill' offers fish and grilled main courses from £2.50-£4.

NELLO PIZZA AND SPAGHETTI HOUSE, 86 Regent Street (Leamington Spa 22070)
Open: Mon-Sat 11.30am-11pm, Sun 6-11pm

[P] [S]

Exciting décor is the hallmark of this split level pizzeria where one of the white walls has a tiled, roof-like projection creating the illusion of courtyard eating. The average cost of a three course meal including wine and coffee is around £4, though a home-made pizza alone will satisfy most people. Starters include pastas, soup of the day and prawn cocktail. The choice of eight main course pizzas includes the special pizza Nello with cheese, tomato, tuna, prawns, mushrooms, anchovies, egg, ham and olives – all for about £1.40!

PARKES, 19 Park Street (Leamington Spa 23741)
Open: Mon-Sat 12noon-2pm, 7-11pm

[C] [P]

A décor of green and white with mirrors and plants sets the scene. The menu is quoted as 'merely a guideline' which can be altered on request. Exciting starters include stuffed tomatoes with ratatouille, a bowl of chili topped with cream and chopped onions or crudités with assorted home-made dips (around £1.20). To follow are enormous main courses, with specialities such as pork cooked in sherry at £2.75, or salads, lasagne and pizzas – all about £1.50-£2.20 – and the inelegantly named 'gut expander' (a giant hamburger served on a bun with the largest portion of French fries served in the Midlands) costing around £2. A special children's portion of hamburger and chips is under £1 and there is a list of 'Ice Cream Orgies' – 'for adults only when containing liquor'! To round off the meal a giant goblet of French house wine is around 70p. There is a disco with dancing every night.

THE REGENT HOTEL ★★★ Regent Street (Leamington Spa 27231)
Open: The Vaults Restaurant: Mon-Sat 12.30-2pm, 7.30-11pm. Chandos Restaurant: Mon-Sat12.30-2pm, 6.45-8.45pm, Sun 12.30-2pm, 7-8.30pm, Fast Food Bar: normal licensing hours

C ♫ P ♿

The imposing Regent Hotel in the centre of this famous spa was the largest hotel in Europe when it was built in 1819 and is renowned for its VIP visitors, including Queen Victoria and Napoleon. Today it boasts of three excellent eating places. The Vaults, a transformed basement wine cellar serves an excellent table d'hôte lunch. A choice of six starters, three main courses including sweetbread à la crème and coffee costs just under £5, but a glass of wine at around 60p must be added. The elegant Chandos Restaurant offers a table d'hôte lunch with far greater choice but is likely to go beyond our budget. Fish salad, roast beef and Yorkshire pudding and a sweet from the trolley makes a satisfying meal. If you only want a quick snack, try the Fast Food Bar, where you can choose one of 12 very reasonably priced hot dishes and get a starter and sweet thrown in for as little as £2.50. House wine is 70p a glass.

Ledbury

APPLEJACK, 44 The Homend (Ledbury 4181)
Open: Tue-Sat 12.30-2.30pm, 7.30-10.15pm

S

The cosy 'old world inn' atmosphere is retained here at Applejack where owners Anna and Bob Evans have converted this 17th-century inn into a snug two-storey bistro and antique shop. A racing driver, Bob started the bistro as a hobby while his wife Anna concentrates on the antique business. At lunchtime the menu is chalked on a large blackboard where a limited selection of interesting dishes is offered. A sample meal could be home-made pea soup, guinea fowl casserole with trimmings and a generous helping of rhubarb crumble followed by as much freshly ground coffee as you can drink – all for under £3. The printed dinner menu is more extensive with dishes such as Hoi-sin pork (charcoal-grilled chops with barbecue sauce) at £1.95 or asparagus chicken (marinated in cider with fresh asparagus and cream) at £2.25 to tempt your palate. Vegetables are 50p extra in the evening but with reasonable care the bill need not exceed £5.50. Situated in the main shopping street of Ledbury, this black and white inn is convenient for shoppers and businesspeople.

Leek

THE JESTER AT LEEK, 81 Mill Street (Leek 383997)
Open: Mon-Sun 12noon-2pm, 7-8pm

P ♿

This beige, pebble-dashed restaurant has an inviting, cottagy interior. A good variety of wholesome basic English fare is available and a three-course Sunday lunch with a choice of seven starters, eight main courses and sweets from the trolley comes at around £4. The à la carte menu, with starters, grills and roasts at reasonable prices, includes a lot of fish and seafood. Try fresh salmon at around £3.75, or golden seafood platter at about £3.50. Budget meals at lunchtime cost about £1.75 and include home-made steak and kidney pie, breaded plaice and a Dish of the Day.

Leintwardine

THE COTTAGER'S COMFORT
(Leintwardine 266)

Open: Mon-Sun 12.30-2pm, 7.30-9.30pm

[P]

This quaint cottage-style restaurant and country pub enjoys a pleasing hillside situation overlooking the A4113 Ludlow to Leintwardine road. Historically interesting, the locals know it as the 'Hole and Poker' dating from the time when, in the 19th century, a round hole in the wall, which now forms a window, was used as a serving hatch through which cider was passed to travellers and riders on horseback. An interesting modern history was begun two years ago when computer businessman Dennis Rowan decided to try his hand at a new venture. With no previous experience he and his wife have put in much hard work and enthusiasm to make the Cottager's Comfort the success it is today. From a limited menu of freshly prepared dishes you might choose artichoke hearts and prawns, spare ribs with all the trimmings followed by figs or cheese, all for under £4. Even with house wine at 45p and a cup of coffee you should still have change from £5.

Ludlow

EAGLE HOUSE, Corve Street (Ludlow 2325)
Open: Oak Room: Mon-Sun 12noon-2.30pm, 7-10pm, Pine Room: 9am-7pm

[P] [S]

Known as 'The Eagle and Child' when it was first built in the 17th century as a coaching inn, this half-timbered building still retains evidence of a cobblestoned blacksmith's yard. In the entrance, traces of wattle and daub plastering have been exposed to show the original construction. Extremely fine oak panelling in the Oak Room restaurant came from nearby Acton Scott Hall and Bitterley Court and is an outstanding feature. The three-course lunch is remarkable value at under £3 – you could start with grapefruit and orange cocktail, then savour roast lamb and finish with Queen of Puddings – though there are several other choices for each course. Table d'hôte dinner costs £4.50 and offers a wide selection including roast duckling and chicken al' spagnole. With careful choice, the à la carte menu could be within our budget. A glass of French wine will set you back 50p. If you are after a quick snack, then climb the stairs to the Pine Room, where anything from a pot of tea to steak and chips is available.

PENNY ANTHONY × 5 Church Street (Ludlow 3282)
Open: Mon-Wed, Fri-Sat 10.30am-2pm, 7-10pm

[C] [P] [S]

Close to the castle entrance, a charming Georgian-style building houses this popular little restaurant. Three courses can cost from around £2-£6 depending on your choice. Delicious cold dishes include terrine of duck and salads (about £2) or pâté maison and garlic bread (around £1.25). Snails in garlic, onions and parsley, hazelnut roast and salad, seafood pancakes or lasagne are hot dishes costing about £2.50. Steak is around £5. A glass of French house wine costs about 50p. A more sophisticated and expensive evening menu includes specialities such as pork fillet with sage (marinated in dry white wine and sage) at £4.50, and chicken with pernod, at around £5.50 including vegetables.

Malvern

LE BOL À TOUT FAIRE
2 St Ann's Road (Malvern 3713)
Open: Tue-Sun 12.30-2.30pm, 7.30-10.30pm

It's well worth the short steep climb it takes to reach this charming little restaurant situated just off Malvern's main through road. Inside, you'll find a bright, modern interior complete with pine furnishings and pots of fresh flowers on each table. A fascinating display of embroidery, ceramics and paintings, the work of local artists, decorates the walls. They provide an interesting conversation piece and, if you want an unusual souvenir, many items are offered for sale. The short but imaginative menu is changed regularly and offers such dishes as cream of spinach soup or eggs mayonnaise with hot cheese scones for starter at around 60p, main courses of wholemeal pancakes stuffed with curried beef plus cucumber salad and brown rice or grilled lamb's kidneys in asparagus cream sauce with brown rice for £2.75 and tempting puds such as vanilla ice cream with hot brandied apricot sauce or lemon cream with almond shortcake for around 70p. Coffee and wine will add less than £1 to the bill.

Newcastle-under-Lyme

POSTILLION RESTAURANT, BUTTERY AND AUTHOR'S BAR, THE POST HOUSE ☆☆☆ Clayton Road (Newcastle-under-Lyme 625151)
Open: Postillion Restaurant: Mon-Sun 12.30-2.15pm, 7-10.15pm, The Buttery: Mon-Sun 7.30am-10.30pm, Author's Bar: Mon-Sun 12noon-2pm

C P

Stick with the three-course table d'hôte lunch and dinner menus here, if you want to stay around the £5 limit. Next door is the Buttery which offers a wide range of food from snacks to full meals for all occasions. Ideal for all the family, it has children's favourites such as hamburgers, pork sausages and omelettes plus tempting goodies such as fruit pie and chocolate banana nut sundae. Choose from a selection of cold meats, pâtés and as much salad as you want for less than £2.50.

Pershore

SMALL TALK, High Street (Pershore 3654)
Open: Mon-Sat 9.30am-5.30pm, Sun 10.30am-5.30pm

Painted pink, this eaterie stands out from its more sober-fronted high street neighbours. In true tea shop tradition, you'll find the cheerful restaurant by walking through a patisserie and extensive gift shop. At the rear there is an attractive patio setting for when the weather's fine. Soup here costs 40p and pizza 70p, whilst meat pie with potatoes and peas (£1.60) and ploughman's lunch (£1.20) are examples of the no-nonsense main dishes available. For dessert, there's a large counter of mouth-watering confectionery to delight the most discerning gâteau gourmet. Whatever your choice, the meal (including coffee) will cost much less than £5 per head. You will have to forego a glass of wine as Small Talk is unlicensed.

Shrewsbury

CAVALIER RESTAURANT, PRINCE RUPERT HOTEL, Butcher Row
(Shrewsbury 52461)
Open: Mon-Sun 12noon-2.15pm, 7-10.15pm

C P S

The restaurant has an air of opulence with its oak beams and pillars, rich red carpet, velvet curtains and cartwheel-converted chandeliers. Oil paintings adorn the white walls, which contrast the dark wood setting. At lunchtime here a table d'hôte menu offers a choice of seven starters and main dishes (eg ravioli au gratin, followed by roast leg of pork with apple sauce), plus a sweet from the trolley, all for £4.50. A more adventurous three-course evening meal, with several more options, costs £6. French house wine is 50p a glass.

DELANY'S, St Julians Craft Centre for Shropshire, off Fish Street
(Shrewsbury 60602)
Open: Tue-Wed 11am-5pm, Thu-Sat 11am-9pm

S

A more unlikely place for a restaurant than the vestry of a church is hard to imagine, but Delany's – a vegetarian's delight – looks quite at home among the original wood panels and highly-polished boards and beams. Soups instead of sermons are the order of the day now the old church has become a restaurant and craft centre. Tasty and original dishes such as cauliflower, mushroom and cheese bake and aubergine nut crumble (under £2) are served on the cheerful green-and-white-clothed tables, each equipped with flowers, a pot of fresh ground rock salt, dishes of soft brown sugar and unsalted butter. The menu is short but all the dishes are inexpensive. Bring your own wine!

THE DICKENS RESTAURANT, LION HOTEL ★★★ Wyle Cop
(Shrewsbury 53107)
Open: Mon-Sat 12.30-2pm, 7-10pm, Sun 12.30-2pm, 7-9pm

C P S

The popular, elegant 18th-century Lion Hotel stands in the centre of Shrewsbury. Distinguished visitors have included Disraeli, Paganini and, of course, Dickens. A two-course lunch costs from £2.55 – with good choices including mushrooms in savoury butter, chicken Kiev and peach Melba. A three-course Sunday lunch is offered for around £4.50 and a similar table d'hôte dinner costs between £5 and £5.50 – sardine salad or spaghetti bolognese are examples of appetisers and roasts, curry, chops or braised steak are some of the main courses. House wine comes at 98p per quarter bottle.

DUN COW, Abbey Foregate
(Shrewsbury 56408)
Open: Mon-Sun 12noon-2pm, 6.30-10.30pm

C P

You're not likely to find a more historic eating house than the Dun Cow, reputed to be one of the oldest pubs in England, dating from circa 1085. Thanks to the research efforts of the owners, you can read about its amazing history including the sightings of a ghost in the dress of a Dutch cavalry officer, from the special leaflet they have produced. The dining room is more modern than the rest of the premises but an effort has been made to capture the 'olde worlde' atmosphere with exposed beams, rough plaster walls and some exposed stonework. Dishes on the interesting à la carte need careful selection as some prices will exceed our limit. Trout Sabrina – two trout dressed with almonds and lemon, and lamb Shrewsbury – cutlets of lamb with port wine and honey, are two of the more unusual and less expensive main courses.

THE GEORGIAN EATING HOUSE, 50 Mardol (Shrewsbury 4834)
Open: Mon-Sat 10am-5pm, 6-10pm

[C] [S]

Jeanne and David Pedro recently arrived from Bermuda and scoured the country to find the right restaurant to run. They settled on these charming little premises, ideally situated for cinema-goers, shoppers and riverbank walkers. A table d'hôte lunch of scampi and chips, roast beef and Yorkshire pudding and other choices comes served with vegetables and accompanied by a starter and sweet for around £3. Sandwiches and toasted tea cakes are served before and after the lunchtime period.

JUST WILLIAM'S, 62-63 Mardol (Shrewsbury 57061)
Open: Mon-Sat 11am-11pm, Sun 7-11pm

[C] [S] [♧]

Not far from Shrewsbury's main street is this pretty little wine bar, where a small bow window gives glimpses of a black and white, flower-decked interior. Renoirs and other French prints adorn the walls and an old converted gas lamp adds atmosphere. The food includes home-made soup (around 50p), meat salads (ranging from about £1.75 to £2.25) and the evening hot dishes such as pork-filled vol-au-vents (at around £2.50) are advertised on a blackboard. With desserts at around 70p, the average cost of a three-course meal and coffee is still under £4. There are several house wines to choose from, all around 55p a glass – or if you prefer it, real ale.

THE OLDE TUDOR STEAK HOUSE
Butcher Row (Shrewsbury 53117)
Open: Tue-Sun 12noon-2.15pm, Tue-Fri 7-10.30pm, Sat 7-11.30pm

[C] [P] [S] [♧]

The Steak House restaurant occupies the second floor of fine 16th-century black and white timbered premises. Refectory tables, paintings and bric-à-brac help to create a Tudor atmosphere. Table d'hôte lunch is very good value at around £3. Three courses include soup of the day, a choice of seven main courses such as chicken in red wine and a sweet of the day which could be a delicious chocolate mousse. The à la carte menu is predominantly grills and though more expensive, with care three courses can be enjoyed for around £5.

ROYALIST PIZZA BAR, Church Street (Shrewsbury 52461)
Open: Mon-Sat 12noon-2.15pm, 6-10.15pm

[P]

A side shoot of the Prince Rupert Hotel, this little pizza bar boasts an unusual 'olde worlde' setting with dark oak beams and white-painted reproduction furniture, chandeliers, leaded windows with coats of arms and white embossed walls. As the name suggests, the most popular main course is pizza. There are four varieties to choose from, all freshly prepared, even the base, while you wait. Soup of the day, Siciliana (a tasty concoction of tomatoes, anchovies, Mozzarella cheese, mushrooms and black olives, ice cream and coffee will cost around £2.50 and a glass of French wine will add another 50p to the bill.

THE STEAK BAR, Fish Street (Shrewsbury 52463)
Open: Mon-Sat 12noon-2pm, 6-10.45pm

[C] [P]

Shrewsbury's original steak bar is situated in a quiet side street opposite the Prince Rupert Hotel. On entering the small cocktail bar that leads to the restaurant, a mouth-watering aroma wafts temptingly towards you from the open servery. Inside, the majority of tables are arranged to create intimate dining alcoves, whilst the oak-beamed ceiling and leaded windows add a certain Tudor aura. So, what catches your eye on the menu? Maybe French onion soup (35p), followed by a 6oz rump steak with all the trimmings (only £2.90) and a fruit salad (60p) to finish. Coffee and a glass of French house wine are well within the budget.

Stafford

ANEMOS, 22 Crabbery Street
(Stafford 48940)
Open: Mon-Wed 9am-5pm,
Thu-Sat 9am-5pm, 7.30-11pm

[S] [♧]

The small upstairs dining room of this shop-fronted Greek restaurant serves a cosmopolitan range of light lunches – omelettes, salads, pizzas, pasta dishes and moussaka are all between £1-£2. A more substantial lunch can be enjoyed from a choice of fourteen starters – including soup of the day at 35p, dolmades at 90p or mushroom salad at £1.10. Main course could be sofrito (a Corfu speciality of beef in wine sauce served with a side salad – costing about £2.60), beef Stroganoff (£2.80) or prawn kebab with salad and rice at £2.50. Desserts include gâteaux at about 55p. The evening menu is basically Greek and more expensive, but three courses could be savoured for around £5. A glass of Italian house wine costs about 50p.

HAND AND CLEAVER INN, Ranton
(Stafford 822367)
Open: Mon-Thu 12noon-2pm, 7-10pm,
Fri-Sat 12noon-2pm, 7-10.30pm,
Sun 12noon-1.30pm, 7-10pm

[C] [P] [♧]

The restaurant of this beautiful inn, built as a farm house in 1733, was once the cowshed. The original stalls have been kept and tables installed, but the names of their previous occupants remain: Snowdrop, Poppy, Rosebud, Daisy and Violet among them. Above this area is the old hay loft, and diners can gaze down into the main restaurant. Lunches here are well within the limit – a three-course Sunday lunch at £4 could include Florida cocktail, roast beef and a sweet from the trolley. The same meal for a child is £2. Snacks such as scampi and chips (£1.50), rump steak, chips and peas (£3) or beef salad (£1.75) are available in the bar. A large glass of wine costs about 55p. The sophisticated evening à la carte menu is a little beyond our limit for most selections, but you could *just* manage three courses.

Stoke-on-Trent

CAPRI RISTORANTE ITALIANO
13 Glebe Street (Stoke-on-Trent 411889)
Open: Mon-Sat 12noon-2.15pm,
7.30-11.45pm

[C] [P]

Entering the rear of this little Italian restaurant from the car park has been compared with walking into the famous Blue Grotto of Capri. Blue and green lighting creates the illusion, which is enhanced by scenes of Italy painted on the white stucco walls by proprietor Vittorio Cirillo. Good, home-cooked Italian fare is highly recommended, with minestrone or salami to start at around £1, lasagne, spaghetti, penne alla arrabiata or penne al ragu as the main course, all about £1.70 and delicious desserts such as profiteroles (95p) or orange slices with liqueur (75p). A glass of house wine – Italian of course – costs 50p, leaving plenty of change from £5 for a cup of frothy espresso or cappucino coffee.

THE POACHERS COTTAGE ✕✕
Stone Road, Trentham
(Stoke-on-Trent 657115)
Open: Tue Sat 12noon-2pm, 7-9.30pm

[P] [♧]

This black and white cottage is easily located on the A34, close to Trentham Gardens. The cottage atmosphere has been retained inside, with black beams, natural stone and tapestry upholstered chairs. White linen tablecloths and colourful carpets add a touch of luxury. The lunchtime menu has excellent value roasts and grills. Rollmop herring hors d'oeuvres, roast chicken with trimmings, sweets, coffee and wine will just top £5.

RIB OF BEEF, GRAND HOTEL ★★★
66 Trinity Street, Hanley
(Stoke-on-Trent 22361)
Open: Mon-Sun 12.30-2pm, 7-10pm

[C] [P] [S]

Situated on the lower ground floor of the impressive Trusthouse Forte hotel close to Hanley city centre, the Rib of Beef restaurant boasts some tasty local favourites. Try the excellent table d'hôte menu. For only about £4.50 at lunchtime you can choose Florida cocktail – one of five starters – then take your choice of roast ribs of beef, fish, grilled lamb chops – it's different every day! Try the delicious vegetables and sauces and, if you have room for it, the sweet trolley offers a host of gooey goodies. Dinner is a little beyond the limit of this guide.

ROOSEVELT'S RESTAURANT
24 Snow Hill (Stoke-on-Trent 269544)
Open: Mon-Sun 12noon-12mdnt

[C]

As the name implies, an American-style fast service operates here, the result of co-owner Philip Crowe's long observations in the States. Judging by the hordes of people that frequent the restaurant, the system is a great success. Brown hessian walls, a quarry-tiled floor and Liberty-print tablecloths create a warm, welcoming effect and the many photographs and posters continue the Americana theme. Having started with, perhaps, corn on the cob (55p), you can choose from several hamburger specials, all with French fries and trimmings, costing around £1.70 or £2.50 depending on burger size. Rosé is a house wine option at 60p a glass. At these prices you can afford to splash out on a knickerbocker glory, enjoy a cup of coffee and still get plenty of change from a fiver.

SHOULDER OF MUTTON, Meadow Lane, Fulford (Blyth Bridge 7375)
Open: Thu-Sat 7-10.30pm,
Sun 12noon-2pm, 7-10.30pm

[C] [P]

A village-centre pub which has been modernised and extended to incorporate a grill room with olde worlde appeal. A T-bone steak, plus French fries, garden peas and salad is only about £4.20. Appealing dishes at budget prices are available on the à la carte menu – steak chasseur (£3.60) and golden-fried scampi (£2.90) are examples. All starters are less than £1, whilst desserts cost around 55p. A glass of house wine is 50p.

SPOT GATE, Hilderstone Road,
Spot Acre, (Hilderstone 277)
Open: Mon-Fri 12noon-2pm,
7.30-9.30pm, Sat 7.30-10.15pm,
Sun 12noon-2pm, 7.30-9pm

[C] [P]

Lunch or dinner aboard this Cavalier Steak Bar is certain to be a gastronomic journey you'll never forget, as diners sit in two beautifully restored dining cars from the famous old Bournemouth Belle. Ursula is the name of the first class compartment seating sixteen in luxurious armchair-style seats plus the two small private dining compartments with intimate seating for four. The other, christened Maggie, seats almost fifty in surroundings of beautiful veneer panelling, brass-framed windows, heavy brass hat and luggage racks and comfortable seating with antimacassars from the days of slicked back hair. Meals are more varied than usual in a steak bar with a range of fish, poultry or meat dishes from around £3-£5.50. Half a chicken with sweet and sour is particularly popular at £3.85. The Nicholas house wine is 52p a glass.

Stourbridge

BELL HOTEL ★★ Market Street
(Stourbridge 5641)
Open: Mon-Sat 12.30-2.15pm,
6.30-8.30pm, Sun 12.30-2.15pm

[C] [P] [S]

As one might expect from an area famous for its glass, this seems to be the theme in this restaurant, with large mirrors, glass skylights, glass doors, old leaded windows and glass partitions. Gold-coloured flock wallpaper blends effectively with the red patterned carpet, which together with the neatly-laid tables, old chairs and uniformed waitresses creates a rather timeless atmosphere. A three-course lunch of grapefruit, grilled lamb garni with vegetables and strawberries and cream can be had for around £3.50. Coffee and wine would add another £1 or so, and the prices are the same in the evening.

BISTRO PAPILLON, ROYAL EXCHANGE INN, High Street (Stourbridge 71836)
Open: Mon-Fri 12noon-2pm, 7-10.30pm, Sat 7-10.30pm

♫ P S

A narrow staircase from the cocktail bar of the Royal Exchange leads to this enchanting French Restaurant. Green floral wallpaper sports prints by Lautrec, picture mirrors and wall lights which together with the piped French music create a romantic atmosphere. This room is open-plan with pine tables and chairs adequately spread out. The menu itself provides very interesting reading with a lengthy introduction to the dishes and their origins. You should find a reasonable choice on the lunchtime menu for under £5 for three courses. After, perhaps, egg mayonnaise – an appetiser costing around 65p, try a 'Chef's special' such as bifteck au poivre – best beef steak sautéd in butter with crushed peppercorns, flamed with brandy and finished with cream – at £3.75. If this breaks the budget, both trout and scampi cost much less. A fresh cream sweet could follow that, with excellent coffee. The Chandory house wine is 55p per glass.

THE GALLERY RESTAURANT ✕
121 Bridgnorth Road, Wollaston (Stourbridge 2788)
Open: Tue-Sat 7.30-9.30pm

C S

Just mention the 'restaurant above the butcher's' to anyone in this area and you will be directed to Bill and Janet Harris's popular 'Gallery'. Bill runs the butcher's shop on this main shopping street and Janet is in charge of the successful little eating house above. Lamb chops, sole and scampi feature on the à la carte menu, all at around £3.50. With soup at 50p and trolley desserts around 90p you may have to break the bank to sample the French house wine.

THE OLD WHITE HORSE INN
South Road (Stourbridge 4258)
Open: Mon-Sat 11am-2.30pm, 6-11pm, Sun 12noon-2.30pm

P 🍷

This imposing public house stands close to the entrance of Mary Steven's Park. The table d'hôte lunch menu, for around £3.50 gives a good selection of three courses – try sardine salad, braised ham with Madeira sauce and a delicious sweet from the trolley. A glass of French house wine costs about 50p. The à la carte menu is extensive, and a little beyond our budget, but appetising meals are served at lunchtime in the main lounge.

ROTHSCHILDS WINE BAR
Bordeaux House, Foster Street (Stourbridge 78140)
Open: Mon-Thu 10am-2.30pm, 7-10.30pm, Fri-Sat 10am-2.30pm, 7-11pm, Sun 7-10.30pm

C ♫ 🍷

Don't be put off by the name – prices are very reasonable here! Cane tables and chairs and French prints, together with authentic piped background music create an illusion of France. A self-service system operates. Following the home-made soup starter, fresh crab or lobster and salad are seasonally available at about £1.75, whilst a cold table (offering as much as you can eat!) is always available at just under £2. Plat du jour, priced from about £2-£3.50, may be cod in sherry and cream sauce, pepperpot beef, king prawn and bacon kebabs or barbecued lamb riblets. Desserts include gâteaux, cheesecakes and ice creams which cost around 55p.

TALBOT HOTEL ★★ High Street (Stourbridge 4350)
Open: Mon-Sat 12noon-2pm, 7-9.30pm, Sun 12noon-2pm

C S

This town centre hotel has been popular for many years. The ground floor dining room seats about seventy in comfortable alcoves screened by velvet half-curtains hung from brass rails, and it is here that lunch on weekdays and Saturdays is chosen from a buffet with mainly cold dishes; though a Chef's Special is always provided. The Sunday lunch menu offers traditional roasts of chicken, lamb, beef or pork with all the trimmings, and a starter and sweet for about £3.50. Evening meals consist mainly of grills such as rainbow trout or lamb cutlets. Prices are very reasonable for both table d'hôte and à la carte.

Stourport-on-Severn

LOCK, STOCK AND BARREL
2a High Street (Stourport-on-Severn 6014)
Open: Mon 12noon-2pm, Tue-Sat 12noon-2pm, 7.30-10pm, Sun 12.30-2pm

C ♫ S 🍷

This canal-side bistro specialises in informal suppers by candlelight and the restaurant on the ground floor in quick easy lunches. Lunches are excellent value, with starters such as melon with orange and cherry, choice of a cold table or hot dish of the day and a sweet with cream costing around £3. Family Sunday lunch offers a three-course roast beef meal for just over £4 with a reduced price for children. You can dine by candlelight, after sampling an interesting wine cocktail, on potted pork with hazelnuts, beef braised in beer and lemon syllabub and many more intriguing dishes. In honour of this guide, a '999 Special' comprises three courses, coffee and wine for £5.50.

Stratford-upon-Avon

THE DIRTY DUCK, Waterside
(Stratford-upon-Avon 297312)
Open: Mon-Sat 12noon-3pm, 6-12mdnt

C S

This typically English pub-restaurant is a favourite haunt of the theatre world, due to its olde worlde charm, and its nearness to the Shakespeare theatre. Apart from serving meals before and after performances, they also offer a good lunch here. Why not choose roast duck at about £4, and eat it while you watch the swans sail by on the Avon? Other main dishes range in price from £2.50 to £4.50 with plaice fillet and braised kidneys as representative examples. There are ten or so starters with prices up to £1 and a sweet or cheese costs about 60p. French house wine is sold by the glass at around 55p.

GROSVENOR HOUSE HOTEL ★★★
Warwick Road
(Stratford-upon-Avon 69213)
Open: Mon-Sun 12noon-1.45pm, 6-8.45pm

C P

Just five minutes' walk from the Royal Shakespeare Theatre is this elegant, family-run hotel. You can enjoy a three-course table d'hôte lunch in the luxurious restaurant for around £4.20. The menu offers basic English fare – roast beef, chicken or lamb are main dishes, with goujon of sole with tartare sauce or lentil soup as appetisers. Hot apple pie and fresh cream or a sweet from the trolley complete a satisfying meal. Dinner at £5.20 includes sardine salad or ham cornets with savoury rice as starters and cod à la creole or boeuf bourguignon as main course dishes. A glass of wine costs 60p.

HATHAWAY TEA ROOMS, 19 High Street (Stratford-upon-Avon 292404)
Open: Mon-Sat 9am-5.30pm, Sun 11.45am-5.30pm

S

Although the name suggests otherwise, this impressive building, with its olde worlde atmosphere goes a good deal further back than Shakespeare's era – the original site dates back to 1315. The tea rooms are reached by passing through the shop up the Jacobean staircase to the tiny landing, which houses a superb grandfather clock. Once inside, you will find everything you expected – dark oak beams, white walls, an open fireplace and antique dressers and tables. A good old-fashioned lunch menu offers traditional dishes such as roast beef and Yorkshire pudding or steak and kidney pie, each for about £1.70, spotted Dick, apple and raspberry tart, both around 55p or banana split at a little more.

HORSESHOE BUTTERY AND RESTAURANT, 33-34 Greenhill Street
(Stratford-upon-Avon 292246)
Open: Mon-Sun, 9am-10pm

[P]

Handy for pre-film and theatre snacks, this bay-windowed, country-style restaurant with its charming mock-Tudor façade lies opposite the cinema and just fifty yards from the famous clock tower. An exceptionally good value table d'hôte lunch still costs less than £3 for three courses (eg, soup, steak and kidney pie, home-made fruit pie), wine and coffee. A special two-course meal costs around £2. Both are served in a warm, friendly atmosphere.

THE OPPOSITION RESTAURANT
13 Sheep Street
(Stratford-upon-Avon 69980)
Open: Tue-Sat 12noon-2.30pm,
Mon-Sat 6-11.30pm

[S]

No need to feel bloodthirsty to enjoy the steakburger – Macbeth style. It's innocent enough to look at with its topping of melted cheese. Other varieties (including Texan and American styles) are well worth trying, as they are made to the proprietor's own recipe by a local butcher. Pizzas (all around £2), spaghetti and pastas are also available, and there's a small list of 'specials' including sirloin, fillet or rump steak, veal and chicken tagliatelle with prawn and wine sauce. Choose a large or small glass of house wine.

THE THATCH RESTAURANT
Cottage Lane, Shottery
(Stratford-upon-Avon 293122)
Open: Mon-Sun 9am-6pm,
Tue-Sat 7-10.30pm

[P]

Next to the famous Anne Hathaway's Cottage you will find this delightful thatched restaurant with its olde worlde

dining room and rustic canopied terrace. Here you can enjoy a fine traditional English lunch with three courses, including roast beef and Yorkshire pudding followed by a slice of home-made apple or lemon meringue pie for about £4. Cream teas are good value at £1. A glass of French wine costs around 50p. The evening menu, in fact, has a distinct French flavour. A table d'hôte Pre-Theatre supper is only £3.

Sutton Coldfield

PIMPERNELL, 59/61 Birmingham Road (021-354 9808)
Open: Tue-Sat 12noon-2.30pm, 6-10.30pm

C

Just the place to eat before or after a film at the nearby cinema. Green and red tasteful décor complements the excellent and inexpensive cuisine. The à la carte menu offers dishes from many countries and is well within our budget. Particularly good value fare may be sampled from the Daily Special lunchtime menu. Soup – such as asparagus – is only 20p and main courses at £1.65 could be roast beef, chicken casserole or grilled plaice. Desserts at 25p include apple and raspberry pie. A large glass of house wine is 50p. It would be very difficult to exceed the budget here!

RISTORANTE STEFANO
358 Birmingham Road (021-373 8576)
Open: Tue-Sat 12noon-2.30pm, 7-10.30pm, Sun 12noon-2.30pm

C S

Black beams and pillars contrast strikingly with the white embossed ceiling and walls of this little Italian restaurant created out of a former shop. Value for money is the keynote of the daily menu, which offers such starters as soup of the day at 35p, assorted salamis at 75p or smoked mackerel salad at 90p. Main course dishes include rigatone napolitaine (£1.25), halibut steak Mornay, chicken chasseur or roast of the day – all at £1.85. Home-made desserts such as fruit crumble (35p) or lemon meringue pie (55p) complete a satisfying meal. A large glass of Italian wine costs 50p. Sunday lunch is excellent value, with three courses for less than £4. Appetisers include melon in port or prawn cocktail, main courses a choice of four roasts, halibut, chicken provençale or salad and there is a good selection of sweets from the trolley.

WYNDLEY LEISURE CENTRE
Clifton Road (021-354 2259)
Open: Mon-Sun 10am-4pm

P

Not only track-suited fitness fanatics here – businesspeople, shoppers and local senior citizens all queue up for the excellent food served at this Leisure Centre lunch bar. Jean Adderley and Judith Hewett produce a tempting display of cooked meats, quiches and pastas which may be accompanied by a jacket potato and a good selection of salad items. Excellent gâteaux, fruit flans or lemon-meringue pies complete the array of home-made fare. For around £1, you could sample soup, hot and tasty bubble and squeak, a large baked potato, coleslaw and a slice of walnut gâteau. The lunch bar is not licensed, but a well-stocked drinks bar is adjacent so carry your wine through.

Upton-upon-Severn

CROMWELLS, 16/18 Church Street
(Upton-upon-Severn 2447)
Open: Mon 9.30am-2.15pm,
Tue-Sat 9.30am-2.15pm, 7.15-10pm

Oliver Cromwell is reputed to have waved to a pretty lady at an upstairs window of this charming black-and-white half-timbered cottage. With a craft shop at the side, the rear houses a bistro with exposed brick walls and beams, leading on to a walled garden where children may let off steam. Upstairs is 'Oliver's Bar' where diners may sip an aperitif and study the blackboard menu. A typical lunch menu could be home-made vegetable soup at 95p, prawn and cheese vol-au-vents with a tossed salad (totalling £2.50) and lemon syllabub at around 95p. The dinner menu offers more choice – seven possibles for each course including frog's legs as a starter! Stilton and onion soup costs 95p, scrumpy chicken £3.35 and Cromwell gâteau or lemon syllabub 95p. With a glass of French Cromwell wine at 65p a glass, you will just about keep within our budget.

Warwick

CINDY'S, 48 Brook Street
(Warwick 43504)
Open: Mon-Sat 9.30am-5pm

[C] [S]

Only about twenty people can be seated in this country kitchen style restaurant found above a tempting delicatessen, so booking in advance is advised. Dominated by pine furniture, Lowrie prints and paintings for sale by a local artist, it offers freshly prepared dishes attractively displayed on the large pine dresser. During summer, home-made quiches and pies accompanied by a selection of salads and fresh fruit sponges are the bill of fare. In the winter months, delicious soup and hot main dishes are available.

NICOLINI'S BISTRO, 18 Jury Street
(Warwick 45817)
Open: Mon 9.30am-2.30pm,
Tue-Sun 9.30am-10.30pm

[C] [P] [S]

Located on one of the main thoroughfares of the city is this delightful little restaurant with its stripped pine chairs, potted plants and effective spot lighting. A well-stocked glass counter displaying fresh salads and tempting sweets immediately attracts the eye, and other dishes are available, such as tasty home-made pizzas. A three-course meal with a glass of wine will, on average, be from £3-£4.

ZARANOFF'S, 16 Market Place (Warwick 42708)
Open: Tue-Sun 12noon-2.30pm, evenings Mon-Sun by reservation

♫ P S

Zaranoff's has the outward appearance of a delicatessen but inside is a thirty-six seater restaurant of truly international appeal. The emphasis is on Hungarian fare, but proprietor Josef Zaranoff, a half-Latvian, half-Russian ex-wrestler and his Midland-born wife Vicky, prepare gourmet delights to tempt palates from Wales to Japan. An interesting example of the lunch-time menu from the 'English Table' is as follows – home-made creamy vegetable soup, Wakefield rabbit with Kelly's sauce, including fresh vegetables, and potted cheese with home-made pickled onions and walnuts. This costs around £3. In the evening, meals are served by prior arrangement, when a large variety of unusual items are often available – from shark meat to pigeon.

Waterhouses

THE OLDE BEAMS (Waterhouses 254)
Open: Tue-Sat 12noon-2pm, 6.30-10pm, Sun 12noon-2pm

P

In the centre of the village is this charming white stone and brick-built house with shuttered windows. Originally an inn, it was built in 1746, and the restaurant has exposed ceiling beams, refectory tables and Windsor chairs. Table d'hôte menus for lunch and dinner offer three courses, with good choices, for £3.75 and £4.30 repectively. At lunchtime a cold buffet table is available for £2.50. Appetisers include kipper mousse and main courses beef curry Madras or roast sirloin of beef garni. All the food is home-made, including a selection of delicious sweets on the trolley. A glass of wine costs from 65p-80p. The à la carte menu offers imaginative fare, much of which is within our budget. On fine days guests may enjoy the beautiful gardens at the rear.

Wolverhampton

LE BISTRO STEAKHOUSE
6 School Street (Wolverhampton 24638)
Open: Mon-Sat 12noon-2.30pm, 6-11.30pm

♫ S

A variety of bottles hanging against white walls, black wrought-iron partitions, and red-patterned carpet create a welcoming atmosphere in this first-floor restaurant, belying the corner premises' rather dreary exterior. The kitchen is supervised by owner 'Steve' Kyriakov who makes sure that Greek specialities such as moussaka (about £2) and afelia (around £2.50) are cooked to perfection. Lunchtime table d'hôte menus offer a choice of Greek or English food for around £1.50 with a sweet 35p extra. The inevitably Greek house wine costs 50p a glass.

PEPITO'S, 5 School Street (Wolverhampton 23403)
Open: Mon-Sat 12noon-2.30pm, 6-11pm, closed 3 weeks in Aug

♫ P S

For those who like Italian food, Pepito's offers the real thing in a pleasant modern restaurant with glass partitioning providing a degree of privacy. Owner Mr Catellani supervises the cooking while his wife, helped by two young ladies, looks after the customers. The two-course table d'hôte lunch is good value at around £1.50, with a choice of four starters and a main course pasta dish or, perhaps, goulash or a roast – there are seven or eight items to choose from. Just a few à la carte alternatives are available at lunch time, but in the evening à la carte takes over, the average price for a meal being about £5. A glass of Valpolicella is about 60p.

NATURAL BREAK, 17 Mealcheapen Street (Worcester 29979)
Open: Mon-Fri 10am-5pm,
Sat 9.30am-5pm

S

Brown-tiled tables and natural pine create an informal, cottagey atmosphere in this popular rendezvous, where proprietors Sandra Jackson and Nigel Wolfenden pin notices of local societies' meetings on the wall alongside paintings by local artists which are offered for sale. The board menu lists a choice of eight interesting salads at around 25p – potato, carrot, mushroom, apple, celery and walnut – ideal to accompany the home-made savoury flans and quiches which only cost about 55p. Desserts include home-baked apple pie, meringues and pastries – freshly prepared every day. Coffee here is said to be the best in Worcester.

BOLTON-LE-SANDS
MORECAMBE
LANCASTER
GISBURN
LANCASHIRE
CLEVELEYS
ST MICHAELS-ON-WYRE
BLACKPOOL
BROUGHTON
KIRKHAM
SAMLESBURY
BURNLEY
FRECKLETON
PRESTON
BLACKBURN
SOUTHPORT
ROCHDALE
PARBOLD
ORMSKIRK
BOLTON
OLDHAM
WIGAN
GREATER MANCHESTER
MANCHESTER
ASHTON-UNDER-LYNE
MERSEYSIDE
STOCKPORT
HAZEL GROVE
LIVERPOOL
WEST KIRBY
ALTRINCHAM
HALE
WILMSLOW
KNUTSFORD
ALDERLEY EDGE
PRESTBURY
MACCLESFIELD
CHESHIRE
CHESTER
CONGLETON

The North West

The dark, sulphurous shadow of long-established industry lies obliquely across the region, but you won't have to venture far from Merseyside or Manchester to discover a countryside as varied as it is beautiful. To the north the Ribble Valley boasts the wild, dramatic Trough of Bowland and the Rossendale Forest and the Fells rise up to the Pennine Range, whilst to the west the coast has sandy beaches for sun-worshippers and Blackpool for fun-lovers.

The southerly Cheshire Plain is rich agricultural land – home of the famous full-flavoured Cheshire cheese. Cheeses are a feature of the region and include crumbly Lancashire cheese which fills many a cheese and onion pie. The pie shops of Lancashire are an integral part of the way of life. Torpedoes (like flattened Cornish pasties), meat and potato pies, and whist pies – bite-sized ovals filled with minced pork in jelly – are sold in most of them.

The workers of Lancashire have always been enthusiastic meat-eaters, with mutton and lamb from the hardy sheep of the harsh Pennines the basis of a great variety of dishes. Chunks of lamb, slowly cooked in huge earthenware pots while the women toiled at the looms, made up the famous hot pot – topped with potatoes a meal in itself. Cooked meats abound – corned mutton and beef, or 'elder' – cooked and pressed cow's udder similar in taste to tongue. Only the bones of the animal are discarded – even the stomach lining is 'dressed' to make tripe, the small intestine makes chitterlings and lamb's stones (testicles) are delicious marinated and fried with parsley. Fresh blood is used to make the esteemed black pudding – still a star attraction at stalls, particularly in Bury Market.

9

Fleetwood hake and Morecambe Bay cockles, whelks, shrimps and crabs are delicacies growing in popularity.

Baking thrives in these parts, with the universal nutty oatcake or 'haverbread' an exciting alternative to wholemeal bread. Lancashire has produced the famous 'parkin' made of ginger and treacle.

Muffins, crumpets, Eccles cakes, Bury simnel cake and sad cakes of Rossendale – why not throw calorie caution to the winds and sample some of these delights in the restaurants listed here?

Alderley Edge

NO. 15 WINE BAR, 15 London Road
(Alderley Edge 582354)
Open: Mon-Sat 12noon-2pm,
7-10.30pm (Fri-Sat 7-11pm)

[P] [S]

The blackboard menu offers starters including pâté at about 95p and prawn cocktail at around £1.15 and hot main dishes such as moussaka, lasagne, chili con carne and tagliatelli, all for around £1.50. Prawn or trout salads are about £1.95. Desserts at around 65p include Jamaican fudge cake. A good selection of wines is available by the glass at about 60p. In summer you can eat in the walled and well-tended garden.

Altrincham

THE CRESTA COURT HOTEL ☆☆☆
Church Street (061-928 8017)
Open: Lodge: Mon-Sat 12noon-2pm,
6-10pm, Sun 12noon-2pm
Quarterdeck: Mon-Sun 12noon-2pm,
6.30-11.15pm (Sun 6.30-10pm)

[C] [♫] [ஃ]

This bright, new hotel has two steak bar restaurants. The Tavern Lodge offers the usual combination of steak, chicken, scampi and fish costing from £1.85 to about £3.55 all served with vegetables. The Quarterdeck is a little more sophisticated, with main dishes from over £2 to £4 and a good selection of vegetables in addition to those included in the price of the meal.

GANDERS, 2 Goose Green
(061-941 3954)
Open: Mon-Thu 12noon-3pm, 7-10.30pm,
Fri 12noon-3pm, 7-11pm, Sat 12noon-4pm, 7-11pm, Sun 7-10.30pm

[C] [S]

Surprisingly, goose is not on the very varied menu of this pleasant wine bar and bistro, housed in a 300-year-old cottage in a quiet alley close to the town centre. A dozen appetisers range in price from 45p for home-made soup to £1.40 for avocado with crab. Tuna fish pâté, ham and prawn cornets, rollmop herring or 'Cranks' vegetarian salad are other tasty choices. Lancashire hot pot is a good, traditional main course for £1.65, but why not go overboard and try fondue bourguignon – a bargain at £2.75 per person? You will need to have three other people with you to sample this delicacy. Desserts are in the 50p-60p bracket and include such delights as passioncake, fresh strawberries and cream and 'real' sherry trifle. Large or small glasses of wine are served – at 70p or 50p respectively.

THE OLD HALL, Stockport Road
(061-928 2965)
Open: Mon-Sun 12noon-2pm, 7-10pm
(Sat 7-10pm only)

[♫] [P] [ஃ]

Value-for-money food consists mainly of unpretentious grills such as gammon with two eggs, or fresh trout with chips, roll and butter for about £2.40. Starters include rollmop herring at around 75p and home-made soup at 50p or so, and a sweet from the trolley costs about 65p.

Ashton-under-Lyne

CORNICHE GRILL, Oldham Road
(061-339 5469)
Open: Mon-Sun 12noon-2.30pm,
6-10.30pm

[S] [ஃ]

Car dealers, Wm Monk claim that this gallery restaurant overlooking the car showroom is a new idea 'direct from Paris', and the first of its kind in this country. Grills are the main feature on the menu with rump steak for as little as £3 or so, and all dishes include French fries or jacket potato and a roll and butter. Sweets and cheese and biscuits are also included in the price of the main course. For about 60p you can choose a connoisseur coffee such as a Monte Carlo (with Cointreau) or a Brands Hatch (with whisky), or have a 'customised' coffee to suit your taste.

Blackburn

KENYON'S STUDIO BUTTERY
31 Penny Street (Blackburn 60347)
Open: Mon-Wed 9am-5pm, Thu 10am-1.30pm, Fri 9am-5pm, Sat 9am-4.30pm

[P] [S]

This sparkling, modern coffee shop in the centre of town is a self-service style operation offering good food at remarkably low prices. A three-course meal starting with soup of the day at about 25p, followed by lasagne or steak and kidney (both less than £1 but the most expensive savoury dishes on the menu) and completed with Black Forest gâteau at around 40p is excellent value.

Blackpool

THE AMERICAN DINER
48 Clifton Street (0253 27656)

Open: Sun-Thu 10am-1am, Fri-Sat 10am-2am

C ♫ S

Stars and stripes on the ceiling and gigantic portraits of Johnny Cash, John Wayne and other Transatlantic notables adorning the walls, give this American diner an air of authenticity which is emphasised by Country and Western music. Excellent value food includes a range of imaginative burgers, chargrills, 'greens 'n things' and all-time favourites such as scampi or chicken. Prices are from £1.30 for a standard burger to around £4 for rump steak. The table d'hôte menu offers a good selection of three courses for £1.60 + 10% service. An appetising choice is French onion soup, gammon and pineapple with vegetables and a sweet such as cherry flan from the display table. A glass of good French house wine is 60p. Every bill in excess of £2 qualifies for a voucher. Three vouchers collected in any two-week period may be used to reduce the next bill by £1.

THE DANISH KITCHEN
Vernon Humpage, Church Street (Blackpool 24291)
Open: Mon-Sat 9am-5.30pm

S

Pine tables and pine beams with mock gas lamps adorn this bright, clean, split-level serve-yourself operation in the centre of town. Freshly made soup is about 30p and there is a tempting array of Danish open sandwiches (crab, prawn, beef, smoked salmon etc) from 55p, salads from 65p, omelettes from 70p and pizzas from 90p. The Danish pastries from 27p, are excellent. A glass of wine is about 50p.

Bolton

THE DROP INN and BUMBLES BEE-STRO, THE LAST DROP ★★
Bromley Cross (Bolton 591131)
Open: Inn: Mon-Sun 12noon-2pm, Bee-stro: Mon-Thu 7-10.30pm, Fri-Sat 7-11pm, Sun 3.30-9.30pm

C ♫ P S

A collection of derelict 18th-century farm buildings has been imaginatively converted to create a modern shopping and hotel complex with traditional village atmosphere. The Drop Inn pub even sports a honky-tonk piano to accompany evening sing-songs, as well as oak beams and a blazing log fire. Bar snacks are served in the evening, but it's at lunchtime that the food scene is best, with an excellent, self-service lunch for around £3. The stone-floored Bee-stro, with its low-arched ceiling, wood and brick surfaces and candlelight, offers main course, salad selection, starter and sweet (try Jamaican bananas), for about £3.50. The menu is changed monthly and includes fish, salad, burger and one or two more unusual dishes.

THE LAMPLIGHTER
26 Knowsley Street (Bolton 35175)
Open: Mon-Fri 12noon-2pm, 5.45-10.30pm, Fri 12noon-2pm, 5.45-11pm, Sat 12noon-11pm, Sun 3-9pm

Pictures, prints and posters of the Victorian era cover the walls, and gas lamps and stuffed animals' heads add to the overwhelming 19th-century atmosphere. Every dish is given the name of a Victorian cigarette card character; the Knife Grinder's Delight, for instance, is an outsized kebab of fine beef, onions, mushrooms, bacon and tomato on a bed of rice, and the Knocker's-Up Nosh – a juicy rump steak with garden peas and a garnish of cress, tomato and potatoes. Fresh fruit, ice cream or cheese is included in the main course price, so nothing tops our limit.

Bolton-le-Sands

WILLOW TREE, By Pass Road (Hest Bank 823316)

Open: Tue-Fri 9.30am-1.45pm, 4.30-8.30pm, Sat 4-9pm, Sun 11.30am-9pm

[P]

This single-storey building with its neatly tiled roof and white stucco walls is just the place to feed the family. Service is prompt and efficient in the two well-appointed, wood-panelled dining rooms, where a lunch of soup or fruit juice, minute steak, lamb chops or grilled plaice, served with new potatoes or chips and peas, a sweet and coffee, is likely to cost around £3.50. The reasonably-priced evening menu offers more choice.

Broughton

THE ORCHARD, Whittingham Lane (Broughton 862208)
Open: Tue-Sat 12noon-2pm, 7.30-9.30pm, Sun 12noon-2pm

[C] [♫] [P] [♧]

The cluster of buildings which forms 'The Orchard' includes a barn now used for functions. Natural stone walls and beams are a foil for brass, copper, china and pictures, the general effect being neat, bright and cheerful. The set lunches are excellent value, three courses costing from £2.50-£3 on weekdays and from about £2.75 on Sunday, the main course giving several choices including traditional roasts. The à la carte menu is reasonable but you would have to use some care in choosing a three-course meal.

Burnley

SMACKWATER JACKS, Ormerod Street (Burnley 21290)
Open: Mon-Sun 12noon-12mdnt

[S] [♧]

A town centre steak and hamburger joint set in a stone and brick-built cellar. The lighthearted menu is written in brash Americanese – start with fruit juice ('we got orange an' we got tomato') and move on to a 'hillbilly chili' – ('the way Pa likes it') – at about £1.45. For dessert there's deep dish apple pie, banana split, cheesecake 'frigate' and various sundaes, all under or around £1.

Chester

THE CHESTER STEAK HOUSE
St Werbergh Street (Chester 43264)
Open: Mon-Sat 11.30am-10.30pm, Sun 12noon-10.30pm

[C] [P] [♧]

The interior of this modern restaurant is decorated in restful colours with Romanesque motifs. A fairly extensive menu offers dishes to suit all tastes from the 'Continental quickies' (pizza, lasagne etc) to the 'Great British specialities' such as roast beef and Yorkshire pudding. Prices are reasonable and although some steaks may exceed our limit, a substantial three-course meal would cost around £4 with coffee.

THE COURTYARD ××
13 St Werburgh Street (Chester 21447)
Open: Mon-Sat 10.30am-2.30pm, 6-10pm

[C] [♫] [♧]

This popular gourmet restaurant is set around a pretty courtyard, within the city walls and the sound of the Cathedral bells. Upstairs at lunchtime a 'help yourself' smørgasbørd operates. A la carte lunch includes sirloin steak at around £3.50, lamb cutlets at about £2.50 and a selection of starters and sweets. Dinner is more adventurous with such delights as lambs' sweetbreads braised in Madeira, but it is more expensive. There is also an evening bistro offering a very reasonable fixed price buffet.

DEERINGS, Mercia Square, Frodsham Street (Chester 23469)
Open: Mon-Sat 12noon-2.30pm, 5.30-10.30pm, Sat 5-11pm, Sun 5-9pm (summer only)

[P] [S] [♧]

This modern glass-fronted restaurant, with its separate wine bar, is to be found in a shopping precinct close to the city walls. The interior is of unusual design with iron and wood arches forming banquettes at one end of the room and an open-plan area with mock-Gothic ceiling at the other. An extensive menu offers a three-course meal with coffee and wine for around £5. To be on the safe side however choose from the excellent selection on the more modestly priced set menu: there are only three starters but chicken provençale, Cumberland grill and deep-fried fillet of plaice served with lemon wedge, home-made tartare sauce and fried croquette potatoes are among the main dishes. Puddings such as the giant éclair filled with ice cream and topped with chocolate sauce and the apple, fruit or lemon meringue pies are all freshly made on the premises. Coffee may be taken in place of dessert at no extra charge; otherwise coffee and a glass of wine are additional, but still within our budget.

THE GALLERY, 24 Paddock Row (Chester 47202)
Open: Mon-Sat 12noon-2.30pm

[♫] [P] [S]

Owner Edward Jones has created a refreshingly-different eating place along the lines of a conservatory with earthy brown carpets and tree-green walls. A beautiful array of pot plants add to the atmosphere. Meals too are a little out of the ordinary. Soup of the day is laced with sherry and cream and main dishes include asparagus and cheese-filled crêpes and rainbow trout – pan fried with almonds and cream. Situated at one end of one of Chester's Rows in the centre of town it is also the ideal rendezvous for shoppers. Price is right here too – three-course lunch with coffee and wine will cost around £4.

PIERRE GRIFFE WINE BAR
4/6 Marcia Square (Chester 312635)
Open: Mon-Fri 12noon-2.30pm, 7-10.45pm, Sat 12noon-2.45pm, 5.30-10.45pm, Sun 12noon-2pm, 7-10.45pm

[P] [S]

Close to the Cathedral, this very popular wine bar has brown walls and carpeting which give emphasis to the attractive pine ceiling. A long bar counter has a good display of salads and meats. The menu is displayed on a blackboard and three courses can easily be savoured for around £3. Start with French onion soup at 60p, then try pork goulash with rice, Malayan chicken salad or minced beef curry – all at around £1.50. Cheesecake costs 50p, gâteaux 55p. A good choice of wines are available by the glass at 50p.

SIR EDWARD'S WINE BAR
30 Bridge Street (Chester 24921)
Open: Mon-Sat 12noon-2.30pm, 6.30-10.30pm (11pm Fri and Sat)

[C] [♫] [P] [S]

This cosy little wine bar enjoys an attractive situation on street level beneath one of Chester's famous 'Rows'. Inside, walls of open brick-work, 200-year-old wood panelling and dark paintwork are adorned with old books, posters and pots. Green gingham tablecloths and flickering candles contribute to the intimate atmosphere and enhance the simple décor. A good selection of starters include avocado, pâté and home-made soup (with fresh ingredients). Top of the price range is the smoked pork chop at around £2.55, and if this was chosen along with the top-priced main course of prime beef steak at about £3.50 with French fried potatoes and a side salad (priced separately) the total, with dessert and freshly percolated coffee (with cream) would well exceed the £5 budget. However a meal of corn-on-the-cob (hors d'oeuvres), gammon steak with peaches and side salad, gâteau and coffee would total only around £4. Service is at the customer's discretion. As one would expect from a wine bar, there is a comprehensive range of wines available with red, white or rosé house wine selling at about 60p per glass.

THE SWISS CELLAR
Lower Bridge Street (Chester 20841)
Open: Mon-Sun 12noon-10pm

[C] [♫] [P] [S]

Mr Keller owns this basement restaurant, and he has contrived to give it a Swiss flavour visually as well as gastronomically. You can spend as little or as much as you like here – from cheese on toast at about 65p to a steak at around £4 including vegetables. Particularly good value is the Chef's Special three-course lunch – perhaps soup, braised chicken with onions and mushrooms, and fruit trifle at around £3.50. The à la carte dinner menu is international but with some Swiss specialities such as entrecôte steak Zurich at around £4.20 and a choice of fondues. Dishes from other parts of Europe include Wiener schnitzel and escalope of veal Zingara at about £4.20. There is a table d'hôte menu for dinner, too, offering three good courses, with plenty of choice, for less than £5. The wine list ranges over Europe and house wine comes at around 75p a glass.

Cleveleys

SAVOY GRILL, 6 Bispham Road (Cleveleys 85 3864)
Open: summer: Sun-Mon 11.30am-7pm, Tue 11.30am-8.30pm, Wed-Sat 11.30am-10pm, winter: Tue-Fri 11.30am-7pm, Sat-Sun 11.30am-9pm

[P] [S]

A popular, corner-house restaurant near the seafront, the Savoy Grill is well-known for its friendly atmosphere and unpretentious food. Soups and pies are all home-made by proprietor Mrs Dorothy Richardson, and a set three-course meal including soup, steak and mushroom pie and ice cream can be had for the extremely modest price of £1.50. A special children's menu lists old favourites such as fish fingers, beefburgers or roast beef and ranges in price from 75p-£1, though apart from these budget meals, a full à la carte also operates. Wine costs 60p a glass.

Congleton

THE GINGERBREAD COFFEE SHOP
3 Duke Street (Congleton 71627)
Open: Mon-Tue 9.30am-4.30pm, Wed 9.30am-1.30pm, Thu-Sat 9.30am-4.30pm

[P] [S]

Twin sisters, Joanna Downs and Pamela Beardmore, run this quaint cream-and-brown painted restaurant. Many of the dishes, such as chicken casserole, savoury flan, pizza and pâté are around £1 and all are served with vegetables or salad. Starters, at around 35p, include grapefruit segments and soup of the day. A sweet such as home-made fruit pie with fresh cream or meringue glacé costs about 50p.

Freckleton

THE SHIP INN (Freckleton 632393)
Open: Quarter Deck Restaurant: Mon-Sun 12noon-2.30pm, 7-9.45pm, The Galley: Mon-Sun 12noon-2.30pm, Sat 8-10.15pm

[C] [♫] [P]

The Ship was built about ten years ago on the site of a hostelry of the same name which dated back to 1630. The interior is designed along the lines of a ship, with a 'Sharp End' bar and another called the Galley. In the latter you can get a help-yourself lunch called 'Scandhovee' for about £2.60, which is very popular locally. You can take an à la carte meal in the Quarter Deck Restaurant but it would be all too easy to top the £5 mark. The speciality is fish with even the salads weighted on the side of seafoods. The table d'hôte lunch is well within limits, three courses costing around £3.50 – melon, grilled pork chop and apple sauce with vegetables, followed by sherry trifle, is an example of what to expect. A glass of house wine is 45p.

Gisburn

COTTAGE CAFE, Main Street (Gisburn 441)
Open: Mon 12noon-2pm, Tue-Sun 11.30am-6pm

With its low-beamed ceilings and warmth of welcome from proprietors Mr and Mrs Farnworth, the Cottage Café lives up to the traditional charm suggested by its name. Home cooking – the steak and kidney pie and home-cooked ham are particularly good – is accompanied by chips and peas. A meal will cost well under £4, and a half bottle of wine around £1.50.

Hale

HALE WINE BAR
106-108 Ashley Road (061-928 2343)
Open: Mon-Thu 12noon-2pm, 7-10pm, Fri-Sat 12noon-2pm, 7-11pm

[P] [S] [🍷]

Two dress shops were transformed into this fashionable wine bar by enterprising owners, Nick Elliot and Tim Eaton. Victoriana is the theme of the two rooms which are on different levels. Downstairs, children may sample half portions at lunchtime. An excellent menu offers starters such as cheese and tuna pâté or quiche Lorraine for around £1, main courses for about £2 include lasagne, moussaka, tagiatelle and prawn salad. Puddings cost around 80p and Jamaican fudge cake, lemon soufflé cake or chocolate mousse are some of the choices. House wine is 60p a glass. Lunch here is a treat for the weary shopper or jaded office worker.

Hazel Grove

THE GEORGIAN HOUSE, 399-401 London Road, (061-483 5517)
Open: Mon-Sun 12noon-2.30pm, 6-11pm (Sun 5-11pm)

[P] [🍷]

You'll recognise the Georgian House by its attractive bow-windowed frontage and, as the name might suggest, here is a place where you can enjoy fine English cuisine. Go there for lunch and you'll find a special value treat awaits you in the form of a 6oz rump steak served with vegetables, tomato, cress and French fried or baked potato, roll and butter and choice of sweet for the amazing all-inclusive price of £2.30. Cheaper combinations include salmon with salad or French fries for £1.70 and half a roast chicken with vegetables and potatoes at £1.75. Certain dishes are available at half price for children. The evening menu offers a more extensive range of steaks, roasts and fish dishes at an average price of £5.30 for three courses including wine and coffee.

Kirkham

THE GEORGIAN RESTAURANT
Blackpool Road, Newton-with-Scales (Kirkham 685896)

Open: Tue-Fri 12noon-2.30pm, 7-10pm, Sat 12noon-10.30pm (closed between 2.30pm and 5pm in winter), Sun 12noon-7pm

[♬] [P] [♲]

Situated on the Preston-Blackpool road, this modernised yet unpretentious restaurant has a friendly, welcoming atmosphere. The menu for weekday lunches and all day Sunday is very reasonably priced and includes roast beef or pork with all the trimmings at around £2.25 and freshly-made prawn salad at about £2.50. Sweets from the trolley, such as banana boats or peach melba cost around 75p. The à la carte menu for lunch or dinner includes some quite expensive items.

Knutsford

SIR FREDERICK'S WINE BAR
44 King Street (Knutsford 53209)
Open: Tue-Sat 12noon-2.30pm, 6.30-10.30pm

[C] [♬] [P] [S]

You'll enjoy the relaxed and friendly atmosphere at this pleasant town centre wine bar. Décor is simple with rough-cast walls and arches decorated with posters and block board prints. A limited à la carte menu is accompanied by an ample wine list. A three-course meal here will cost around £4 with a choice of cold table and Continental salads or hot dishes such as gammon steak with peaches cost around £2.

Lancaster

OLD BRUSSELS, 53 Market Street (Lancaster 69177)
Open: Mon-Thu 8am-6pm, Fri-Sat 8am-10pm

[C] [♬] [P] [S] [♲]

Old Brussels is a family-owned and run restaurant serving good food, reasonably priced and nicely presented. The budget lunch (three-courses) starts at about £1.50, but it is possible to have a good, filling meal, or a roast lunch menu from around £2 with starter and sweet. The 'special' lunch includes steaks, duck or trout and ranges in price from £4-£6. Four house wines may be bought by the glass at about 45p.

SQUIRRELS, 92 Penny Street (Lancaster 62307)
Open: Mon-Sat 12noon-2pm, 6-10pm, Sun 7-10pm

[C] [P] [S]

The smart brown-and-cream exterior of this city-centre wine bar attracts hungry shoppers and wine buffs alike. Inside, the cavernous, cellar-like atmosphere has a pleasing effect and complements the good range of food. Main courses include chili con carne and Lancashire goulash at around £2.25, with filled baked potatoes, pâté, pies and salads as possible (and cheaper) alternatives. With home-made soup as your starter, and a slice of full-cream gâteau for sweet, you have a tasty and wholesome three course meal at under £5. House wine costs around 45p a glass.

Liverpool

CASA ITALIA, Temple Court, 40 Stanley Street (051-227 5774)
Open: Mon-Sat 12noon-10pm

[♬] [P] [S]

This bright, bustling pizzeria, surrounded by more sombre city buildings, instantly commands attention. The menu lists a dazzling selection of pizzas and pastas, averaging around £1.75. If the Italian hors d'oeuvres are sampled (around £2), plus one of the delicious sweets from the trolley, espresso coffee and a glass of wine, the meal will still cost much less than £5.

D'ANNA, Armour House, Lord Street (051-709 1177)
Open: Mon-Sat 11.30am-10.30pm

[C] [P] [S]

In the heart of 'Scouseland', close to the Mersey, you will find this small, unpretentious restaurant decorated in restful green with alcoves and dark oak tables. The bill of fare covers a broad spectrum, from omelettes at around £2 to fish dishes ranging from £2 for plaice to around £4.50 for Dover sole. Grills are similarly priced and cold buffets, including prawn salad, are around £2.50.

EVERYMAN BISTRO, Hope Street (051-708 0338)
Open: Mon 12noon-2pm, Tue-Fri 12noon-2pm, 6-11.30pm, Sat 6-11.30pm

[S]

This interesting bistro is situated in the basement of the Everyman Theatre in the centre of town. Blackboards display a menu based on fresh produce and it is easy to eat three courses here for around £2-£2.50. Home-made soup or quiche lorraine are two of the starters with dishes such as spicy Caribbean pork, broccoli cheese, salads and casseroles as main courses. There is a selection of home-made sweets, various cheeses and live yoghurts to finish with.

LA GRANDE BOUFFE, 48a Castle Street (051-236 3375)
Open: Mon 10am-3pm, Tue-Fri 10am-11pm, Sat 11am-3pm, 7-11pm

[P] [S]

La Grande Bouffe is a typical French-style basement café. French pictures adorn the walls. The menu is on a blackboard and dishes include home-made soup such as potato and watercress at about 45p, quiches for around 60p, beef sausage meat and spinach pie for less than £1 and Armenian lamb or rare roast beef for about £2. Cold dishes include fresh mackerel with salad at about £1.40. Desserts (50p-70p) are also home-made. It is a self-service operation – ideal for a quick, tasty meal. French house wine costs around 55p a glass. The à la carte evening meal is likely to be beyond our limit.

ST GEORGE'S HOTEL ★★★★ St John's Precinct, Lime Street (051-709 7090)
Open: Buttery: Mon-Sat 10am-10pm

[C] [P] [S]

The stylish modern Buttery of this sumptuous hotel serves a comprehensive range of food. For a quick snack, toasted sandwiches, hamburgers of all varieties, pizzas, ravioli and egg dishes are on the huge menu for around £1 to £3.50. There is also plenty of scope for a three-course meal within our budget. A choice of seven starters includes minestrone with Parmesan at about 50p. A good selection of fish and grills from about £2-£5 make a substantial main course. Sweets range in price from around 40p-80p.

ZODIAC COFFEE HOUSE, ADELPHI HOTEL ★★★★ Ranelagh Place (051-709 7200)
Open: Mon-Sat 12noon-10.30pm, Sun 12noon-10pm

[C] [P]

No fortunes told here, but your luck's in as far as having a good meal at a reasonable price is concerned. Set lunch costs from £3-£3.50 all in, with a choice of main dishes including salmon pancakes, omelette princesse or a selection of cold meats and salads from the buffet. The à la carte menu offers a standard range of dishes at slightly higher prices, but still within the limit. House wine is about 50p a glass.

Macclesfield

DA TOPO GIGIO, 15 Church Street (Macclesfield 22231)
Open: Tue-Sat 12noon-2pm, 7-10.30pm

[P] [S]

Half-way down the quaint, cobbled street of this old silk-manufacturing town is this informal restaurant, named after the famous Italian mouse. Fresh produce is put to good use in the thick minestrone soup – only 60p but almost a meal in itself – chicken carbonara or salmon cooked to choice, both under £2.50. Home-made sweets start at 50p, so a three-course lunch can cost as little as £3.25 here. Italian house wine costs around 55p a glass.

Manchester

THE CAFE, 3-5 Princess Street, Albert Square (061-834 2076)
Open: Mon-Sun 12noon-4am

[S]

Just the place for the late-nighter, this modern-fronted steak and burger restaurant is in the city centre. As well as the char-grilled steaks and pure beefburgers there is a good selection of 'Cafe Extras' such as poussin Continental – a baby chicken cooked in a rich wine sauce with a hint of garlic for around £3. For the vegetarian there are the veg-burger and the Cafe-casserole, both under £2. Sweets, including fresh cream Black Forest gâteau, rum baba, sorbets and cheesecakes range from 75p-85p. Wine is about 50p a glass.

DANISH FOOD CENTRE, Royal Exchange Buildings, Cross Street (061-832 9924)
Open: Copenhagen Restaurant: Mon-Sat 12noon-3pm, 6-12mdnt, Danmark Inn: Mon-Sat 10am-8pm

[S]

This popular Danish eaterie is situated in the city centre, within the Royal Exchange Buildings. A beautifully-decorated three-tier cold table provides the centrepiece of the main restaurant, though a help-yourself choice to as much as you like from the appetizing array of dishes offered here will pass the £5 mark a little. Of course, you can always plump for the nourishing open sandwich known as smørbrød. Snaps and a good wine list are available, although the Danish lagers are enthusiastically recommended!

FARMHOUSE KITCHEN
42 Blackfriars Street (cnr Deansgate) (061-832 7001)
Open: Mon-Sat 9am-7pm (8pm Thu)

[P] [S]

The Farmhouse Serve-yourself Kitchen attracts shoppers and businessmen to its convenient location on the fringe of the city centre. Hot and cold dishes are available at very reasonable prices and the excellent salad selection has proved particularly popular. Of the hot meals, the chicken in wine sauce is worth trying as are the fried haddock and cheese or quiche, all around £1.25. An extremely nourishing three-course meal with wine can be had for around £3.

KWOK MAN ✕✕ 28-32 Princess Street (061-228 2620)
Open: Mon-Sat 12noon-5am

[S]

Just the place for anyone suffering from night starvation! There are around one hundred authentic Cantonese dishes to choose from, some quite exotic such as shark's fin and chicken soup, Chung Yau chicken with spring onion and brandy sauce and fried crab claw, but if you're with a group, the set menus are recommended. With different selections for 2 to 5 people, they offer a good introduction to Chinese-style eating at a cost of £4-£5 per person.

Table d'hôte lunch is also reasonably priced, three courses with coffee can be had for around £2.

THE LANCASHIRE FOLD, Kirkway, Alkrington, Middleton (061-643 4198)
At the junction of Mount Road and Kirkway and not far from M62 junction 20
Open: during normal licensing hours
Restaurant: Tue-Fri, Sun 12noon-2pm, 7-10pm, Sat 7-10pm

[C] [P] [&]

For those who prefer to get away from the city centre, The Lancashire Fold may provide the answer. This modern extension to a pub has a brick-and-timber décor and comfortable furnishings. Although the à la carte menu is not cheap, it is possible to choose a three-course meal within the £5 limit. Choose chilled melon at around £1, suprême de poulet Maryland with additional vegetables at around £3.45, a sweet from the trolley or cheese at around 75p and you are left with just enough for a glass of wine. At lunchtime you can get a good table d'hôte meal for about £3.

THE LOOSE BOX, 34 Deansgate (061-834 4423)
Open: Mon-Thu 12noon-12mdnt, Fri-Sat 12noon-2am, Sun 6pm-12mdnt

[S]

This small, attractive restaurant in the centre of Manchester serves Brazilian (the nationality of proprietor Mr Shahvaee) and French food. The décor is reminiscent of South America, with its tiled floor, rough-cast walls and cane ceiling. There's plenty on the interesting menu that will break the bank, but a selection such as mushrooms Acapulco, bife alà Brasilia (beef and chili beans in fresh yoghurt) and coupe Copacabana will kéep you well within the budget.

MARKET RESTAURANT
30 Edge Street (061-834 3743)
Open: Tue-Sat 6.30-11pm

Energetic owners Su-Su Edgecombe and Elizabeth Price have breathed new life into an almost-dead part of the city with their delightful new restaurant. Pale primrose walls offset with dark green woodwork and simple stone flooring create a plain but pleasing effect, with a smattering of pictures, prints and bric-à-brac to add interest. Candles on the tables and lace curtains are the finishing touches. A starter such as chilled Lebanese cucumber soup made with yoghurt, cream and fresh mint costs around 75p, and could be followed by spinach and mushroom pancakes au gratin (£1.75). Finish with a sweet such as French gooseberry tart at around 75p and add a glass of house wine at 60p and you are well within the budget.

PIZZERIA BELLA NAPOLI
1 Kennedy Street (061-236 1537)
Open: Mon-Sat 12noon-11.30pm, Sun 6.30-11.30pm

[P] [S]

This friendly basement eating house has typical Italian-style décor, stuccoed walls and tiled floors. Being much smaller than the Pizzeria Italia, its sister restaurant across the city, tables can be hard to come by at peak periods. The slick young staff serve a variety of pastas and pizzas, such as cannelloni ripieni (pancakes filled with beef, eggs and spinach – £1.80) or pizza marinara (mozzarella cheese, anchovy, olives, tuna and prawns in tomato sauce – £2). Sweets run from 80p-£1, so you can easily afford to splash out on half a carafe of house wine.

PIZZERIA ITALIA, 40-42 Deansgate (061-834 1541)
Open: Mon-Sat 12noon-11.30pm, Sun 6.30-11.30pm

[P] [S]

A corner-sited pizza house on two floor-levels, Pizzeria Italia is decorated in the true Italian style with tiled floors and lusty pot plants. Low-priced dishes including soups, fish and chicken supplement the enormous and varied plate-sized pizzas, excellent value at under £2. Service is snappy, operated by well turned-out and efficient all-Italian staff. House wine is 65p a glass.

RAJDOOT RESTAURANT ✕✕
St James House, South King Street (061-834 2176/7092)
Open: Mon-Sat 12noon-2.30pm, 6.30-12mdnt, Sun 6.30-12mdnt

[C] [♫] [S] [&]

One step inside the door of the Rajdoot Indian restaurant is a step into a different world. Waiters in their national costumes wait to greet you – the atmosphere is sultry and authentic. An extremely wide and varied menu is available and the specialities of the house are the Tandoori murghi (£3.80). Tandoori fish and Makhan chicken at around £2.60 or lamb pasanda at a little less. A set meal of Tandoori murghi, shish kebab, nan, rogan josh, prawn masalla, rice, dessert and coffee is excellent value at around £5.

SAM'S CHOP HOUSE × Back Pool Fold, Chapel Walks (061-834 8717)
Open: Mon-Fri 12noon-3pm

If you enjoy a lunch in a place which oozes in friendly charm, Sam's Chop House is a must for you. Set in a back alley, below street level, the décor is plain and simple. Stone walls are adorned by large prints and hanging mock oil lamps enhance the cosy atmosphere. Mrs Morton, the motherly manageress, will welcome you as 'pet' or 'darling' while she or her equally-friendly waitresses serve you with good standard English fare: various steaks from between £4-£5, lamb cutlets and roast chicken garni at around £3-£4 are examples. Extra large portions of scampi or plaice are served for gluttons.

Morecambe

COFFEE SHOPPE, 35 Princes' Crescent, Bare (no telephone)
Open: summer: Mon-Sat 9.30am-5.30pm, Sun 10.30am-5.30pm, winter: Mon-Sat 9.30am-4.45pm

P

This typical, pleasant little tea shop is set in a row of shops, just off the sea front. Salads, home-cooked meat pies, cakes, pastries and sandwiches are available and very reasonable and tasty three-course meals can be had for less than or around £2. Try home-made soup, followed by cottage cheese and peach salad then finish with one of Heather Millen's luscious creamy cakes.

Oldham

MOTHER HUBBARD'S
270 Manchester Street
(061-652 0873)
Open: Mon-Sun 11.30am-11.30pm

C P

The cupboard is far from bare at this modern, detached fish restaurant. A variety of fresh fish, delivered daily from Grimsby, ensures that you're in for a piscine treat. A smart interior features spindled wooden divisions (to allow that little bit of privacy at tables) and a Georgian-style bar. The friendly waitresses serve a simple starter, plus main fish dish (scampi, halibut, haddock or plaice with all the trimmings, and a coffee) with ice-cream to finish at a cost of £1.50-£3.50 depending on your fish choice. A glass of Nicolas house wine is 50p.

Ormskirk

TOWER AND STEEPLE
15 Church Street (Ormskirk 72017)
Open: Tue, Wed, Fri 10am-2.30pm, 7-10.30pm, Thu 10am-4pm, 7-10.30pm, Sat 10am-4pm, 7-11pm, Sun 12noon-2.30pm

P S

Lunches are particularly tempting here, with ham and pineapple, grilled plaice and dish of the day all around £2. A three-course Sunday lunch offering a variety of roasts and desserts from the trolley can be had for just over £3. The dinner menu includes a host of seafood starters and a variety of steaks and grills.

Parbold

THE WIGGIN TREE, Parbold Hill (Parbold 2318/2593)
1 mile east of Parbold, 2 miles from junction 27 of the M6
Open: Mon-Sun 12noon-2.15pm, Mon-Fri 7-10pm, Sat 7-11pm, Sun 4.30-9pm

C P

Versatility is the keynote of this 18th-century, stone-built cottage restaurant. Whilst retaining its olde-worlde charm, with oak-beamed ceilings, stone fireplace and treadle sewing machine tables, it is nonetheless able to cope with a steady flow of hungry customers. Waitresses dressed as serving wenches will bring you the interesting menu, from which it is possible to choose a three-course meal for as little as £2.50. Try a starter of black pudding followed by fried whiting with a choice of vegetables or salad and potatoes and finish off with a home-made dessert or ice cream. A la carte eating is also possible if care is taken to keep within the budget and, at the other end of the scale, good bar meals are always available. Wine costs about 60p a glass.

Prestbury

PRESTBURY PLACE, New Road (Prestbury 828423)
Open: Wed-Sat 12noon-2pm, Tue-Sat 7.30-10pm

[P]

Built at the end of a row of 17th-century cottages, this 'home from home' is friendly, relaxed and informal with a simple green décor. The menu, chalked up on a blackboard, includes quiche seafood at around £1, Mexican beef casserole, Alabama chili or chicken on rice all around £2.25 and an excellent cheesecake at about 65p. Good quality wines are available by the glass.

Preston

ALEXANDERS, Winckley Street (Preston 54302)
Open: Mon-Fri 12noon-2.30pm, 7-10pm

[C] [P] [S] [&]

Originally a 19th-century coach house and stable, this elegant building is set in a courtyard in the centre of town. A sumptuous atmosphere is created inside with fawn and burgundy suede-look wall covering, dark-wood panels and 'picture' mirrors, and the whole effect is enhanced by subtle lighting from mock-Victorian wall lamps. A very good table d'hôte menu is available at prices around £2.50. Changed twice weekly, it offers superior main courses such as chicken Americaine and grilled gammon with mushrooms. An ambitious selection of dishes appear on the à la carte menu which is rather more expensive – but very tempting, the fillet of plaice at £3.50 being particularly good. There's a list of 18 wines to choose from, including some Italian house 'plonk' at around 55p a glass.

LA BODEGA, 21 Cannon Street (Preston 52159)
Open: Wine Bar: Mon-Thu 11am-3pm, 7-10.30pm, Fri-Sat 11am-3pm, 7-11pm, Sun 7-10.30pm, Bistro: Mon 11.30-2pm, Tue-Sat 11.30-2pm, 8-11pm, Sun 8-10.30pm

[P] [S]

Upturned barrels as tables, wine posters and gingham tablecloths exude a Continental air echoed in the names of dishes such as paella and chicken Basque style. Steak forms the basis of most dishes on the menu, try the Drunken Bull – sozzled in red wine and brandy for under £4. Lunchtimes are self-service.

THE DANISH KITCHEN, 10 Lune Street (Preston 22086)
Open: Danish Kitchen: Mon-Sat 9.15am-5.15pm, Steak Kitchen: Mon-Sat 12noon-3pm, 6-11pm

[P] [S]

Bright and refreshing, this town centre Danish Kitchen is gaining in popularity with businessmen and shoppers, with its choice of eating styles. Upstairs is the budget self-service operation where Danish open sandwiches, salads, omelettes and pizzas are available, together with delicious pastries and gâteaux. Downstairs is the new Steak Kitchen, where you choose your own steak from a refrigerated display, then see it cooked over charcoal while waitresses serve you with a starter and a glass of wine (around 50p). Pine tables and beams accentuate the fresh, Continental atmosphere.

FRENCH BISTRO ✕ Miller Arcade, Church Street (Preston 53882)
Open: Mon-Sun 12noon-2.15pm, 7pm-12.15am

[C] [♫] [P] [S]

Colourful posters and French wall prints adorn the walls of this candle-lit bistro. Octopus, snails and oysters feature on the impressive list of starters, with main courses ranging from a Frenchman's break (under £1) or quiche lorraine (at around £1.50) to delicious steak salad or pot pourri (chili, pork, beef and chicken served with rice) – under £3. The evening menu is even more tempting, with prawns normande, boeuf bourguignon, chili con carne and many other flavoursome alternatives. A bar downstairs offers over 1000 different drinks.

THE PATIO, TRAFALGAR HOTEL ☆☆☆ Preston New Road, Samlesbury (Samlesbury 351)

On A59 east of Preston at junction with Blackburn road
Open: Mon-Sun 7am-2.30am

[C] [P] [&]

The nostalgic French design of the menu, the costumed waitresses, and the opportunity to eat into the early hours sets the scene. Tiled floors and glass-topped tables, potted plants and a fountain make a refreshing environment. Variety is the order of the day: the French connection is continued with a small selection of sweet and savoury pancakes (for around £2), over the borders to Italy for a choice of pizzas, and further afield for chicken Kashmir shish kebab or American burgers. The home front is not forgotten, with Lancashire hot pot or fisherman's pie (at about £2) and grills. An added bonus is the invitation to help yourself to the free salad while you wait. At lunchtime the carvery choice features a roast, salads and Danish-style open sandwiches.

THE TICKLED TROUT ☆☆☆
(Samlesbury 671)
Open: Kingfisher Restaurant: Mon-Sun 12noon-2.15pm, 7-10.15pm

[C] [P] [&]

The oak-beamed Kingfisher Restaurant with its alcoves, antiques and views of the River Ribble offers a table d'hôte, three-course lunch for around £4.10, consisting of (for example) salad niçoise followed by grilled gammon and peach with a selection of vegetables and potatoes, and a slice of fresh cream gâteau. A price reduction is made for children under ten years. The à la carte menu is beyond our means.

WELCOME INN, Hennel Lane, Lostock Hall (Preston 38569)
2½ miles from junction 29 on the M6
Open: Sun-Fri 12noon-1.45pm, 7-9.45pm, Sat 7-10pm

[P]

Situated on the fringe of Preston, this modern public house boasts an attractive bistro where service is attentive and friendly. Here you will find such delights as chicken in the pot (with beer, mushrooms and shallots) and home-made steak, kidney and mushroom pie, with a good selection of home-made sweets to complement. Numerous different liqueur coffees offered make a satisfying end to your meal.

Rochdale

ALPINE AYINGERBRAU GASTHOF
Whitworth Road (Rochdale 48953)
Open: Mon-Thu 12noon-2pm, 7-10pm, Fri 12noon-2pm, 7-10.30pm, Sat 7-11pm

[C] [♫] [P] [♿]

A taste of Bavaria in the heart of Rochdale – that's the Alpine Ayingerbrau Gasthof. Even the outside of the restaurant has been modelled on its popular namesake at the foot of the Bavarian Alps. Inside, the warm glow of pine weaves a subtle spell, conducive to good eating. The à la carte menu can be pricey, but you'll be well within the budget if you stick to one of the specialities such as Fisch mit Sauerkraut (baked fish with herbs, served on a bed of sauerkraut) at about £2.60 or Jager schnitzel (pork steak in a red wine and mushroom sauce) at around £3.60 and choose the accompanying courses with care. Home-made sweets from the trolley are specially recommended. For lunch, hot or cold buffet is good value at about £3.

MARIO'S PIZZERIA
115 Yorkshire Street (Rochdale 46286)
Open: Mon-Sat 12noon-2.30pm, 6-11.30pm

Mario Andreotti and his English wife make their cellar pizzeria a warm welcoming haven for the hungry. Gingham tablecloths, padded benches and plain white rough-cast walls help to give the place a simple charm which compensates for the fairly predictable menu of pizzas and pastas. Even the most expensive dish – a sirloin steak cooked in Chianti – is still likely to be around £4. A whole three-course meal with a glass of wine will cost little more if you stick to the modest Italian fare.

THE SIR WINSTON CHURCHILL
Bury Old Road (Heywood 60530)
Open: Mon-Sun 12.30-2.30pm, 7-10pm

[P] [S] [♿]

The grill room of this modern public house is attractively furnished and an array of pot plants adds an agreeable freshness to the décor. There are a few items on the menu which exceed the budget, but you could get, say, soup, pork chop or grilled trout with potatoes and another vegetable, sweet, coffee and a glass of house wine for around £5.

YEW TREE INN, Thornham (Rochdale 49742)
Open: Pullman Diner: Mon-Fri 12noon-2pm, 7-10.30pm, Sun 7-9.30pm, Bar: Sun-Fri 12noon-2pm, 7-10pm, Sat 12noon-2pm

[C] [P]

Although you may never have been near Rochdale in your life it is quite possible you've dined in the restaurant of the Yew Tree before. The Pullman coach which adjoins the inn travelled 1 250 000 miles between 1951 and 1968 and at various times was in service on 'Tyne Tees Pullman', 'Master Cutler', 'Queen of Scots' and 'Bournemouth Belle', and has the great honour of having been pulled by that famous locomotive 'Mallard'. Now restored to its former glory, the Pullman Diner can be entered directly from the bar of this typical black-and-white Lancashire Inn. Here seafood pancake costs around £1 and melon and ginger about 80p. Main course prices include vegetables, only a few items exceeding £5. Scampi mornay and êntrecote chasseur are just under £5. A sweet is in the region of 70p and a glass of wine about 50p. Alternatively there is a bar buffet if you only want a snack. In the cellars there's a ghostly horse whose hoofs can be heard clop-clopping on the flags.

St Michaels-on-Wyre

THE CHERRY TREE GRILL
Garstang Road (St Michaels 661)
Open: Mon-Thu, Sat 10.30-11.45am, 12noon-2pm, 5-8pm, Sun 10.30-11.45am, 12noon-2pm, 3-7pm

[P]

This stone-built end-of-terrace house was once the village smithy and is now a small but pleasant grill restaurant. The three-course lunch is all-inclusive for the price of the main course varying between £3-£3.50. A more extensive à la carte menu is available for high tea with sirloin steak or scampi at around £4. To finish there is a tempting array of desserts – how about raspberry Pavlova or orange chocolate sundae?

Southport

PIZZERIA-RISTORANTE PARADISO
120 Lord Street (Southport 40259)
Open: Mon-Sat 12noon-3pm, 5.30-11pm, Sun 12noon-2pm, 5.30-11pm

[S] [&]

With main courses ranging from pizza margherita at just over £1 and spaghetti bolognese at around £1.75 to beef Stroganoff at just under £4 you can be sure of a good meal within our price range. There are six starters priced between 50p and £1.25 and a sweet from the trolley costs about 60p. A glass of house wine is priced at around 60p. The décor is pleasantly simple with white walls decorated with photographs.

VESUVIO, 329 Lord Street
(Southport 42275)
Open: Tue-Sun 12noon-3pm, 6.30-11pm

[C] [P]

Set in a small alleyway leading off Lord Street, this diminutive, attractive restaurant offers a whole range of dishes, from pizzas and pastas to scampi provençale. Venetian pictures and bric-à-brac are complemented by cream and brown walls and Chianti bottles. Particularly tempting is a three-course menu, available at lunchtime and in the evening, for only £2.50. A choice of six starters includes mussel cocktail, pâté maison and minestrone soup. Main dishes offer a choice of English or Italian – plaice, chicken, pork chop or trout for patriots or lasagne, spaghetti bolognese or cannelloni for those with a more exotic palate. Desserts are apple pie, crème caramel or ice cream. House wine comes at 50p a glass.

Stockport

GEORGIAN HOUSE
59-61 Buxton Road (061-480 5982)
Open: Mon-Sat 12noon-2.30pm, 6-11pm, Sun 5-11pm

[P] [&]

The bow-windowed Georgian House restaurant on the A6 doesn't go in for frills but you can get good, reasonably-priced meals there, with half-price portions of certain dishes for children. The special two-course lunch is particularly good value. A half roast chicken, garnished, served with vegetables, roll and butter and a choice of sweet costs about £1.75; replace the chicken by a 7oz rump steak and the price goes up to a moderate £2.30. The à la carte menu, too, is modestly priced, starters costing between 35p for soup and £1.40 for smoked trout. The price quoted for main course includes vegetables, roll and butter and a sweet or cheese and biscuits. Only lobster salad at around £6 is beyond reach and the Georgian specialities are all near the £4 mark. A glass of wine costs about 60p.

THE WISHING WELL, 26a Bramhall Lane South, Bramhall (061-440 8970)
Open: Tue-Thu 12noon-2pm, 6.30-10pm, Fri-Sun 12noon-2pm, 7-10.45pm

[C] [P] [S]

This rather special Yugoslavian restaurant is in an unlikely location above a greengrocery in one of Manchester's desirable residential suburbs. Vlado Barulovic, the proprietor, features some of his country's mouth-watering dishes in the superb value set lunch which will only set you back around £3 – and coffee's included. Try Podverak ad Curetine (sauerkraut and onions with roast turkey) or Bosanki Lonac (beef and pork with vegetables in wine). The evening à la carte will call upon a strong will if you are going to spend under £6, and has more emphasis on international meat and fish dishes. Mr Barulovic, will, however, prepare a Yugoslavian speciality to order.

West Kirby

WHAT'S COOKING?
34 Banks Road (051-625 7579)
Open: Mon-Sat 12noon-11.30pm, Sun 1-11.30pm

[C] [♬] [S]

The bright cream and green exterior of this first-floor restaurant is just as inviting as its name. Ideal for the shopper, What's Cooking? is located close to the town centre and specialises in American-style cuisine. The premises have recently been enlarged to cut down the huge queue that is always outside! Menu selections include beefburgers with a choice of toppings plus home-made dressing, pizzas, steaks and chicken or 'mouth-watering, mammoth salads'. Chili con carne (just under £2) or spare ribs (around £2.20) are interesting alternatives. A full three-course meal with a glass of wine will cost about £4.

Wigan

ROBERTO'S, Rowbottom Square (Wigan 42385)
Open: Restaurant: Mon-Sat 11.30am-2pm, 7-10pm. Pizza Bar: Mon-Sat 11.30am-2pm

[C] [♬] [🍷]

Nestling in what were once the cellars of the local newspaper, this pine-tabled restaurant, with its pot plants and pictures, offers pastas, pizzas and inexpensive 'English' meals of the chicken or plaice and chips variety in a pizza bar next door, and an excellent table d'hôte menu in the restaurant. A three-course lunch, such as egg mayonnaise, cannelloni and sherry trifle works out at only £2.30. A glass of the Italian house wine costs 60p.

Wilmslow

GREYHOUND STEAKHOUSE
Wilmslow Road, Handforth (Wilmslow 23193)
Open: Mon-Sat 12noon-2.30pm, 6-11.30pm, Sun 12noon-2.30pm, 7-11pm

[C] [♬] [P] [S] [🍷]

This Schooner Inn steakhouse, about ten miles south of Manchester features natural stone combined with timbers from Fleetwood pier. For starter you can have soup (about 50p) or prawn cocktail (around £1) and main courses (the price includes an ice cream sweet or cheese) vary from fillet of plaice with lemon, tartare sauce, peas and jacket potato or chips at the £3 mark to a mixed grill (steak, gammon, lamb, sausage and kidney with tomato, peas, jacket potato or chips) at about £5. House wine will set you back around 50p a glass. Lunchtime snacks such as shepherd's pie or filled rolls are available at the bar.

RUMPLESTILTSKINS
2d Hawthorn Lane (Wilmslow 532472)
Open: Mon-Sat 12noon-2.30pm, 7-11pm

[C] [S] [🍷]

The impish spirit of Rumplestiltskin presides over this small but colourful restaurant. High-backed bench seating creates a feeling of privacy in a room filled with hay-rakes, yokes and other agricultural paraphernalia and hung with saleable paintings. The £4.65 set lunch could consist of egg mayonnaise, roast chicken and bacon with vegetables and potatoes of the day, followed by lemon soufflé and coffee, though other choices are available. The à la carte menu is very tempting with dishes such as beef Wellington and scampi Africainne *willing* you to break the budget. A glass of red or white house wine costs 45p a glass.

Yorkshire and Humberside

The picture of a cold, unyielding North – all mills and mines – is beginning to fade as more and more people recognise Yorkshire as an area of outstanding natural beauty. The one-time largest county in England, now re-shaped and adjoined by Humberside, covers over 4 000 000 acres of unspoilt moorland which centuries ago inspired writers such as Charles Dickens and the Brontë sisters. Their words, vibrating with a barren atmosphere and evoking the harsh, cruel world of Wuthering Heights, have left an enduring impression. Yet in reality, there is rather a different face to Yorkshire – full of warmth and breathtaking scenery.

In early days, the remoteness of

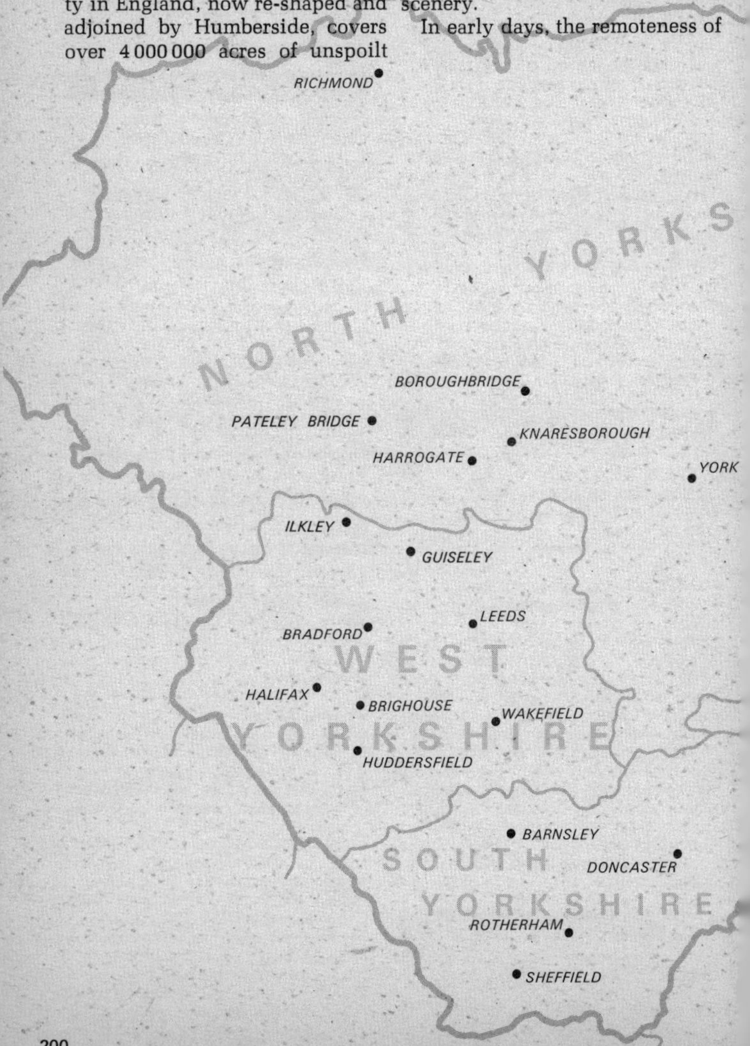

this region meant that most families had to rely upon their own resources. They kept hardy mountain sheep and fine pigs (notably a breed known as the Large White), baked their own bread, made their own cheese and filled in the gaps with pies of all descriptions and plenty of oatcakes – a mixture of fermented oatmeal and milk, which in the 19th century were exported from Yorkshire to London.

Nowadays, Yorkshire is famous for many tasty foods. Fine, smoked York hams, from the well-built legs of the Large White, are famous throughout Britain, while the mild, crumbly Wensleydale cheese is ever popular and usually eaten with apple pie. As every self-respecting Yorkshireman knows: 'An apple pie without cheese is like a kiss without a squeeze.'

No list of Yorkshire delicacies would be complete without a mention of the county's most renowned dish – Yorkshire Pudding. Originally introduced to act as a kind of edible sponge to catch the juices from roasting meat, it is now a traditional part of Sunday lunches throughout the country, though in the North it is often served on its own, as a starter.

Savoury dishes aside, the Yorkshire region yields rich Harrogate toffee, toasted teacakes, many local gingerbreads and dozens of variations on the theme of parkin – a traditional snack for Guy Fawkes night, made from butter, sugar, treacle, flour, eggs and ginger. Bilberry pie is another firm favourite. A browse through the following pages will equip you with all the necessary information needed to seek out your Northern favourites.

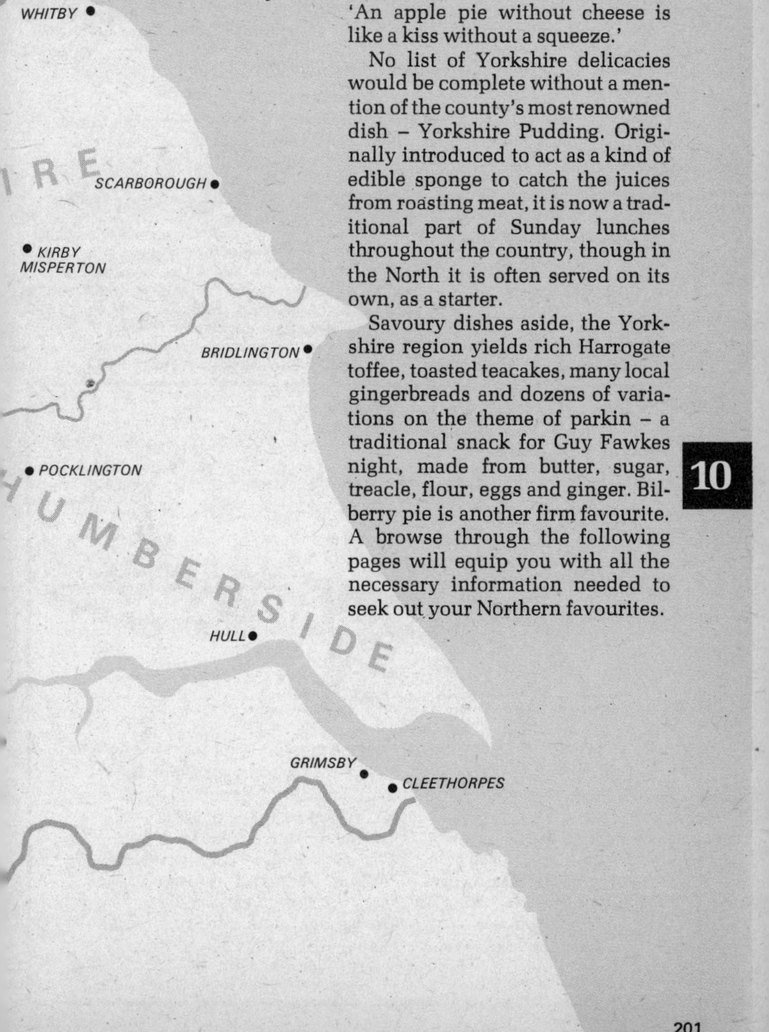

Barnsley

BROOKLANDS RESTAURANT
Barnsley Road, Dodworth
(Barnsley 84238/6364)
Open: Mon-Sun 12noon-2.30pm, 6.30-9.30pm

[P]

Within 500 yards of the M1 is this single storey building housing three dining rooms, each featuring splendid displays of fresh fruit and wines. Over 400 wines are on offer, some by the glass at around 35p. Meals are exceptionally good value, a three-course lunch costing about £3.20. The choice is excellent and imaginative (try chicken poche à la crème – chopped, poached chicken with mushrooms in a cream sauce). Chef's special dishes are also included, such as moussaka or roast pork. You are also invited to ask for more – 'and it shall be freely given'!

QUEEN'S HOTEL ★★ Regent Street
(Barnsley 84192)
Open: Mon-Sat 12noon-2.30pm, 6.30-9.30pm; Sun 12noon-2pm, 7-9pm

[C] [S]

An imposing Victorian three-storey building, conveniently close to the railway station and town centre, houses this cheerful split-level restaurant where décor is in the best tradition of Victorian design. Main courses in the Carvery and Buffet are around £2 and £1.50 respectively. Starters are from 50p upwards and desserts cost about 70p. There is also a selection of snacks, 'quickies' and 'fillers' – sandwiches, salads and savoury pancakes.

Boroughbridge

THREE ARROWS ★★★ Horsefair
(Boroughbridge 2245)
Open: Mon-Sun 12.30-2pm, 7.30-9.30pm

[C] [♫] [P]

This restaurant has a long, tree-lined entrance through lawns and gardens. Elegant though it is, the place is not ruinously expensive. Table d'hôte lunch and dinner for around £4 and around £5 respectively, offer three courses of honest-to-goodness English fare, with a selection of vegetables, though the à la carte can work out too dear unless you drop one course. Beef Strogonoff and duckling with cherry or orange sauce are two of the less expensive choices. A large glass of French house wine is around 50p.

Dancing is available at weekends.

Bradford

THE VINTAGE, 18-22 Hall Ings
(Bradford 27463)
Open: Mon-Sun 11.30am-2.30pm, 5.30-11.30pm

[C] [P] [S] [&]

This steak house in the city centre, with its warm and pleasing décor in red and gold, is designed in Victorian style. There are two rooms, each with arched 'cellar' ceilings and a smart bar with comfortable seating and 18th-century pictures. Mainly grills, steak, chops and chicken dishes are served with salad and vegetables and it is not difficult to stay within £5, particularly with the special lunch menu which is likely to cost less than £4 with VAT included.

Bridlington

CLEO'S, Prince Street
(Bridlington 75661)
Open: summer Mon-Sun 12noon-11.30pm, winter Mon-Wed 12noon-3pm, Fri-Sat 12noon-11.30pm, Sun 12noon-6pm

[P] [&]

This bright and attractive restaurant, with a décor predominantly red, prides itself on being able to suit all tastes by serving pizzas, salads and burgers plus a variety of snack-type 'specials' alongside a more formal à la carte selection. Traditional dishes such as home-made steak and kidney pie are on hand for the less adventurous, children are catered for with sausages, beefburgers or fish-fingers and chips, while other dishes are aimed modestly at the 'gourmet' (try the chef's own beef Stroganoff). A delicious selection of home-made sweets and ices are available, with liqueur coffee to follow.

THE OLD FORGE, Main Street, Sewerby (Bridlington 74535)
Open: Mon-Sat 10.30am-5pm, 7.30-10pm (Fri–Jul & Aug only), Sun 10.30am-5pm (evening by appointment)

[♫] [P] [&]

One of a double row of stone-built fishermen's cottages of some age and interest, modernised and converted from its more recent use as a blacksmith's forge, the Old Forge is a convenient eating place for visitors to Sewerby Hall with its gardens, museum and zoo. With children's portions at about half the price of the regular meal, this is a particularly attractive restaurant for the whole family. Service is efficient and a good selection of English fare is offered, locally-caught fish being a speciality with fried haddock around £1.80.

Brighouse

BLACK BULL HOTEL, Thornton Square
(Brighouse 714816)
Open: Mon-Sat 12noon-2pm

[P] [S]

The homely restaurant of the Black Bull Hotel with its rose-patterned wallpaper is an ideal place for shoppers and motorists who enjoy a traditional English lunch. With a choice of starters and good basic sweets, a 'roast beef and Yorkshire' meal complete with coffee and a glass of wine will cost about £3.50. Grills are more expensive, but fillet steak garni, accompanied by a starter and a sweet will still be within budget.

Cleethorpes

CAVALIER STEAK BAR, THE LIFEBOAT HOTEL
Promenade, Kingsway
(Cleethorpes 67272)
Open: Mon-Fri, Sun 12noon-2pm, 6.30-10.15pm, Sat 6.30-10.15pm

[C] [P] [S]

The Lifeboat Hotel overlooks the North Sea, so the lounge bar, where you can sip an aperitif, has a nautical theme. The restaurant, with contrasting white chipboard décor and dark wooden cubicles under a beamed ceiling, also has nautical pictures and fittings. A special lunch menu operates from Mondays to Fridays – you can enjoy soup, steak and kidney or roast chicken, apple pie, coffee and a glass of wine for just over £3. Typical choices on the à la carte menu are pâté (80p), lemon sole (£3.15) and gâteau (70p). A glass of French house wine is 45p.

Doncaster

BACCHUS, 44 Hallgate
(Doncaster 20232)
Open: Mon-Sat 12noon-3pm, 6pm-12mdnt, Sun 7.30-12mdnt

[C] [♫] [S] [&]

It's tempting to believe that Bacchus, the god of wine, also knew a thing or two about the importance of good quality food – his disciples certainly believed they inherited the powers inherent in what they ate. If you're feeling adventurous you might like to try some escargots (snails) for a starter and spicy kebabs served on a bed of rice with pitta bread, yoghurt and fresh green salad sounds like a mouth-watering main course. Evenings are table service only, when the bill can nudge the £5 limit if you're not careful, but you queue at a self-service counter for lunch, choosing from a menu chalked on a blackboard offering a stew of the day for about £1.80, and other English dishes ranging from £1.50 to £2.60. The wine list is extensive and reasonably priced (including four house wines at 55p a glass) – and there's even live music for good measure. From Monday to Saturday, drinks are cheaper during 'Happy Hour' – 6-7pm.

THE EQUESTRIAN WINE BAR
High Street, Bawtry (Doncaster 711057)
Open: Mon-Sat 11am-3pm, 6-11.30pm, Sun 6-11.30pm

[C] [♫] [P] [S] [♧]

No, you can't take your horse inside this two-storey wine bar overlooking the old market place, but there are murals of racing and showjumping scenes to justify the name. On the ground floor the main room serves bar meals for lunchtime and evening. Home-made minestrone soup is hot favourite here and, along with lasagne, spaghetti or quiche at around £2 per portion, appears chalked on a blackboard menu behind the bar. The first-floor restaurant is open evenings only with waitress service, offering a more varied menu, also with an Italian bias. A typical meal might be melon (£1), spaghetti bolognese (£2.20) and a scrumptious gâteau from the trolley. House wine is Italian too, and costs 50p per glass.

INDUS ✕ 24 Silver Street
(Doncaster 23366)
Open: Mon-Sat 12noon-2.30pm, 7pm-12.30am, Sun 7-12mdnt

[C] [♫] [S] [♧]

This is a town-centre Indian restaurant providing an eastern atmosphere with a good variety of dishes from the sub-continent, ranging from very mild dishes such as chicken kurma or murgh masallam to the very hot vindaloo, or the more subtly spiced chooza masala and the Indus special tandoori chicken, with prices from about £2 to £3 inclusive of accompanying sauces and rice. English grills are also available. Eastern fruits such as lychees are served and there are ice creams to be had including kulfi (Indian ice cream with nuts) at around £1. Coffee with cream and a glass of house wine add a little under £1 to the bill.

REGENT HOTEL RESTAURANT
Regent Square (Doncaster 64336)
Open: Mon-Sat 12noon-2pm, 6-10pm, Sun 12noon-2.30pm, 7-9.30pm

[P] [S] [♧]

At the edge of Doncaster's main shopping area, this restaurant serves, in the words of our inspector, 'good, substantial, no-nonsense' meals matched by low prices. Sunday lunch (roasts or trout) table d'hôte is about £4, the weekday three-course business lunch (various home-made pies, chicken or plaice), about £2. In the evenings, an à la carte menu only is available, with three courses priced by the main dish. Apart from fillet steak, all these are within our budget – from plaice and tartare sauce at £3 to sirloin steak at £5. Starters include home-made pâté or ravioli and a choice of various ice creams or Chef's Special sweet of the day concludes the meal. A glass of Spanish house wine costs 50p.

TOTO'S PIZZA RESTAURANT,
36-38 East Laithgate
(Doncaster 63712/63801)
Open: Mon-Sat 12noon-2.15pm, Mon-Thu 6-11.30pm, Fri-Sat 6–12mdnt

[C] [P] [S] [♧]

If you're doing a day's shopping in the town, where better to break for lunch than this centrally situated (near the famous market) Italian restaurant. You'll recognise it by the brightly decorated picture windows, and the inside furnishings of glass-topped tables, stainless-steel chairs, and the splendid deep blue, green and red colour scheme. Specialities of the day are chalked up on a blackboard, and these can include trout meunière (around £2.90) and suprême de volialle at around £3.10, including vegetables. The menu lists seven pasta dishes – lasagne, ravioli, cannelloni and spaghetti – and ten different kinds of pizza ranging in price from about £1.50-£2. Sweets are priced from about 85p and there's a good selection of wines available.

VINTAGE STEAK BAR,
Cleveland Street (Doncaster 64786)
Open: Mon-Sun 11.30am-2.30pm, 5.30-11.30pm

[S]

A Victorian flavour here, with red furnishings and mellow wooden chairs and tables. The varied menu offers fourteen starters from about 40p, including smoked trout, iced melon and fried scampi, with a selection of fish, omelettes, grills and salads to follow. Each main course dish, such as steak, duck, chicken, lamb and pork, is served with French fried potatoes, tomato and garden peas and costs from £3.50 for lamb to £5 for steak. A sweet or cheese and biscuits may be chased down by a potent liqueur coffee in the restaurant or bar-lounge, and there's a separate room available for private parties and receptions. The central position of the Vintage Steak Bar is another plus.

Grimsby

THE LANTERN BISTRO
Freeman Street
(Grimsby 56480)
Open: Mon-Sat 11.30am-1.30pm, Tue-Sat 7-10.30pm

[♫] [P] [S]

Cheerful French music greets visitors to this rustic bistro, which has captured the flavour of France in its décor of plain wooden tables and colourful posters, adverts and pictures of Paris. It's a great find on one of Grimsby's busiest shopping streets, close to the indoor market. Lunchtime dishes, chalked up on two blackboards, include starters such as salami and prawn salad at 50p and main courses such as roast pork and apple sauce or moussaka, both around £1.50 and served with vegetables and croquette or new potatoes. Fresh cream desserts add the finishing touch, and French house wine is a bargain at around 50p a glass.

Guiseley

HARRY RAMSDEN'S, White Cross
(Guiseley 74641)
Open: Mon-Sun 11.30am-11.30pm

[P]

Claiming to be 'the most famous fish and chip restaurant in the world', this biggish restaurant has changed hands many times since one Harry Ramsden first opened up over sixty years ago. Outside the mainly brick building, several benches are interspersed along a verandah for 'eating out'. Inside, the smartly-dressed waitresses scurry between the many pot plants with high efficiency. After a soup or fruit juice starter, you can choose from any one of nine main fish dishes, all at under £3 and including chips, bread and butter and a drink (children's portions are about £1). If you're not already full up, a strawberry sundae or choc'n'nut dessert will soon put that right!

Halifax

DA CAMILLO, Southgate
(Halifax 54573)
Open: Mon-Sat 12noon-2pm, 7-11pm

[S]

Conveniently sited over a central pedestrian precinct in a busy shopping area is this second-floor pizzeria. The simple décor is predominantly deep brown with cork and plaster walls. Red linen tablecloths add a splash of colour. Business lunch and the fixed evening menu consist of tasty Italian dishes – cannelloni, lasagne, spaghetti bolognese, plus a selection of salad all in the £2 range – including a starter. Coffee is extra and a sweet can be had for under 30p, bringing the total with wine to around £3. Sirloin and fillet steak served with mushrooms, peas and jacket potato or salad are also available but will add another £2 on to your bill.

Harrogate

APOLLO RESTAURANT, 34 Oxford Street (Harrogate 504475)
Open: Tue-Sat 12noon-2.30pm, 6-11pm

[♫] [P] [S]

Apollo is a first-floor city centre restaurant, situated close to the multi-storey car park. The classical décor of Ionic pillars is reminiscent of the Parthenon and the atmosphere is enhanced by the Greek music in the background. Dishes offered are international, with a Greek bias, but most of those appearing on the à la carte menu are too expensive for a meal around £5. However, a three-course lunch with home-made soup of the day, a main course of fish, grill, chicken, a Greek special or salad, and home-made fruit pie or Greek sweet, coffee and wine can be had for around £4. Seating is mostly in curtained cubicles.

BETTY'S, 1 Parliament Street
(Harrogate 64659)
Open: Restaurant: Mon-Sat 11.45am-2pm. Tea-room: Mon-Sat 9.30am-5.30pm

[P] [S]

There are two eating places in Betty's – a tea-room where tea and cakes or more substantial grills and salads can be had throughout the day, and a lunchtime restaurant offering an excellent three-course lunch such as selected hors d'oeuvres, roast chicken, savoury stuffing and vegetables and Yorkshire curd tart with double cream for around

£3.50. Tasty home-made cakes and pastries are also sold in the confectionery department at the entrance. Betty's enjoys a fine view across the Montpelier Gardens.

THE EMPRESS, Church Square (Harrogate 67629)
Open: Mon-Fri 12noon-2.30pm, 7-10.30pm, Sat 7-10.30pm, Sun 12noon-1.30pm

In a stone building on the edge of town, with rich gold, turquoise and purple Regency décor and tasteful fittings, the restaurant is on the first floor, above the ground-floor lounge bar. A three-course businessperson's lunch including a choice of varying hot dishes or cold meat salad, served with potatoes and two veg is particularly good value at around £2.70 and even the extensive à la carte comes easily within our limit except in the case of a few speciality dishes. Children are also well catered for with a specially-designed menu complete with children's puzzles which they can take away as a souvenir.

OPEN ARMS, 3 Royal Parade (Harrogate 503034)
Open: Tue-Sun 12noon-2pm, Tue-Fri 6pm-10pm, Sat 5.30-10pm

S

True to its name, this town-centre restaurant offers a warm welcome with a glowing red décor, oak-clad walls and a menu designed to tempt the family. Meals are reasonably priced with emphasis on traditional fare – omelettes, roasts, grilled meat and fish dishes. A three-course children's lunch consisting of a couple of roasts or haddock – costs around £1.95, and the house specialities including beef steak pie, made with golden short-crust pastry and served with vegetables of the day are good value at around £1.90.

TUDOR RESTAURANT, 3 Ripon Road (Harrogate 68701)
Open: Mon-Sat 12noon-2pm, 6-11pm

P S

This old, gracious, stone-built Victorian house boasts a comfortable oak-panelled bar and restaurant. Close to the exhibition and conference centre, it is ideal for business lunches, which for around £4, consist of three-courses with an excellent choice of main dishes: home-made steak and kidney pie, chicken à la king, prawn or crab salad, braised oxtail and deep fried chicken with pineapple. Apart from ice cream or cheese and biscuits there is a tempting choice of sweets from the trolley. The à la carte menu prices dinner out of this guide. Wine by the glass is about 45p.

VANI'S, 15 Parliament Street (Harrogate 501313)
Open: Mon-Sat 12noon-2pm, 6-11.30pm, Sun 6-11.30pm

C S

This Italian restaurant has a casual, easy atmosphere guaranteed to soothe the most jaded shopper. The décor is imaginative, with cast-iron tables with round Italian marble tops, wicker-seated bentwood chairs and a basically red background. Starters include home-made soup and pâté and various seafood appetisers, most of which cost around £1.20. The list of pastas and pizzas is impressive and they mainly cost around £1.50. There is a good selection of home-made sweets from the trolley. Three courses will cost you about £4 and wine may be bought in half carafes for around £1.70.

Huddersfield

PIZZERIA SOLE MIO, Units 3 and 4, Imperial Arcade, Market Street (Huddersfield 42828)
Open: Tue-Fri 12noon-2.30pm, 5-11.30pm, Sat 12noon-11.30pm, Sun 5.30-11pm

S

Here you will discover Italy in the heart of Huddersfield, in a shopping arcade. Outside it has a terrazza and canopy blinds, inside roughcast walls, open brickwork, ceramic tile-topped tables and high-backed ladder chairs emphasise the Italian atmosphere. There is an extensive menu of home-made pastas including lasagne and cannelloni at around £1.50. The formidable list of pizzas range in price from under £1.25 to £1.75. Imaginative starters, including snails, are available and wine by the glass or carafe.

Hull

PECAN PIZZERIA, 32 Silver Street (Hull 226651)
Open: Mon-Tue 12noon-2.30pm, 6-11pm, Fri-Sat 12noon-2.30pm, 6-11.30pm, Sun 6-11pm

As part of an imposing stone Victorian building in the heart of Hull's commercial district, the Pecan could be taken for another finance house. Even inside, there are strong overtones of the

Stock Exchange, with lofty ceilings, classical pillars and arches and Victorian décor. But enthusiastic Italian waiters in red-check shirts, contemporary music and an extensive, mainly Italian menu dispel any stodgy banking atmosphere. The menu is almost a meal in itself with its mouth-watering descriptions, but tread carefully as far as the specialities are concerned. If you stick to the interesting starters, pizza or pasta dish and a sweet you should spend around £5.

Ilkley

CAFE KONDITOREI, Spa Flats, The Grove (Ilkley 601578)
Open: Mon-Sat 12noon-2.30pm, 4-5.30pm

[P] [S]

Converted from one of the old spa hotels, all the produce served in this café is home-made. Lunches start at noon and high teas after 4pm, when children's portions are available. Cork walls and classical pillars create an elegant, restful atmosphere. Soups are home-made and are delicious eaten with hot herb or garlic bread (about 55p for the two). Special dishes of the day include seafood vol-au-vents with chips and salad for around £2. Danish open sandwiches – try chicken with peach and Waldorf salad at £1.40, omelettes and salads are also served. Desserts range from 40p-80p and examples are lemon or fruit-filled pancake, sherry trifle and a variety of continental gâteaux and torten. A glass of Italian house wine costs 50p.

Kirby Misperton

BEAN SHEAF RESTAURANT ✕✕
(Kirby Misperton 614)
Open: Tue-Sun 12noon-2pm

[P]

This single-storey wayside cottage, converted and extended, offers a comfortable respite to the motorist, and to visitors to Flamingo Land Zoo. On entry, a comfortable lounge bar decorated in quiet fawns and browns leads through to a large, colourful dining room divided in two by an arch with classical pillars. Evening meals are rather above our limit but three-course lunches, weekdays and Sundays are very good value at around £3.50. All dishes are prepared personally by the proprietor and include such main meals as sweetbread villeroy (sliced, fried and served with the chef's special sauce), escalopes of pork Milanaise and chicken fried American style. An extensive wine list offers a choice of over 100 reasonably-priced wines.

Knaresborough

LE MELANGE, 8 Bond End (Harrogate 863899)
Open: Wed-Mon 12noon-2pm

[C] [♫] [S]

'French cooking at its very best' boasts the menu, and the standard certainly attracts a thriving custom to this small, stone-built restaurant. The evening menu nudges our price limit, but lunch can be taken without fear of overspending. Try a minute steak, mixed grill or individual shepherd's pie (all served with a selection of vegetables) and round it off with one of the reasonably-priced sweets and coffee. During the summer months a cold buffet table is available offering various meats and fish and a choice of salad for around £2.25. Wine (French, of course) is around 65p a glass. A special businessperson's lunch costs £3.

Leeds

THE ALLERTON, Nursery Lane, Alwoodley (Leeds 686249)
Open: Mon-Fri 12noon-2pm, 7.15-11pm, Sat 7.15-11pm

[C] [P]

The tasteful restaurant is dominated by the ceiling, which is buttressed by low, shallow arches. The table d'hôte lunch is excellent value at around £3 and includes a choice of four starters, seven main courses and sweets from the trolley. There is a set three-course special dinner which includes steak or scampi at about £4 and there is also an extensive à la carte menu from which it is possible to keep within the limit of the guide by choosing dishes carefully. A speciality of the house is fondue bourgignon – cook your own tender steak pieces to an accompaniment of tasty sauces.

KENNETH MARLOW'S FISH RESTAURANT, 62 Street Lane (Leeds 666353)
Open: Tue-Fri 12noon-2pm, 6-10pm, Sat 12noon-2pm, 6-10.30pm, Sun 4.30-10pm

Fish is the order of the day at this restaurant set in a modern development close to the northern ring road. A small bar with a few seats leads into an open-plan restaurant with bold green décor. All main courses feature fish – fried, except when in salad form, and chipped potatoes are included. No fancy fare is offered, but a wholesome three-course meal can be had at around £3.60.

NEW INN, Wetherby Road, Scarcroft (Leeds 892029)
Open: Mon, Wed-Sat 12noon-2.30pm, 7-10.30pm, Sun 12noon-2pm, 7-10pm

[P]

This modern pub and restaurant stands by the roadside and has extensive lawns. The fawns and browns of the pleasant décor blend well with the exposed brickwork and coloured spotlights. Pictures of Falstaffian scenes decorate the walls. Only the set lunch menu at £3.25 qualifies for the limited budget meal as the à la carte menu would need very careful choice to keep to a bill of around £5. For lunch, starters include ravioli au gratin and Florida cocktail, with roast pork or lambs liver with onions for main course.

NEW MILANO ✕✕ 621 Roundhay Road (Leeds 659752)
Open: Mon-Fri 12noon-2.30pm, Sat 7-11.30pm

[C] [P] [S] [♧]

On a main road into the town stands this smart, ground floor restaurant; an oasis in the desert of shops around it. Food is English and Italian - expensive in the evening but well within our means for lunch. A table d'hôte menu offers a choice of eight starters and seven main-course dishes served with vegetables of the day. A sweet from the trolley or cheese completes a very substantial meal for around £3.20, with coffee extra. Red or white house wine is available by the carafe, or at 60p for a large glass.

THE TRAVELLER'S REST
Harewood Road, East Keswick (Collingham Bridge 2766)
Open: Mon-Fri 12noon-2pm, 7-10pm, Sat 12noon-2pm, 6.30-10.30pm, Sun 12noon-1.30pm, 7-10pm

[C] [♫] [P] [♧]

This first-floor restaurant enjoys a prime location overlooking the beautiful Wharfe Valley. The small Tudor-style room with its dark wood beams and furniture, partitioned cubicles and rich brown carpeting provides a cosy, restful eating place for about forty people. Main courses comprise grills and fries, with a choice of steaks at the top end of the price scale. It is possible to overdo the limit here, but it is also quite easy to stay within £5 with a meal such as smoked mackerel, followed by deep-fried breast of chicken with sweetcorn and pineapple plus a choice from the sweet trolley, coffee and a glass of wine.

THE VINTAGE STEAK BAR
Merrion Street (Leeds 454312)
Open: Mon-Sun 11.30am-2.30pm, 5.30-11.30pm

[C] [♫] [P] [S] [♧]

Soft lighting, a red and brown colour scheme, cubicles with red velvet dividing screens and walls adorned with Edwardian motoring and cycling prints create comfortable surroundings in the steak bar with adjoining large bar. The à la carte menu includes fourteen starters with soup of the day at about 50p. Main dishes range from lamb cutlets at around £3 to pepper steaks or tournedos Rossini at about £5. A special menu which changes daily offers less expensive meals – for example soup or grapefruit cocktail for around 50p, roast pork or braised steak for around £1.10, minute steak for about £2 (all served with potatoes and two veg) and plaice and chips for about £1.60. Sweets are in the 50p-70p range and coffee is very reasonable at about 27p. A glass of house wine is around 52p.

Pateley Bridge

BRIDGEWAY RESTAURANT
1 High Street (Harrogate 711640)
Open: Tue-Wed, Fri-Sun 12noon-2pm

[P] [♧]

This first-floor restaurant overlooks the valley of the River Nidd in upper Nidderdale where the road bridge spans the river. Dark oak tables, wheelback chairs, light oak-clad walls and a beamed ceiling complete the rustic feeling. Home-made country fare is a special feature, from lentil soup at 60p to English kidneys braised in red wine sauce (£2.20), roast topside and Yorkshire pud and roast Nidderdale turkey – both around £2.50. Home-made fruit pies with fresh cream cost 60p and a glass of Italian wine is 50p.

Pocklington

BAYERNSTUBL, 4-6 Market Place (Pocklington 2643)
Open: Mon-Sun 12noon-10.15pm (10.45pm Sat)

[P] [S] [♧]

This converted pantiled cottage in the centre of town is furnished in natural wood to emphasise the Bavarian atmosphere. The popular lunchtime menu is basically English fare with sandwiches, home-made fruit pies and gâteaux at extremely reasonable prices, enabling one to eat a three-course meal for about £1.80. A meal from the main 'Speisekarte', written in German with English subtitles, will probably cost you around £4.50. Start with krabben salat (prawn cocktail), then sample a rich, spicy German dish such as paprika huhn (paprika roasted chicken) and round it off with apfel strüdel and cream.

Richmond

THE BLACK LION HOTEL
Finkle Street (Richmond 3121)
Open: Mon-Sun 12noon-2pm, 7-9.30pm

[P]

Once a coaching inn, this quaint 17th-century building has a restaurant on the first floor with a low, beamed ceiling, white décor, wheelback chairs and 19th-century prints. Meals are honest-to-goodness English fare, well-prepared, pleasantly served and excellent value, with a table d'hôte three-course lunch at around £3.60 and a three-course dinner at about £5. Main dishes include roasts, hot pot, curry, steak and kidney pie and pork chops in cider. Home-made desserts include fresh gâteaux. House wine costs 55p.

Rotherham

THE DUNGEON, Wortley Road, Kimberworth (Rotherham 557701)
Open: Mon-Fri 12noon-2.30pm

[P] [S]

Below The Drawbridge pub you will find the Dungeon. Simulated rock and cave décor, solely illuminated by coloured lighting from electric storm lanterns, sets the scene. Lunches are excellent value and the menu offers a wide choice of starters, main courses and sweets. The most expensive choice costs around £5.50, the least expensive, close to £3. Seafood platter, sirloin steak garni, gammon steak and omelettes are usually available; or you may select from the Drawbridge cold buffet table where cold meats, continental sausage, fish and mixed salads are all individually priced and an average plateful will cost around £2.

Scarborough

MEDI'S, Crown Crescent
(Scarborough 72406)
Open: Mon-Sun 5.30-11.30pm

Italian and Greek background music imparts a cheerful foot-tapping atmosphere in this recently opened pizza parlour on the South Cliff side of town. A bright décor in white and pink with mirrors and arched pillars is complemented by the use of spotlights and soft inset ceiling lights. Potted palms and other plants add the final touch. The huge pink and white menu offers pasta and pizza dishes at around £2 (many under), burgers – home-made and served on a bun with salad and French fries – at around the same price and charcoal-grilled kebabs are £4.

Sheffield

ASHOKA, 307 Eccleshall Road
(Sheffield 686177)
Open: Mon-Thu 12noon-2pm, 6-12mdnt, Fri-Sat 12noon-2pm, 6pm-1am, Sun 12noon-2pm, 7-12mdnt

What the Ashoka lacks in ethnic décor and atmosphere it more than compensates for by the range and quality of its Indian cuisine. Main courses, all eastern variations on a theme of chicken, fish or meat, are reasonably priced at around £2.50.

Sundries such as chapatis, poppadams, Bombay duck and vegetables are all extra, but two or more people could dine in style very easily for around £4.50 per head by sharing a selection of dishes. For that special celebration, a party of six can order a lamb masallam – a leg of lamb marinated in a rich sauce with herbs and spices, roasted and then carved at your table. It is served with ghee rice and costs around £30. But you'll have to warn the chef you are coming – he requires two days notice if he is to prepare this masterpiece to your satisfaction. Authentic starters and sweets can be had for around 80p.

DAM HOUSE RESTAURANT, Crookes Valley Park (Sheffield 661344)
Open: Mon-Sat 12noon-2.30pm, Tue-Sat 7-11pm

C P S

A more peaceful setting in which to enjoy a meal would be hard to find, particularly so close to the heart of a city. The 18th-century Dam House is set in a lush green valley with a terraced patio/garden overlooking a boating lake which was once a small reservoir (hence the name). Food is predominantly English, with the traditional Yorkshire pudding with onions and gravy featuring as a starter. Main dishes on the three-course lunch menu, which costs around £4 include the tried-and-true favourites, beef and kidney hotpot and home-made steak and kidney pie. A glass of house wine, cheese and biscuits and coffee with cream will add another £1.30 or so to your bill. Beware of dinner prices; the extensive à la carte menu in the evening is likely to be rather more than £5. For the energetic, there's disco dancing until the small hours each weekend, at no extra charge.

THE ROBIN HOOD, Millhouses Lane (Sheffield 360649)
Open: Mon-Fri 12noon-2pm, 6.30-10.30pm, Sat 6.30-10.30pm, Sun 12noon-2pm, 7-10.30pm

C P S

Basically a steak bar, this is a fast-moving restaurant operation with mostly grills and fries served in the spacious dining room with its dark oak fittings and from a modern kitchen openly on show. All meals include jacket or chipped potatoes and peas or a salad. Children are made welcome; a special Junior Choice menu provides a list of half portions at around £1.50.

LA TRATTORIA ROMANA, 438 Eccleshall Road (Sheffield 665491)
Open: Mon-Sun 6.30-11.30pm

Enjoy a relaxed and informal atmosphere and authentic Italian fare in this small trattoria with its plain, scrubbed pine tables and chairs, flower decorations, wine bottles and open wooden staircase to the first floor. A short list of specialities of the day is displayed on the blackboard, while on the main menu patrons are likely to find their usual Italian favourites plus a selection of veal and steaks done in the Italian manner. Pastas and pizzas range in price from about £1.50-£2, polli and veal dishes are around £3.80 and steak specialities range from about £3.50-£4.60. Various exotic ices are offered for dessert at around 75p.

WAGGON AND HORSES, Abbeysdale Road, Millhouses (Sheffield 361451)
Open: Mon-Sun 12noon-2.45pm, 7-11.30pm (Sun 10.30pm)

C P

Part of the Falstaff taverns group, this two-storey, stone-built inn overlooks a pleasant recreation area. A three-course lunch is served here daily, when for about £3 you can sample a plain but wholesome range of dishes against a charming background of exposed stone walls, oak beams and wrought-iron screens. Typical choices from the menu would be soup, grapefruit cocktail or juices followed by mixed grill, steak and kidney pie or fried plaice, plus a sweet such as mandarin cheesecake. Specialities and à la carte dishes are reasonably-priced, although you may have to forgo sweet or starter if you plump for something like beef Stroganoff or fillet steak. The Sunday lunch menu, offering two roast dishes and other choices is inexpensive.

Wakefield

STONELEIGH HOTEL AND RESTAURANT ❀❀ Doncaster Road (Wakefield 69461)
Open: Mon-Sun 12noon-2pm

[C] [P] [⚘]

Once a row of elegant Victorian terraced houses, this smart hotel is located close to the Trinity rugby league club. 'Quality' is the key word in the sophisticated dining room where full silver service is employed to complement high class international cuisine. Dinner (as may be expected), outsteps the budget, but a good table d'hôte lunch is within our means at around £4.50. There is a choice of eight starters followed by nine main-course alternatives such as lemon sole mornay, grilled lamb chop with mint sauce or sauté of beef with tomato. Finish with the pick of the sweet trolley, fresh fruit or cheese.

THE VENUS RESTAURANT
51 Westgate (Wakefield 75378)
Open: Mon-Sat 12noon-2.30pm, 6.30-11.30pm, Sun 12noon-2.30pm, 7-11pm

[C] [♬] [P] [⚘]

Those who venture beyond the somewhat unimpressive side-street entrance of the Venus restaurant will be pleasantly surprised by the warm, sumptuous interior, with oak panelling and gold dralon furnishings. The menu is rich in English and Greek cuisine with some Greek speciality dishes such as kebabs and afelia (pork fillet cooked in wine sauce with coriander and cream) – both around £3.50 including rice or Greek salad, but the à la carte menu will require careful selection to keep the costs around £5, particularly as prices quoted do not include VAT. The three-course table d'hôte lunch is ideal, offering traditional dishes such as fish, roasts or salads, with one Greek special for around £3.50 Though part of the Bull Tavern, children are catered for with half portions of selected dishes – at half price.

Whitby

KHYBER PASS RESTAURANT AND GRILL
(Whitby 603500)
Open: summer: Mon-Sun 11.45am-5.30pm,
winter: Sat-Sun 11.45am-5.30pm

[⚘]

The wandering road from the harbour up on to the West Cliff is called the Khyber Pass – the name has been adopted by this single storey café which overlooks the beach and harbour entrance. At lunchtime three courses are priced by the main dish – from sausage at £2 to roast beef and Yorkshire pudding at around £3.40. Whitby crab salad is offered at £3.20. Starters include soup of the day and a selection of six desserts offers home-made fruit tart and custard and crème caramel. Junior Choice at £1 is served all day – choose from fish fingers, fish, sausage, beans, eggs – any of these with chips, ice cream and a glass of squash. The evening menu is more sophisticated – curries, kebabs, fish and grills all cost over £3, so three-courses can only be enjoyed with the cheaper main dishes.

MAGPIE CAFE, 14 Pier Road
(Whitby 2058)
Open: Mon-Thu, Sat-Sun 11.30am-2.30pm, 3.30-6.30pm

[⚘]

At the quayside you will find this converted merchant's house with its distinctive bow windows and black-and-white exterior. Beside the fish-landing harbour, it is well placed to specialise in fresh Whitby seafood from the dockside. Proprietors Sheila and Ian McKenzie claim that their menus provide a meal to suit *all* tastes. A Magpie Special Lunch for about £2.50 offers home-made soup of the day as one starter, home-made steak pie, chips and peas and a choice which includes fresh cream sherry trifle or strawberry flan, Black Forest gâteau or apple pie. The Magpie Special Fish Lunch at £3 offers a choice of Whitby crab, prawn cocktail or potted shrimps as appetisers, cod or haddock with chips and a selection of about ten sweets. With both lunches a pot of tea is included, since The Magpie is unlicensed, but since there is a choice of four liqueur mousses in each case, you won't be totally on the wagon! A special children's meal for just over £1 offers sausage, beans and chips, jelly and ice cream and a glass of orange. Paintings by local artists adorn the white walls of the dining room.

York

BETTY'S OAKROOM RESTAURANT AND TEA ROOM, St Helen's Square (York 22323)
Open: Mon-Sat 12noon-2pm, 5.15-9pm (closed Mon-Wed evenings in winter)

P S

This three-storeyed corner-house complex was the haunt of the boys of No. 6 Bomber Squadron during World War II, but today's fare won't cost you a bomb! The main restaurant is in the basement and takes its name from the all-oak furnishings. A three-course meal here such as minestrone soup, fried fillet of plaice with full garnish and Swiss sherry trifle to finish, is around £4. Above, in the cafeteria you can dine on fruit juice, roast beef and Yorkshire pud, plus a gâteau for less than £3.

BIBIS, 115-119 Micklegate (York 34765)
Open: Mon-Fri 6-11.30pm, Sat 12noon-2.15pm, 6-11.30pm, Sun 12.15-2.15pm, 6-11pm

P S

Very Italian, this ballroom-sized ground-floor restaurant with its granite-topped tables, black salt and pepper mills, deep green ceiling and tiled floor. Very Italian the food, too, with a wide selection of pastas and pizzas as well as blackboard-listed specials such as chicken, fish, or steak dishes. Starters include fresh Whitby crab when in season, buttered corn-on-the-cob, and honeydew melon, and there is a selection of home-made desserts and flambé ice creams. A three-course meal is likely to cost around £3 to £4.

CHARLIE'S BISTRO, County Hotel, Tanner Row (York 25120)
Open: Mon-Thu 12noon-2pm, 6-11pm (closed Mon evenings), Fri-Sat 12noon-2pm, 6-12mdnt

P S

This little bistro on the ground floor of the County Hotel is decorated in 1920s style, with pictures of Charlie Chaplin around the walls. The choice of dishes à la carte includes peppered fillet steak with baked potato and salad at about £3 and York gammon with egg and chips at about £2.50, and there are a number of delicious sweets around 50p as well as mouth-watering sweet crêpes (a little more expensive). For a really cheap meal you'd find it hard to beat the two-course lunch costing about £1. This consists of soup followed by a choice from items such as home-made steak and kidney pie, seafood salad and lasagne.

DREAMVILLE, King's Square (York 36592)
Open: Mon-Sun 10am-11pm

[S]

Dreamville is exactly what it sounds – an American-style food-fantasy, with a colourful gangster theme. The entrance is reminiscent of a fun-fair or amusement arcade, and opens up on to an ice cream parlour. The menu lists all kinds of burgers named after shady characters such as Al Capone, Frankie Yale and Lucky Luciano, and they range in price from £1.50 to just over £3 depending on size and content. Other dishes include fish'n'fries, lasagne, charcoal grilled spare ribs and real Texas style chilli, all at the £2 mark. Finish with a luxurious ice cream extravaganza (thirty-six varieties available) and perhaps an American style milk-shake or ice-cream soda.

PUNCH BOWL HOTEL, Blossom Street (York 22619)
Open: Mon-Sat 12noon-2.30pm, 7-11pm, Sun 12noon-2pm, 7-10pm

[C] [♫] [P]

You can imagine yourself in an old coaching inn when you take a meal at the 18th-century Punch Bowl. In fact this is what it once was, but later it became first an almshouse and then a dwelling house. Now refurbished as a hotel and steak house, the Punch Bowl offers a very reasonable table d'hôte meal of starter, main dish and dessert, the price varying with the main dish chosen. An example is grapefruit cocktail, steak and kidney pie with vegetables and potato, and apple pie and cream at around £3.50. Coffee with mints and a large glass of house wine together add only about 90p! Choosing a £5 meal from the à la carte menu is easily done – the price includes vegetables and a sweet or cheese.

RISTORANTI BARI, 15 The Shambles (York 33807)
Open: Mon-Sun 11.30am-2.30pm, 6-11pm

[C] [♫] [P] [S]

Do you fancy Sophia Loren? A 'scalloppe' of that name, made of fillet of pork with cheese, brandy, and tomato sauce, costs about £3.80 (including vegetables) in this Italian pizzeria. The range of *paste* and *pizze* includes lasagne or cannelloni at around £1.80, spaghetti bolognese at around £1.70, and the Chef's special pizza at about £2. A glass of house wine is around 60p and coffee costs 45p or thereabouts for espresso or cappuccino.

TIGGA, 45 Goodramgate (York 33787)
Open: Mon-Sat 9.30am-10pm, Sun 5.30-8pm

[C] [♫] [P] [S]

'Tigga', housed in a renovated Tudor merchant's home, combines a needlecraft centre and a gift shop with an enterprising restaurant operation. Proprietors Rodger and Rosalie Kilvington are now specialising in 'Taste of England' dishes. Many combinations of three courses come within the region of £5, though you could exceed this with an à la carte dinner. Those who would like to sample the traditional meal of Yorkshire pudding served as a starter, roast English beef with appropriate vegetables, apple pie served with cheese, and coffee must order a couple of hours in advance and be prepared to exceed our limit. But if you're looking for a cheaper evening meal there are a number of supper dishes, and at any time of day Tigga Burgers may be your choice. There is a quick lunch at about £1.85 which is particularly good value and a children's version at around £1.

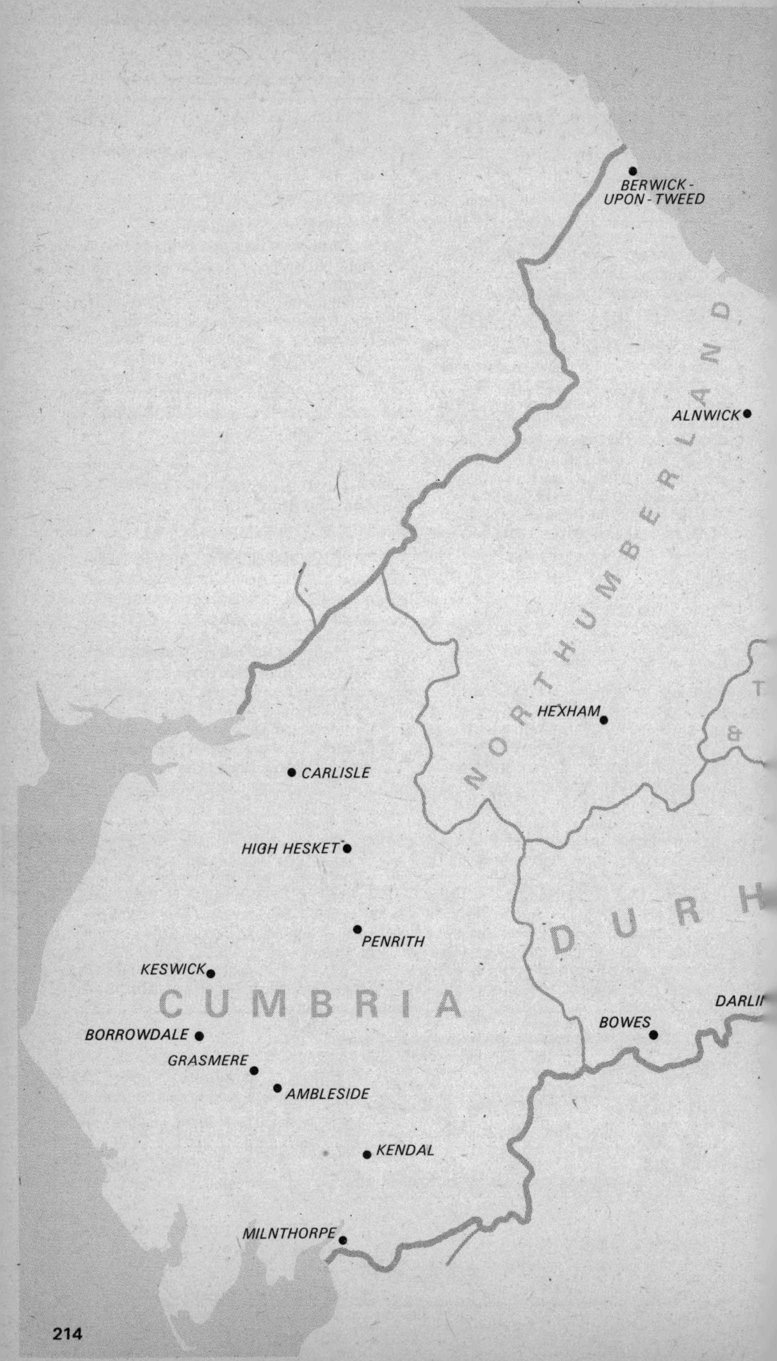
BERWICK-UPON-TWEED
ALNWICK
NORTHUMBERLAND
HEXHAM
CARLISLE
HIGH HESKET
PENRITH
KESWICK
CUMBRIA
BORROWDALE
GRASMERE
AMBLESIDE
KENDAL
MILNTHORPE
DURH
BOWES
DARLI

The North and the Lakes

Here we have a contrast of rugged Northumbrian coastline, bleak industrial areas and a magnificent landscape of outstanding natural beauty, and, like the land, the food of the North of England also has some interesting contrasts. On the one hand there's the plain wholesome food of a region historically beset by hard times, and on the other recipes liberally laced with rum, rich in dried fruits and Barbados sugar introduced to Whitehaven and other northern ports from the West Indies.

The grandeur that is the Lake District is known to tourists from all over the world. Its heather-clad mountains and glassy lakes create an outdoor paradise which stimulates even the weakest appetite and encourages tourists to buy the sweet and tasty regional specialities such as rum butter, Grasmere Gingerbread and the renowned Kendal mint cake – a peppermint candy designed as a compact energy source for walkers and climbers. Butter is a favourite ingredient in many local sweets – notably butter fudge, toffee and shortbread.

A familiar feature at pub lunches, or on the breakfast tables in these parts, is the Cumberland sausage. This meaty specimen is nine inches long, well stuffed with pork and a liberal flavouring of herbs. Cumberland ham, baked, glazed and, perhaps, served with a rich Madeira sauce, appears on menus throughout the Lake District as a 'local speciality'. Mutton from the hardy Herdwick sheep is used in a variation in Lancashire Hot Pot known as 'tatie pot' consisting of a potato base topped with lamb chops, sliced black pudding and onions. Housewives in the area also use this meat in a dish known as 'Cumberland Sweet Pie' which combines minced mutton with dried fruit, lemon juice, brown sugar, mixed peel and spices encased in a light pastry, but this has not yet found its way into many public eating houses.

Where lakes abound there is no shortage of freshwater fish. Salmon and trout are, of course, the most popular here and most restaurants will feature these fish. In Northumbria, Tweed salmon served poached is a notable delicacy. Oak-smoked kippers from Craster and other east coast fishing ports are a tasty teatime treat while pease pudding with boiled ham is a true Geordie favourite. You will find most of these and many other local dishes at the restaurants within the following section.

Alnwick

HOTSPUR HOTEL ★★
(Alnwick 602924)
Open: Billy Bones Buttery: Mon-Sun 12noon-2pm, summer: 7-9.30pm, winter: 6-9.30pm
Percy Restaurant: summer: Mon-Sun 7-9pm, winter: Mon-Sun 7-8pm

[♫] [P] [S]

Billy Bones was piper to the Duchess of Northumberland in 1815, when the Duke leased Hotspur House to him. There he established a hostelry. In 1971, a local business man turned it into a hotel again and converted the stable into the Billy Bones Buttery, where horse brasses on the walls proclaim the building's former use. Here you can get a super lunch for about £2 – soup or fruit juice, a choice of four main dishes likely to include a roast, fish, and cold meat with salad, and an 'English' sweet – perhaps fruit crumble with custard or a sponge pudding. The à la carte menu is also within our budget, with basket meals including pork sausage, tomato, onion and chips at around £1.25 and – at the other end of the scale – deep-fried seafood selection with chips at over £2. Steak is the most expensive bar meal, costing £4. Starters include soup and fruit juice and sweets are ice cream-based, costing up to 90p. House wine costs about 60p a glass. The Percy Restaurant (Percy is the family name of the Dukes of Northumberland) does a table d'hôte dinner at around £5, which is excellent value, but the à la carte menu is rather out of our league.

Ambleside

ALEXANDER RESTAURANT, Lake Road (Ambleside 3096)
Open: Mon, Wed-Sun 10.30am-2.15pm, 5.30-9.30pm

[C] [P]

Above a coffee room that's been recently converted from a shop, this homely restaurant offers good value food at sensible prices. A three-course lunch (eg, grapefruit segments, roast Scotch lamb with mint sauce and trimmings, plus meringue glacé to finish) costs just £2.50. The set dinner is £4.50, with rainbow trout meunière and gammon steak as two of the four main dish options. In addition to this, an à la carte menu provides several other delicacies, one of which is sure to tickle your taste buds. Nicolas house wine costs 55p per goblet.

GEMINI RESTAURANT, Lake Road (Ambleside 2528)
Open: Feb-Nov: Mon-Sat 10am-6.30pm

[P] [S]

A friendly, informal family-run roadside restaurant with large rear car park. Three small open-plan areas create a comfortable atmosphere and a good selection of wholesome hot dishes are provided. Starters include grapefruit and mandarin cocktail at around 50p and main courses, predominantly grills, range in price from around £1.50-£3.80 with specialities such as duckling à l'orange or sole in prawn and mushroom sauce – both about £4.50. There is an excellent choice of desserts from around 48p-68p. Special children's dishes are around £1. Try grape or apple juice which costs about 30p a glass – no fermented grapes here as the restaurant is unlicensed.

THE JACARANDA RESTAURANT
Compston Road (Ambleside 2430)
Open: Mon-Fri 12noon-8.30pm, Sat 5-8pm, Sun 12noon-8pm

[P]

There's a touch of nostalgia in the name of this neat little restaurant. The jacaranda is a beautiful flowering tree found in the tropics, notably the Caribbean island of St Lucia where proprietors Mr & Mrs K Stead gained much of their catering experience. Malawi and Nairobi were also bases for the Stead's work abroad and prints and pictures of these places lining the wall are a colourful feature of the restaurant's interior. However, this taste for the foreign is not extended to the menu which offers mainly grills, fish and salads. Almost any combination will come within our limit; a sample meal would include home-made chicken liver pâté with hot buttered toast at 80p, rainbow trout meunière with vegetables and potatoes or full salad for £2.80 (a more expensive choice), fresh cream dessert chosen from display (60p) and coffee and wine for less than £1.

Berwick-upon-Tweed

KING'S ARMS HOTEL ★★ Hide Hill (Berwick-upon-Tweed 7454)
Open: summer: Mon-Sun 8-9.30am, 12noon-10pm, winter: Mon-Sun 12noon-2pm, 6.30-9pm

[C] [P] [S]

The King's Arms was once a coaching inn, a regular stop for the London to Edinburgh Highflyer – 18th-century equivalent of the Flying Scotsman. Today its oak-panelled dining room which functions as a buttery at lunchtimes recalls those days, with the adjacent Highflyer restaurant. The buttery menu includes salads from around £1.75, pastas and pizzas at about £1.50-£2, fish and meat dishes ranging from £2.60-£3.50 and grills at over £2.20. The restaurant's prices range from about £2.70 for haddock or spaghetti to around £4 for sirloin steak. You may buy a three-course table d'hôte Sunday lunch for about £4.50. The Hunting Lodge bar does lunches, including farmhouse soup for around 40p and hot pies and chips for around £1.

POPINJAYS, 30 Hide Hill (Berwick-upon-Tweed 7237)
Open: Mon-Sat 9.30am-6pm

[P] [S]

Georgina Home-Robertson is the enthusiastic owner of this farmhouse-style coffee shop which boasts a walled patio at the rear with ruined stables providing a dramatic backcloth. Coffee shop Popinjays may be, but down market it definitely is not. Food here is simple but nicely prepared with salads at around £1 and various hot dishes including basic grills and omelettes at about 75p. All ingredients for a good three-course meal are here except for a glass of wine – Popinjays is unlicensed.

QUEEN'S HEAD HOTEL ★ Sandgate (Berwick-upon-Tweed 7852)
Open: Mon-Sun 7.30-9.30am, 12noon-2pm, 7-9.30pm

[P] [S]

One of two Berwick hotels owned and run by Mr Geoffrey Young and his family, the Queen's Head lies at the bottom of Hide Hill, near the river. The pleasant restaurant with its dark oak furniture and flock wallpaper offers three-course table d'hôte lunch at around £3.50 with coffee extra. There is also an à la carte menu with fish, entrées and roasts at prices ranging from £2.50

to £3, the total cost working out between £4.50-£5 for three courses.

RAVENSHOLME HOTEL ★★
Ravensdowne
(Berwick-upon-Tweed 7170)
Open: Mon-Sun 7.30-10am, 12noon-2pm, 6.30-9.30pm

C ♬ P S 🍷

Geoffrey Young owns this hotel and he and his family run it personally. The Ravensholme has two restaurants, a downstairs Wallace Room with Wallace tartan carpet, and an upstairs Gold Room. The Wallace Room offers a good range of dishes including fried fillet of Eyemouth haddock or two lamb chops and various steaks on the à la carte menu, and three courses can cost around £5-£6. An excellent table d'hôte lunch offers three courses for under or around £4. The Gold Room serves bar lunches and suppers in summer.

THE RUM PUNCHEON RESTAURANT, Golden Square
(Berwick-upon-Tweed 7431)
Open: Mon-Sat, 9.30am-9pm

C ♬ P S

You can't linger late over dinner here, but this oak-clad 18th-century restaurant is certainly worth a visit. The Stoddart family has been in business selling groceries, wines and spirits there since 1834. In the restaurant you can buy a three-course lunch for something around £3 or the main course only for about £2, as well as separate à la carte dishes such as scampi, steak or salmon, all at between £2-£3.50. Substantial bar lunches are also served, with main courses from just over £1 to about £3 and sweets from 45p upwards. A large glass of wine will cost you around 50p.

Borrowdale

THE YEW TREE, Seatoller
(Borrowdale 634)
Open: Tue-Fri, Sun 12noon-8pm, Sat 6-9.30pm

C P 🍷

Nestling at the foot of the spectacular Honiston Pass, this whitewashed restaurant was originally built as two cottages in 1628. Massive oak beams and a slate floor emphasise the antiquity of the dining room, with its wheelback chairs and wooden tables. Food is simple and wholesome. Try ham and vegetable broth with a roll as a starter for 60p. Smoked salmon at £1.50 is one of the more expensive appetisers. Main courses offered are grills, omelettes and salads. Speciality of the house is ham and egg (£2.20) and 'more ham and egg' (£2.90). Cumberland sausage with salad and mushrooms is £2.20. A very tempting selection of sweets include pot of chocolate (55p), brandy meringue (60p) or bilberries and cream (75p). Starred items on the menu are available in smaller portions for children at two-thirds of the full price. A range of wines are offered by the glass for 60p.

Bowes

ANCIENT UNICORN HOTEL ★★
(Teesdale 28321)
Open: Mon-Sun 11.30am-2.30pm, 6-9.30pm

C P 🍷

This attractive coaching inn, built around a cobbled courtyard, has been offering accommodation and refreshment to weary travellers since the 16th century. Prices in the restaurant of this two-star hotel are somewhat beyond our limit so we are concentrating on the very reasonable and extensive bar snack menu. A sample of dishes available are sardine and tomato salad for starter at 90p, chicken curry with rice and peas at about £2 and, to finish with, a sweet chosen from a selection at 75p. Coffee is 35p and a glass of wine won't break the bank at 55p per glass.

Carlisle

THE CENTRAL HOTEL ★★ Victoria Viaduct (Carlisle 20256)
Open: Mon-Sun 12noon-2pm, 7-9pm

C ♬ P S 🍷

A comfortable and popular Greenall Whitley hotel managed with great style by Stanley Cohen. Bar lunch here is excellent with a good ploughman's at about 65p, a wide range of cold and hot dishes for around £1 and specials including scampi at about £2. Outstandingly good value, too, is the Central's table d'hôte dinner at about £5.50. A glass of house wine costs in the region of 40p.

THE CITADEL RESTAURANT, 77-79 English Street (Carlisle 21298)
Open: Mon-Sat 11.30am-10.30pm, Sun: normal licensing hours

C ♬ P S 🍷

Is this the ideal haunt? Certainly the friendly ghosts keep coming back for more. So, it seems, do the patrons who claim to have seen several unearthly apparitions in this 100-year-old citadel, including a wizened old lady and a chap in 18th-century garb. The restaurant is situated above a tangle of ancient passageways which once led to the cathedral and old jail. Now it's handy for the station and shops. Warm and bright, it serves straightforward no-nonsense meals at fairly reasonable prices. Particularly good value are a three-course shopper's lunch at about £2, and the à la carte seafood dishes, none of which will set you back more than £3. A glass of house wine costs about 50p.

THE CROWN AND MITRE ★★★
English Street (Carlisle 25491/33354)
Open: Belowstairs Restaurant: Mon-Fri 12.30-2.30pm, 7-10pm, Sat-Sun 7-10pm, Coffee House: Mon-Sat 9am-10.30pm, Sun 10am-10pm

[C] [♫] [P] [S] [♧]

The Belowstairs restaurant is a little on the dear side, but it is not difficult to stick to a £5 limit and eat well. Starters begin at about 65p for fresh orange or grapefruit juice pressed to order and include a delicious gazpacho at around 85p. Of the main dishes, grilled calves' liver and bacon at around £2.50, Dover sole from £5 and fillet steak with mushrooms and red wine sauce at about £6 are good value. The Coffee Bar offers starters from around 25p, salads, fish and grills from about £1, as well as toasted sandwiches and a choice of children's specials, all at around 70p.

CUMBRIAN HOTEL ★★★ Court Square (Carlisle 31951)
Open: during normal licensing hours, Victoria's Restaurant: 12noon-2pm, 7-9.30pm. Cumbrian Kitchen: summer: 9.30am-9.30pm, winter: 10am-8pm

[C] [P] [S] [♧]

As its name implies, the Cumbrian's well-appointed main restaurant has a Victorian décor. The à la carte menu is very English, but rather expensive, although the table d'hôte lunch at about £4 and dinner at around £5.75 are both excellent buys. The Cumbrian Kitchen is a different matter altogether. You can have a snack and a cup of coffee here, with change from £1.50, or a substantial meal with a glass of house wine for less than £4. Bar snacks, available at lunchtime, include chicken salad at about £1.50, and an Albert's Special (half a French loaf buttered and filled with just about everything) at about £1.20.

THE MALT SHOVEL, Rickergate (Carlisle 34095)
Open: during normal licensing hours, Brew House Restaurant: Mon-Sat 12noon-2pm, 7.30-9.30pm

[C] [♫] [P] [S] [♧]

The Brew House Restaurant has a most appropriate décor of malt sacks and malt shovels and is very bright and clean, with comfortable chairs and a relaxed, intimate atmosphere. The lunch menu prices start at around 75p for a ploughman's. A T-bone steak garni at about £4 apart, none of the main dishes costs much more than £2.50. But the Malt Shovel is at its best in the evening, with nineteen starters at prices ranging from around 40p-£1.50, and a superb selection of fish dishes, poultry, roast grills and entrées at prices that average out around £4. Incidentally, Robert Burns slept at the Malt Shovel, we are told. It's a pity he missed the food.

Darlington

RISTORANTE BACCUS
145-147 Northgate (Darlington 67078)
Open: Mon-Fri 11am-2pm, 7-11.30pm, Sat 7-11.30pm

[C] [P] [♧]

Five minutes walk from the town centre, this small Italian restaurant specialises in attentive service and interesting surroundings. An intimate cocktail bar is linked to the dining room by an ornate arch. Wrought iron interwoven with 'vines' and paintings of food and wine complete the scene. An excellent-value three-course lunch, with five choices of starters, seven choices of main dishes and five of desserts only costs £1.70. You could have sardine salad, minute steak with vegetables of the day and pineapple fritter. For lunch or dinner an extremely comprehensive à la carte menu offers a host of starters, fish, pasta, poultry and veal dishes, over a dozen Italian beef specialities, salads and sweets, many of which are well within our limit. Scallambra house wine is 50p per large glass.

TAJ MAHAL TANDOORI
192 Northgate (Darlington 68920)
Open: Mon-Sun 12noon-2.30pm, 7pm-12mdnt

[C] [♫] [P]

A small, intimate restaurant situated very close to the town centre, the Taj Mahal offers unbelievable value with its three-course lunch for only £1.60. The lunch menu includes twelve Indian dishes such as chicken curry and prawn and four English dishes including rump or sirloin steak with soup or fruit juice to start and a sweet to follow. A prominent feature of the dining area is a large Eastern-style mural covering one wall, the other three walls are hung with soft drapes, and the Indian atmosphere is enhanced by traditional background music. The à la carte menu offers a large variety of dishes with many tandoori specialities for around £2-£3. A selection of wines cost 75p per glass.

Durham

THE BROTHERS RESTAURANT AND WINE BAR KITCHENER, 4 Framwellgate Bridge, Milburngate Centre (Durham 46777)
Open: Mon-Sun 12noon-3pm, 7-11.30pm

C P S

Situated in the shadow of the Gothic cathedral and castle is this olde worlde eating place. The fact that it is run by two brothers (and their wives and mother) accounts for the name, but they have developed this to incorporate a monastic theme in style and décor – though the food is anything but frugal! Eight-ounce jacket potatoes with a choice of fillings, a dozen assorted salads and at least three hot dishes a day, including 'Brothers pot' (stewed beef and vegetables) at about £3, give plenty of scope for inexpensive eating. For those who have made no vow to poverty, there is a comprehensive (and more pricey!) à la carte menu. A glass of Spanish house wine costs around 75p.

ROYAL COUNTY HOTEL ★★★★ COFFEE HOUSE, Old Elvet (Durham 66821)
Open: Mon-Sat 10am-8pm, Sun 10am-5pm

C ♫ P S

Youngsters enjoy their meals in this attractive buttery as there is a menu of children's favourites such as bangers and mash at about 75p and sweets (including 'Thunder and Lightning' – ice cream, golden syrup and whipped cream!) at around 45p. À la carte dishes are reasonably priced and you can choose an appetising meal such as soup with roll and butter, fried breast of chicken with banana fritter, chips and peas, a slice of chocolate gâteau, coffee and house wine for around £5.60.

PIZZERIA LA CANTINA, North Road (Durham 46050)
Open: Tue-Sat 12noon-2.30pm, Mon-Sat 6.30-10.30pm

C ♫

Once inside this second-floor restaurant, one could almost be in an eating place in Rome or Florence. Inside, there are no windows and lighting is by coach lamps. Italian music strums gently in the background and Italian posters and Chianti bottles decorate the brick and rough-cast walls. A gallery dining area completes the scene with large wagon wheels and halved barrels set into the walls. An excellent selection of pasta and pizza dishes are offered, all for around £1.80, so that a three-course meal could easily be had for around £4 including wine.

THE SQUIRE TRELAWNY, 80 Front

Street, Sherburn (Durham 720613)
Open: Tue-Sat 7.30-9.45pm

[C] [P]

Away from the city centre, this tiny, low-ceilinged bar and restaurant has a wealth of heavy old beams, horse brasses, harnesses and stirrups, set off by heavy rough-cast walls. Subtle lighting is by coach lamps. The à la carte menu is pricey, but an excellent-value 'snack' menu is served from Tuesday-Thursday inclusive. A choice of minute steak, scampi, roast chicken or gammon and apricot – all served with chips and peas – cost £2.25. Soup of the day at 65p and a sweet from the trolley at around the same price, complete a satisfying three-course meal. A large glass of wine is just over 60p.

Grasmere

THE SHEPHERD'S CROOK, Stock Lane (Grasmere 342)
Open: Mon-Sun 12noon-3pm, 6-8.30pm

[P] [&]

An old-English atmosphere is created inside this quaint roadside restaurant by the small-paned leaded windows, soft low lighting and walls lined with willow-patterned crockery. Separate menus are offered for lunch and dinner, priced at an average of £3 and £4 respectively, for three courses. The emphasis is on good, homely cooking and warm friendly service. Try the rainbow trout with almonds served with two vegetables and a choice of four types of potato or salad for around £3, followed by a helping of home-made fruit pie and cream (just over 60p). In the evening prawns au gratin or the farmhouse grill (lamb chop, sausage, bacon, egg, mushroom and tomato) may take your fancy.

THE SINGING BIRDS RESTAURANT
Town End (Grasmere 268)
Open: Mar-Nov: Mon-Sun 10.30am-3pm, 3.30-6pm, 7-9.30pm

[C] [P]

Close to Dove Cottage and the Wordsworth Museum is a quaint white cottage housing an antique shop and restaurant. Inside, rough-cast walls, dark beams and brass and copper bric-à-brac emphasise the rustic atmosphere. All the lunch menus include a host of home-made dishes. 'Light' lunches include soup of the day with granary bread for around 75p, savoury flan or quiche served with an interesting salad for about £2.75 and open sandwiches such as 'shrimps in a crowd' for around £1.75. Three-course à la carte lunches vary in price from £4 upwards and include pâté maison, home-made chicken and mushroom pie or spaghetti bolognese. A three-course Sunday table d'hôte lunch for about £5.50 offers excellent choices – try egg and prawn surprise followed by chicken chasseur or lamb's kidneys turbigo. French or German house wines cost around 50p a glass.

Hexham

HADRIAN'S WALL (Hexham 81232)
Open: Mon-Sun 12noon-2pm, 7-9pm

[P]

Overshadowed by the Roman wall, this smart ivy-clad inn dating back over 250 years enjoys a well-deserved local reputation for its good food and efficient service. A four-course lunch of home-made soup, a fish dish, a main course of steak and kidney pudding, lemon sole, curry or trout plus a sweet and coffee with cream is still around £5, including wine.

High Hesket

THE ASTRA (Southwaite 541)
Open: Mon-Sun 11am-10pm

[P] [&]

If you want a meal on your journey, without the time-consuming business of finding your way round a strange town, you could do much worse than stop at the Astra. This modern brick-built complex stands on the A6 half way between Carlisle and Penrith. Uniformed waitresses give efficient, speedy service in the restaurants, where you can have a good three-course lunch and coffee for around £4 (less than £2 for children under ten, no charge for those under three). For this you may choose as a starter fruit juice, soup, or a relish. Main dishes include home-made beefsteak pie and roast chicken with stuffing, and there is a choice of four sweets such as sherry trifle or apple pie and custard. A snack menu includes a two-course lunch for around £3 and ploughman's at about £1.30. A minimum of 50p per head is charged in the restaurants. A glass of French house wine costs about 50p.

Kendal

BARNABY RUDGE, Tebay
Open: summer: Mon-Sat 11am-3pm, 6.30-10.30pm, Sun 12noon-2pm, 7-10.30pm

winter: Mon-Sat 6.30-10.30pm,
Sun 12noon-2pm

[P]

Two or three minutes drive from the M6 (Junc 38) through the Tebay village will lead you to this quaint little restaurant, with its bow-windowed frontage. The equally 'olde worlde' interior abounds with gleaming brass and copper, and mature wooden pillars and beams. A lunch of soup, ham and mushroom pizza with French fries, and hot apple strudel with fresh cream can be had for a mere £2.80. Coffee with cream and a glass of wine will add about 80p to your bill. Evening prices are much the same on a more extensive menu, although the sirloin or fillet steak at £3.95 could take your total just over the limit. For a sweet try the house special of toasted waffles with spiced apple, nuts and cream.

CHERRY TREE RESTAURANT,
24 Finkle Street (Kendal 20547)
Open: Mon-Sun 10am-9.30pm, (closed early Thu in winter)

[S]

The entrance to the Cherry Tree lies up an alleyway. The main first-floor restaurant is very bright and clean, with good dark oak furniture and excellent quality crockery. The décor has white rough-cast walls and beams. You can buy hot and cold snacks here and Danish open sandwiches, as well as a four-course lunch for about £2.80. Dinner costs very little more and offers an excellent choice with salmon, veal, chicken and turkey well within the budget. A glass of house wine costs about 50p.

THE MASH TUN, The Brewery Arts Centre (Kendal 25133)
Open: Mon-Sat 10am-2pm

[P] [S]

The Mash Tun is housed in a converted stone-built brewery. The food is under the personal supervision of Avril Leigh and Elaine Wright of The Castle Dairy. Popular with local business folk and farmers, The Mash Tun offers a choice of pies and flans, roast chicken leg, silverside of beef and fresh trout all at around £1.50, and all with chips or salad, as well as a great variety of similarly-priced fish or cold meat salads. There is a choice of three sweets for about 50p.

THE WOOLPACK HOTEL ★★★
Stricklandgate (Kendal 23852)
Open: normal licensing hours.
Ca Steean Restaurant: Mon-Sat 12.30-2pm, 7-10pm, Shepherd's Pie Buttery, summer: Mon-Sat 10am-9.30pm, winter: Mon-Sat 10am-6.30pm

[C] [P] [S]

The Ca Steean Restaurant offers fine food in elegant surroundings. A three-course meal can be had from the à la carte menu for around £5, if you stick to the lower price range, or there is the table d'hôte at around £3.50 for lunch and around £5.25 for dinner with hot grill-style main courses or cold buffet. The Shepherd's Pie Buttery is a more casual eating place with pine-clad walls and lantern-style lighting where a three-course meal costs around £3. Bar snacks include a hamburger bap with onions at about 50p and a good ploughman's lunch at around 75p. A glass of wine costs around 50p.

Keswick

BAY TREE, 1 Wordsworth Street (Keswick 73313)
Open: summer: Mon-Sun 10am-4.30pm, 7-9pm, winter: Mon-Sun 7-9pm

[P] [S]

This attractive terrace restaurant and guesthouse is easy to spot by its cheerful canopy and corner position. Victoriana is the style for interior décor, with old prints and highly-polished tables and chairs. The three-course dinner menu is just out of our range at £6-£8, but lunchtime choices (changing daily) include delights such as stuffed deep-fried mushrooms at £1.35, sirloin steak (£3.95) and roast meat salad at around £2.

DERWENTWATER HOTEL ★★★
Portinscale (Keswick 72538)
Open: Mon-Sun 8.30-9.30am, 12noon-2pm, 4-5pm, 7-8.30pm

C P

A friendly, informal hotel this, in a superb position close to the shores of Derwentwater. An excellent bar lunch will set you back a little over £3. Cold platters include, incidentally, a 'rock dub' of smoked salmon, prawns, sardines, tuna, pilchards and herrings with salad at just under £3 and a vegetarian dish of cheese, pineapple, carrot and salad for around £2. Every item on the special children's menu costs in the region of 75p. The dinner menu is priced a little over the odds for this book and is aimed more for the hotel guests than casual trade. La Chiqua is the Spanish house wine and sells at about 50p a glass.

THE DOG AND GUN, 2 Lake Road (Keswick 73463)
Open: Mon-Sun, during normal licensing hours

C P

A genuine old coaching inn, this, and one of the oldest pubs in Keswick. The intimacy of its low, beamed ceiling and, in winter time, the welcoming open fire, make the Dog and Gun popular with locals and visitors alike. Food is prepared by the proprietress and is available at any time during opening hours. Prices are just a little higher than the average pub but the food is worth that bit extra too. Ploughman's lunch is around £1.40, or for around £3, you can enjoy home-cooked ham with jacket potato, pineapple, and fresh garden salad. Prime rare roast beef, jacket potato and tossed salad costs another 40p or so. Beef curry and rice, interestingly garnished with tomato, peach, and cucumber is another speciality. Sweets such as chocolate orange pot or coffee ice cream are spiked with liqueur and cost around 95p. Wine by the glass is around 55p.

YAN TYAN TETHERA, 70 Main Street (Keswick 72033)
Open: summer: Mon-Sun 12noon-3pm, Tue-Sun 6.30-10pm, winter: Mon-Sun 12noon-2.30pm, Thu, Fri, Sat evenings by appointment only

P S

No Chinese chippy this, as you might think, for 'yan, tyan, tethera, etc' is how they count sheep in Borrowdale. The owner, Simone Boddington, is a very nice, jolly lady and runs what is clearly a very happy ship. The day menu includes starters from around 50p to £1.30, hot dishes, including Cumberland sausage, from about 70p to £2.50, and fish from about 80p to £2.50. In the evening, Simone's specialities have a bias towards seafood. But they are popular, so do book. 'No service charge or gratuities please' the menu says. 'Just come back again!' English wines are a speciality here, you can have a glass of white wine which costs about 70p.

Milnthorpe

CROOKLANDS HOTEL BUTTERY AND COFFEE SHOP (Crooklands 432)
Two minutes from the M6 (No. 36 interchange) on the A65 going towards Kendal.
Open: Mon-Sun 7am-2.30pm, 6.30-9.30pm. Closed winter evenings

P

The buttery of the Crooklands Hotel is a small bright and cheerful restaurant, well worth knowing about. You can get a good lunch here, including home-made soup with roll (about 65p) and the 'pie of the day' (around £2.25 with vegetables). On summer evenings you can have a fresh salad.

Newcastle upon Tyne

BLACKGATE RESTAURANT, Milburngate House, The Side (Newcastle-upon-Tyne 26661)
Open: Tue-Fri 12noon-2.30pm, 7-10.30pm, Sat 7-10.30pm

[C] [♫] [🍷]

This is a place for home-made food. All bread rolls, ice creams, desserts, petit fours and pâtés are freshly prepared on the premises. The table d'hôte lunch menu lists combinations of dishes in the region of £3.75-£5.25. Choose an unusual starter such as cheese and avocado mousse followed by roast leg of lamb with rosemary, a sweet (what better than pistachio ice cream?) and coffee. Prices are rather higher for dinner. Wine is French and around 65p a glass.

CAVALIER STEAK BAR, DENTON HOTEL, West Road (Newcastle-upon-Tyne 742390)
Open: Mon-Fri 12noon-2pm, 7-10.30pm, Sat 7-10.30pm, Sun 12noon-2pm, 7-10.30pm

[P] [🍷]

The impressive Denton Hotel's steak bar has a bright cocktail bar and an intimate, beamed restaurant with subdued lighting. Soup is around 35p and there is a fine choice of steaks, fish and poultry. Gammon steak is about £2.50 and Cavalier mixed grill is excellent value at around £3.60 – both served with potatoes, peas and salad garnish. A sweet from the trolley is about 75p and a glass of house wine costs around 50p. A 'Junior Cavalier Menu' is available for children.

COFFEE HOUSE, NORTHUMBRIA HOTEL ★★ Osborne Road (Newcastle upon Tyne 814961)
Open: Mon-Sun 10am-11.30pm

[C] [P] [S]

The Scandinavian pine décor of this attractive buttery is complemented by a long menu with Norwegian subtitles. The Coffee House serves Danish pastries, lunchtime snacks such as seafood pancake at about £1.50 and full three-course meals. Home-made soup of the day, a main dish such as asparagus and cheese pancake or fillet of plaice and a generous slice of fresh cream gâteau will leave you plenty of change from £4 to sample a really excellent cup of coffee and a glass of Spanish house wine.

THE FALCON, Prudhoe (Prudhoe 32324)
Open: Mon-Sat 12noon-2pm, 6.30-10pm, Sun 12noon-1.45pm, 7-10pm

[C] [P] [🍷]

The grill room of this modern pub has picture windows the full length of one wall, giving a view of the surrounding countryside. Clean lines and simple furnishings, with an open grill bar where you can sit on comfortable high stools, and separate tables and chairs if you prefer more sedate seating arrangements, gives a feeling of uncluttered elegance. The menu is unpretentious and you can get a good three-course meal very reasonably. Starters, which include smoked mackerel at around 75p, range in price from 30p to £1.50. Main dishes include pork chop at £2, fillet of plaice at around £2.40 and mixed grill in the region of £3.50, all served with chipped or croquette potatoes, and there are various salads, all priced at £1.80. Desserts range from about 30p for ice cream-based sweets to 65p if you select from the trolley. For children there is a special 'Mr Menu' which includes a main meal, an orange, ice-cream (and the menu itself!), all for 85p. House wine is 57p a glass.

GIOVANNI'S PIZZERIA, 11 North Street (Newcastle upon Tyne 28741)
Open: Mon-Sat 12noon-2.30pm, 6-11.30pm, Sun 7-11pm

[C] [♫]

A comfortable pizzeria where boothed seating and soft Italian music create an authentic atmosphere accentuated by the charming Italian waiters. The whole scene is warmed by the glow of red flock décor and red linen tablecloths. Cuisine is predominantly Italian and pizzas are particularly good value at just around £1.50 and for those who prefer plain English fare, an omelette or gammon steak can be had for around the same price at lunchtimes. The evening menu is more expensive.

THE GOLDEN BENGAL RESTAURANT, 39 Groat Market (Newcastle upon Tyne 20471)
Open: Mon-Sat 12noon-2.30pm, 6-11.30pm, Sun 7-11pm
[C] [♫] [P] [S]

Soft Indian background music and a décor of Indian murals capture an Oriental atmosphere in this city centre restaurant. Soup or fruit juice are followed by chicken curry, keema pillau with vegetable curry or roast chicken and vegetables, with a sweet or fruit to complete the meal. The à la carte menu contains a wealth of Indian specialities – curries mild and hot, medium hot or very hot – at around £1.80. Biriani dishes served with vegetable curry are in the £2.70-£3.80 range and Tandoori clay oven-cooked chicken or king prawns are around £2.80-£3.80. Fruit such as guava or mango served with fresh cream is about 65-75p.

RISTORANTE ROMA ✕
22 Cullingwood Street
(Newcastle upon Tyne 20612)
Open: Mon-Sat 12noon-2.30pm, 7-11.30pm

[C] [♫] [P] [S] [♧]

As a gesture to Italian culture the menu has everything from chariot races to Chianti bottles and offers Sophia Loren (a juicy steak dish) and Gina Lollobrigida – the Chef's secret on a plate in the à la carte menu. Who could ask for more? Further temptations are artichoke hearts in a cream sauce and lobster mornay, plus a star-studded list of sweets headed by crêpes suzette and banana, peach or pineapple flambés. Midday budget items include lasagne or cannelloni for around £1.25, sole or chicken for less than £2 and sirloin steak for around £2.25!

Penrith

OLD VICTORIA HOTEL, 46 Castlegate
(Penrith 62467)
Open: Mon-Sun 12noon-2pm, 7-10pm

[P] [♧]

The two bar lounges of this quaint, roadside hotel are all aglow with copper-topped tables, crackling fires and old oak beams dripping pewter and brass. Meals such as prawn cocktail with brandy and cream, followed by steak, fish, gammon and other hot dishes, a ploughman's or sandwiches (ranging from approximately 50p-£5.50) may be taken here. At dinner time the same menu applies, but there's also a more expensive five-course dinner menu.

WAVERLEY HOTEL ★ Crown Square
(Penrith 63962)
Open: summer: Mon 10am-2pm, 7-8.30pm, Tue-Sat 10am-8.30pm, Sun 12noon-2pm
winter: Mon-Sat 12noon-2pm, 7-8.30pm

[C] [P] [S]

On the fringe of the town centre is this very popular hotel dining room with a small, intimate cocktail bar. The attraction is very reasonably-priced home-made food and fresh vegetables. The main menu includes barbecued spare ribs, steak and kidney pie and beef curry, all for around £2 and a selection of pizzas for around £1.50. Various dishes of the day cost from £1, and there is a newly-opened cold buffet table from £1.25. A choice of home-made sweets cost about 50p, with a glass of French house wine at around 50p.

Sunderland

DENTS, 3 Whitburn Bents Road
(Whitburn 292572)
Open: Mon-Sat 12noon-10pm, Sun 12noon-6pm

[C] [P] [♧]

The après-ski atmosphere of this small cheerful restaurant should give you a good appetite. The polished wood, rough, white-painted walls and ski-ing gear complete the ski lodge look. Instead of ski-slopes, however, the gaily-canopied frontage overlooks the sea. The day-time menu includes home-made soup served with delicious, home-baked rolls for 60p, fresh-cooked-to-order pasta dishes at about £2, or stuffed baked potatoes from 55p. The evening menu spans fast food (burgers, etc) and more imaginative (and more expensive) dishes such as veal Savoyarde or smoked pork in creamy mushroom sauce (about £4).

THE MELTING POT, 9 Maritime Terrace (Sunderland 76909)
Open: Mon-Sat 12noon-2.30pm, 6pm-12mdnt

[C] [P] [S]

Gold drapes covering three walls create a warm, comfortable atmosphere in this intimate Indian restaurant situated in Sunderland's pedestrian precinct. The "lunchtime special" menu, offering a choice of soup or fruit juice, ten traditional Indian dishes such as chicken or prawn curry, five English dishes including rump steak, plus sweet, is superb value at £1.50. The extensive à la carte is also well within our budget but you'll have to be prepared to drink more as the wine is sold in a minimum of half bottles at around £2.

SCOTLAND

The fountain, Glasgow

Glencoe Hotel, Carnoustie

The Mill Hotel, Tynet

Soroba House Hotel, Oban

The Green Park Hotel, Pitlochry

Edinburgh and the Border Regions

Edinburgh, Scotland's capital, is one of Britain's best loved cultural centres, where a unique blend of old and new attracts thousands of tourists each year to the International Festival of Arts and the Tattoo – a military extravaganza enacted on the ramparts of the Edinburgh Castle. The heart of the city is the Old Town which runs from the Castle down the Royal Mile to Holyrood Palace, the residence of the Queen when she is in Edinburgh. In striking contrast to the maze of narrow streets, wynds and courtyards of the Old Town, and separated from it by that unique shopping area of Princes Street with its beautiful gardens alongside, stands the New Town – a stately masterpiece of 18th-century urban planning. Panoramic views of the Firth of Forth to the east and the Pentland Hills can be enjoyed atop Arthur's Seat or Calton Hill.

A cosmopolitan city, it offers ethnic food to suit all nationalities, while still retaining many of the traditional dishes appreciated by both locals and tourists alike. There is nothing quite like a heaped plate of spicy haggis, neeps and chappit tatties (turnip and mashed potatoes) to make you feel you've 'arrived' in Scotland. Scottish shortbread, a buttered biscuit made in rounds or individual shapes, is a best-selling souvenir as is Edinburgh rock – a soft fruit-flavoured sweet. Less well known are the scones, black bun (a rich fruit mixture, spices and brandy encased in a short pastry) and herrings from the local fishing port of Newhaven. The finest oats have always been produced in this region and are used to make porridge (a thinner version than its English and Irish counterparts and served with salt rather than sugar), oatcakes and some home-made soups. To the south and west of Edinburgh is the beautiful Border Country. A tapestry of rolling hills, farmlands, glistening streams and charming historic towns, this region has a character all of its own. The site of many Border battles, the towns of Jedburgh, Kelso and Melrose are distinguished by fine abbeys whose stately ruins stand as a noble memorial to a less peaceful time. It was in this area that the 19th-century novelist, Sir Walter Scott drew his inspiration for works such as Ivanhoe and a visit to his stately home, Abbotsford, is the highlight of many a Border tour. Farther west to Dumfries and Galloway are found memorials to the great bard himself, Robert Burns. The rivers in these parts yield abundant fish, notably the River Tweed, renowned for its salmon which can be tasted at some of the restaurants mentioned within.

DUMFRIES
&
NEWTON STEWART
CASTLE DOUGLAS
DALBEATTIE
PORTPATRICK
KIRKCUDBRIGHT

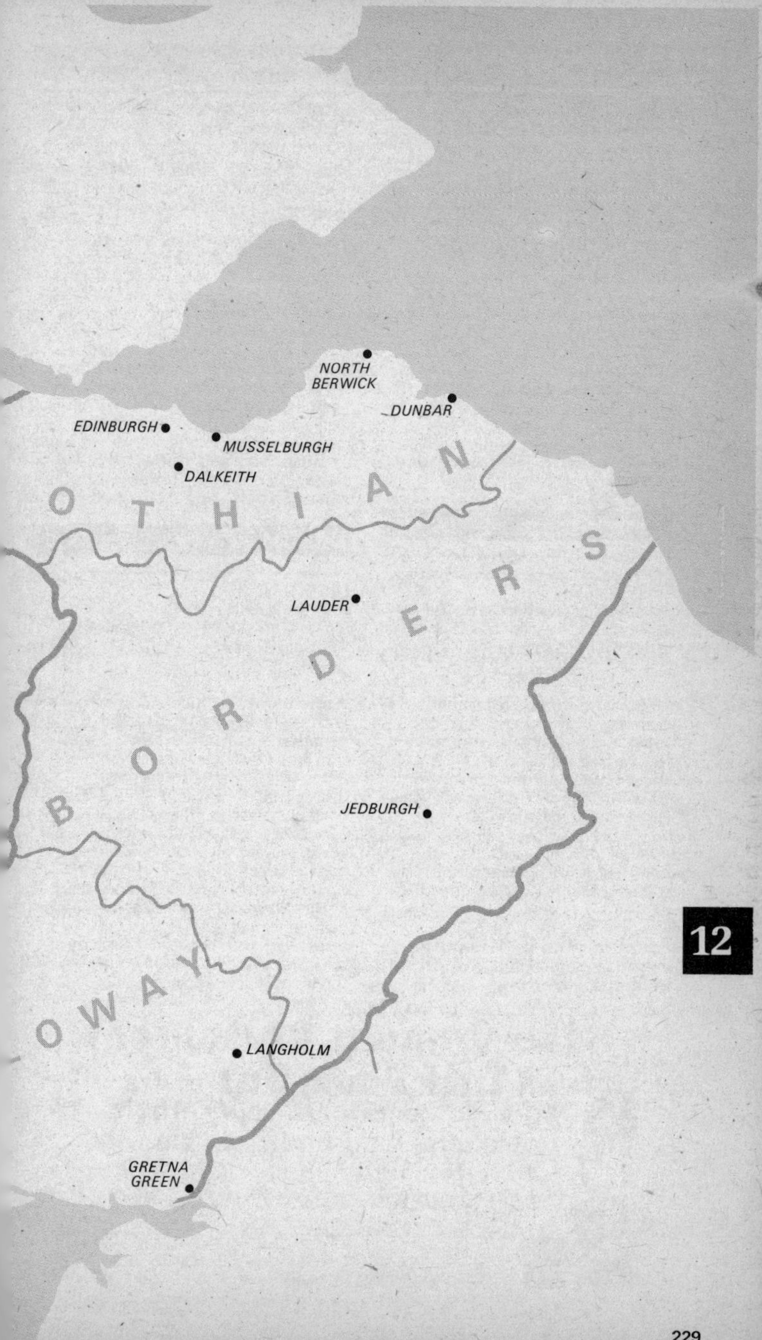

NORTH BERWICK
DUNBAR
EDINBURGH
MUSSELBURGH
DALKEITH
OTHIAN
LAUDER
BORDERS
JEDBURGH
OWAY
LANGHOLM
GRETNA GREEN

12

Castle Douglas

ROSE COTTAGE, Gelston
(Castle Douglas 2513)
Open: Mon-Sun 9am-5pm

[P]

This cottage restaurant, with its lovely gardens, in the rural village of Gelston, two miles south of Castle Douglas, is a veritable haven from the ravages of inflation. Where else could you enjoy soup, followed by gammon steak with chips and vegetables, plus home-made gâteau to finish, for about £2.50? Amazingly, children's portions bring this price down even lower. As well as a choice of nine main dishes, friendly owners Mr and Mrs Donaldson offer generous Devonshire teas for 70p. Coffee is about 20p a cup, but you'll have to forego the wine as the restaurant is unlicensed.

Dalbeattie

THE GRANARY, Barend, Sandyhills
(Southwick 663)
12m south east of Dalbeattie on the A710
Open: Mon-Sun 7.30-9pm

[P]

This renovated farm building retains its rustic character and charm, with whitewashed stone walls, a timber-vaulted ceiling and tiled floor. An excellent table d'hôte meal is served here, and although the choice of dishes is limited, the food itself is most creative, offering dishes such as tomato and orange soup, moussaka (a mammoth portion) with fresh vegetables and salad, followed by a tempting array of home-made sweets such as meringue nests with strawberries and cream. With a glass of house wine at around 50p, you will just exceed £5, but its worth it!

Dalkeith

GIORGIO PIZZA & SPAGHETTI HOUSE, 128 High Street
(031-663 4492)
Open: Mon-Sun 12noon-2.30pm, 5pm-1am

[C] [P] [S]

Grapes, hanging bottles, wrought-ironwork and lighting by lanterns convey the atmosphere of an Italian bistro, and indeed owner Mr Crolla does come from a village near Rome. Pasta dishes are prevalent as may be expected, and £1.70 or so will buy a substantial main course such as lasagna al forno or spaghetti marenara. A three-course business lunch for around £1.70 offers exceptionally good value, and high teas are served from 5pm to 7pm. If you want a special meal, you may prefer to choose escalope Garibaldi or bistecca pizziola, either of which costs about £3.75.

Dumfries

OPUS, 95 Queensberry Street
(Dumfries 5752)
Open: Mon-Wed, Fri-Sat 9am-5pm, Thu 9am-1pm

[P] [S]

A bright, cosy restaurant decked out with red tables and much wood panelling, but tricky to locate. You'll find it up two flights of stairs above a fabric shop. Snacks are served throughout the day, but at lunchtimes a blackboard menu offers a bewildering variety of goodies. Take your pick from several salad bowls and cold meat for just £1. Or how about the hot dishes? Spicy vegetable pie and lasagne (both £1) are the most popular. Desserts, calculated to test a weightwatcher's resolve, include cheesecake and fresh cream gâteau. The eaterie is unlicensed, but try the excellent coffee.

Dunbar

CAFE GRECO, 88 High Street (Dunbar 62749)
Open: summer: Mon-Sun 10am-10pm, winter: Mon-Sun 10am-7pm

C S ♧

The vibrant modern colour scheme of black, white and orange spills out of this restaurant to transform the tall, narrow stone-built listed building which houses it. Open from noon to 10pm in season, Café Greco caters well for visitors to the East Lothian coastal town, offering a wide range of hot and cold snacks including omelettes, curries and salads. A satisfying three-course meal can be had starting with home-made soup and including either a Continental main course such as scampi provençale or a more traditional steak or fried chicken dish. Rounded off with fruit pie and cream or gâteau and a glass of wine, dinner can cost you around £4.50.

Edinburgh

AEROGRILL, Edinburgh Airport (031-344 3272)
Open: Mon-Sun 11.30am-9.15pm

C P S ♧

Children, more than anyone, regard a visit to an airport as a special occasion, though a family outing of this sort can often work out to be rather hard on Dad's pocket. Not so if you lunch at the Aerogrill, where a children's menu with matching prices is available on request. Apart from a selection of grills, omelettes, salads and fish dishes, a full three-course meal, including ¼ litre carafe costs little more than £4.

BAR ITALIA, 100-104 Lothian Road (031-229 0451)
Open: Mon-Sun 12noon-4pm

♫ P S ♧

Pizza delle Stagioni, with tomatoes, mozzarella, ham, salami, clams, mushrooms, artichokes and green peppers, costs around £2.50 and you have a choice of nine other varieties, the cheapest being a pizza margherita for about £2. In the same price range you can choose from fourteen pasta dishes, and there are also a number of more straightforward dishes such as roast chicken with chips or grilled sirloin with chips at around £3. A starter and a sweet could add two or three pounds to the bill, but if you're watching the pennies you could choose soup and ice cream (the cheapest choices).

BRUNO'S, 8-14a Morrison Street (031-229 7521)
Open: Mon-Sat 12noon-2pm, Sun 5.30pm-12mdnt 5.30pm-12.30am (1.30am Fri-Sat)

S

Bright red canopies provide a distinctly Continental façade to this popular Italian restaurant, close to the city centre. Inside, the Italian influence is reflected in the warm red of the décor and carpeting, dark wood furniture, lanterns and polished copper lighting. The whole effect is enhanced by the friendly Italian waiters dressed in red shirts, embroidered with a bold 'B', and black trousers. An extensive menu covers the whole range of Italian cuisine from the humble pizza, starting around £1.80 to the bistecca dello chef (Chef's speciality steak) from about £4. With a speciality starter of pâté, pizza Bruno and a choice of sweet including torte or gâteau you have a three-course meal for around £4.50. A glass of wine costs about 55p.

CAFE CAPPUCCINO, 15 Salisbury Place (031-667 4265)
Open: Mon-Sat 9am-8.30pm

P S ♧

The menu includes a wide variety of omelettes, salads, toasted sandwiches and filled rolls, all very reasonably priced, and if you are looking for a real meal there is an equally wide choice of fish or meat dishes which, with vegetables, mostly cost between £1 and £2.50. There is a good selection of ice-cream confections with prices around 50p. The Café Cappuccino is not licensed but you can take your pick from twenty non-alcoholic beverages of which cappuccino coffee is one.

THE CAPRICE, 325-331 Leith Walk (031-554 1279)
Open: Tue-Sat 12noon-2pm, 5.30-11pm, Sun 6-11pm

♫ P S ♧

Green mosaic frontage and a display of flags – mostly European – make it easy to distinguish this Italian restaurant from afar. The inside is functional and divided into several areas. Choose, if you can, the section nearest to the wood-burning stove and you will be able to see your pizza (there are fifteen varieties priced under £3.10) being prepared and cooked. You don't have to eat pizza though, and it's the table d'hôte lunch – a choice of two, in fact – which makes the Caprice so popular at mid-day. Fruit juice or soup, a main course which might be a small steak or an Italian speciality such as cannelloni, a sweet, coffee or tea, all for about £2.50 can't be bad value, yet there is a cheaper lunch with only the main course changed. The choice is wider than for the more expensive meal, including a pasta or pizza, salad, omelette, lamb chasseur and beef and vegetable pie.

LE CHÂTEAU, Spittal Street
(031-229 1181)
Open: Mon-Sat 12noon-2.30pm, 6-11pm

C ♫ 🍷

From its impressive frontage you might expect Le Château prices to be well above our limit, but Bill and Bridget Morgan's restaurant is recommended for good food at reasonable prices, for its bright and comfortable interior, and friendly atmosphere. Starters include a house pâté, prawn cocktail for around £1.10 and piping-hot soup at 50p or so. There is a choice of four or five dishes and of the usual grills at around £3.50. Among the house specialities are lasagne and chicken.

CRAWFORD'S, 31 Frederick Street
(031-225 4579)
Open: summer: Mon-Sat 8am-11pm (7pm winter)

S 🍷

This one of the very handy Crawford's chain of restaurants, catering for families and shoppers. The ground-floor restaurant's décor has a country theme with pine wood and terra-cotta ceramic tiles. As with most Crawford's you can get a quick and reasonably-priced meal from the attractively laid out cold counter, or if you prefer, there is a tempting range of flans, pies and casseroles. To finish with, the range of gâteaux befit one of Scotland's best known bakeries.

DANISH KITCHEN, 124 Princes Street
(031-226 6669)
Open: Mon-Sat 9.30am-4.50pm

S 🍷

On the mezzanine floor of Austin Reed at the west end of Princes Street, the self-service Danish Kitchen provides very good food at a reasonable price, in most pleasant and comfortable surroundings. You can choose from freshly-made soup, Danish open sandwiches, salads, toasted sandwiches and omelettes. There is a tempting selection of sweets and freshly-baked pastries, and beverages include tea, coffee, fruit drinks, and milk shakes. Indeed a satisfying meal here need cost no more than £2.50 including wine.

DENZLER'S ×× 80 Queen Street
(031-226 5467)
Open: Mon-Sat 12noon-2pm, 6.30-9.50pm

The Swiss origins of the Denzler husband-and-wife team are revealed in both wine list and menu. Lunchtime starters at under £1, include Swiss fruit juice, main courses such as escalope de porc Cordon Bleu and êntrecote chasseur cost from around £2.50. Dinner menu is more adventurous and more expensive – you'll find it difficult to keep within our limit. The wine list offers a good selection and a glass of the house wine costs around 60p.

THE DORIC TAVERN × 15-16 Market Street (031-225 1084)
Open: Mon-Sat 12noon-2.30pm, 6-9.30pm

S

If local lawyers and journalists gather in a restaurant, it's a sure sign that you'll get value for money. With a set three-course lunch for under £3 and four-course dinner for under £4, prices are hard to beat. Filling British dishes such as boiled silverside and dumplings or haggis and turnips are featured. The extensive à la carte, which includes an excellent mixed grill for about £2.50, is also very good value. Mr McGuffie, proprietor for the last quarter-century, believes in traditional service.

FORTROSE GRILL, 71 Rose Street
(031-225 8012)
Open: summer: Mon-Sat 11am-10pm, Sun 12.30-10pm, winter: closed Sun

S 🍷

Rose Street, with its boutiques and up-market restaurants is the 'in' shopping and eating area of Edinburgh. The Fortrose Grill is small and simple, the welcome and service friendly and informal. There is a good-value business lunch at about £2 and the à la carte menu is quite reasonable, with soup and 'fruity' starters up to 50p. Salads, pastas, and omelettes are in the £2-£3 range and a mixed grill of steak, sausage, bacon, tomato, mushroom and chips is one of the most expensive meals at around £4.40. Sweets are variations on the theme of ice cream, coffee is around 28p and a glass of house wine about 65p. The menu finishes with the words 'Servis non compris' which doesn't mean 'I don't understand how the washing machine works' but suggests discretion when tipping.

MADOGS, 38 George Street
(031-225 3408)

Open: Mon-Sat 12noon-3pm, 6pm-1am

[C] [♫] [S]

This is very much an American restaurant with an American movie-hero theme to its décor and a limited but interesting menu which includes dishes made from materials specially imported from the States by the young American owners. The staff are American, friendly, and efficient, and the music American and rather loud. The lunch menu includes Kosher pastrami at around £1.90 and New England clam chowder at about £1.20. The dinner menu can be expensive, but there are a number of main fish or char broiler dishes at around £4.40.

THE PANCAKE PLACE, 130 High Street (031-225 1972)
Open: Mon-Sat 10am-9pm,
Sun 11am-9pm

[S]

Occupying a prime position in the city's historic Royal Mile, this restaurant, as its name suggests, specialises in pancakes large and small, sweet or savoury. The limited range of starters offers soup of the day or fruit juice at prices around 30p. You then launch into the mind-blowing array of savoury pancakes; hot ones with such fillings as haddock Mornay, bacon and maple syrup (an American favourite), and chicken curry, all under £2, and a selection of 'cool crisp salads', cheeses, ham, chicken or egg, served with two thin pancakes, mayonnaise or pickle on a bed of lettuce, tomato or cucumber for around the same price. If you have enough room to spare (the menu does warn that all sweet pancakes can ruin your diet) try an 'American' – three sweet pancakes layered with butter and served with a jug of maple syrup for about £1. A couple of 'spoon size' pancakes topped with sliced banana and cream cost 65p.

POST HOUSE HOTEL ☆☆☆
Corstorphine Road (031-334 8221)
Open: Buttery: Mon-Sun 10.30am-10pm

[C] [P] [S]

Very handy for the zoo, this bright and modern buttery serves anything from large and colourful double-decker sandwiches to a three-course meal. Try the 'platter' menu which offers juicy steaks or scampi with chips and vegetables (all good nourishing stuff!) plus a sweet, washed down by a glass of French house wine, all for around £4.50. Babies are well-catered for here with 'strained dinner' or boiled egg and buttered fingers – and everything consumed within earshot of the animals!

THE QUERNSTONE, 4-8 Lochrin Buildings (031-229 5319)
Open: Restaurant: Mon-Sat 12noon-2.30pm, 5-10pm, Ice-cream Parlour: Mon-Sat 10.30am-10pm, Sun 1-9pm

[C] [♫] [P] [S] [👪]

The Italian family Boni own and run The Quernstone, a restaurant and ice cream parlour famous hereabouts for its ice-cream and extremely popular – particularly with King's Theatre folk, both audiences and performers – for its good, but inexpensive, home-cooked food. Italian dishes include various spaghettis at around £2.25 and pizziola steak at around £4. Boniburgers and Quernstoneburger Specials are around the £2 mark.

THE STABLE BAR, Mortonhall Park, 30 Frogston Road East
(031-664 0773)
Open: normal licensing hours
Restaurant: Mon-Sun 12noon-2pm

[♫] [P] [👪]

Adjacent to the Mortonhall Caravan Park but occupying an 18th-century coach house, this bar/restaurant is situated in an extremely pleasant environment. Open for lunches only, the daily changing menu offers a limited choice but good value for money. A typical lunch gives the choice of two starters, three main courses and two sweets. The most expensive combination being pâté, braised ham with vegetables and gâteau which would cost around £2.80. With the addition of coffee and wine this meal will still be around £3.60.

TATTOO GRILL, ROYAL SCOT HOTEL ☆☆☆☆ 111 Glasgow Road
(031-334 9191)
Open: Mon-Sun 12noon-2.30pm, 6-9.30pm

[C] [♫] [P] [👪]

Pick your dishes from an interesting menu garnished with Scottish dialect. A simple Angus steak rejoices in the name of the Aberdonian, whereas gammon with pineapple and cherry is known as the Tam o'Shanter, and they exist, so the menu says 'tae mak ye full'. Other choices are the 'wee tasties' (sandwiches), 'cauld cuts' (a selection of cold meats and salad) and various sweets 'tae tickle your palate'. A posh terrace restaurant in the same hotel offers a weekday-only set lunch at around £4.50.

Gretna Green

THE AULD SMIDDY RESTAURANT
Headless Cross (Gretna 365)
Open: summer: 8am-7pm, winter: 8am-6pm

[P] [S] [👪]

Although you can no longer elope here with your sweetheart, you can enjoy a pleasant snack or full meal at very reasonable prices. Tucked just behind the world-famous blacksmith's shop, this low-ceilinged restaurant is festooned with brass bric-à-brac. A three-course lunch (which might consist of soup, roast beef with horseradish sauce, followed by apple tart) is still under £3, so even with coffee (24p) and a glass of wine (55p) you are well within the budget.

Jedburgh

THE CARTER'S REST ✕ Abbey Place
(Jedburgh 3414)
Open: Mon-Sun 12noon-2pm, 6-9pm
(closed Sun in winter)

[♫] [P] [👪]

This restaurant is built of stone plundered from the nearby Abbey, whose ruins dominate the outlook and was the local 'Penny' School for a hundred years or so from 1779, then a real Carter's Rest for patrons of Jedburgh's horse fair. Today it offers excellent grills, bar lunches and dinners, as well as a popular Sunday cold buffet. You can eat à la carte very well for around £5 here, even allowing 60p for a glass of wine, or make do with bar snacks. Hot buffet lunch specials include beef olives with trimmings at about £2.40 and a £1.20 ham omelette.

Kirkcudbright

THE COFFEE POT, 5 Castle Street
(Kirkcudbright 30569)
Open: summer only: Mon-Sat 10am-5pm, 6.45-8.30pm

[C] [S]

The Coffee Pot with its bow-windowed frontage is a snug little restaurant just across from the old castle in the centre of historic Kirkcudbright. George and Rona Bower have devised an interesting à la carte menu to tempt the tourist and shopper alike at prices of around £5. Starters include mushrooms provençale and seven main courses include fried local trout and roast venison. Rum baba and raspberries St Moritz are desserts.

Langholm

TH' AULD ACQUAINTANCE, 88 High Street (Langholm 80573)
Open: Wed-Thu 10.30am-6.30pm, Fri 10.30am-7.30pm, Sat 10.30am-8pm, Sun 10.30am-7pm

[P] [S] [🍷]

Wood panelling, Regency wall-lamps and oak beams add a definite character to this homely, L-shaped restaurant. You can choose from four starters (all under £1), and follow with any one of a dozen fish and meat grills, which range from £1.70 to £4 (except sirloin steak at £5). Trolley-borne sweets are around 75p, whilst half bottles of wine from the list start at £1.50. For those just feeling peckish, a snack menu offers sandwiches and rolls at modest prices.

Lauder

THE BLACK BULL HOTEL
(Lauder 208)
Open: Mon-Sun 8am-9.30pm

[♫] [P] [🍷]

The jangle of harness and sound of posthorns no longer announces the arrival of travellers in need of rest and refreshment, yet The Black Bull retains the atmosphere of a coaching inn. Built in the 18th century, it survived the coming of the railways and has been revived and modernised to cope with the swing back to road transport. Bars are open during normal licensing hours and wine may be purchased by the glass. In the elegant dining room you can enjoy lunch at around £3.75 but the dinner menu is just out of our reach. The three-course lunch offers five or six main dishes including roasts. For a cold meal or snack, try the Harness Room Grill, where you can feast your eyes on relics of coaching days whilst enjoying your choice from the bar menu. This includes a three-course lunch at around £2 and ploughman's at about £1.

Musselburgh

CAPRICE, 198 High Street
(031-665 2991)
Open: summer: Mon-Sat 12noon-12mdnt, Sun 4pm-12mdnt, winter: Mon-Sat 12noon-2.30pm, 5.30-12mdnt, Sun 4pm-12mdnt

[♫] [P] [S] [🍷]

'Our succulent pizzas are cooked in the traditional manner in a wood-fired oven to give them that extra taste of quality. Even the wood used, Scottish pine, is chosen because it adds the required flavour. . . .' That's how Cavalier Victor Alongi introduces his customers to his pizzeria cum Italian restaurant. The sixteen different home-made pizza specialities have deservedly gained Victor and his son Alfredo a renowned reputation. A medium-sized pizza (12in diameter) provides a very generous meal for the average eater, but for those with voracious appetites the large pizza (15in) will prove a challenge. A choice from the extensive à la carte menu costs around £5 with wine, but two table d'hôte lunch menus offer good value at around £1.30 for three courses.

Newton Stewart

THE SALAD BOWL, 8 Albert Street
(Newton Stewart 3026)
Open: Mon-Sat 10am-6.30pm, 8-10.45pm (10pm Etr-Oct)

[S]

You're assured of a warm welcome at this pleasant little restaurant, which is ideally placed to catch all the town's passing trade. Inside, the rough-cast walls are ornamented by hanging plants, display cabinets and an antique clock. Tables are of wood with laminated tops. The buffet luncheon consists of soup, plus an array of eye-catching cold meat salads at only £1.20 including coffee. Fish predominates on the high tea menu, with a deep-fried haddock, for instance, costing £2.30 (again including a hot drink). In the evening a more adventurous, up-market menu offers a wide choice of starters and main dishes, but still within the budget if you choose carefully (eg stuffed tomato, trout meunière and apple tart is around £4.50). House wine is 60p per glass.

North Berwick

LA BONBONNIERE, 1 Station Hill
(North Berwick 3622)
Open: Mon-Sat 10am-6pm,
Sun 11am-6pm

[P]

Tapestries by owner Mrs Moss lend a personal touch to the stone-walled, homely interior of this small, street-level coffee shop. This is a family concern, with true home cooking and friendly atmosphere. Good, basic meals such as liver and onions, casserole, or mince, are suitably priced; three courses will cost around £3. La Bonbonnière is not licensed.

Portpatrick

THE OLD MILL HOUSE
(Portpatrick 358)
Open: Apr-Oct: Mon-Sun 10.30am-10pm

[P]

This picturesque, whitewashed old mill house, set amid beautiful gardens complete with trout stream and heated outdoor pool, ground its last barley in 1929 and the miller is said to haunt the premises still. Food includes a table d'hôte lunch menu of good British fare costing something over £3. A luscious Galloway steak can be sampled from the à la carte menu for about £4 and fresh Solway salmon is another tempting local dish. An interesting bar menu offers a wide selection of less pricey dishes including special children's meals for around 65p for such favourites as bangers, fish or pizza fingers or salad with chips. A three-course children's menu for younger hungers costs around £1.50. High teas range from around £2.45 to £4.45 according to the main dish chosen, with cheese and egg salad at the lower end and grilled sirloin steak at the top. This price is inclusive of hot home-baked scones with butter and jam, home-baked cakes and tea.

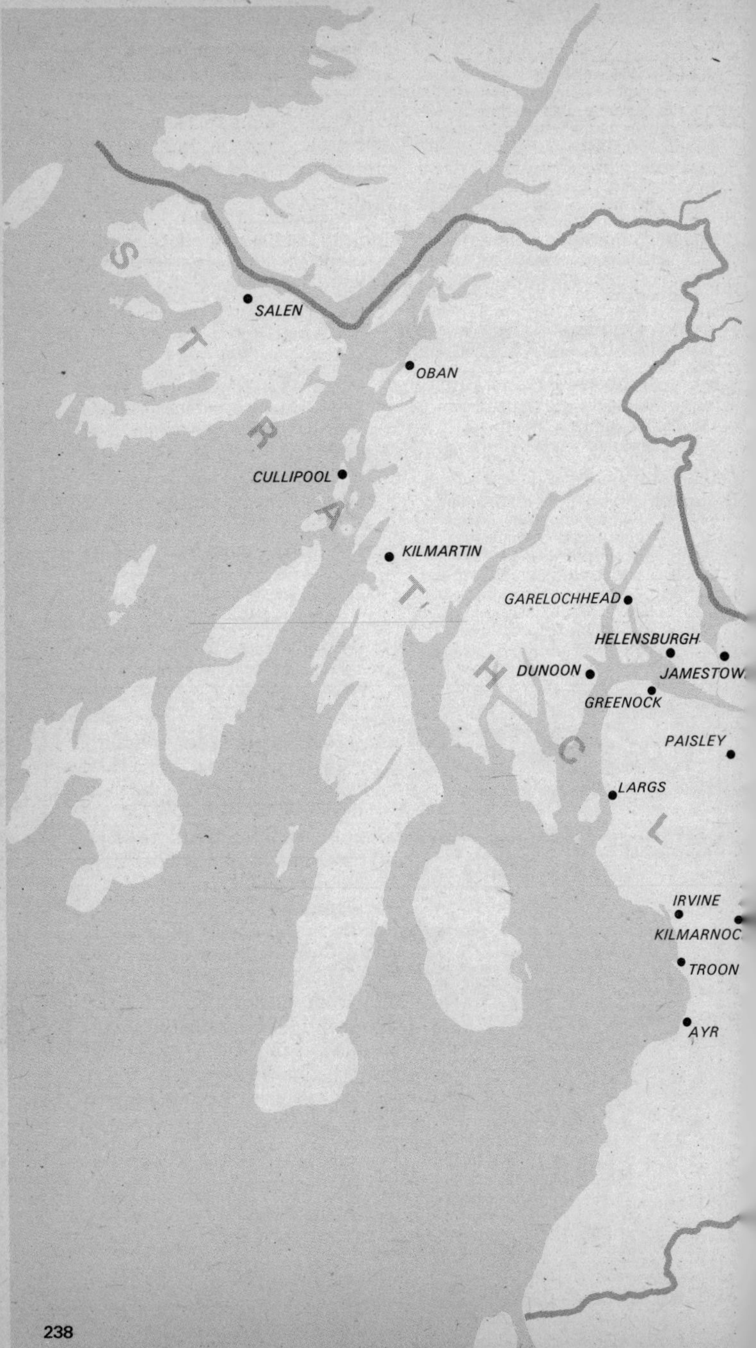
S
T
R
A
T
H
C
L
SALEN
OBAN
CULLIPOOL
KILMARTIN
GARELOCHHEAD
HELENSBURGH
DUNOON
JAMESTOW
GREENOCK
PAISLEY
LARGS
IRVINE
KILMARNOC
TROON
AYR

Glasgow and the West

The largest city in Scotland, Glasgow tops a million inhabitants in the sprawling commercial and industrial community where Georgian elegance and Victorian splendour vie for attention. Notable representatives are the Gothic Cathedral and the world-famous Art Gallery at Kelvingrove Park. The city straddles the River Clyde, which runs through a fruit-farming valley overlooked by rolling hills where noble castles such as Craignethan and Bothwell stand as testimonies to an eventful history.

The fierce beauty of the West is legendary – where gold and silver sands line the rugged coastline, sea lochs slice deep into the lofty mountains and mysterious islands and headlands beckon the curious. The Isle of Arran with its jagged mountains – a microcosm of Scotland itself – and the Mull of Kintyre, immortalised in song by Paul McCartney are only two of many. This region of majestic lochs, including Loch Lomond, may not boast the Loch Ness monster, but Loch Morar is reputed to house an aquatic dinosaur from Mesozoic times at least equal in size to Nessy.

Loch Fyne – a vast sea loch set in an area of devastating beauty – is renowned for the best and fattest herrings in Britain and local curers split and smoke these herrings to produce fine, very large kippers.

There is a wealth of good food to be sampled in these parts. Cock-a-leekie – fowl simmered with cut leeks and with prunes added for sweetening, is a nourishing broth and stoved howtowdie – casseroled chicken with onions, potatoes and lashings of butter is a very satisfying dish. In the south, Ayrshire roll is a popular meal – bacon cured with salt, saltpetre, sugar and vinegar, then boned and made into long rolls to mature – is delicious grilled.

For dessert a cloutie dumpling is just the thing – a sweet boiled pudding with dried fruits, treacle, cinnamon and mixed spices boiled in a cloth. If this is too filling, a bap may suffice – a soft, flat oval made from slightly sweetened dough and eaten warm. One speciality you probably will not find in the establishments listed in the following pages is rumbledethumps – a Scottish version of bubble and squeak pepped up with onions or chives.

Ayr

THE BEEFHOUSE (STATION HOTEL)
★★★ Burns Statue Square (Ayr 63268)
Open: Mon-Thu, Sun 12noon-2.30pm, 6-10pm, Fri-Sat 12noon-2.30pm, 6-11pm

C ♫ P S ♧

One of a chain of Reo Stakis eating houses, this spacious restaurant has over sixty pine tables, individually lit to create a very attractive setting. Overhead, two large arches give the low ceiling a pleasing vault-like effect. With main courses being chiefly beefsteak, there's need to select carefully if you're not to exceed the budget. However, farmhouse-style Scotch broth (50p), beef'n'greens – mountain-high strips of beef over shredded lettuce with toasties (£3.20) and a fresh fruit salad (85p) will just leave you enough for a coffee with cream. Around 60p secures a glass of house wine.

CARLE'S RESTAURANT ✕ 27 Burns Statue Square (Ayr 62740)
Open: Mon-Sat 12noon-10pm

P S ♧

A bright and airy restaurant with comfy half-moon chairs, circular tables and futuristic hanging lights. Upstairs, starters range from soup at 55p, to an exotic prawn cocktail at £1.50. There is a choice of seven main courses costing between £2.20 and £3.50 – in the middle of this price range is the very popular roast chicken garnished with Ayrshire bacon and tomato, whilst lemon meringue pie is a delicious dessert option at 70p. A glass of Mr Carle's house wine is about 55p. On the ground floor, a coffee-shop style operates with cold meat salads, omelettes or roast of the day, all at very reasonable prices.

THE COFFEE CLUB, 37 Beresford Terrace (Ayr 63239)
Open: Mon-Sat 10am-10pm

♫ P S

This small and friendly establishment is situated near to Burns' Statue Square in the centre of Ayr. The clubby atmosphere extends to comfortable seating and low-level tables, making this a place to relax while you take your meal. An interesting variety of snacks, salads and light meals are served with a creative flair. Snacks range from pizza to substantial open sandwiches and there are a number of filling dishes such as ravioli, risotto, or chili con carne at around £1.50, and for the same price you can have a portion of savoury flan with salad. Sweets include pastries, fruit flan, and waffles, at prices around 65p.

THE COPPERFIELD
242 Prestwick Road (Ayr 67905)
Open: summer: Mon-Sat 10am-9pm, winter: Mon-Sat 10am-6pm

C P S ♧

David himself would have felt quite at home amid the dark wooden beams of this pseudo-Dickensian eating house. Doubtless, he would have tucked into home-baked goodies (proprietor Mrs Holland's forté) with relish. Menu prices, although alas a long way from Mr Micawber's ideas on costs, are very low indeed. A full three-course meal is still only around £2.50 – remarkable, considering all prices include VAT. Meals are traditional – roast beef, potatoes and veg, haddock, chips and veg or ham and peach salad – the kind of choice to suit a whole family's tastes, and even sirloin steak with all the trimmings comes to under £4. Wine costs around 45p per glass.

THE COUNTRY CLUB
63-65 Newmarket Street (Ayr 62667)
Open: Mon-Sat 9am-6pm

C P S

Especially in winter, you must sample the piping hot soup served at the table from a shining copper pot in this popular restaurant in Ayr's main shopping street. It is delicious, and only costs around 30p. In fact, for about £2.30 you can have genuine haggis with garden vegetables, *and* a starter and sweet, or cheese, or coffee on the table d'hôte lunch menu. Only turkey and gammon or sirloin steak cost more. The snack lunch menu offers ten different dishes such as scrambled egg on toast, macaroni au gratin or mutton pie at around £1 with a side salad. Even à la carte is not entirely beyond reach, and includes omelettes at about £1.50, roast chicken at around £2.70 (hot or cold, with salad). Vegetables will add about £1 and a sweet (all ice cream-based) between 70p and 90p. Wines, too, are very reasonably priced, with a glass of Sauterne or Lutomer Riesling costing around 50p.

JACOBITE, 7 Carrick Street (Ayr 67568)
Open: Mon-Sat 9am-11pm, Sun (summer only) 12noon-9pm

♫ P S ♧

The long, narrow shape of the Jacobite has been well utilised to cater for a wide variety of needs. At the front, fast food and snacks are served – such as the

Jaco-burger (with gammon and cheese) for under £1. Beyond, the dining area serves breakfast, dinner and everything in between. All meals are well under £5. There's a three-course special at about £3, which may include soup, steak pie and fruit flan – all home-made. Apart from being ideal for family eating, the Jacobite, with its wide doors, and a room set apart from the main throng, is suitable for the disabled. It is easy to pick out the attractive awning and bow windows of the Jacobite in Ayr's shopping precinct. Inside, dark oak browns associated with the Jacobean period are highlighted by brasses and a collection of old bottles.

OLDE WORLDE INN
48 Newmarket Street (Ayr 62392)
Open: Mon-Sat 12noon-2.30pm, 5-11pm, Sun 5-10pm

[C] [♫] [P] [S] [♧]

Whether Robbie Burns, whose statue stands some 100 yards away, would have felt at home in this 'olde worlde inn' is debatable, but he would have been assured of a good basic meal at a fair price. This member of the Reo Stakis chain, has panelled walls and beams, with a rough stone archway creating a break in the interior. Main course prices include a starter, but sweets are extra. However, haddock, chicken, gammon or beefsteak burger, all for around £3 should fill you up and keep you within the budget. The special lunchtime menu is particularly good value, at around £2, and includes in the main course choice, lasagne and spaghetti Bolognese.

PLOUGH INN, 231 High Street (Ayr 62578)
Open: Mon-Sun 11am-2.30pm, 5-11pm

[C] [♧]

This Reo Stakis 'Olde Worlde' Inn is typical of the chain, with almost a North American flavour in its mellow lighting and unostentatious but comfortable furnishings. In the restaurant, a waitress-served meal of Scotch broth, prawn cocktail, pâté or fruit juice, followed by a main course such as steak, chicken or haddock costs around £4 (including appropriate vegetables, potatoes and a roll or chunky bread and butter). Apple pie and cream or Black Forest gâteau cost around 65p. There is a three-course children's menu too, for little more than £1, making this a good place to take the family. House wines are available by the carafe or glass.

THE TUDOR RESTAURANT
6-8 Beresford Terrace (Ayr 61404)
Open: Mon-Sat 9am-9pm

[P] [S] [♧]

The Tudor Restaurant may not be anything like authentic 16th-century, but for the family it offers a good meal at very reasonable prices. A table d'hôte lunch is still under £2 and includes soup or fruit juice, a main course such as beefsteak pie, cold meat with salad, or haddock and chips, and a sweet or cheese. There is a special children's menu at around £1.20. High tea, which comes with a pot of tea, bread, scone, jam and a cake (all home-baked), gives a considerable choice, from eggs on toast at around £1.60 to entrecôte steak at around £3.10, and again there is a children's version for considerably less. The restaurant is not licensed.

Cullipool

LONGHOUSE BUTTERY, Isle of Luing (Luing 209)
Open: Mon-Wed & Sun 11am-5pm, Thu-Sat 11am-8pm

[P]

It's well worth the journey from the Scottish mainland across the Island of Seil and then the 90-second car ferry to this beautiful little island of Luing. The high spot of a visit must be this converted, whitewashed croft which incorporates a white and pine-clad restaurant with dispense bar and small gallery where partner Edna Whyte displays and sells gifts bearing her 'Old Rectory' designs. The other half of the partnership, Audrey Stone, is to be seen serving the delicious meals including such delicacies as buttery venison pâté, and fresh Luing prawns, served on wholemeal bread with crispy salad. Home-made sweets include the mouthwatering triple meringue with cream for 80p. A three-course lunch with coffee and wine costs in the region of £3.80. Unfortunately, the special dinner, including fresh lobster or salmon, would over-stretch our pocket.

Cumnock

THE ROYAL HOTEL ★★
1 Glaisnock Street (Cumnock 20822)
Open: Mon-Sat 12noon-2pm, 5-6.30pm, 7-9pm, Sun 12.30-2.30pm, 5-6.30pm, 7-9pm

[P] [S] [♧]

It is a well-deserved compliment to this traditional and comfortable hotel that local businessmen are regular customers. In the attractively lit dining room, a conventional choice of dishes is very well presented, and very well priced. Three lunch courses focusing on roast sirloin (with perhaps banana fritters or green figs with cream to follow) will not cost much over £3, and even if you go for the fresh salmon, you'll still be spending well under £5. The very substantial high tea might cost £4.50 for a mixed grill, tea, scones, and cakes. Dinner will be around the £5 mark.

Dunoon

IMPERIAL GRILL, 72 Argyll Street (Dunoon 3155)
Open: summer: Mon-Sat 12noon-3pm, 5-11pm, winter: Mon-Sat 12noon-3pm, 5-10pm (closed Wed)

[♫]

Dunoon, the principal town on the beautiful Cowal Peninsula, boasts this modern grill room in its main street. Particularly good value is the three-course business lunch which offers a varying menu of simple fare including such main dishes as farmhouse grill, roast pork and apple sauce or fried fillet of haddock. Along with a choice of two starters and sweets the whole meal costs around £2. A more extensive à la carte offers an evening meal for around £5 including a glass of French wine in the region of 55p. A substantial high tea of main course grill, pot of tea and bread and butter costs around £2. After this you may just feel like sampling the Imperial's pièce de résistance – freshly-baked cakes and scones from their adjoining bakery.

East Kilbride

HONG KONG, 46-48 Kirkton Park (East Kilbride 20112)
Open: Mon-Sat 12noon-12mdnt, Sun 2pm-12mdnt

[C] [♫] [P]

Here is a Chinese restaurant with a certain individuality. Décor is unmistakably oriental with golden dragons set against black walls, and the à la carte is extensive and fairly typical, but it's the speciality teas, desserts and wine list which makes this restaurant stand out from the rest. You'll have to choose carefully if you're to keep within the limit on the à la carte menu but the set dinners, comprising six courses, coffee with cream and mint chocolate, offer excellent value at around £5. If you forgo the starter on the à la carte menu you might just afford a special sweet such as the Hong Kong Special – a delicate concoction of peaches, sparkling wine, soda water and angostura bitters costing £2.70 for two persons. Otherwise save your pennies for one of the sixteen unusual teas such as 'gunpowder green tea' described as an 'attractive clear fragrant liquor' at £1 per pot for two, and a cocktail from the imaginative list of twenty-six. Wine is sold by the glass for 45p, but if you prefer a bottle there are seventy-nine names to choose from.

MUSHROOM, Princes Square (East Kilbride 23222)
Open: Mon-Sat 12noon-2.30pm, 5-10pm

[C] [P] [S] [♿]

One of the Stakis organisation's 'Olde Worlde Inns'. Don't be misled by that, the genuine timbers and chintzes will not be in evidence. But you will find fast food, freshly cooked and not overpriced. Sirloin steak at around £4 includes peas, chips or baked potato and a starter. Alternatives are haddock, chicken or gammon. Sweets or cheese are around 65p. Situated in the middle of a modern shopping centre in Scotland's oldest 'new' town, the Mushroom is convenient and well-used by families and businessmen.

Garelochhead

RISTORANTE AUGUSTO, Main Street (Garelochhead 810570)
Open: summer: Tue-Sun 12noon-3pm, 6.30-9.30pm, winter: Tue-Sat 7-9.30pm

[C] [♫] [P] [S]

An unassuming little Italian restaurant on the main road, distinguished by the enterprise of proprietor Augusto Vitrano. He provides a novel contrast to an otherwise traditional Italian atmosphere as he sings, dances and generally entertains his customers, dressed in his kilt. The limited menu is pasta and pizza-based and a three-course meal of minestrone soup, spaghetti vongole (with clams, onion and tomato) and zabaglione (traditional sweet made with egg yolks, sugar and Marsala), including a cup of espresso coffee, is just within our budget.

Glasgow

AD-LIB (MID ATLANTIC)
111 Hope Street (041-248 7102)
Open: Mon-Sat 12noon-2am, Sun 6pm-1am

[C] [♫] [S] [♿]

With stainless steel floor (yes, floor) and furniture, painted brick and hessian-hung walls covered with original movie posters of yesteryear, check tablecloths and excellent service from friendly staff, this American diner, opposite Glasgow Central Station, is a good place for a quick lunch or a leisurely evening meal. A selection of American hamburgers, served with chips, salad and a choice of pickles, is available. Hamburgers are available at prices from around £2.50. Main courses include kebabs, vegetarian pancakes, and Texas-style chili and prices range from £2 to around £5 – the latter for a T-bone steak with accompanying vegetables. Sweets include pancakes with hot fudge and cream, and American cheesecake with fruit and cream, which explains, perhaps, the diner's popularity with children. A business lunch of ¼lb hamburger with potatoes and salad, pancake, and coffee is available at the £2 mark. A glass of an Italian house wine costs about 70p.

THE CARVERY, EXCELSIOR HOTEL
★★★★ Glasgow Airport (041-887 1212)
Open: Mon-Fri 12noon-2.30pm, 6.30-10pm, Sat-Sun 12.30-2.30pm, 6.30-10pm

[C] [P] [S]

If you are awaiting a flight, or the arrival of a flight, what better place to while away the time than in this modern carvery, situated just a hundred yards from the main terminal building. Suitably soundproofed to exclude all aircraft noise, the restaurant is a spacious room with comfortable seating and modern décor. A standard carvery menu is offered for lunch and dinner with an additional charge of about 50p in the evening. The chef will carve from a choice of beef, lamb or pork and there are the traditional accompaniments: roast potatoes and a selection of vegetables. Starter, sweet and coffee are included in the set prices of £5.50 and £5.90 for lunch and dinner respectively. A ½-bottle of house wine costs £1.

COPRA, 336 Argyle Street
(041-221 2460)
Open: Mon-Sat 9am-7pm

[C] [S]

Mr Joe Guidi has acquired a loyal and regular clientele since his family took over the Copra almost twenty years ago. Regular favourites such as lamb chops (two) and spaghetti bolognese appear on the otherwise varied menu each day, but there is also an extensive selection of entrées that changes daily offering such dishes as curried chicken, grilled rainbow trout with lemon or roast lamb. With both starters and sweets at around 50p it is not impossible to have a very satisfying meal here for around £2.50. Whilst this restaurant closes early, Mr Guidi also operates, and welcomes you to, the Alhambra Restaurant, 350 Argyle Street, which stays open until 10.30pm and offers a similar menu. Wine is sold by the half bottle at around £2.

DELTA RESTAURANT
283 Sauchiehall Street (041-332 3661)
Open: Mon-Sat 10am-7.30pm

[♫] [S]

Situated at the western end of Sauchiehall Street, this tartan-floored basement restaurant with pine-clad walls welcomes you with soft music for a three-course meal which includes such wholesome dishes as Loch Fyne herrings in oatmeal or sizzling roast pork with apple sauce at around £3. Smart waitresses serve morning coffee, lunch and, after three o'clock, high tea consists of a main dish such as fried fillet of haddock withFrench fried potatoes plus a pot of tea and buttered toast for about £2.30.

HANSOM BAR, THE FOUNTAIN RESTAURANT XXXX
2 Woodside Crescent (041-332 6396)
Open: Mon-Fri 12noon-2.15pm, 6.15-10.15pm; Sat 6.15-10.15pm

[C] [♫] [P] [S]

Not so much a bar, more a sort of bistro is the Hansom, downstairs in the elegant Georgian building which houses the upmarket Fountain Restaurant. There is always a good choice of cooked dishes available, such as mussel and onion stew at around £3 and Hansom Pie at about £2.50, for example. The Hansom is very popular and inclined to be crowded at lunchtime, but the atmosphere is friendly and relaxed nevertheless. House wine (Spanish) costs around 65p a glass.

MOUSSAKA HOUSE
36 Kelvingrove Street (041-332 2510)
Open: Mon-Sat 12noon-3pm, 6-12mdnt, Sun 6.30-11pm

[C] [♫] [P] [🍷]

'The best value in town' is the claim made for this restaurant's lunchtime menu at about £1.80 – and they could be right. As the name suggests, a variety of moussaka dishes are the main feature, but kebab, stuffed pepper, or plainer dishes are also available. Soup and sweet are kept simple. It should be easy to choose an appetising meal of Greek specialities for about £5 from the à la carte. Try houmous (chick pea 'pâté') at about 75p, moussaka special (mince, aubergines, courgettes, potatoes, cheese and tomatoes) for about £2.50 and a sweet from the trolley for about 60p. A red and brown colour scheme, a plastic vine draped over a wooden archway and Greek music contribute to the Mediterranean atmosphere.

RAMANA, 427 Sauchiehall Street (041-332 2528/2590)
Open: Mon-Sun 12noon-12mdnt

[C] [♫] [S] [🍷]

Never tried Indian food? Try Ramana then, for the well-designed menu explains what each dish contains and how it is cooked. The lounge bar, too, is well-designed with lush Kashmir furniture. Tandoori dishes (cooked in a charcoal-fired clay oven) are the house speciality – there's chicken tandoori with salad at around £2.90 or sheesh kebab Turkish (made with fillet steak) served with rice, salad and sauce at £4.25. And especially recommended for the 'beginner' are birianies and pillaus, priced between about £1.70 (for vegetable pillau) and £3.20 (for scampi biriani). If you're still not convinced that Indian food is for you, there's a list of Western dishes too, so you can choose fish and chips or grilled steak if you must. The businessperson's lunch at something over £1.25 is very popular – doubtless for the oriental atmosphere which wafts the diner away from Glasgow for a little while, as well as for the good, low-priced food. The house wine is Italian and costs around 70p a glass.

THE SPAGHETTI FACTORY
30 Gibson Street (041-334 2385)
Open: Tue-Sun 12noon-12mdnt, Mon 5-12mdnt

[♫] [S] [🍷]

An extremely popular basement restaurant located in the student quarter, where an extravaganza of 'endless amusement combined with science' awaits you. The odd menu (in both size and content) lists a host of original dishes peppered with several outrageous tips on Italian eating – 'place fork in centre of pasta – twirl until fork is full. Try not to fall over' – plus other bits of whimsical information on the dishes. Typical main courses include spaghetti bolognese and pizza, both under £2 and hamburgers from around £1.95-£2.65. There is an attractive selection of sweets, and as the place is unlicensed, you are invited to bring your own favourite tipple. Highly recommended for anyone young at heart who enjoys good food and marvellous atmosphere.

Greenock

BANGALORE INDIAN RESTAURANT, 119 West Blackhall Street (Greenock 84355/6)
Open: Mon-Wed 12noon-12mdnt, Thu-Sat 12noon-12.30am, Sun 5-12mdnt

Just off the main Glasgow-Gourock road

is this modern Indian restaurant. Decorated in traditional style, the interior is dimly lit and the walls have dark flock wallpaper decorated with Asian paintings. There is seating for about 100 at white-clothed tables; some in cosy alcoves offer a more intimate dining place. An extensive menu of Indian dishes is offered with prices around £1-£2 per main dish; beef roghan josh, a spicy dish in tomato and onion sauce, is recommended. Tandoori specialities such as shaslik or tandoori chicken are about £3.50. Chicken jal frazy or chicken begum behar are only around £2.50. The businessperson's lunch is excellent value at around £2 for three courses. A large glass of house wine is about 75p.

Helensburgh

SANGAM INDIAN RESTAURANT
45 Sinclair Street (Helensburgh 4817)
Open: Mon-Sat 12noon-12mdnt,
Sun 5-12mdnt

[C] [P] [S]

You'll find this spacious, well-appointed restaurant on the first floor of a corner site in Helensburgh's main shopping area. Maroon wallpaper and curtaining, plus imitation oil lamps, create a cosy, intimate atmosphere. A variety of typical Asian food (for instance, beef byriani or shami kebab with salad – both around £2.50) is augmented by 'western dishes' such as steak and chips (£4) or prawn omelette (£2.30). A midday feature is the special three-course lunch, which is very good value at £1.50. House wine, though, is a little expensive at £1, albeit in a large glass.

Irvine

THE COFFEE CLUB, 142 High Street
(Irvine 71572)
Open: Mon-Sat 10am-10pm

[S]

The restaurant's décor of black seating against a crimson wall, combined with clever lighting, produces a striking effect. Snacks, light meals and desserts are served with a creative flair, as in the other Ayrshire Coffee Clubs, but here you can obtain more substantial meals too – sirloin with chips and salad at around £4 for instance – and the restaurant is licensed, a glass of house wine coming at about 55p. There is a soda fountain and pizza parlour adjoining.

Jamestown

WHITELAW'S AMERICAN DINER
207 Main Street (Alexandria 54864)
Open: Mon-Fri, Sun 12.30-2.30pm,
7-11.45pm, Sat 12.30-2.30pm,
7-11.45pm

[P] [S]

If you like a friendly atmosphere in bright surroundings, this American diner is the answer. Portions are generous and the food is good. Starters such as soup of the day, stuffed peppers and a half portion of chili con carne are almost a meal in themselves. Prices range from 35p to just over £1. As well as the inevitable range of excellent budget burgers found in this style of operation, main dishes include gammon steak with pineapple rings and brown sugar (about £2.70), chicken served with honey (around £3.50) and scampi (less than £3). A selection of desserts include burnt almond parfait at 80p. A glass of wine costs 50p.

Kilmarnock

THE COFFEE CLUB × 30 Bank Street
(Kilmarnock 22048)

Open: Mon-Sat 10am-10.30pm

♫ P S ♲

Friendly, speedy service and a pleasant décor, with roughcast walls, alcoves and tiffany lamps make this a popular meeting and eating place. Snacks are served upstairs, while full meals may be enjoyed in the basement. Assorted starters are from 45p – for a choice of soup and fruit juices. Ravioli, corn-on-the-cob, pâté and pickled herring are among more expensive items. A galaxy of grills from £1.60-£4.95 offers a 'veal choppie', Scotsman's grill (haggis, peas, carrots and chips) or Italian grill (meat balls, onion, tomato sauce and spaghetti) to name a few. Fish dishes and 'a few foreign foods' are also available. Ravioli, lasagne, chili con carne and spaghetti bolognese cost between £1.25-£1.50. Curries are around £2.50-£3. A delicious selection of desserts is certain to tempt you – lemon meringue pie for only 45p is hard to resist.

Kilmartin

KILMARTIN HOTEL
(Kilmartin 244/250)
Open: Mon-Sat 11.30am-2pm, 6-9pm, Sun 12.30-2pm, 6.30-9pm

P ♲

Situated some thirty miles south of Oban on the A816, this traditional roadside inn has built up a local reputation for its good food and friendly atmosphere. All items from the extensive light meal menu are served in a simple six-tabled dining area, after you've ordered at the lounge bar. A starter such as home-made soup is 35p, whilst fried, breaded scampi (£1.70) and minute steak with onion rings (£3.30) are two of the more popular main dishes. Strawberry gâteau is a recommended dessert at 60p. If you book in advance, a more formal meal can be had in an intimate, candlelit dining room, but at £5.50 it's stretching our budget. Wine is very reasonable at 45p per 6oz glass.

Lanark

SILVER BELL, 26 Bannatyne Street (Lanark 3129)
Open: Mon-Sat 11am-9pm, Sun 12.30-2.30pm, 4.30-6.30pm

C P ♲

Situated in the centre of a town that boasts its own racecourse, the Silver Bell takes this as its theme with prints of racehorses decorating the walls. High-backed chairs and dark beamwork add character, and the warm, relaxed atmosphere is enhanced by the friendly local waitresses. A table d'hôte lunch menu is offered at around £3.50 for three-courses such as fresh melon, braised liver and sausages, followed by pear belle Hélène. Tea or coffee costs around 30p extra. The à la carte dinner menu is more extensive with sirloin steak (£4.50) and rainbow trout (£3.50) featuring on the menu, but be prepared to pay at least £2 more than lunch for your three courses. You may prefer high tea (around £2.50) which includes a main course such as farmhouse grill or French-fried chicken and bacon, tea, scones, cakes and bread. Wine is served by the glass at around 50p.

THE TAVERN, Riverside Road, Kirkfieldbank (Lanark 3163/2537)
Open: Mon-Sat 12noon-2pm, 6.30-9pm

P

Ideal for the motorist, this white-painted tavern has a very popular lounge bar with a small wood-panelled restaurant adjoining. The à la carte lunch and supper menus are very reasonably priced, with the emphasis on grills. French fries, garden peas and carrots are included in the price of all main courses. A plateful of mouth-watering beef steak pie comes at around £1.50. A really satisfying three-course meal can also be enjoyed at somewhere between £2 and £2.50. Basket meals are very popular at around £1.50 and a glass of wine still costs less than 50p.

Largs

GREEN SHUTTER TEAROOM
28 Bath Street (Largs 672252)
Open: Mon-Sun 10am-6pm
Closed: Oct-Mar

P ♲

Just across the road from the sea, this restaurant commands a unique view of the beautiful Isle of Cumbrae. A three-course meal is excellent value – home-made soup of the day is about 35p and a wide selection of grills includes haddock with peas and chips (around £1.75) or gammon steak with pineapple (about £2.35). Sweets include home-made apple tart with cream, meringue nest with fruit and cream and brandy snaps with cream and ice cream – all less than 65p. A special 'Kiddies Corner' menu (for kids of ten and under) offers beefburgers, sausages, or fish-fingers with peas and chips and ice cream novelties for about £1.

NARDINI'S, Esplanade (Largs 674555)
Open: Mon-Sun 12noon-3pm, 3.30-8pm

[♫] [P] [&]

A popular seaside establishment catering mainly for holidaymakers in the season; but the enterprising proprietor of Nardini's keeps his winter trade going by offering a three-course meal at around £2. Just what you get for this money depends upon the day of the week – fish and chips on Monday, steak and kidney pie on Wednesday, lasagne on Thursday, for instance, but there is a selection of grills, omelettes, etc, if you do not fancy the 'dish of the day'. In the summer you can have a substantial lunch or high tea for well under £5. A variety of salads are on offer at £1.25 and the special children's menu offers smaller portions at smaller prices – for example tomato soup, sausage and beans, and knickerbocker glory (and what meal would please most children more?) would set you back about £1.50. Grown-ups in knickerbockers have to pay over £1 for their glory, but there are a number of other tempting sweets for about half that price. A glass of house wine is around 55p. You can get dinner here too, served from 8pm to 10pm, but the bill would almost certainly exceed £5.

Mauchline

LA CANDELA, 5 Kilmarnock Road (Mauchline 51015)
On the A76 to Dumfries
Open: Mon-Sun 12noon-2pm, 6.30-10pm

[♫] [P] [&]

Despite the evident Italian influence, the extensive menu is quite cosmopolitan, with the French and English getting a decent look in. The décor, is continental and romantic, with alcoves to ensure privacy. The lunchtime choice is adequate but fairly basic, its great disadvantage being cost at around £3. The dinner menu caters for both the wealthy and the more penny-conscious, with Italian dishes taking the lead in the low-cost league. Pasta dishes range from £1.50-£2. Sweets cost well under £1; starters range from 60p to £2.

Motherwell

LAKESIDE RESTAURANT
Strathclyde Country Park
(Motherwell 54280)
Open: Mon-Sat 12noon-3pm, 7-11pm, Sun 12noon-3pm, 4-7pm

[P] [&]

Enjoying a magnificent setting amid this rambling country park, the Lakeside Restaurant, as its name suggests, overlooks a picturesque man-made lake which dominates the park. While watching the antics of yachtsmen and wind surfers from their cosy retreat, diners may choose a lunch from the table d'hôte menu for around £3 (£3.50 on Sunday). Simple, wholesome fare is the order of the day with main courses such as fried haddock, gammon steak and chef's roast of the day served with vegetables, boiled potatoes or French fries. In the evening the choice is between the three-course table d'hôte at £4.94 offering more adventurous dishes such as chicken Kiev and sole à la crème, and the high tea menu which offers more simple dishes and misses out on starter at an inclusive price of £2.75 for adults and £1.75 for children. An extensive à la carte is available but prices are beyond our budget. A glass of wine costs 60p.

Newton Mearns

THE COFFEE CLUB, 114 Ayr Road (041-639 6888)
Open: Mon-Sat 10am-10.30pm

[C] [♫] [P] [S]

You'll have to come early for lunch or dinner to this popular, cosy little coffee shop, as demand far outweighs the seating availability. Situated in a block of ten shops on the main A77 road to Ayr the soft brown interior with cork tiles and lots of pot plants offer shoppers and travellers alike a peaceful haven in which to relax and enjoy a meal such as soup of the day, egg, cheese, bacon and sweetcorn flan served hot with salad and coleslaw, cheesecake, Viennese coffee for around £3. You'll have to forgo the glass of wine as the Coffee Club is unlicensed.

Oban

THE BOX TREE, 108 St George Street (Oban 4641)
Open: Apr-Nov: Mon-Sat 9am-10pm, Sun 6-10pm

[S]

Simplicity is the attraction of this unlicensed restaurant. Uniformed staff give friendly, attentive service in a floral wall-papered environment. Sit in your individual dining booth and choose from the short, simple menu. Lunch has an emphasis on salads (about £2), although fried Hebridean haddock (about £2.80) is also available. Dinner includes more expensive scampi and grilled gammon or steak, but will still cost around £4 for the three courses. Pâté with oatcakes for a starter sounds a pleasant departure from the norm. Burger snacks and sandwiches are also served if you want to keep the total bill beneath £2.

CORRAN HALLS RESTAURANT
Esplanade (Oban 4566)
Open: May-Oct: Mon-Sun 10am-8pm

Mrs Violet Lockhart and her daughter Barbara aim to provide a service to Oban's many summer visitors and particularly to hungry children. The restaurant is handily placed for theatre-goers and boasts a pretty garden for 'eating out'. The à la carte menu provides a choice of three-course meals from a list of five starters, a dozen main dishes served with potatoes and vegetables and a selection of sweets, for around £4. The most expensive main dish is entrecôte steak garni at about £5, the least expensive is Scotch pie and beans at around £1.50. A choice of salads are also offered. A glass of house wine is around 60p.

THE GALLERY RESTAURANT
Gibraltar Street (Oban 4647)
Open: summer: Mon-Sun 9.30am-5.30pm, 6-11pm, winter: 9.30am-5.30pm, 6-8pm, Closed: mid-winter

P S

Iain Reid is justly proud of his smart little restaurant situated in the busy town centre. Open all day, the Gallery offers hot or cold snacks and full three-course meals. In the evening the atmosphere is transformed as lights sparkle on the attractive watercolours adorning the cream walls. A three-course dinner may cost about £3.50, though if you select grilled sirloin steak, this alone will cost around £4. Scampi or roast chicken are good value at the £3 mark. A selection of tempting cheesecakes and gâteaux are available for dessert. A glass of house wine costs about 55p.

McTAVISH'S KITCHEN, George Street (Oban 3064)
Open: Restaurant: summer: Mon-Sun 12noon-3pm, 5-11pm, Self-service: summer: Mon-Sun 9am-10pm, winter: 9.30am-5pm

S

Oban lives for and by its visitors and no-one does more to provide good wholesome food and entertainment in comfortable and congenial surroundings than James and Jeremy Inglis at McTavish's Kitchen. Their large, modern, purpose-built premises overlooking the sea, houses a downstairs self-service food bar seating 150 and a clean and bright upstairs restaurant with room for 270, as well as the Laird's Bar and the predatorily named Mantrap Bar. Food in both restaurant and self-service is very good of its kind and not expensive. As you might expect, this is the place for Scottish specialities and you can have a three-course meal including 'haggis and neeps' or Loch Fyne kippers for around £4.60. An added attraction during the summer evenings is the folk cabaret which can be enjoyed from 9pm in the restaurant. The unlicensed self-service restaurant offers no-nonsense eating-house fare at very reasonable prices. Helpings are generous and the dishes such as roast chicken (£3.55) or haddock and chips (£2.95) are well-cooked and presented with flair.

SOROBA HOUSE HOTEL (Oban 2628)
Open: Mon-Sun 7.45-9.30am, 12noon-2.30pm, 7-10pm

[P]

Take the A816 Lochgilphead Road out of Oban, for approximately one mile to David and Edyth Hutchinson's Soroba House Hotel standing in nine acres of its own grounds with commanding views over Oban to Mull. A very comfortable and pleasant hotel it is too, drawing something like 70% of its restaurant and bar trade from Oban folk. Although dinner is out of our league you can enjoy a four-course lunch here for around £4, comprising starter such as grapefruit and mandarin cup followed by soup of the day, then a main dish of roast half chicken with French fries and salad garnish or fried golden queen of scallops with vegetables. Sweets, including ice cream and various gâteaux, are chosen from the well-laden trolley and coffee is offered at 35p.

THE THISTLE HOTEL RESTAURANT
Breadalbane Place (Oban 3132)
Open: Apr-Sep: Mon-Sun 12noon-2.30pm, 5-9.30pm

[P]

Whatever you do, don't come to Oban without trying the excellent locally-landed seafood. And Robert Silverman's Thistle Restaurant is the place for it. The décor is old-fashioned, but the white tablecloths are clean, the service prompt and efficient. Starters include rollmop herring and salad at around £1 and sweet pickled herring and salad at about the same price. There is a wide choice of fish dishes including poached fillet of sole Mornay, fried scampi and grilled locally farmed trout at prices from around £2.50-£5, but lobster Thermidor, alas, breaks the budget. There is also a good choice of roasts and grills at prices ranging from about £2.75-£4. The table d'hôte menus are excellent value, the three-course menu offering good choices at around £3 (plus VAT) and the four-course menu including such dishes as egg mayonnaise, potage du jour, roast Angus beef and horseradish with vegetables, and Scotch cream trifle, is a feast at less than £5. A glass of French house wine is about 60p.

Paisley

CARDOSI'S, 46 Causeyside Street (041-889 5339)
Open: Mon-Sun 11am-11pm

[P] [S]

After seventeen years of running the same restaurant in the same town, the Cardosi family has had plenty of time to get to know its clientele and how to please them. They cater for all tastes by operating a café and take-away counter as well as the first-floor restaurant and dispense bar, where it's possible to get a good three-course 'business lunch' for around £1.85. A typical choice of dishes from this menu would include cream of asparagus soup, 'haggis, neeps and tatties' and banana crumble and custard. A reasonably-priced à la carte

menu is always available, along with its list of chef's specialities – Mexico steak, chicken Kiev or Napoli steak with all the trimmings – and yes, you will still get change from £5. Wines may be bought by the carafe, the half-carafe or by the glass at around 50p.

Salen, Isle of Mull

THE PUFFER AGROUND ✕ Aros
Open: mid Jan-mid Oct: Mon-Sun 12noon-2.30pm, 6-9pm, winter (reservations only): Fri-Sat 8-10pm

[P]

No need to find your sea-legs on this ship, though you may have doubts, as the restaurant's design is strikingly based on that of a Clyde 'Puffer', and maritime paintings line the walls. No less striking is the selection of American candies that greet your entrance. The restaurant shares its home in a row of converted roadside cottages with a craft shop. Excellent use is made of fresh local produce and as far as possible, each meal is individually prepared. Fisherman's pancake or shellfish soup with brandy and cream live side by side with more conventional, and cheaper starters. A main course salad or casserole will cost about £3.50, though you can spend more, and sweets such as baked treacle sponge or fresh peach and cream roll, about 60p. Service is simple but very friendly.

Troon

CAMPBELL'S KITCHEN, 3 South Beach (Troon 314421)
Open: Tue 12noon-4pm, Wed-Sun 12noon-4pm, 7-9.30pm

[P]

Opened during 1979, Campbell's Kitchen already has a homely atmosphere. Red and white floral décor and red-stained pinewood chairs give a pleasant ambience, but the main attraction is the delicious smell of home-baking. At the counter is a display of meringues, gâteaux, and scones, all at about 45p per portion. A 'special meal', including a fruit juice or soup, and a hot dish of the day, is available at about £1.50. Alternatively there is a choice of salads or various omelettes at about £1.50. Campbell's Kitchen welcomes disabled diners.

THE COFFEE CLUB, 18 West Portland Street (Troon 311394)
Open: Mon-Sat 10am-10pm

[♫] [P] [S]

In this friendly, relaxed atmosphere it is possible to enjoy excellent coffee (by the mug if you prefer it that way), and there is a good selection of appetising snacks and savoury dishes from which to choose. Imaginative, and presented with flair, the food available is excellent value for money – an omelette, pizza, or Italian dish such as spaghetti, will cost you between £1 and £1.50. The restaurant is not licensed.

Wishaw

ANVIL OLDE WORLDE INN
254 Main Street (Wishaw 75546)
Open: Mon-Sat 12noon-2.30pm, 5-10pm, Sun 6.30-10pm

[C] [♫] [S]

In Wishaw's main street, this member of the Stakis chain of Olde Worlde Inns, is a popular lunchtime venue for local business people. The emphasis is on convenience, with good value, standard menus of the chicken, gammon and steak variety. Accompaniments are chips or baked potato and peas, with a salad garnish. A three-course meal will cost £3.40-£5.70.

Central, Tayside and Fife

The most popular touring area in Scotland is the Trossachs, an afforested area encompassing the beautiful Lochs Katrine, Achray, Venachar and Ard and the Queen Elizabeth Forest Park. It was just north of here that, during the 17th century, Rob Roy MacGregor, a powerful red-haired Highlander immortalised in Sir Walter Scott's novel, robbed the rich to help the poor – a Scottish Robin Hood.

To the north east is the university city of Dundee. This bustling industrial city has little to offer the tourist but it does give its name to one or two edible mementoes that are popular worldwide – Dundee cake and Dundee marmalade. The bitter orange marmalade was first made by a Dundee housewife, Mrs Jean Keiller. She was given a load of Seville oranges bought from a storm-bound Spanish cargo ship and finding them too bitter to eat,

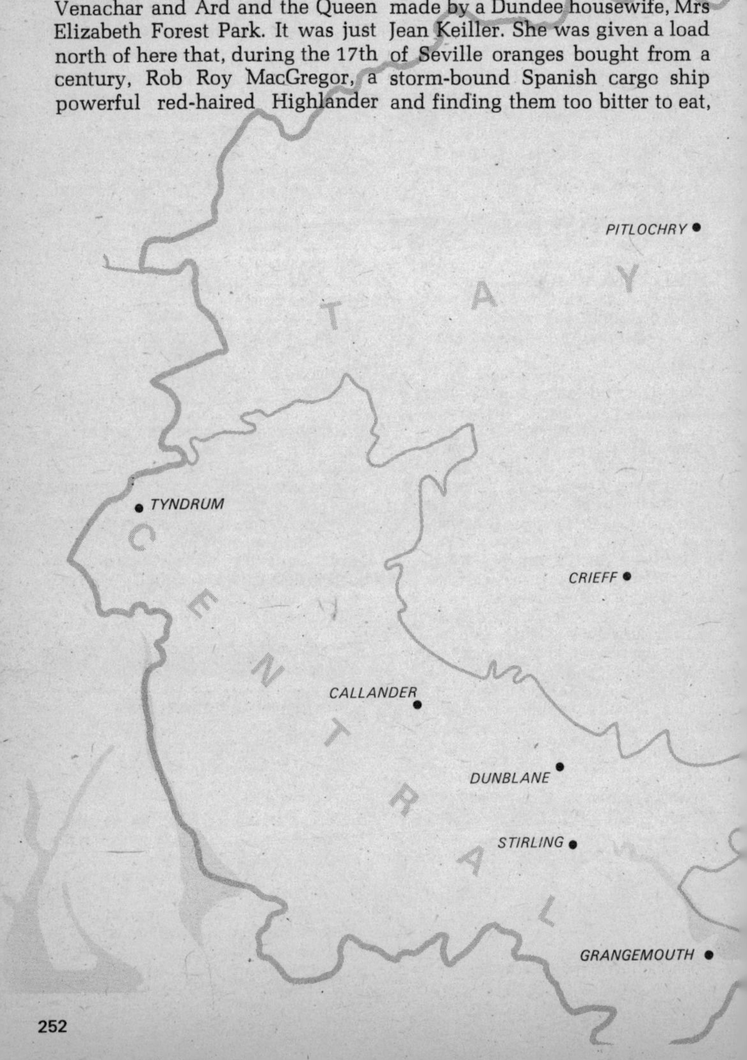

but not wishing to waste the fruit, she produced a jam now sold all over the world as Keiller's Dundee marmalade. The rich fruit Dundee cake was originally made for christenings but now finds its way onto many a Sunday tea table. Another teatime treat in these parts is the Arbroath Smokie – a smoked haddock originating from the town of the same name situated just north of Dundee.

South of Dundee stands the charming old city of Perth. Known as 'the fair city', Perth was the capital of Scotland long before Edinburgh assumed that honour in 1450, and just outside the city is Scone Palace where Scottish kings were crowned. A town of equal importance in Scotland's history is the ancient crag-borne town of Stirling whose castle became the royal residence of the Stuart kings from 1392.

Indeed it is still possible to feast like a king here with, perhaps, a hearty bowl of Scots Broth – thick with barley and vegetables as a warming starter, followed by a freshly-caught salmon from the River Tay.

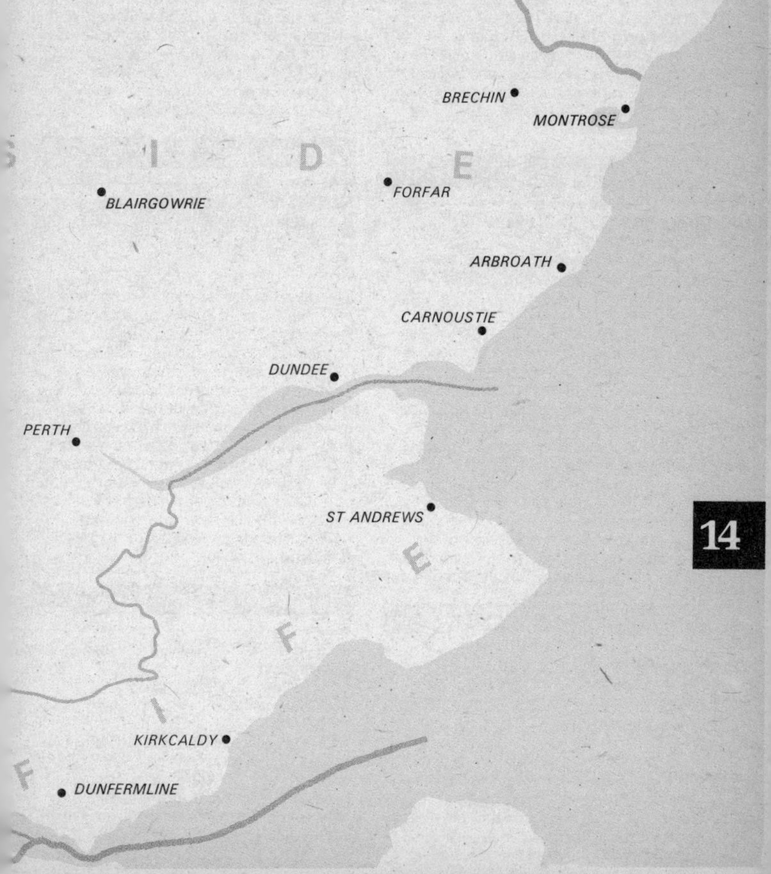

Arbroath

HOTEL SEAFORTH ★★ Dundee Road
(Arbroath 72232)
Open: summer: Mon-Fri, Sun 12.30-2pm, 6-9pm, Sat 12.30-2pm, 6-9.30pm

[C] [P] [wine]

This attractive hotel restaurant boasts an array of tempting dishes for the hungry holidaymaker. Representative of the items on the lunch menu are melon cocktail, grilled pork chops with vegetables and sherry trifle, plus coffee, for the modest price of £3.50. The four-course set dinner (only available until 8pm) costs around £5 and includes the old favourite – roast beef and Yorkshire pudding. Later in the evening an extensive à la carte menu operates, but here the budget-conscious will have to choose very carefully. High teas (served between 6-7pm) vary in price from £3 to £4 and amongst the popular grills are Arbroath smokies and gammon with pineapple. Standard table wine is 60p a glass.

Blairgowrie

THE HUB, 23 High Street
(Blairgowrie 2038)
Open: May-Oct Mon-Sat 10am-9pm, Sun 3pm-9pm Nov-Apr Mon-Sat 10am-5pm

[P] [S] [wine]

Well named, 'The Hub' is a town-centre restaurant with unusual circular windows, split-level dining area and modern décor. The emphasis is on the popular grills, roasts, salads and fish dishes, all reasonably priced. In fact you could have entrecôte steak with all the trimmings plus soup, a sweet such as sherry trifle, coffee and wine for an inclusive price of around £4. For the busy shopper an afternoon tea including a pot of tea, toast, scone and butter, cake and biscuit costs only £1.

Brechin

NORTHERN HOTEL ★★ 2 Clerk Street
(Brechin 2156)
Open: Mon-Sun 12.30-2pm, 5-6.30pm, 7-8.30pm

[C] [P] [wine]

For those who relish a proper 'sit down' meal within the realms of a tight budget, this hotel is the ideal place. A three-course lunch, such as salami salad, scampi and tartare sauce, followed by home-made apple pie (plus coffee) costs around £3.50, dinner just over £4. Snacks in the bar and satisfying high teas are also available.

Callander

PIPS, 23 Ancaster Square
(Callander 30470)
Open: summer: Mon-Sat 10am-7pm, Sun 11am-7pm, winter: Mon-Tue 10am-4pm Thu-Sun 10am-4pm

[P] [wine]

This eye-catching little restaurant snuggles in a corner of the Square. From the outside, attractive laboured brasswork, tinted windows and a sophisticated striped canopy invite further inspection. The interior is equally striking with white laminated tables and chairs and a bold décor with pictures mounted on hessian walls. Salads and home-baking are the specialities of the house, and desserts are served with lashings of cream. Great value at around £2.50 per head.

Carnoustie

GLENCOE HOTEL ★★ Links Parade
(Carnoustie 53273)
Open: Mon-Sun 1-2pm, 7.30-9pm

[C] [P]

The name Carnoustie is synonymous with golf, and this neat, family hotel has the distinction of overlooking the famous championship golf-course. Table lamps and soft music create a soothing atmosphere in the dining room, and the patio extension provides an ideal eating place with views of the golf-course. Lunch and dinner are both table d'hôte, dinner being five courses, with coffee. There is an excellent choice of tempting main course dishes such as grilled fillet of lemon sole Sorrento, cold baked gammon salad or beef and pheasant pie.

Crieff

THE HIGHLANDMAN, East High Street
(Crieff 4265)
Open: Mon-Sat 10am-7pm, Sun 12noon-7pm

The premises of The Highlandman, once a garage showroom and filling station, have been converted into pleasant restaurant-cum-tearoom, where one can get anything from a cup of tea and a piece of home-made shortbread to a full three-course meal, anytime from morning to evening. Main dishes include sirloin steak or scampi at around £3.25, gammon steak at about £2.25, or various grills from around £1.25. Incidentally, disabled persons will find access easy.

STAR HOTEL ★ East High Street (Crieff 2632)
Open: Mon-Sun 12noon-2pm, 4.30-6pm (High Tea), 7-9pm

[C] [P] [S] [♧]

The pleasant surroundings of the panelled dining room which overlooks the main street of this attractive Perthshire town provides an ideal venue for shoppers and tourists alike. Lunchtime specials such as fried fillet of haddock with lemon, grilled liver and onions or pizza – all served with French fried potatoes and two vegetables of the day-cost only £1.10. Starter, a sweet and coffee would add less than £1 extra to the bill. The à la carte menu is more extensive but still reasonable offering grilled Tay salmon, chicken Suedoise (sautéed in a delicious sauce of mushrooms, cream and white wine) or Wiener schnitzel for around £3. A high tea menu served from 4.30-6pm offers a selection of grills or cold meat salad with French fries and vegetables, tea, bread and butter, scones and cakes in a price range of £1.95 to £4. A glass of house wine costs around 50p.

Dunblane

FOURWAYS RESTAURANT
Main North Road (Dunblane 822098)
Open: summer Mon-Sat 9.15am-6pm, Sun 10am-6pm, winter: Mon-Sat 9.30am-6pm, Sun 10am-6pm

[P] [♧]

This small restaurant and gift shop enjoys a prime position within walking distance of the magnificent 15th-century cathedral and the Bishop's Palace and is consequently very popular with tourists. A friendly and caring staff serve mainly grills and home-made soups or pies. Top lunch price (inclusive of VAT) is around £4.80 but one can eat well for a lot less (for example, soup plus home-made steak and kidney pie with apple tart to follow is under £3). Unlicensed.

Dundee

LYRICS RESTAURANT
37 Union Street (Dundee 22117)
Open: Mon-Sat 12noon-2.30pm, 5-11pm

[C] [♬] [P] [S] [♧]

The Lyric Restaurant offers good food American style in comfortable surroundings. The à la carte speciality menu includes Yankee bean soup (a hearty mixture of red kidney beans, lima beans, tomatoes, onion, celery and garlic!) for around 60p; Brunswick Chicken (a warming dish of chicken with noodles) about £2.80 and apple brown Betty – a dessert served with ice cream which has been found in American cookbooks since the 18th century and costs less than 80p. You can drink as much American blend coffee, with milk or cream, as you like for around 60p.

OLDE WORLDE INN, 124 Seagate (Dundee 21179)
Open: Mon-Sat 12noon-2.30pm, 5-10.30pm, Sun 6.30-10pm

[♬] [S] [♧]

Handy for the new Wellgate shopping centre and opposite the main bus station, this is a typical Reo Stakis steakhouse, serving items from the organisation's standard menu. Main course items range from about £2.60 for a fillet of haddock to £4.40 for prime Angus steak and include a choice of starters. Biscuits and cheese or apple pie with cream cost about 85p. The children's special three-course meal with a soft drink is very good value at around £1.20. Wine costs about 60p a glass.

QUALITY INN, City Square (Dundee 24755)
Open: Mon-Sat 9am-6.30pm

[C] [S] [♧]

Kids will love this town centre eatery, particularly when they see the 'Food and Fun menu' full of tempting goodies and six 'Hungry Bear' puzzles to keep them occupied while their meal is being prepared. There's a pretty good deal for grown-ups too, with a three-course lunch for only £2.40, for a meal such as minestrone soup, prawn and mushroom risotto with additional vegetables and meringue glacé. Wine is not available by the glass, only quarter bottles. The à la carte is just as reasonable, concentrating on grills, fish and omelettes for £2 and there is even a selection of 'waist preserver' dishes for the calorie conscious.

Dunfermline

OLDE WORLDE INN, BELLEVILLE HOTEL
6 Pilmuir Street (Dunfermline 21076)
Open: Mon-Thu 12noon-2.30pm,

6-10pm, Fri-Sat 12noon-2.30pm, 5-11pm

C P S

Another of the Reo Stakis chain, this restaurant is situated on the first floor of a three-storey, stone building near the centre of Scotland's former capital. Bar lunches are marvellous value, with three courses such as egg mayonnaise, roast of the day and apple pie with cream, plus coffee, costing only £2. The à la carte menu, also for the budget-conscious, offers a choice of seven main dishes, featuring gammon steak with peach at around £3 (this price includes a starter such as delicious farmhouse broth). A special 'children's choice' costs £1.20. Desserts are around 70p and house wine 60p per glass.

Forfar

AUGUST MOON, 114 Castle Street (Forfar 64105)
Open: Mon-Sat 11.30am-2pm, 5-11.30pm, Sun 4-11.30pm

For those who think that all Chinese restaurants have a stereotyped appearance with very little individuality, a visit to August Moon will prove a pleasant experience. No embossed wallpaper or Chinese lanterns here. This little eating place has a charm and character all of its own, with white rough-cast walls and cosy Tudor-style banquettes. A comprehensive à la carte menu offers the usual complement of Oriental dishes plus a selection of European ones. The price of all main courses includes boiled rice, and a heated stand is laid on your table to keep the whole thing hot. Most dishes are around the £2-£3 mark and, a set meal for two of fried spring roll, sweet and sour pork, chicken with cashew nuts and vegetables, mixed vegetables, egg fried rice plus coffee or tea offers excellent value at just over £6.

Grangemouth

THE DUTCH INN, Main Street, Skinflats (Grangemouth 483015)
Open: Mon-Sun 12noon-2pm, 6-11.30pm

C P

Décor here is a pleasing blend of natural stone and timber, smart modern carpeting and soft furnishings. The à la carte menu offers cuisine to suit most palates. Starters range from 25p for fruit juice to £1.60 for smoked salmon. Potted shrimps are £1. Grills from £2.50 include salmon steak, gammon and T-bone steak. Prawn or chicken curries and meat salads are all £2.75. Potatoes and vegetables are included in the price of all main courses. Desserts such as fruit cocktail cost 50p, gâteaux are 60p. A glass of Hirondelle wine is 50p.

Kirkcaldy

GREEN COCKATOO RESTAURANT
275-277 High Street (Kirkcaldy 3310)
Open: Mon-Sat 9am-5pm (closed Wed)

C P S

At the north end of the High Street, you'll find a bakery and confectioner's shop. Go through the shop and up some stairs and on the first floor you will find the Green Cockatoo, a traditional Scottish tearoom with polished wood panelling, fresh white linen on the tables, and friendly service. Tea is obviously *the* meal here, with all those delicious scones and cakes downstairs, but the lunch menu is good value too with the most expensive dish – fresh salmon and salad – priced at about £3. Sweets include Bakewell tart and custard, fresh cream gâteau and ice creams. Coffee costs about 25p and a glass of wine around 60p. On the second floor is a grill room, the 'Drouthy Crony' with a more limited menu at similarly moderate prices.

THE PANCAKE PLACE, 28 Kirk Wynd (Kirkcaldy 4982)
Open: Mon-Wed 10am-5.30pm, Thu-Sat 10am-10pm

[♫] [P] [S]

Housed in a converted stone building dating from 1779, this is a comfortable restaurant specialising in pancakes-with-everything. You can start with soup, but there is a choice of twelve snack-sized pancakes with intriguing fillings such as ham and peach, each costing around 75p. For your main course, large savoury pancakes such as chicken and pineapple (about £1.50) or Rocky Mountain Burger for less than £1 are recommended. Alternatively you can try one of seven crisp salads, served with two thin pancakes. There are a dozen varieties of sweet pancakes available for dessert. Costing around £1, 'Pippin', a large pancake with a hot apple and cinnamon filling topped with cream is a gourmet's delight.

Montrose

CORNER HOUSE HOTEL ★★
High Street (Montrose 3126)
Open: Mon-Sun 12noon-2pm, 4.30-6pm

This attractive hotel restaurant is run efficiently by friendly waitresses who will serve you a three-course lunch with coffee and a glass of Hirondelle for less than £3. The daily changing menu features the old favourites such as fried haddock, lasagne, roasts and omelettes for around £1.30. Later in the day a high tea menu is available with main courses such as gammon steak and chips or cold York ham salad at around £2.50 including a selection of vegetables, home-made scones, cakes and tea. The à la carte menu is rather more pricey but with careful selection a meal for around £5 is possible.

Perth

HUNTERS' LODGE, Bankfoot (Bankfoot 325) 6m north of Perth off A9 at Bankfoot services turn-off
Open: Mon-Sun 12noon-2pm, 5-9pm

[P] [🍷]

The good Scots tradition of high tea is a feature of this country restaurant on the southern outskirts of Bankfoot. Served between 5-7pm it combines the best of two meals for around £3.50, with a choice of grills or salad, tea and scones. In the bar beefsteak pie, curry, Arbroath smokie and pickled kippers (about £2) feature amongst a wide range. The restaurant à la carte offers an interesting selection of starters (try Blairgowrie Treat, a compôte of melon, raspberries and apples for under £1) main courses and sweets. Careful choice should keep you within the budget.

OLDE WORLDE INN, CITY MILL HOTEL, West Mill Street (Perth 28281)
Open: 12noon-2.30pm, 5-10.30pm

C P ♧

Convenient, fast food of the steaks, chicken and haddock variety is served in a 19th-century mill which has been converted into a modern hotel of the Reo Stakis organisation. The mill stream and wheel which can be seen through plated glass in the hotel's lounge bar and reception area. Main course prices, between £2.75 and £6 include soup, but sweets or cheese are 65p extra. Wine is around 50p per glass.

THE PANCAKE PLACE, 10 Charlotte Street (Perth 28077)
Open: summer: Mon-Wed 10am-5.30pm, Thu-Sun 10am-7.30pm,
winter: Mon-Sat 10am-5.30pm

S ♧

This specialised eaterie, with its informal tea-room atmosphere, was the first to pander to pancake fans in central Scotland (other sister restaurants have since opened at Edinburgh, Kirkcaldy and St Andrews). After fruit juice or soup of the day (around 30p), you can sample a giant burger (£1.10), chicken and pineapple (£1.50) or any one of six crispy salads from £1.20 to £1.70. And to follow? How about 'Florida' – a large pancake topped with ice-cream, peaches and fresh whipped cream – just one of a dozen exotic desserts guaranteed to ruin your diet! An average three-course meal, with coffee and half a bottle of wine comes to about £4.50.

THE PENNY POST ✕ 80 George Street (Perth 20867)
Open: Mon-Sat 12noon-2pm, 7-10pm

C P S ♧

A cosy little restaurant which should appeal to those who find historic connections of interest, for the 18th-century building that houses The Penny Post was one of the earliest post offices, dating back to 1773. The bar downstairs is, in fact, the old Post Office counter. The à la carte menu offers such dishes as home-made Scotch broth at around 50p, and the Penny Post Special (strips of beef cooked in red wine, mushrooms and cream and served on a bed of rice) at around £4.25 and this gives a good indication of the sort of prices prevailing. The cheaper lunch menu includes beefsteak, kidney and mushroom pie or fish at about £2.

QUALITY INN, St John's Square (Perth 25093)
Open: Mon-Sat 9.30am-6pm

S ♧

These Trusthouse Forte restaurants are favourites with many people. This one is certainly quick and convenient if you are shopping or sightseeing. Supplementing the usual THF menu of omelettes, grills and salads is a table d'hôte lunch (two courses at around £1.85, three £2) and a high tea (including tea and toast) at about £1.85. The premises are not licensed.

Pitlochry

GREEN PARK HOTEL ★★★ (Pitlochry 2537)
Open: Mar-Oct inclusive, Mon-Sun 8.30-9.30am, 12.30-2pm, 6.30-8pm

P ♧

If you take pleasure in having your meal in beautiful surroundings, try the Green Park Hotel. This enlarged country house is set amongst lawns and fine trees, with a view across Loch Faskally. Inside, the dining room is very clean and bright. There are no à la carte meals, but the owners, Graham and Anne Brown, offer a good selection of dishes for a three-course lunch at around £4, including service and VAT. You could start with Mortadella salad, follow with beef kromeski garni and finish with sliced peaches and cream. Lunch on Sunday is more restricted and a little more expensive than on weekdays.

THE LUGGIE, Rie-Achan Road (Pitlochry 2085)
Open: Apr-early Nov: Mon-Sun 10am-9pm

A 'luggie' is a milkmaid's bucket – appropriate since this quaint little restaurant was originally the byre of an old dairy farm. Inside, the raftered roof, white-painted rough-cast walls and stone fireplace are very welcoming. Ian and Diana Russell, the owners, ensure that home-baking and local produce are a main feature of all the fare. Lunchtime offers the choice of a self-service cold table and an excellent selection of cold meats, duck, salmon and smoked mackerel, accompanied by a variety of original salads, assorted gâteaux and fresh fruit salads, or hot dishes such as grills which are served at the table. The main course in either case will be around £3, with starters and sweets for about 60p-£2. The dinner menu offers a much wider choice of hot dishes but the price is likely to bring the full meal outside our budget.

St Andrews

THE PANCAKE PLACE, 177-179 South Street (St Andrews 75671)
Open: Mon 10am-10pm, Tue-Wed 10am-5.30pm, Thu-Sun 10am-10pm

♬ P S

The interior of this attractive speciality restaurant is surprisingly rural, with a beamed ceiling, natural stone and white-painted plaster walls. Pancakes may be sampled as a starter, main course or dessert. Soup of the day is about 30p, or you can start with a savoury pancake such as ham and peach or haddock Mornay for around 75p. For a main course you could choose a Rocky Mountain burger at about £1.10 A range of salads are also available including chicken, ham, cheese and egg, prices ranging from around £1.20-£1.80. There is a choice of a dozen sweet pancakes for dessert. 'Pippin' is filled with hot apples and cinnamon and topped with cream. A glass of house wine costs about 50p.

Stirling

BOMA RESTAURANT, KINGSGATE HOTEL ★ Kings Street (Stirling 3944)
Open: Mon-Sun 8am-10pm

S ♧

In their residential hotel, right in the town and handy for the railway station and Thistle shopping centre, Sandy and Jean Wallace have opened the 'Boma' Restaurant. Real zebra skins brought back from East Africa set the black-and-white theme of the décor. A lunch of soup or fruit juice, followed by a main course (from around £2.50 for chicken or ham salad, roast chicken or haddock fillet to around £3.80 for grilled sirloin steak garni) is available daily. Sweets, cheese and coffee are not included in the price. High tea includes a starter such as egg mayonnaise, a savoury dish with chips, scone, cake and tea at prices from about £3.60. Half portions of appropriate dishes are served for children and high chairs are available if required.

THE RIVERWAY RESTAURANT✕
Kildean (Stirling 5734)
Open: summer: Mon-Fri 9am-7pm
Sat 9am-9pm, Sun 12noon-7pm
winter: Wed-Sun 10am-7pm

♬ P ♧

Half a mile from the town centre, on the road to the Trossachs, just off the M9 motorway and yet enjoying a panoramic view of the River Forth, the Riverway Restaurant is well-known for its excellent cuisine at reasonable prices. The three-course table d'hôte lunch costs under £3 and is good nourishing food in ample portions. High tea, the main evening meal including grills, is about the same price. The Saturday night dinner-dance, with live music, costs about £6.

STATION HOTEL ★★ 56 Murray Place (Stirling 2017)
Open: Mon-Sun 12noon-2.30pm, 5-10.30pm

C ♧

The Reo Stakis 'Olde Worlde' Inn in the Station Hotel offers their standard menu (as for 'The Plough' at Ayr). The wattle ceiling and dark oak settles may not be genuine antiques but the atmosphere is right for an enjoyable meal, with full waiter service, at very reasonable prices. Bar snacks include haggis, bashed neeps (mashed turnips to Sassenachs) and champit tatties (three guesses?) at around £1.20. House wines cost around 50p a glass.

Tyndrum

CLIFTON COFFEE HOUSE, A82/A85 junction (Tyndrum 242)
Open: Apr-Oct: Mon-Sun 8.30am-5.30pm

P

You'll be pleasantly surprised by the prices of this cheerful Tayside eaterie. It is part of a smoothly-run tourist complex that includes craft, book and whisky shops. Inside, the décor is predominantly white with strategically placed hanging baskets and hand-crafted pottery. There is an air of quality here, despite it being a self-service operation. A wide range of starters include barley broth and cullen skink (the traditional fish-based soup). Various main courses are available throughout the day, such as beef curry (£1.50), haggis with neeps and tatties (turnip and potato) at £1.40 and venison hotpot (around £2). Wine comes at about 55p a glass, or help the meal down with a schooner of sherry at 45p.

Highland and Grampian

The majesty of the Scottish Highlands is undeniable. Here is everyone's image of Scotland – a land of misty mountains, romantic glens and deep wooded gorges; a land where the scent of heather mingles with the haunting sound of bagpipes. A land almost unchanged since the castles rang to the voices of larger-than-life clan chiefs who ruled the north and gave to Scotland a most cherished part of her heritage – the tartan.

Tourists and inhabitants alike have good reason to marvel at the beauty of this region, and they are in distinguished company. Queen Elizabeth and the Royal family reside during the late summer months in Balmoral Castle by the bonny banks of the River Dee, and Glamis Castle, the childhood home of the Queen Mother, lies to the south east.

High-class tables are seldom without some form of Highland delicacy, be it smoked Scotch salmon, choice steaks from the famous Aberdeen Angus beef, venison from the stately Highland deer or the first grouse of the season. For the sweet tooth, noble Highland desserts include Atholl Brose – a potent concoction of oatmeal, heather honey and whisky,

blended together with whipped cream, or Cranachan – another cream and oatmeal mixture, this time with fresh raspberries (some of the best in Britain are grown here) thrown in, and a nutty topping of toasted oatmeal.

There is, of course, a more humble side to Highland fare. From Aberdeen there comes the Finnan Haddie – a haddock originally given its distinctive flavour by smoking in black peat and sphagnum moss; the peat used to smoke and flavour the fish while the moss was flared to partly cook the flesh. Although the 'smokey' taste is now achieved by more modern methods, a dish of Finnan Haddie steamed in milk and butter is still a delight to the palate. This fish is also the main ingredient in a soup known as Cullen Skink made from haddock, sieved potatoes and onions in a fish stock.

And what can be said about whisky – Scottish gold – the drink that has gained so much favour in all corners of the world and knows no rival?

All of the most famous malt whiskies are distilled here and there are guided tours of many of the distilleries for the keen tippler. But have a good meal first!

Aberdeen

THE LANTERN RESTAURANT
101 Crown Street (Aberdeen 55440)
Open: Mon-Sat 12noon-2pm, 7-10.30pm

C P S

The Chef's Specialities menu is incredibly good value for lunch or dinner. Green bean salad is one of the delicious starters, costing around 75p. Casserole of kidney and sweetbreads (about £3) and poached salmon bonne femme (just over £3) are two of the main courses, both served with generous portions of vegetables.

OLDE WORLDE INN, Holburn Street (Aberdeen 56442)
Open: Mon-Sun 12noon-2.30pm, 5-11pm (10pm Sun)

C P S

Reo Stakis Olde Worlde Inns have a definite appeal for inveterate meat-eaters. Main course prices, from around £2.75-£5 and including haddock, chicken and various steaks, cover a starter as well as vegetables and a roll and butter. Sweets are about 70p and a glass of wine costs around 60p.

OLIVER'S, CALEDONIAN HOTEL ★★★
Union Terrace (Aberdeen 29233)
Open: Mon-Sat 12noon-2.30pm, 6-11.30pm, Sun 6.30-11pm

C S

This steak and hamburger grill is named after Oliver Hardy who, along with his buddy Stan, dominated the American screen comedy in the 1930s. The restaurant is superbly appointed, in ultra-modern design, with the all-black décor and contrasting chrome fittings giving a most striking and exciting effect. The menu is designed on a poster-style sheet and the various courses are given film-jargon titles, 'Reel 1, Take 1' (starters), 'The Main Feature', 'The Supporting Role' and 'Epilogue' (desserts). A 'Way Out West' burger costs between £2.50-£3. Main courses include French fries or baked potato and fresh green salad with an accompanying choice of dressing. Along with soup at about 60p, pie at around £1 and a glass of house wine at about 65p, these meals fit easily into a limited budget.

QUALITY INN, 1 Union Bridge (Aberdeen 50459)
Open: Mon-Sat 9am-6.30pm

C S

This modern eating house provides a quick service for shoppers and holidaymakers, with a ground-floor coffee shop and upstairs restaurant. The restaurant menu is reasonably priced (gammon steak around £2.10, seafood platter about £2.75), with a waist-preserver menu for the figure-conscious and a children's menu including an exciting variety of ice-creams.

VICTORIA RESTAURANT
140 Union Street (Aberdeen 28639)
Open: Mon-Sat 10am-7.30pm

S

Enjoy a nicely-presented yet inexpensive meal right here. The à la carte menu includes a selection of starters – soup, fruit juice or grapefruit cocktail all around 50p; main dishes such as omelettes, grills, salads and fish which, with vegetables, are likely to cost between £1.75 and £3.50, and sweets at 50p or more. Very popular is a three-course lunch at around £2.40.

Aboyne

THE BOAT INN, Charleston Road (Aboyne 2317)
Open: Mon-Fri 12noon-2.30pm, Sat-Sun 9am-11pm

P S

This small inn affords good views of the River Dee, and meals at thoroughly reasonable prices. At lunchtime try macaroni cheese or shepherd's pie, either of which comes at around £1.60 High tea offers main dishes ranging from bacon and egg (about £2.20) to crab (around £3.30) or rump steak (just over £3.80), all served with chips and vegetables and with toast, pancakes, cakes and a pot of tea included in the price. The dinner menu includes home-made pâté at about 75p or sirloin steak garni at around £4.40.

Beauly

THE SKILLET, The Square
(Beauly 2573)
Open: Apr-Oct, Mon-Sat 9.30am-8pm, Sun 11am-8pm

[P] [S] [&]

The Skillet is an ideal place for the hungry tourist. The simple but wholesome fare is reasonably priced at around £2.50 for a three-course table d'hôte lunch and from around £3.50 for a full dinner. The à la carte menu offers a good selection of grills, fish and salads at an average price of £2.75, with bread and butter or toast plus tea included.

Buckie

THE MILL MOTEL, Tynet
(Clochan 233)
Open: Mon-Sun 12.30-2pm, 7.30-9pm

[C] [♫] [P]

Only fifteen years ago this old mill was still in production, now it is a character restaurant. Evidence of milling is everywhere and the lounge bar extends into the original lofts. The dining room offers table d'hôte lunch and dinner menus. Lunch is around £3.50 and the choice is excellent but the four-course dinner is the pièce de résistance. Tynet pâté is one of eight delicious starters, with fillet sole Bercy as an entrée. Main courses include sweetbreads chasseur.

Evanton

FOULIS FERRY, 1½ miles S of Evanton on A9 (Evanton 830535)
Open: Mon and Wed-Sat 10am-10pm, Sun 12noon-6pm

[P]

Who pays the Ferryman? It's not important in this white-painted, converted cottage restaurant where the Ferryman once lived and where reasonably-priced meals are now served. Salads, quiches and simple, home-baked meals are available daily, with Italian house-wine at around 55p a glass. Choose with care at dinner time and an exotic à la carte meal can work out at around £5.

Forres

THE ELIZABETHAN INN ✕✕ Mundale
(Forres 72526)
Open: Mon-Tue, Thu-Fri 12.30-1.30pm, 7.30-8.30pm, Wed 12.30-1.30pm

[P]

An authentic cottagey atmosphere and honest-to-goodness home-cooked fare can be found about two miles west of Forres. Built of stone and close to the River Findhorn, the interior has brick and stone walls, Victorian and antique tables and chairs and a rare air of relaxation. Meals are table d'hôte and it is advisable to book for lunch which at around £3 is much in demand. A three-course dinner with excellent sweets from the trolley is about £5.

Fort William

THE ANGUS RESTAURANT
66 High Street (Fort William 2654)
Open: summer: Mon-Sat 10am-10pm, winter: Mon-Sat 12noon-10pm

[S] [&]

The Angus first-floor restaurant and ground-floor lounge bar has been strikingly created from former shop premises. Red is the colour theme of the well-appointed restaurant which offers a three-course meal from around £3. Grills predominate the à la carte lunch and dinner menus, and particularly recommended is the salmon steak, available in season for around £3.75.

McTAVISH'S KITCHEN, High Street
(Fort William 2406)
Open: Restaurant: Easter and mid-May to end Sep Mon-Sun 12noon-3pm, 5-10.45pm. Self-service: Mon-Sun summer: 9am-6pm or later

[♫] [P] [S]

Excellent food, folk cabaret acts (summer evenings) and obliging staff are features here. Although prices in the main restaurant are rather near the limit, a three-course meal including 'A Taste of Scotland' dishes such as Tweed Kettle (a 19th-century Edinburgh dish of poached salmon fillet cooked in white wine, carrots and onion topped with a light cream sauce) for around

£4.50. The ground-floor Laird's Bar and self-service restaurant offer a less pricey selection of meals.

MERCURY MOTOR INN ☆☆☆
Achintore Road (Fort William 3117)
2m along the A85 to Glasgow
Open: Mon-Sun 12noon-2pm, for bar lunches, 6.30-9.30pm (9pm winter) for à la carte dinners

C ♫ P ♧

Panoramic views from the dining room over Loch Linnhe are a bonus here. 'Bar Bites', as the Mercury calls them, include salad bowl lunches at around £3. The à la carte dinner menu boasts 'Taste of Scotland' dishes including pickled Mallaig herring, haggis wi' neeps and typically Scottish soups (at around 70p).

THE MOORINGS HOTEL, Banavie (Corpach 550)
Open: Mon-Sun 12.30-2pm, 6.30-9.30pm. Lunches served May to Oct only.

P

Take the A82 Inverness road out of Fort William, turning off on to first the A830 and then the B8004 for Banavie. You'll get a three-course table d'hôte dinner here for around £5-£6 and a table d'hôte lunch for about £3.75. Main courses from the lunch menu are also served singly at around £1.75 per dish. The restaurant licence permits alcoholic drinks with a full meal only. The Sinclairs do their own cooking.

THE STAG'S HEAD HOTEL ★★ High Street (Fort William 4144)
Open: Restaurant: Mon-Sun 12.30-2.30pm, 6.30-9pm.
Bar Snacks: 11am-2.30pm

C P S

A stag's head motif on the carpet and expensive dark oak furniture set the scene. The à la carte lunch and dinner menu is a little pricey for our needs but includes a good choice of reasonably-priced starters, and a selection of fish or meat dishes, all at under or around £3. But the bar lunches are the thing – chicken chasseur around £1.20, roast haunch of venison in port sauce costs about £1.80 and a fresh salmon salad £4.

Grantown-on-Spey

CRAGGAN MILL RESTAURANT
(Grantown-on-Spey 2288)
Open: summer: Mon-Sun 12.30-2pm, 6-10pm winter: Mon-Sun 7-10pm

P

A plain and rustic style is favoured by proprietors Bruno and Ann Bellini. Cuisine is a winning mixture of Italian and English, as the stylish menu reflects. A starter, such as mussels in wine or mushrooms and Stilton soup, should be followed by scampi provençale or chicken in brandy (both are under £3.75). Interesting sweets are available for under £1.

Inverness

BALMORAL RESTAURANT
19 Queensgate (Inverness 33198)
Open: Mon-Sat (also Sun Jul and Aug)
Snack Bar: 8am-5.30pm,
Restaurant: 11am-7pm

S ♧

The Balmoral is a popular family restaurant offering good food and friendly service both in the Snack Bar and in the Smorrebrod Restaurant. Snack bar prices range from 40p for filled rolls to about £3 top whack, for steak. The recently-opened Smorrebrod, on the first floor, offers a tempting array of open sandwiches (with salad) at around £2.

CABERFEIDH RESTAURANT
CALEDONIAN HOTEL, Church Street (Inverness 35181)
Open: Mon-Thu 12noon-2.15pm, 5-11pm, Fri-Sat 12noon-2pm, 5-12mdnt

C ♫ P

The Caberfeidh Restaurant, a modern grill room attached to the hotel, offers visitors a sustaining selection of goodies in comfortable surroundings. A typical three-course meal could include grapefruit cocktail at 60p, fried scampi with lemon and French fries or salad bowl for £3.30 and chocolate mousse (also 60p). A glass of wine will bring the bill to just over £5. For only £1.35 you can have a business lunch.

CRAWFORDS PIZZA RESTAURANT
Lombard Street (Inverness 34328)
Open: Mon-Sat 10am-11pm,
Sun 12noon-6pm

S ♧

This bright, modern pizzeria is conveniently situated in a pedestrianised shopping precinct. Inside, tiled floors and stucco walls with mirrors, are in pleasant contrast to the city atmosphere outside. There are twelve varieties of pizza to choose from, as well as salads, open sandwiches and canneloni. Even with wine it would be difficult to spend more than £5. Visit the Smørgasbrød Restaurant too.

Invershin

INVERSHIN HOTEL (Invershin 202)
Open: Mon-Thu 12noon-3pm, 7-9pm, Fri and Sun 12noon-3pm, 7-9.30pm, Sat 12noon-3pm, 7-10pm

P

You'll be encouraged to eat Scots at this traditional Highland hotel. Successful consumption of 'freshly-killed Highland haggis with tatties', roast ribs of Angus beef, and sweet little Cloutie dumplings, should leave you with a sense of achievement. And the old Scottish trait of getting good value for money holds true, too – lunch will be under £4, dinner around £5. Local fish features on all menus, and is strongly recommended.

Kingussie

WOOD'N'SPOON RESTAURANT
3-7 High Street (Kingussie 488)
Open: summer: Mon-Sat 10am-9.30pm, winter: Mon-Sat 11am-2.30pm, 6-9.30pm.

C S

The high-ceilinged restaurant has hessian walls, natural pine partitions and a self service counter where home-made cakes, quiches and other goodies are arrayed. In the evening starters include home-made smoked fish pâté at around £1. Chef's specials include venison casserole and poached salmon, both served with baked potato and vegetables for around £3.75. Arbroath smokies are always available. Sweets from the trolley have fresh cream.

Leckmelm

LOCH BROOM RESTAURANT
(Ullapool 2471)
Open: summer only: Mon-Sun 9am-9pm

P

Enjoy commanding panoramic views of brooding Loch Broom while you partake of entrecôte steak garni and apricot flan with cream. This restaurant, housed in an elevated wooden chalet close by the loch, offers a relaxed, comfortable atmosphere and a very reasonably priced à la carte menu. A three-course meal will cost around £5.

Lochton

T'MAST, Lochton House (A957, 6m SE of Banchory) (Crathes 543/585)

Open: summer: Mon-Sun 12noon-2.30pm, 7-10pm

P

Formerly a grocer's shop, then a tea-room, this pub-cum-restaurant with its sun lounge extension now acts as a modern oasis for Grampian travellers. Lunchtime prices here are exceptionally low. For example, a simple starter, roast pork with apple sauce and peach Melba only comes to about £3. A typical high tea offering is gammon with pineapple (also at £3), including a hot drink, toast and cakes. Prices for dinner and supper are only fractionally higher, with sirloin steak garni top whack at about £3.50.

Peterhead

COFFEE SHOP, Fraserburgh Road (Peterhead 71121)
Open: Mon-Sun 7.30am-11pm

C P

Inside Peterhead's newest and most modern hotel, the Waterside Inn, you will find this glowing Coffee Shop which offers a wide range of meals. Quick snacks include mushrooms and bacon on toast (about £1.10), pizza (around £1.50) or salads (from about £2). A three-course meal could include cream of chicken soup (about 50p), a grill such as farmhouse grill (gammon with egg, mushrooms, tomatoes and chips at around £2.20) and a meringue glacé (about 80p) or a thick slice of fresh cream gâteau (around 70p).

Thurso

PENTLAND HOTEL, Princes Street (Thurso 3202)
Open: Mon-Thu 12noon-2pm, 6.30-8pm, Fri-Sat 12noon-2pm, 6.30-9pm, Sun 12.30-2pm, 6.30-8pm

S

In the bright, cheerful dining room of the Pentland, you can be tempted by an extensive à la carte lunch, dinner, or to combine the best of two meals, a high tea (5-6pm). A three-course lunch can easily cost under £4 and may include roast Caithness ribs of beef, or for 'a few dollars more', fresh Thurso salmon. Bar lunches served during the week are again very reasonably priced, and may offer Irish stew or Goa curry from £1.20.

Tomintoul

GLENMULLIACH RESTAURANT
(Tomintoul 356)
2m south of Tomintoul
Open: Mon-Sun 10am-6.30pm

P

The Lannagan family have built their dream restaurant from scratch. Father and sons did the building work, mum took over the decorating. The result is a pleasant, modern, cottage-style building set amongst forested hills. Inside, a wood-burning stove, red-pine fittings and a cheerful atmosphere defy the occasional Scottish mist. Food-wise, the emphasis is on home-baking and Scottish fare. Day-time self-service prices can be as low as £1.75 for three-courses.

Ullapool

FAR ISLES, North Road (Ullapool 2385)
Open: Mon-Sun 12noon-2.15pm, 5.30-9.30pm

P S

This attractively decorated, modern restaurant and bar on the northern outskirts of this picturesque little fishing village serves reasonably-priced wholesome food. Dishes include fresh Loch Broom scallops with savoury rice and salad, or escalope of pork Cordon Bleu, French fried and croquette potatoes with veg for around £3.40.

WALES

The Red Lion Hotel, Llangorse

Park Hill Hotel, Betws-y-Coed

La Gondola, Swansea

Plantagenant House, Tenby.

The Cliff Hotel, Cardigan

The Nags Head Hotel, Garthmyl

Wales

Spectacular mountains, haunting lakes, hostile, barren hills and a dramatic rugged coastline are matched in this country of passionate Celts by an exciting and varied cuisine.

Flocks of the small breed of Welsh sheep populate the rocky hills, where wild thyme gives the sweet, succulent meat its characteristic flavour. Small cutlets and chops are served almost everywhere, but specialities are honeyed lamb shoulder with rosemary or saddle of mutton with rowanberry sauce. Many a best end of neck ends its days in a bowl of cawl, the traditional soup packed with vegetables and herbs – a meal in itself for labouring shepherds and miners alike.

Mid-Wales boasts an abundance of game – braised pheasant or Welsh woodcock and goose with spicy apple sauce have been the pride of Montgomery for many a year. Lake Vyrnwy and the River Dovey yield excellent salmon and trout. Trout with bacon often served in Wales is the British counterpart of *truites au lard* of Brittany.

The Irish Sea has been plundered for centuries for Gaelic delicacies. Swansea has the largest fresh fish market in Wales – frequented still by the famous Penclawdd cockle women. Cockles are used in cockle pies, cockle oatmeal

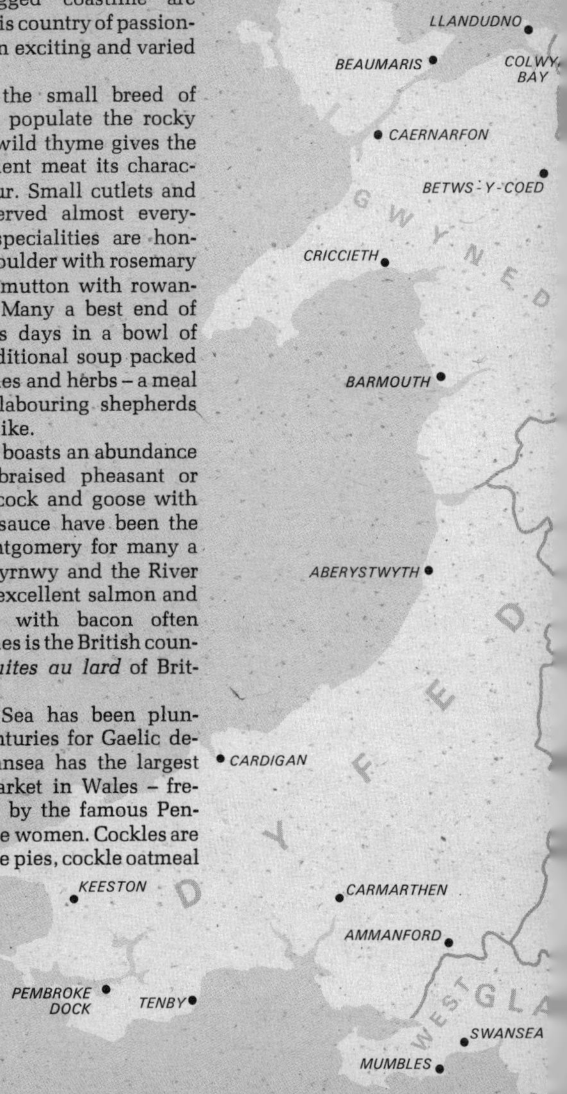

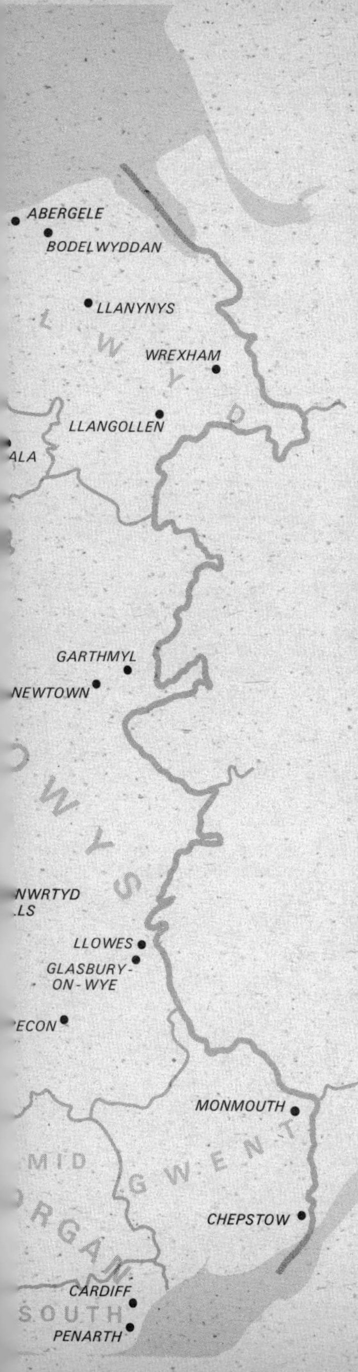

cakes, pancakes and even in stew – often accompanied by mussels, clams or scallops. Scallops and bacon and oyster soup are two delicious Gower dishes. Another fruit of the sea is laver – a smooth, fine seaweed also sold in Swansea market and processed to make a caviar-like purée. The famed laverbread is used with oatmeal to make cakes on the griddle.

The griddle or bakestone is used everywhere in Wales for cooking pancakes, oatcakes and Welsh cakes – bursting with sultanas and raisins and a treat served hot with butter, sprinkled with sugar, cinnamon and jam or honey.

It is impossible to think of Wales without the leek, and sure enough, it's put to good use here. Leek pasties, tarts and flans are universal, but a notable speciality is Anglesey eggs – boiled and covered in cheese sauce, then surrounded with a mixture of leeks and mashed potato. Pumpkins used to rival leeks in Gower and Welsh settlers in the United States probably introduced pumpkin pie there. Now you have to make do with vegetable marrow or squash pie – every bit as tasty.

And as for the Welsh Rarebit, that nourishing snack – it isn't even made from Caerphilly cheese, but from hard cheeses such as Cheddar or Cheshire with a dash of Worcestershire sauce – and who wants to go to Wales for that anyway? Certainly not worth asking for it in any of these eating places!

Abergele

BULL HOTEL, Chapel Street (Abergele 822115)
Open: Mon-Sun 12noon-2.30pm, 7-8.30pm

[♫] [P] [S]

Emphasis is on good home cooking in this traditionally furnished inn, with a friendly, relaxed atmosphere. The dining room menu operates for lunch and dinner and offers basic English fare, with three courses costing from £3-£4.50. Home-made fruit pies or sherry trifle with cream are around 50p.

Aberystwyth

THE CAMBRIAN HOTEL ★★
Alexandra Road (Aberystwyth 612446)
Open: Mon-Sun 12noon-2pm, 6.30-8pm (7.30pm Sun)

[P]

The atmosphere is warm and friendly and the food is home-cooked, hot and well served. Three-course table d'hôte lunch is around £3.50 and includes a choice of basic English roasts or salad. The four-course table d'hôte dinner has cheese and biscuits as the fourth course. Roast dinners are around £3.50, steak dinners around £5.

CAPRICE, 8-10 North Parade (Aberystwyth 612084)
Open: Jun-Oct Mon-Sun 9am-8.30pm; the rest of the year Mon-Fri 9am-5.30pm (Closed: winter: Wed)

[C] [♫] [S] [♧]

Crabs straight from the harbour are a speciality at Jill and Alun Evans's cheerful restaurant. A three-course meal, with soup or fruit juice, a main course of roast, poultry or fish, and a sweet such as fruit tart and custard costs about £2. The à la carte menu is equally modestly priced, with starters from 35p for fruit juice to around £1.20 for prawn cocktail, main courses are up to about £4.

MARINE HOTEL, Marine Parade (Aberystwyth 612444)
Open: summer: Bar and dining room: Mon-Sun 12.30-2pm, 7-9.30pm, winter: 12.30-2pm, 7pm onwards, Grill room: Mon-Sat 7-9.30pm

[C] [♫] [P] [S] [♧]

This Welsh hotel is Welsh owned, and the lamb on the menu is Welsh too. Lunch at around £3 cannot be bad value, and here one has a choice of four starters, a main course followed by a pudding or lighter sweet and coffee. The table d'hôte dinner offers a wider choice than the lunch menu at around £4.50. There is also a snack menu, with sandwiches and ploughman's lunch supplemented by sausage (about £1.30) and fish or chicken (about £1.30) all served with chips. Omelettes are priced from 85p. A meal from the cold table is £1.80.

Y DEWIN BISTRO, Ffordd Portland Road (Aberystwyth 617738)
Open: High season: Mon-Sat 12noon-2pm, 5-10pm, rest of the year: Mon-Sat 5-11pm (closed Wed)

The owner, Sian Myrddin, has succeeded in creating a Celtic atmosphere. Murals and paintings by a local artist enhance the effect with 'Lord of the Rings' themes. Menus are in Welsh and English, though no attempt has been made to translate pizza or quiche lorraine into either language! All food is home-cooked. Specialities are cawl and syllabub.

Ammanford

EXECUTIVE RESTAURANT
46 High Street (Ammanford 4442)
Open: Tue-Sat 10.30am-2pm, 7.30-10pm

[P]

Fresh from running a busy pub, owners Bobby and Ray Moring have taken a daring plunge and converted the property adjoining their home (once a vicarage) into a restaurant. A lunchtime platter of fish and chips, roast pork or roast beef with vegetables of the day costs a little over £1, with sweet and starter prices kept very low. Bobby Moring's delicious trifle is the most popular dessert. A three-course evening meal here would be likely to take the best part of your fiver, but for fresh fish and generous cuts of meat, it represents good value for money. Rioja wines are a speciality of the list, but San Fernando is sold by the carafe.

Bala

NEUADD Y CYFNOD, High Street (Bala 520262)
Open: summer: Mon-Sun 9am-9pm, winter: Mon-Fri dinner only

[C] [P] [S]

In this imposing building, a long school hall, with its panelled walls and high ceilings, Gwyn and Ann Evans offer a taste or two of traditional Welsh cooking. Menus, with parallel text translations, include lunch at around £3 (half price for children), dinner at about £3.20 (again just over half price for children) and a particularly Welsh dinner, that includes a glass of mead, at just over £3.20. Welsh farmhouse soup, with local salmon and lamb figure among the alternatives in all three meals. A speciality of the house is an authentic Welsh tea at around £1.50.

Barmouth

THE ANGRY CHEESE, Church Street
(Barmouth 280038)
Open: summer: Mon-Sun 12noon-2pm, 6-10.30pm, winter: Fri-Sat 6-10.30pm

Inside this attractive restaurant, the décor is 'neo-rustic' with pine tables, banquettes and rush-seated chairs. Bar snacks are available, and the three-course set menu costs around £3.60. There's a choice of two items in each course, featuring main dishes such as pork schnitzel with beurre noisette or Chicken Grandmère. Vegetarians are tempted by such dishes as fruit and vegetable kebabs or peanut and parmesan pancake. If you go à la carte, potatoes and fresh vegetables of the day are included in the price.

Beaumaris

HOBSON'S CHOICE × 13 Castle Street
(Beaumaris 810323)
Open: May-Sep: Tue-Sat 12noon-2pm

[C] [P]

Lunch only comes within our budget at this charming 16th-century converted bakehouse. Chef Ian Mirrless provides superb kitchen or duck liver pâté with granary or French bread for around 70p and delicious home-made soup at 50p. Local scallops with mushrooms, cheese and white wine sauce is a dish to delight at £3.55. Home-made sweets are 60p.

Betws-y-Coed

PARK HILL HOTEL ★★ Llanrwst Road
(Betws-y-Coed 540)
Open: Mon-Sun for dinner, beginning 7-7.30pm (booking essential)

[C] [P]

If 'home-made and fresh' appeals to you then you'll like this hotel restaurant. Choice is necessarily limited as proprietors John and Jenny Waite do the cooking and serving themselves. The

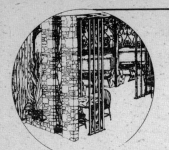

table d'hôte dinner at around £4.75 offers a choice between soup, fruit juice and one other starter (pâté perhaps), at least two main dishes (a roast, coq au vin, plaice meunière and baked gammon in cider are examples), three sweets (raspberry tart and cream, peach lorraine, blackcurrant cheesecake for instance) or cheese and biscuits, plus tea or coffee. Just one thing – it's advisable to book well in advance.

Bodelwyddan

THE CROFT, FAENOL FAWR MANOR ✗✗ (Rhuddlan 590784)
Open: Mon-Sun 12noon-2.30pm, 7.30-11pm

Ⓒ 🎵 Ⓟ

Faenol Fawr is a restaurant (a bit expensive for us) in a manor house built in 1597, but the Croft is *really* old, dating back to the early part of the 13th century. Here, you can take a pleasant yet inexpensive meal chosen from the Supper Bar menu. Starters include home-made soup at around 35p and Arbroath smokies at about £1.50. There are casseroles – duck and blackberry at around £2.20 and local pheasant in red wine (around £3) and meat platters

for about £2 – with help-yourself salad and jacket potato included in the price. A home-made sweet will add 75p or so. House wine is available at about 60p.

Brecon

RED LION INN, Llangorse (Llangorse 238)
Open: Mon-Sun 12noon-2pm, 7-9.30pm

Ⓟ 🐾

A warm Welsh welcome is assured in this two hundred-year-old inn close to the famous Llangorse lake. Situated deep in the heart of the Brecon Beacons National Park, it is an ideal holiday stopping-place. Meals in the bar include snacks such as Chef's terrine, roll and butter at about 70p, cottage pie or lasagne at about £1.40. More substantial dishes such as chicken Red Lion style, Veal Cordon Bleu or beef chasseur cost around £3. An à la carte meal may be had in the dining room, but this could prove beyond our means. House wine costs around 60p a glass.

Caernarfon

PLAS BOWMAN, High Street (Caernarfon 5555)
Open: Mon-Sat 12noon-1.30pm,

The Red Lion Inn
Llangorse, Brecon.

This delightful Country Inn has 10 Bedrooms (5 with bath and 5 with shower).

The restaurant, open to residents, serves an à la carte menu every evening, Monday to Saturday, from 7 - 9.30pm and also offers an extensive wine list.

Bar snacks and meals are served in the bar every lunchtime and evening from 7 - 9.30pm.

Cold buffet is served in the bar every Sunday lunchtime, between 12.00 noon and 2pm.

Telephone Llangorse 238

6-9.30pm, Sun 12noon-1.30pm, 7-8pm

[S]

Built in 1334 for the High Sheriff, Thomas Bowman, this three-storey property now houses Posi Williams, North Wales Chef of the Year 1980, who cooks fresh meats, fish and vegetables for a menu which changes daily. Just over £5 will get you three courses, coffee or tea and a glass of wine for lunch *or* dinner. The set menu offers about four choices for each course. Appetisers could include avocado vinaigrette, pâté of the house or sardine salad. Salmon with hollandaise sauces, beef Stroganoff or stuffed marrow are examples of main course dishes.

THE STABLES RESTAURANT AND HOTEL ☆☆☆
(Llanwnda 830711/830413)
Open: Mon-Sun 12noon-1.45pm, 7-9.45pm

[C] [♫] [P]

By far the best in the food line that Caernarfon has to offer is to be found at Mrs Jenny Howarth's Stables Restaurant, some three miles outside the town, on the A497 road to Pwhelli. Formerly the stables to Plas Fynnon, the building was very cleverly and tastefully converted for its present use in 1972. The menu is a long and impressive one but the locals, who ought to know, swear by the barbecued spare ribs starter, ham and asparagus mornay, grilled trout with almonds, local lamb chops in wine sauce and pineapple flambé, all around £2.75. A table d'hôte menu is also available for around £5.50 and about £4 at lunchtimes. The piped music is agreeable and discreet and live entertainment is frequently provided.

Cardiff

THE BUNGALOW CAFE, 15 High Street (Cardiff 26932)
Open: Mon-Sat 10am-5.30pm

[S]

The Bungalow Café has been established in Cardiff for all of seventy years. Opposite the entrance to Castle Arcade, and very handy for Cardiff Castle, The Bungalow offers a fairly comprehensive menu covering morning coffee, lunch, afternoon tea and grills in an old-fashioned tea house setting. Starters range from around 40p to £1, roasts and poultry from about £2-£3, grills from around £2.20-£3.50, fish dishes from £2-£3.50 or so and sweets from around 45p upwards. The restaurant is reached through a cake shop via a small takeaway bar selling pasties, steak pies, cottage pies etc. The Bungalow is unlicensed.

THE HIMALAYA RESTAURANT, 24 Wellfield Road (Cardiff 491722)
Open: Mon-Sun 12noon-3pm, 6pm-2am

[C] [♫] [S]

The best Indian food in Cardiff is the local verdict on Bakshi Suleman's restaurant. The Himalaya has a vaguely Oriental décor. Biriani dishes, chicken curries and meat or prawn curries cost from around £2 to £2.50. The restaurant is licensed and sells a half bottle of Spanish wine for about £1.50. Be warned: the helpings are enormous.

THE PLYMOUTH ARMS RESTAURANT, St Fagans
(Cardiff 569130)
Open: Tue-Sat 12noon-2.30pm, 7-9.30pm

[C] [P]

You take the A48 Swansea road out of Cardiff, following the signs for the Welsh folk museum, to reach St Fagans and The Plymouth Arms. You can get a good bar lunch for around £1.75 and a substantial three-course table d'hôte lunch for about £4.50, which includes the choice of sirloin steak bordelaise. The à la carte menu is comparatively expensive, but a three-course dinner at around a fiver, with a glass of white wine is just about possible.

SAVASTANO'S, 302 North Road
(Cardiff 30270)
Open: Mon-Sat 12noon-2.30pm, 7-11.30pm (Thu-Sat 12mdnt)

Giacomo Savastano's restaurant doesn't strike one as particularly Italian, for the décor is plain and the furniture pine. But his food is very Italian, very good and – as Italian restaurants go – extremely reasonably priced, with soups around 55p, pastas at about £2, a number of fish, chicken or veal dishes at around £2.50 and steaks from about £3.20. A carafe of Italian wine costs around £2.50 and a glass about 55p.

YE OLDE WINE SHOPPE, Wyndham Arcade, St Mary Street (Cardiff 29876)
Open: Mon-Sat 12noon-2.30pm, 7-11pm

[C] [♫] [P] [S]

Don't be put off by the name. This must be the best-stocked wine bar in Cardiff and well worth a visit, for its friendly bars and bright little bistro. The

downstairs bar and bistro serve the same food at the same prices – appetisers at around 50p to £1.50, a choice of cold table platters at about £2, or Chef's Specials from the £2.75 mark which include pork Americana (fillet cooked in wine with peaches and brandy flambé) and Malayan chicken (a hot spicy curry). Gâteaux and cheesecakes are about 60p a portion – the cost of a large glass of house wine.

YR YSTAFELL GYMRAEG
74 Whitchurch Road (Cardiff 42317)
Open: Mon-Fri 12noon-2pm, 7-11.30pm, Sat 7-11.30pm

[C]

Yr Ystafell Gymraeg (The Welsh Room to you) is just that, with its Welsh-weave drapes, Welsh tapestry curtains, Welsh Tourist Board posters, the inevitable Welsh dresser and a Welsh menu (with English sub-titles). The owners sound Italian and, indeed, proprietor Umberto Palladino is, but his wife is just about as Welsh as it is possible to be. Starters include Penclawdd Cockles at around £1. Poultry dishes range in price from around £3 for Chicken Snowdonia. Home-made fruit pies, gâteaux and trifle range from between 70p-£1.20. A glass of French-bottled house wine costs about 50p.

Cardigan

THE BELL HOTEL, Pendre
(Cardigan 2629)
Open: Mon, Sat 11am-11pm, Tue-Fri 12noon-2pm, 7-9pm

[C] [P] [S]

Malcolm and Jenny Wood have a good lunchtime trade at The Bell. Hot dishes in the restaurant include steak and kidney pie at £1.50, and deep-fried scampi at around £3. The evening menu includes fresh local sea trout at around £3.

THE BLACK LION HOTEL
High Street (Cardigan 2532)
Open: Mon-Sat 12noon-2.30pm, 8-10pm

[♫] [S]

The Gegin Fach restaurant does a first-class three-course meal for around £5. Try the meals in baskets at prices from £1.50 upwards, served in the lounge. Burgers at around £1.20-£1.50 are also available.

CLIFF HOTEL ★★★ Gwbert-on-Sea
(Cardigan 3241/3242/2517)
Open: Mon-Sun 12.45-2pm, 7-9pm

[C] [P]

This restaurant offers an interesting choice of menu but unfortunately, the à la carte is beyond our reach. There is a good table d'hôte lunch and dinner at around £4.50 and £5.50 respectively. For starters hot consommé with profiteroles, main course – hot crab Gwbert style with new potatoes and tomato provençale, and a choice of sweets from the trolley. A glass of the Italian carafe wine costs around 65p.

Carmarthen

THE OLD CURIOSITY, 20a King Street (Carmarthen 32384)
Open: Mon-Tue 10am-5pm, Wed-Fri 10am-9.30pm, Sat 10am-10pm
[C] [♫] [P] [S]

The Old Curiosity is much, much more than a convenient place for a coffee, a snack, or a meal. The Indian salad contains brown rice, not white, and vegetarians may choose from a number of appetising dishes. The seafood salad at around £2.50 is excellent, and omelettes include mushroom, ham or chicken all at around £1.50. 'Gap fillers' at around £1 include curry butter prawns and bacon-wrapped bananas.

QUEENSWAY RESTAURANT
Queen Street (Carmarthen 5631)
Open: Mon-Sat 10am-2.30pm,

6.30-11pm

[C]

This ground-floor restaurant and first-floor wine bar opens on to a sun-trap roof garden. Steaks are popular in the restaurant, where the à la carte menu includes Chef's specials priced about £3. Meals served from the wine bar include plaice and chips or roast beef and Yorkshire pudding at around £4 or steak and chips at under £4.

Chepstow

CASTLE VIEW HOTEL ★★ Bridge Street (Chepstow 70349)
Open: Mon-Sat 12.15-2pm, 6.30-9pm, Sun 12.15-1.45pm, 6.30-8.30pm and normal licensing hours

[P] [S]

As its name suggests this charming, creeper-clad hotel is opposite Chepstow Castle. Meals in the bar include imaginative soups such as salmon and cucumber, cawl and celestial soup – potato, carrot and onion with sherry. Prawns au gratin is a popular main course choice. Restaurant dishes include West Country pork chop with apple, onion, cheese and cider or plaice fillet poached in white wine with mushroom and cream sauce at around £3.60, including vegetables. Sweets such as lemon syllabub with sherry costs about 80p.

Colwyn Bay

MELFORT HOTEL ★ Llannerch Road East, Rhos-on-Sea (Colwyn Bay 44390)
Open: Mon-Sun 12.30-2pm, 6.30-7.30pm

[P]

Enjoy dinner in the relaxed, spacious dining room of this small private hotel located just off the West Promenade. Good, home-made food is offered at around £4 for three courses, which could include oxtail soup, followed by roast beef and Yorkshire pudding and gooseberry tart and custard.

Criccieth

BRON EIFION COUNTRY HOUSE HOTEL ★★★ (Criccieth 2293)
Open: Mon-Sun 8.30-9.30am, 1-2pm, 7.30-9pm

[P] [ ]

Bron Eifion was built in the 1870s as the summer residence of slate master John Greaves. Its main hall boasts superb wall panelling and a magnificent central galley of pitch pine. The hotel's three-course lunch is about £4.50 (including service) and gives a tempting choice of starters and desserts. A glass of wine costs about 70p.

Garthmyl

THE NAG'S HEAD HOTEL
(Berriew 287/537)
Open: Mon-Sat 10.30am-2.30pm, 6-10.30pm, Sun 12noon-2pm, 7-10.30pm

[P]

Modern, colourful décor is the hallmark of the small restaurant at The Nag's Head, where Mr and Mrs Emilio Moreno attend personally to your needs. The atmosphere is cosy and intimate in the small bar where you can drink while you wait for your excellent meal. Particularly recommended is the table d'hôte – for example, you can eat Spanish omelette, roast chicken Cuban style and apple pie for under £5.

Glasbury

LLWYNAUBACH LODGE ★★
(Glasbury 473)
Open: Mon-Sun 12noon-2.30pm, 7.30-10.30pm

[C] [♫] [P] [♣]

Llwynaubach Lodge enjoys a peaceful situation in the Wye Valley with ten acres of grounds including their own trout-filled lake and an outdoor swimming pool. At lunchtime during the week, hot and cold bar snacks and salads are available from £1-£3. Chef's carving table offers hot roast joints in the evenings and for Sunday lunch.

Llandudno

CAPTAIN'S TABLE RESTAURANT
Gloddaeth Street South (no telephone)
Open: Mon-Sun 12noon-2.30pm, 6-9.30pm

[S] [♣]

Paintings and sketches decorate the walls of this first-floor restaurant off the main street. With minute steak at around £3 and roast chicken at around £2.50, a three-course meal can be enjoyed for under £5. Children's portions are available at reduced prices.

COFFEE SHOP AND POOLSIDE BAR, EMPIRE HOTEL ★★★ Church Walks (Llandudno 77260/77269

Open: Mon-Sun 11am-3pm, 6-10pm

[C] [P]

The range of five starters (predominately fishy!) cost from 70p-£1.50. A variety of salads, rainbow trout and charcoal chicken are just some of the main courses that enable you to keep within the budget. Desserts are around 60p, the same as the glass price for the very palatable house wine.

PLAS FRON DEG HOTEL
48 Church Walks (Llandudno 77267)
Open: Mon-Sun 12.30-2pm, 6-9.30pm

[C]

Lunch and dinner menus priced from around £4.50 offer a limited but real choice, with dishes such as pork in cream and sherry sauce or chocolate roulade to tempt the taste buds. 'A Taste of Wales' menus are a feature of Plas Fron Deg, too, and well worth trying.

Llangollen

GALE'S WINE AND FOOD BAR
18 Bridge Street (Llangollen 860089)
Open: Mon-Sat 12noon-1.45pm, 6-10pm (also Sun Jun-Oct)

[P] [S]

There are ninety wines on offer at Richard and Jill Gale's Wine and Food Bar, including two vintage ports and eight wines sold by the glass, at prices from about 50p-55p. The atmosphere is very friendly and welcoming, the menu written on a blackboard behind the bar. The food is outstandingly good for this kind of operation and very reasonable, with home-made soups at around 50p, a choice of pâtés at around 75p and seven hot dishes from around £1.50-£2. Very popular are pork and apple Stroganoff at around £1.70 and beef in Guinness at about £2.

ROYAL HOTEL ★★★ Bridge Street (Llangollen 860202)
Open: Mon-Sun 12noon-2pm, 7-9.30pm (10pm Sat)

[C] [P] [S] [♧]

There are views of the River Dee from the restaurant of this Trusthouse Forte hotel which offers all the usual lunchtime platter and Blue Plate Special offers. The à la carte menu is on the expensive side, but the three-course table d'hôte lunch at about £4.50 and dinner at around £5 are excellent value. A good, more modest bar lunch or evening meal is possible at around £2.

Llanwrtyd Wells

DOL-Y-COED HOTEL
(Llanwrtyd Wells 215)
Open: Mon-Sat 12noon-2pm, 7-8pm

[P]

Everything a simple country hotel should be, the creeper-clad Dol-y-coed overlooks the River Irfon on the outskirts of the village. Log fires, dark, rich wood, old prints and unpretentious comfort exude a peaceful atmosphere. The three-course lunch (under £4) and dinner (under £5) present a small choice of good, fresh food. Bar meals such as home-cooked cold ham and various salads at under £2 are available.

Llanynys

THE LODGE, Llanrhaeadr Hall
(Llanynys 370)
Open: Mon-Sat 9.30am-5.15pm

[P] [♧]

The Lodge combines the display of fashions (from many parts of the world) and objets d'art with the provision of tasty inexpensive food. The accent is on snacks, with filled baps, Welsh rarebit, hamburger, and several other items, all at under £1, but there are more substantial dishes including salads (cheese, ham, prawn or chicken) for between £1.50-£2 and savoury pancakes or omelettes for less than £2. Sweets and pastries are home-made. A wide variety of beverages is available – but the Lodge is not licensed.

Llowes

RADNOR ARMS (Glasbury 460)
Open: Mon-Sat 12noon-3pm, 7-10.30pm

[P] [♧]

This small, pleasant country pub is a converted house with white-painted walls. The atmosphere in the dining area with its high, beamed ceiling, is informal and relaxed. A good selection of food is chalked up on the blackboard menu with home-made soups at about 70p, quiches at around £2, lasagne or Cheshire pork and apple pie, both about £2.50 and mackerel in white wine costing a little more. There is a good selection of sweets at around £1.

Monmouth

KING'S HEAD HOTEL ★★★ Agincourt Square (Monmouth 2177)
Open: Mon-Fri 12.30-2pm, 7-9pm, Fri 12.30-2pm, 7-10pm, Sun 12.30-1.45pm, 7-9pm
Coach House: Mon 6.30-11pm, Tue-Sat 12noon-3pm, 6.30-11pm

Table d'hôte lunch costs around £4.50, but the dinner menu is £6 or more. More informal lunches well within the budget are served in the cocktail bar – a cold buffet selection with interesting, fresh salads costs about £1.85, and hot dish of the day might be a casserole, pasta dish or steak and kidney pie. To the rear of the main hotel, is the Coach House. Colourful plants are arranged on the very pleasant patio area. Prices on the pub-snack menu range between 50p and £2. In the grill room, the usual selection of grills is enlivened by Barnsley chop at £2.65 or Polynesian prawn and pineapple curry at about £5.

Mumbles

LA GONDOLA, 590 Mumbles Road
(Swansea 62338)
Open: Tue-Sun 12noon-2.30pm, 6.30-11pm

[C] [P]

Apart from his native Italian, Proprietor Aldo Grattarola speaks English very

well, and gets by in French and German, so it follows that he should keep a cosmopolitan menu. À la carte choices include gammon Oriental, fillet Stroganoff, Dover sole meunière and lasagne verdi al forno – a pretty cosmopolitan bag, you'll agree! More modest is the set lunch menu offering four choices of roast, plaice, trout or steak and kidney pie with vegetables and potatoes, plus a sweet and starter, around £3.

Newtown

BEAR HOTEL ★★★ Broad Street
(Newtown 26964)
Open: Mon-Sun 12noon-2pm,
6.30-9.30pm

Formerly a coaching inn, the Bear has all the atmosphere anyone could wish for. Food is available in the bar and the two grill rooms: the Spinning Wheel and the Severn. Bar snacks are served in the evening and are mainly substantial, including steak and kidney pie or chicken and chips. The restaurants serve an excellent three-course dinner with a large choice for each course, including baked honeyed lamb or chicken Marengo at around £4.50.

Pembroke Dock

HILL HOUSE INN, Cosheston
(Pembroke 4352/5344)
Open: Mon-Sun 12noon-2pm, 7-10pm

C P

There's a touch of Welsh patriotism at this early Georgian inn, with Welsh gammon and lamb featuring on the table d'hôte menu amongst a good choice of international dishes. The beers are mainly Welsh brews – and the impressive Victorian-style, mahogany bar on the ground floor was made by local craftsman John Owen Hughes. There is a comfortable, welcoming atmosphere. The table d'hôte in the charming dining room is around £6 but does include a glass of house wine. Bar meals are good value, with home-made soups and pâtés at 50p and 75p respectively, and prawn Normandy (with tartare sauce, apple and tomato purée) at £1.80, or fresh local trout.

Penarth

L'APERITIF, CAPRICE RESTAURANT, ✕✕✕ The Esplanade
(Penarth 702424)
Open: Mon-Sat 10.30am-2.30pm,
7-10.30pm, Sun 10.30am-2.30pm

C ♫ P S

Situated below the Caprice Restaurant (superb cuisine but too expensive for us!) L'Aperitif operates from the same kitchen and offers good unpretentious food at very reasonable prices. Starters include home-made soup of the day at around 40p, potted shrimps at about £1.20 and mixed hors d'oeuvres at around £2. Dishes include lamb cutlets, peas and chips at just over £3 and fillet steak garni, with chips, at about £4.50. Sweets include a choice of gâteaux and fruit tart with cream in the 50p-80p range. The three-course Sunday lunch is very good value, the price list for the main course being inclusive of starter and sweet and costing about £4. Starters offer a choice of soup, fruit juice or Florida cocktail, the third course can be a fresh cream dessert or cheese and biscuits.

Swansea

THE DRAGON HOTEL ☆☆☆☆
Kingsway Circle (Swansea 51074)
Open: The Birch Room: Mon-Sat 12.30-2.30pm, 7-9.30pm
The Dragon and Viking Buttery:
Mon-Sun 12noon-2.45pm, 6-10.45pm

C ♫ P S

The Birch Room's à la carte menu is on

the expensive side but a choice of table d'hôte lunches at prices from about £4.50, the three-course table d'hôte dinner at around £5 and the four-course one at the £5.75 mark are all excellent value. The Buttery prices are extremely competitive, with plaice at less than £3, pizza Norseman at around £1.75 and gammon steak at around £3. Prices of the lounge-bar salads run from £1.50 upwards.

GREEN'S BURGER RESTAURANT
50 St Helen's Road (Swansea 41901)
Open: Mon-Sun 11.30am-2.30pm
6-11.30pm (all day during summer)

[C] [♫] [P] [♧]

Green's restaurant is all scrub-top tables, green-shaded wall lamps and green napkins. 'We're the greatest' is the house motto and Swansea's younger set would probably agree. Starters include spare rib in BBQ sauce at about 70p. There is a good choice of 4oz or 8oz burgers here. Alternatives include a monster T-bone steak or a pizza at about £2.25. Desserts such as home-made apple pie, gâteaux and rum baba are around 70-80p. A glass of the house wine costs around 60p. Green's boasts a DJ on weekday evenings and live entertainment on a Sunday.

Tenby

THE BUCCANEER RESTAURANT
St Julian's Street (Tenby 2273)
Open: Etr to Christmas,
Mon-Sun 12.15-2pm, 6.30-10.30pm

[C] [P]

Hot and cold appetisers at the Buccaneer range from fruit juices to lobster cocktail or prawns in garlic butter (around £2), fish dishes from plaice to grilled Dover sole, and grills from lamb cutlets to Porterhouse steak. Desserts include fruit fritters and cheesecake from around 60p-£1.

HOI SAN RESTAURANT
Tudor Square (Tenby 2025)
Open: Apr-Sep Mon-Sun 12noon-11.45pm, Oct-Dec, Mar Thu-Fri 6-11.45pm, Sat-Sun 12noon-11.45pm

[S]

A friendly, enthusiastic Cantonese atmosphere is to be found here in the centre of Tenby. Chopsticks are laid out to test your dexterity and help is at hand should you fail the test. Special home cooking evenings are laid on when unusual family-style dishes are available. The choice of special dinners is impressive. Particularly recommended are braised Indian corn with chicken and fried beef with soya beans and garlic sauce at around £2.50.

THE LION'S DEN, ROYAL LION HOTEL ★★ High Street (Tenby 2127)
Open: summer: Mon-Sun 12noon-2pm, 6.30-10pm (winter: closed Sun)

C

The Lion's Den restaurant and bar, with its dark oak settles and cosy alcoves, is a favourite meeting and eating place for Tenby folk and visitors alike. The cheap three-course lunch with roast chicken, plaice, steak and kidney pie and omelettes all around £2.75 and a special menu for children at around £1.75 are excellent value as is the à la carte menu, with main course dishes ranging from pizza to fillet steak Rossini. Real turtle soup or salad niçoise are two interesting appetisers, both at around 60p and sweets from the trolley are about 75p.

NORMANDIE HOTEL, Upper Frog Street (Tenby 2227)
Open: Mon-Sun 12noon-2pm, 7.30-10pm

♫ S

The restaurant, formerly stables,

positively bristles with chunky stone walls and gnarled beams. Lunchtime bar snacks are very popular and extremely reasonably priced. The restaurant's lunches include roast beef, turkey and ham or chicken all at around £3.50.

PLANTAGENET HOUSE, Quay Hill (Tenby 2350).
Open: Etr-Oct: Mon-Sun 10am-10.30pm

[C] [♬] [S] [♧]

Pamela Stone and her partners aim to provide a comprehensive, good quality service at no-nonsense prices. Three-course meals are available throughout the day at around £3.90 for adults and about £2.30 for children. The Children's Choice menu is priced at below £1.50.

Wrexham

THE WELSH KITCHEN,
7-9 Church Street (Wrexham 263302)
Open: Mon-Sat 10am-2.30pm

[C] [♬] [S]

Exposed roof timbers set the scene and there is a good choice from soup or pâté and any one of four or five main courses, all for around £2.50. Chef's Specials cost around £4.25. Home-made desserts such as fruit pie and cream cost about 55p.

Glossary

afelia Greek dish of pork fillet, red wine, cream and coriander

antipasti Italian appetisers

apfel strüdel apple in very thin pastry

Arbroath smokies haddock specially cured at Arbroath

baklava Greek sweet of flaky pastry filled with nuts and steeped in syrup

beef blanquette beef stew made with a white sauce

beef kromeski creamed mixture of meats wrapped in bacon and deep-fried in butter

beef Stroganoff strips of steak cooked with onions and mushrooms, with sour cream and sherry

beef teriyaki Japanese dish of sliced beef marinated in soy sauce, ginger, garlic and mirin

Berliner apfel kuchen German apple cake

biriani meat and rice dish flavoured with spices and saffron

bistecca pizzaiola beef steak with tomatoes, garlic and basil

blanquette de veau veal casseroled in white sauce

boeuf bourguignon beef casseroled in red wine with onions, bacon and mushrooms

bouillabaise Marseilles assorted fish and shellfish cooked in white wine, garlic, saffron and olive oil

brochette cooked on a skewer

cacciatore Italian hunter's-style sauce – with mushrooms, herbs, shallots, wine, tomatoes, ham and tongue

cannelloni tubular pasta stuffed with meat and served with sauce

carbonnade of beef beef slices, onions and herbs braised in beer

chapatis Indian unleavened bread

chasseur French hunter's-style sauce of mushrooms, tomatoes, wine, garlic and herbs

chateaubriand thick fillet or rump steak

chicken Kiev young whole chicken or chicken breast rolled and stuffed with garlic butter, rolled in fresh breadcrumbs and fried in oil

chicken à la king diced chicken with mushrooms and pimentoes in a white sauce with sherry, whisky and slivered almonds

chicken Basque style chicken cooked with onions, green peppers and tomatoes

chicken florentine chicken cooked in oil, with spices and spinach

chicken kurma mildly spiced chicken cooked with cream and nuts

chicken paesana chicken peasant-style, with bacon, potatoes, carrots, marrow and root vegetables

chicken spatchcock 'despatch cock' – small broiler, jointed and grilled at speed

chicken supreme boned chicken breast served in a thick, bland chicken stock

chicken Veronique chicken casseroled in white wine sauce with grapes

chili con carne kidney beans, minced beef, tomatoes, pimento or chili pepper and spices, with slices of raw onion

chocolate Bavarois rich, chocolate custard, set with gelatine and topped with whipped cream

chop suey stir-fried meat in gunpowder sauce, served with rice

chow chow Chinese preserve of orange peel, ginger etc

chow mein fried noodles with a topping of stir-fried meats and vegetables

clam chowder spicy clam soup

coq au vin chicken flamed with brandy and casseroled in red wine with mushrooms, bacon, onion and herbs

consommé clear soup served hot or cold

croûtons small pieces of bread toasted or fried

crudités an appetiser of raw vegetables, usually served sliced, grated or diced

Cumberland sausage a giant herb-filled sausage, containing rosemary, thyme and sage

cumquat plum-sized fruit with sweet rind and acid pulp

d'agneau grillée poivre vert lamb grilled with green peppers

devilled pôissin whole, young chicken in a hot, spicy sauce

dolci Italian pastries and cakes

dolmas vine leaves stuffed with rice and herbs

dolmades (dolmadakia) vine or cabbage leaves stuffed with rice and minced meat, braised in white sauce

dondurma makli Egyptian ice cream flavoured with mastic

egg à la Russe eggs in mayonnaise with diced vegetables

en croûte in a pastry crust

escalope of veal champignoise thin slice of veal served in mushroom sauce

escalope of veal cordon bleu breaded veal with a cheese filling

escalope of veal Holstein thin, boneless slice of veal, breaded, with fried egg and anchovies

escargots snails

fetta best-known Greek cheese, made of goat's, or ewe's milk, white and crumbly

fettuccine matriciana thin noodles served in tomato sauce, bacon or pork and sheep's milk cheese

Florida cocktail grapefruit and orange appetiser

fondue *either* melted cheese with white wine in a tureen, into which bread is dipped, *or* bite-sized pieces of beef, dipped into boiling oil in a tureen and eaten with a variety of sauces

fricasée browned pieces of meat braised with seasonings and vegetables and served in a thick sauce

gazpacho icy cold, seasoned soup with raw onions, garlic, tomato, cucumber and green peppers

gnocchi Italian dumplings

goulash beef or veal casseroled with paprika, peppers, onions and vegetables, served with sour cream

gulab jam a traditional Indian sweet

haggis boiled sheep's tripe stuffed with oatmeal, onions, chopped sheep's liver, lights and heart

horiatiko Greek rye bread

houmous Greek chick pea and sesame appetiser

jugged hare jointed hare casseroled in a mixture of herbs, onions, cloves and port or stout

kalamari squid

kateifi Greek sweet of sugared thin noodles, almonds, walnuts and syrup

kedgeree flaked fish served in a mixture of rice, eggs and butter

kleftedes spicy Greek meat balls

kleftiko Greek 'bandits meal' of lamb cooked with bay, oregano and spices

kosher pastrami lamb or beef sausage cooked in unadulterated oils

kotopoullo chicken roast with spring beans and Greek herbs

kotta kebab skewered chicken with peppers and tomatoes

kulfi Indian ice cream with nuts

lamb's kidney's turbigo kidneys chopped in batter with mushroom and sausage pieces, glazed with white wine and tomato

lamb marechella pieces of lamb fried in egg and breadcrumbs

lamb masallam whole leg of lamb or lamb pieces marinated and cooked with rare Indian herbs

lamb pasanda marinated lamb slices cooked in cream or yoghurt and mild spices

lasagne thin layers of noodle dough, baked with tomato, sausage meat, chicken liver, ham, white sauce and grated cheese

lobster bisque rich soup made from lobster, cream and brandy

lobster musalla lobster cooked with curry powder

longaniko sausage Greek sausage made with minced pork marinated in wine and smoked

marchand de vin steak poached in red wine with shallots or onions

Marsala red dessert wine from Sicily

masala Indian herbs

medaglione round fillets of beef or veal

meringue glacé Chantilly meringue served with ice cream and sweetened, whipped cream

meze (mezedes) a selection of Greek speciality dishes

mignonette small pieces of tenderloin of beef, pork or veal

milanese Milanese style: breaded, fried with Parmesan cheese and often served with saffron rice

Mortadella salad salad served with Bologna sausage

moules marinières mussels simmered in white wine and garlic

moussaka Greek dish of layers of aubergines and minced meat, topped with a white sauce and baked

mousseline a variety of Hollandaise sauce with whipped cream

moutons au haricots casserole of mutton, beans and potatoes

mozzarella soft, unripened cheese with a sweet, bland flavour, made from buffalo's milk in Southern Italy, cow's milk elsewhere

nan levened Indian bread

navarin of lamb mutton casserole with turnips

neeps Scottish turnips

noisettes choice, boneless meat usually taken from loin or rib and cut into a round shape

normande Norman style – usually cooked in white wine with gudgeon, crayfish, oysters, mussels, shrimps, mushrooms, cream or with truffles

oregano herb of the marjoram family

paella Spanish saffron rice dish with assorted seafood and/or meat

paprika huhn German paprika-cooked chicken

pâté de foie gras duck or goose liver pâté

Pavlova meringue meringue filled with ice cream and fruit such as raspberries or strawberries

peach Melba peach served in syrup with vanilla ice cream and raspberry sauce

pear Hélène pear with vanilla ice cream and chocolate sauce

Peking duck roast duck eaten wrapped in a pancake

penne carbona macaroni with ham, cream, eggs, cheese and nutmeg

pillau rice and meat cooked together in spices

pitta flat, round bread

pizza capricciosa chef's speciality pizza

pizza margherita pizza named after Italy's first Queen – tomato, mozzarella cheese and basil represent national colours

pizza marinara pizza with garlic and tomatoes

pizza napoletana classic pizza with anchovies, ham, capers, tomato, mozzarella cheese and oregano

pizza proscuitto ham pizza

pizza quattro stagioni pizza with a different topping for each quarter

pizza romana pizza with onions

pizza sardenaria pizza with sardines, anchovies, tomatoes, black olives and garlic

pizza siciliana pizza with black olives, capers and cheese

pizzaiola steak see bistecca pizzaiola

plaice meunière plaice sautèd in butter, garnished with lemon and parsley

plaice niçoise plaice served with lettuce, tomatoes, green beans, hard boiled eggs, tuna, olives, green peppers, potatoes and anchovies

polla (i) chicken (Italian)

poppadams parchment-thin discs of lentil flour, fried in very hot oil

pork tonkatsu Japanese pork in batter

potage French soup

pot-au-feu stockpot of meat and aromatic vegetables

profiteroles small choux pastry puffs filled with cream and covered with chocolate sauce

quiche shell of unsweetened pastry filled with egg custard and cheese etc

ragout stew of meat with olive oil, garlic, tomatoes, carrots and herbs

raita Indian yoghurt

rashmi kebab chicken minced with onions, chillies, fresh mint, coriander, herbs and spices